Still Counting

Achievements and Follies of a Nonagenarian

Edward B. Marks

Hamilton Books
an imprint of
University Press of America,® Inc.
Lanham · Boulder · New York · Toronto · Oxford

Copyright © 2005 by
Edward B. Marks

Published by Hamilton Books
4501 Forbes Boulevard
Suite 200
Lanham, Maryland 20706
UPA Acquisitions Department (301) 459-3366

PO Box 317
Oxford
OX2 9RU, UK

Library of Congress Control Number: 2004112554

ISBN 0-7618-2985-7 (paperback : alk. ppr.)

For Vera

TABLE OF CONTENTS

ACKNOWLEDGEMENTS

Warm acknowledgments are due to the following who read advance chapters of this memoir and contributed helpful suggestions: Adelina Ardittis, Bill Egan, Norman Gilbertson, Joan Griffiths, George Klein, Katie Marks and Haven North. Special thanks to Jason Thompson for reading chapters and for his encouragement and constructive ideas on the concept and content of this memoir;

Special thanks to Katie Burke, Editor-in-Chief of Pomegranate Communications, and Joanne Hively, who read the entire manuscript at a critical stage and made valuable suggestions;

To Michael Barad and Vivian Barad for their constant encouragement since the project's inception and their creative guidance with regard to the formatting of the text. In the case of Michael, recognition of his persistent skill in fashioning the index;

To Ronni Kass for overall design of text and illustrations;

To Vivian Barad, Yvette Branczyk, Rhoda Clark, Carol Diamond, Hugh Downs, Gail Nauheim Kaufmann, Susan Kellermann, Katie Marks, Lucky Marks, Ambassador Joseph Verner Reed, Reynaldo Reyes, Tony Schuman, Alison Seiler and the U.S. Agency for International Development for providing photographs.

Dedication of the book to my wife Vera insufficiently reflects her abiding inspiration, enthusiasm, and practical hand in its production, including hours of typing, and apt editorial input along the way;

While others helped in the design and composition of this memoir, the responsibility for its content is solely mine. To dig back into the past for verification of twentieth century world refugee problems and their impact on U.S. immigration I have had to rely pretty much on my own recollections. I am not a research scholar and in these years I have relatively few surviving contemporaries. Fortunately, as a pack rat for most of my life, I've retained a substantial amount of relevant source material.

Thanks to the *New York Times Magazine* for permission to reprint "The Drys Crusade again but with New Tactics;" *The New Yorker* for permission to reprint "Two Against the Pre-Packs;" to *Playboy* for permission to reprint "Through a Wine Glass Hazily—One of the Wettest Junkets in History;" to Knopf Publishing Group for permission to reprint "Hamlet" from Newman Levy's 1923 book *Opera Guyed*.

THE KENNEDY JUNKET

Another Congressional junket? We'd had our fill of Senators and Congressmen of both parties, wanting to have a look at Vietnam. In mid-1965 the war was hotting up and 'Nam was big news in the U.S.A. Hoards of paratroopers from the Hill wanted to be able to give their constituents an eyewitness report, even if their visit was limited to two or three days. This time it would be a party of four—two senators and two representatives all serving on the Senate or House Judiciary Committees.

After a day of briefing at the embassy, our party of five (I was their escort) set out for Tan Son Nhat Airport. One of the senators was Ted Kennedy of Massachusetts; the other was Millard Tydings of Maryland. John V. Tunney of California, son of Gene Tunney, the former heavyweight boxing champion, and John Culver of Iowa were the two congressmen.

I knew Kennedy slightly; in fact, I had been flown back to Washington to testify before his sub-committee just a few weeks after my arrival in Vietnam as Assistant Director of the U.S. Agency for International Development (USAID) Mission for Refugee Assistance. Kennedy had given me a hard time at the hearing, subjecting me to tough questions. But he had a right to—it was largely at his insistence that USAID had agreed to amplify its help to South Vietnam by establishing a refugee division with its own staff in USAID Saigon and in the twenty-odd provinces having the most serious refugee problems. Kennedy was aware that thousands of refugees had resulted from our military action in support of the South Vietnamese Army. It was only fair for us to help their government assist those who had fled or needed relief to reestablish homes in their villages. Kennedy's questions were penetrating but he was sufficiently considerate to state at the outset that I was an experienced refugee hand who had only recently been assigned to duty in Vietnam.

Our program for the four visitors was to fly north to Danang, an important military base for the burgeoning legion of U.S. troops. The congressional quartet looked dashing; they had outfitted themselves with rakish Australian bush hats and were gung ho for an adventurous trip. Our plane was a two-engined Beechcraft, a distinct relief to me, after flying around in helicopters and STAL planes (Steep Takeoff And Landing—to avoid enemy gunfire.)

We had barely taken off when Kennedy asked me to tell the pilot to overfly Pleiku, a mountainous town which at that moment was the scene of a bloody and well publicized battle. Pleiku was considerably to the west of Saigon and Danang. My doubt that we could change course was vehemently confirmed by the pilot. "No way," he said, "Our flight plan takes us directly to Danang."

The delegation was unhappy at the news. Kennedy said, "Please tell the pilot we want to see him." I returned to the cockpit and informed the young lieutenant who passed the controls to the co-pilot and followed me back to the cabin.

Kennedy repeated the request—it was urgent that they have a look at Pleiku. The pilot doffed his cap and responded, twisting the cap in his hands. "I'm sorry to disappoint you, Senator, but I can't do that. Besides it would expose you to unnecessary risk."

When one of the delegation remonstrated, the pilot was quick to react. "Gentlemen," he said, "you may be important in Washington, but I'm in command of this airplane and I'm under orders to fly you direct to Danang." The delegation was silent. That closed the issue and there was no further mention of Pleiku.

Vehicles awaiting our arrival at Danang airport took us to a large U.S. encampment. After some initial briefing, the delegation began to work the encircling crowd of GIs.

"Anybody here from Massachusetts?" "Who's here from Maryland?" "Did you say you're from Iowa?" All in all, the delegation had a good exposure to the GIs and their problems. Enroute back to the plane we visited a Vietnamese Refugee Camp. That gave them a first-hand look at the refugee situation. They were less jaunty and more reflective on the return flight to Saigon. By then I had been in 'Nam for some weeks and could respond with more assurance to their queries about the refugees and what we were doing to help them.

Back in Saigon, the delegation said they were well satisfied with their visit. They lost no time in sending first-hand reports to their constituents. Other delegations followed. Our team also had to cope with the curiosity of the media, not so much the reporters assigned to Vietnam, as those dropping in from the U.S., France and elsewhere to have a look.

In time the USAID information people handled most inquiring visitors, and our staff was able to focus on the serious logistical problems at hand. I have dealt with these in another chapter of this narrative. Suffice it to say here that our task was complicated by the fact that a shooting war was taking place. We never knew where or when we might be called on to assuage the effects of a military action. Understandably, the military were chary about giving us any advance information of where they were about to strike.

So here I was in Saigon at age 55, separated from my wife and family, flying around in little airplanes and choppers, cooperating with Refugee Minister Dr. Que, consulting with the American Ambassador and General Westmoreland, briefing Congressional delegations, eating in Cheap Charlie's with GIs, working seven days a week, and returning nightly to my small apartment on Doan Cong Buu.

Alone most nights with a chance to think, I asked myself, what was I doing there, what in my life led up to it, and where was I headed in future?

I had a happy childhood, blessed with loving parents and siblings. I enjoyed my boyhood growing up in New York, with every summer either in our Great Neck home or in camp. I made wonderful friendships lasting into adult life. I relished my four years at Dartmouth and my achievements there. I was lucky to find a job in the Depression of 1932 that led to other jobs. While I was working, I earned an MA at Columbia that helped me embark on a career in public service, first, with the Government in Washington, and later abroad with the United Nations. After three years in Geneva, I headed missions in Greece, the U.S. and Yugoslavia. At the outset of 1959, I left international work to become the first Executive Director of the U.S. Committee for Refugees, established to celebrate America's role in the UN's World Refugee Year. Then followed a second Washington job in the Africa Bureau of USAID that involved a fair amount of travel in West African countries. I had hoped to follow that with a choice USAID assignment in London, but instead, because of my refugee experience, I was assigned to head a team in war-torn Vietnam as USAID's Assistant Director for Refugee Assistance.

What next? How could I possibly tell? Married in 1940, I had two children who, with my wife, had accompanied me to Geneva and Athens. In 1965, no families were permitted to accompany American military or civilian personnel in Vietnam. With some bargaining power, I had stipulated that I would spend one year only in Vietnam instead of the customary two-year assignment. Now that year was up.

I've always enjoyed telling stories and I retain fairly vivid memories of most events that shaped my life or struck me as amusing along the way. In writing this memoir I aim to tell my story as it happened. Hindsight is useful, and from a vantage point of many years I've tried to put most things in perspective. I hope to present a reasonably varied picture of a life lived mainly in the twentieth century. Although I've never kept a diary, I have quoted liberally and literally from actual documents that bear witness to significant events. These include a few published articles, some pieces that never made it to publication, and contemporary accounts including a letter describing my visit to the Soviet Union before it was recognized by the United States, my report of a failed strike that I led, and my response to a questionnaire put to me by the U.S. Government International Organizations Employees Loyalty Board. Life has had some tough spots, but I've savored most of it. And it's always been interesting!

THE MARKS FAMILY

GRANDPA BENNETT AND GRANDMA HANNAH

My paternal grandfather, Bennett Marks, was born in 1833 in Kurnik, a small town in eastern Germany that is now part of Poland. He immigrated to the U.S. in 1848 and settled in Troy, New York, probably because relatives had preceded him there. He became a firefighter and later a soldier in the Union Army. To my knowledge, he never saw battlefield action but was a guard on prison trains bringing up captured Confederate soldiers from the South.

My brother once asked him if he had ever shot anybody. Grandpa revealed that he had fired his rifle at a prisoner who was trying to escape. "But I aimed high," he said. Grandpa was very proud of the fact that he was in the honor guard that met Lincoln's funeral train when it passed through New York on its way to Springfield, Illinois. Once dining in Krebs Restaurant in Skaneateles, New York with my wife Vera, I saw his picture in a group of Union soldiers.

Grandpa married Shprintzi Spero near the end of the Civil War, and my father, Edward Bennett Marks, was born in Troy on November 28, 1865. His mother died of a fever when Pop was a year old, and Bennett took his infant son to New York City. During his life, my father made frequent summer visits to his mother's grave. I have a letter from the cemetery in Troy that locates the grave and states that the deceased was the wife of Bernhard Marks.

We know that in subsequent years Bernhard changed his name to Bennett. What is not clear was when and how he took the surname of Marks. My second cousin, Judge James Dannenberg, who has done considerable genealogical research, had a grandfather, James (or Jimmy) Kurnicki for whom he was named. Jimmy and my father were first cousins and lifelong friends. As a child I knew Jimmy and his wife Rae after they moved to New York City. Among our forebears was a man named Marcus, and it's possible Grandpa derived the name "Marks" from that. Whether he was born Kurnicki or Marcus, he must have changed his name to Marks before his wife died.

In New York, Grandpa was a letter carrier for 28 years and a member of the first postmen's union. He and Hannah, the woman I knew as my grandmother, were married shortly after he came to the City. They had three sons, my father's half-brothers, Max, Sol and Mitch. At first they lived on Stanton and other streets on the Lower East Side but later moved to a tenement on East 85th Street in the Yorkville section of Manhattan. My frugal grandmother saved money from Bennett's salary, and in time, possibly with my father's help, bought the tenement in which they lived. I frequently visited there as a boy. She was a resolute, thrifty wife. Whenever I came, Hannah invariably gave me a piece of extremely bitter ginger, with the result that ginger repelled me until I sampled a milder variety. Grandma Hannah was nearly a foot shorter than her six-foot husband. She hailed from Saxony, *"wo die schone madel waxen"* (where the pretty girls grow), and early photos of her confirm the aptness of that adage. Her maiden name was Weiskopf and curiously her hair turned white when she was still a young woman.

Grandpa and Grandma spent every summer with us in Great Neck, in the commodious house my father purchased several years before I was born. I spent many hours hearing his life's tales in a swing hung under a maple tree. He was a patriotic American. I'm told that at the outset of WWI he favored Germany, but his sentiment took a 180 degree turn when America entered the war, and he became a staunch advocate of the Allied cause.

Bennett was an easygoing fellow. He liked nothing better than to down a few beers at Jaeger's, a nearby Yorkville tavern, with several of his cronies. He told us about a companion who knew Grandpa was Jewish. One day, after he'd had a few too many, he turned to Grandpa. "You're a decent chap, Marks," he said, "But your people killed my Lord!" Bennett replied, "Well, you can kill mine if you can catch him!" My sister Phyllis, 12 years my senior, recalled being sent to Jaeger's to "rush the growler," that is, to bring back a pitcher of suds if Grandpa at home was feeling thirsty.

Grandpa died in 1922 when I was 11 years old. After Grandpa died, Hannah sold the Yorkville brownstone and lived for a few remaining years with Sol and his wife, Eda, in an apartment on Riverside Drive near Grant's Tomb.

MIMI AND THE CHUCK FAMILY

I know very little of my maternal grandparents. Henry Schuck was born in Berlin and, with his brother, William, was in the textile business after they immigrated to the United States. Shortly after their arrival here the brothers took the "S" off their surnames. Henry's first wife died after the birth of their second child, and he remarried Sophia Levy. He died before I was born and Sophia lived for only a few years after I was born. Sophia had ten children, including my mother, and could trace her ancestry in America back to the 18th century. She was always proud of that. One of her maternal ancestors was married to Haym Salomon, a wealthy Philadelphia merchant, who gets a footnote in the history books because he helped to finance the Revolutionary army. As a child, Sophia was a playmate of the daughter of Mme. Jumel, whose second husband was Aaron Burr. Once a headquarters for George Washington, the Jumel Mansion at 166th Street and Edgecomb Avenue can be visited today as a museum. I have the copy of a letter written by Henry Levy, brother of my grandmother

Sophia, which describes her wedding to Henry Chuck in June 1861. He writes to a "Cousin Miriam" who has the same first name as my mother, but my mother was not born until October 3, 1875.

The Chuck family for some years summered in Long Branch, New Jersey, where relatives of my father's mother, named Spero, were long established. My mother met my father there when she was ten years old and he was twenty. Reba and Princie Spero, two spinsters, lived with their brother Robert. I vaguely remember them through the haze of years, because we sometimes visited them when I was a child. Robert was known to many as Uncle Robert. I don't recall, if I ever knew, what he did for a living, but he had a great interest in the safety of children. His *S.O.S. Song* achieved a certain popularity:

Stay on the sidewalk, that's S.O.S., S.O.S., S.O.S.
That's just a slogan every kid should repeat,
A timely warning not to play on the street.
Children should listen to Mom and Dad
If you're hurt, they'll feel sad…

After graduation from a New York high school, my mother Mirol or Miriam (she used both), known to all as Mimi, entered the art school at Cooper Union, a venerable institution on the Bowery at 7th Street in Manhattan. Named for Peter Cooper, it was founded in the mid-19th century and was the scene of a crucial speech by presidential candidate Abe Lincoln in 1860 when his Eastern backers brought him to New York in a test of his national appeal.

At Cooper Union, Mimi drew from life, and the drawings my sister retained prove that she was a talented student. My father, a decade after they met, pursued her. They were engaged in May 1897 and married in Vienna Hall on East 59th Street on December 15th of that year.

Our nuclear family included my sister Phyllis, born in 1898 and my brother Herbert, born in 1902, who was nine years and one day older than me. I was born April 22, 1911. I had a plethora of uncles and aunts—my father's half-brothers and their wives and a large contingent of aunts, uncles and cousins on my mother's side. Aside from family, my father had virtually no intimate friends, except for a few of his business associates. One exception was the Albert family of Sydney, Australia, who always visited us on their trips to the U.S. and went abroad with my folks in the summer of 1910. My mother kept a diary of that trip and talks of a gala evening out and "much more," a suspicious nine months before my birth.

My mother liked to take me on excursions. She took me several times each year to the Metropolitan Museum of Art. In adult life, I became a member and marveled not only at their permanent collection but also at their special exhibitions. As a child, I chiefly remember the suits of armor, the painting of Joan of Arc having a vision, and *The Horse Fair* by Rosa Bonheur. *The Horse Fair* had special interest because a nephew of the painter, Lucian Bonheur, lived in the house next to us in Great Neck. He was married to a relative of my mother.

My mother took me to children's theater performances, to the Museum of Natural History, to the zoo, and once, on the subway, to Coney Island. When I was six or seven, she took me to a matinee to see Sarah Bernhardt perform on one of her farewell tours. It was after Bernhardt's leg had been amputated, and she was playing the part of a wounded *poilu*. I remember having a lot of curiosity about the missing leg, but was too young to appreciate the performance.

As a youngster shopping with my mother, I saw the first traffic light in New York City. It was installed in a bronze colored metal tower, about 12 feet in height, at 42nd Street and Fifth Avenue. There was two-way traffic on Fifth Avenue in those days, and the tower was placed right in the middle of the street.

Mimi saw a great deal of her sisters, notably Julie Adelson and Sadie Davis. My folks entertained their siblings and a few cousins, including the Kurnickis. They gave roulette parties to a dozen or more on Saturday nights. They enjoyed musical comedies and operettas, especially if my father was publishing the music, and they periodically went to the Metropolitan Opera, which Mimi relished.

On most important questions, Mimi accepted my father's lead, but in those areas where she felt responsible, she exercised independent judgment. She was a firm but not controlling mother. She was fun to be with, always knew a game to play. When she was widowed and in her nineties, she could still play a wicked game of dominoes or gin.

Once in Great Neck we had a maid of eastern European origin. She answered the phone one day when my mother, who was in New York at the time, called. She left us the following message: MIZMOKS GOLDUP ENSEZ ZUNZ YUKOMOM GOLERUP SEZ NOMER HOWLET IZGONABE GOLERUP*

When we didn't have servants, Mims was an inventive cook, and I looked forward to the meals she prepared. She read a good deal, played countless games of solitaire when Pop was writing his memoirs. She was innately gentle and considerate, and every inch a lady.

My work took me to Washington and abroad for a good part of her later life, but fortunately I saw her on a home leave a month before she died. She was living then, independently though with a companion, in The Adams, a residential hotel at 86th Street and Fifth Avenue.

*(Mrs. Marks called up and says as soon as you come home call her up. She says no matter how late it is call her up.)

MY POP

My pop was a good father, wise, compassionate and a man of high ethical standards. He went to school in Manhattan, and attended City College for a year, but he was essentially a self-educated man. For a time, he sold "notions" (ribbons, thread, needles, scissors, fabrics and other household sewing essentials) for the firm of J.P. Caine, traveling extensively in Westchester County and lower Connecticut.

My father remembered the blizzard of 1888 which paralyzed New York for a few days. He recalled helping a snowbound woman to cross Madison Square Park. Jose Marti, the Cuban revolutionary poet and journalist, then living in exile in New York, described the scene for *La Nacion* of Buenos Aires as "a city silent, deserted, shrouded, buried under the snow . . . For two days, the snow has had New York in its power, encircled, terrified, like a prize fighter driven to the canvas by a sneak punch."

Pop was an early, talented versifier, and won $100 for a triple acrostic in a contest to promote *Doctor Bill*, a play on Broadway:

Don't fail to call in, without further   Delay,
On   Our friend Dr. Bill, the success   Of the day
Consult him Concerning his great   Cure for Blues,
The kangaroo dance That's sure   To amuse
Opinions may differ   On   One play or other
Regarding this one,   Rest assured there's no other
But that it is   Brimful of Brightness and fun
Intensely   Interesting and   In for a run
Long   Live Dr. Bill   Let none miss this year,
London's   Laughing success and the   Latest craze here.

One rainy evening, at a hotel in Mamaroneck, NY, he met another drummer (a traveling salesman) named Joseph W. Stern who was playing the piano. Before the night was out, they wrote the music and lyrics of a song called *The Little Lost Child*. They had it printed up, and my father kept the copies under his bed. At night, they plugged the song—that meant taking it around to cafes and music halls. When it was sung by Lottie Gilson, a popular soubrette of the day, it became a hit, and the two writers decided to publish it themselves. They called the firm Joseph W. Stern & Co. because my father didn't want to give up his job with Caine.

Marks and Stern subsequently scored with another great tearjerker of the 1890s, *My Mother was a Lady*, the chorus of which ran:
My mother was a lady
Like yours you will allow;
And you may have a sister
Who needs protection now.
I've come to this great city
To find a brother dear;
And you wouldn't dare insult me, sir
If Jack were only here.

The firm soon began to publish songs by other writers including *Hot Time in the Old Town Tonight* and *Sweet Rosie O'Grady*. They published Irving Berlin's first song, *Marie from Sunny Italy*, but it was not a success. They also published the first song of Jerome Kern who, for a time, worked in their business. My father remembered Kern as a fellow with green pants who kept pushing to get ahead. An early hit was *My Gal Sal (They Called her Frivolous Sal)* written by Paul Dresser, brother of the novelist Theodore Dreiser.

My father, widely known as E.B., had an early interest in encouraging and publishing the music of African-American composers, including the Johnson brothers, James Weldon and J. Rosamund. They wrote, with Bob Cole, *Under the Bamboo Tree*, *My Castle on the River Nile* and other successes. The Johnsons also wrote *Lift Every Voice and Sing*, known for many years as the Negro National Anthem. James Weldon Johnson was a leading personality of his day. In addition to being a song writer, he was the author of a fine book of Negro Spirituals, *The Autobiography of an Ex-Colored Man* and *Along This Way*. He was one of the first African-American diplomats to serve his country as Consul in Venezuela and Nicaragua. This was in a day (1913-1916) when there were no African-American U.S. ambassadors. I never met James Weldon but knew his brother Rosamund, who after a successful career as a composer, came to work in the Professional Department of what became the Marks Publishing Company when Pop bought out Joe Stern's interest around 1920.

The firm's "Half Hour" editions of classical composers were popular. They published the Paderewski edition of Chopin's compositions, Paul Lincke's *Glow-Worm* and Jessel's *Parade of the Wooden Soldiers*.

Marks published the first serious compositions of my lifelong friend, William Schuman. My father encouraged Bill and me in our popular song writing efforts.

Pop actively headed the firm, publishing both popular and classical music, until his death from pneumonia in 1945. Somewhere along the line, he became a disciple of Marcus Aurelius, and he advocated moderation in all things. Marcus Aurelius counseled "a benevolent disposition, and the example of a family governed in a fatherly manner, and the idea of living comfortable to nature; and gravity without affectation, and to look carefully after the interests of friends, and to tolerate ignorant persons, and those who form opinions without consideration."

E.B. had a contagious zest for life and was generally receptive to fresh ideas. Many times when I or another family member hesitated at the threshold of a new experience, he would say, "Take it in." That expression became a sort of mantra for me through life. I can't say I've always followed that precept but when I act on an impulse I seldom regret it. I've also counseled my children and others to "take it in" as they confront a perplexing decision.

My father deplored the deterioration of Broadway. He was an ardent foe of "payola," the common practice of paying a singer or bandleader to perform a song. He looked back wistfully to the time when a man's word was as good as his bond, and a handshake was sufficient to conclude a deal.

Pop was 45 when I was born, much involved in business, and somewhat less actively engaged in my upbringing than a younger father would have been. But when I was a child he told me wondrous tales of a character he invented named Tommy Bounce, encouraged my interest in sports, especially baseball, and was unfailingly thoughtful and helpful as I grew older. He never directed me much but he never thwarted me. He struck me just once. It was in Great Neck. Ed North, John Bancroft and I went out on a day's hike, but got lost or distracted and didn't get home until after nine o'clock. My mother got very worried, and it was chiefly because of her concern that Pop whacked me when I finally arrived home.

Pop found time to give me special treats. He took me to baseball games where I saw Ruth in his prime. Because he so admired the Babe and Lou Gehrig, Pop was a Yankee fan. Herb and I were rabid New York Giants rooters. Pop was not a boxing fan, but etched clearly in my mind was the evening we saw Joe Louis smash Max Schmeling in 1936. It was a quick fight and Schmeling was, if not a Nazi, just out of Nazi Germany.

I looked forward to summers at our house in Great Neck when Pop and I would play catch and he would join in family games of one-or-two-a-cat. He was a careful horse player who would spend a couple of hours with Racing Form on Friday night doping the horses. Sometimes I would accompany him to Belmont or Aqueduct on Saturday. It was the time of bookmakers, and we would scurry from one booth to another to obtain the best odds on the horses he favored. He also set great store on the performance of jockeys, and made that an important determinant, as well as the horse's form, in selecting a winner. My mother seldom went to the track, and when she did, rarely bet. On one occasion, however, she asked my father to place a bet on Monday Lunch. Pop tried to discourage her. "That nag is nowhere," he said. "It's twenty five to one—play it to place or show." "To win," my mother insisted. "I have a hunch!" Of course, Monday Lunch ran away with the field! Generally my father came home a winner and would give me a small share of his winnings. He was particularly successful in Saratoga, NY, where he and Mimi regularly spent August and took the waters. On vacation, he could study the racing charts more carefully.

Pop found time to write two books. The first, published by Viking in 1934 and titled *They All Sang—From Tony Pastor to Rudy Vallee* was pretty much his own life story. He drafted it, but the final version was written in collaboration with A.J. Liebling, a Dartmouth classmate of my brother Herb, who came to our apartment evenings to work with him. Liebling later wrote for *The New Yorker* and other periodicals and produced several books including a wonderfully comic yarn called *The Telephone Booth Indian*. My mother and I knew him best as a gargantuan gourmand who just about emptied our refrigerator on every visit. *They All Had Glamour—From the Swedish Nightingale to the Naked Lady* was written by my father alone and published by Julian Messner in 1944. The hard cover book cost $4.00 in those days! It contains personal and biographical recollections of the great theater, opera and related personalities of the nineteenth century such as Adelina Patti, Lola Montez, Jenny Lind and Lillian Russell. It also has lists of great value to researchers of the actors, singers and impresarios of the century, as well as an extensive compendium of many old-time ballads and songs.

My father was healthy most of his life. He was a great fan of home remedies and when he traveled would take with him a store of bicarbonate of soda, rhubarb and ipecac, Bellans (it was something like Tums and my father swore by it) and other items to allay bouts of indigestion which were not disabling but apparently frequent. In the family tradition of verse writing, which he inaugurated, he celebrated weddings and other occasions with relevant lyrics to popular tunes. Herb, Phil and I on one of his birthdays wrote some verses to the tune of *La Cucaracha* spoofing Pop's foibles and predilections:

Our cuckoo papa, our cuckoo papa,
When he goes away on trips,
He takes the bathroom,
The whole damned bathroom,
Stuffs it all in to his grips.

For some years Pop had regular weekly massages in the evening from a large, vigorous man named Kaiser who spoke with a heavy German accent. Kaiser was at least well in his 70s when I knew him as a child. It was said he had no teeth but could crack nuts with his gums. My father rarely got home before 7 pm, after which we dined, so at times Kaiser appeared when I was already in bed. One morning when I passed through the living room on my way to school I saw a bulky shape under a sheet on the living room couch. It rather frightened me, but I was too timid to investigate. When I met my mother in the kitchen she told me Kaiser had died from his exertions and that they were unable to arrange for recovery of his body until the morning.

In the summer Pop commuted to his office from Great Neck. In the early thirties he decided we should live year round in Great Neck, and from then on, except weekends, he commuted daily to the city on the Long Island Railroad.

My father was still active when we convened to celebrate his 80th birthday on November 28, 1945. Shortly after he came down with a bad case of pneumonia. I was then working for the government in Washington. Herb's wife, Hortie, reached me at the office, "If you want to see your father alive, rush to Mineola Hospital," she said. I took the first available train—a hideous journey, standing most of the way. I had to change at Penn Station, and boarded the LIRR to Mineola. I arrived too late. Penicillin in time would have saved Pop, but it wasn't yet in general use. I returned sadly with Mimi and my family to Great

Neck. Many moving tributes were paid to my father. My mother soon let us know that she wanted to move from Great Neck back to the City.

SONGS FOR A CENTURY

I don't know when my father began calling the Marks Music Company "The House of Hits," but it may have been around 1920 when he bought out Joe Stern's interest and changed the name of the firm.

In that year Marks had one of its biggest successes, *Parade of the Wooden Soldiers* from the Russian revue *Chauve Souris*. Paul Whiteman, the premier bandleader of the day, made a record of *Parade* with *Mr. Gallagher and Mr. Sheen* on the other side, and it sold like wildfire. The firm which had started in one small room on 14th Street moved up to the 20s, then to its own building on 38th Street, then to 46th Street, and in Pop's last years to Radio City/Rockefeller Center at 50th Street. He was keeping pace with the advance of much of the city's business by moving uptown.

I was always interested in songs, and although I never learned to play an instrument, knew the words of many of them that I sang with friends or at home to Phil's accompaniment on the piano. At Camp Cobbossee in the 20s I wrote songs with Bill Schuman. Bill had an astonishing career as a leading American serious composer, President of the Juilliard School and President of Lincoln Center, but in 1928 and 1929 he scored my lyrics for *Lovesick* and *Who'll Close the Window in the Morning*. *Lovesick* which Herb called the syphilis song, was published by the firm and recorded by Bert Lown and his orchestra, but it never made the charts.

WHO'LL CLOSE THE WINDOW IN THE MORNING?

Believe me darling when I say
I never knew until today
I had a chance for a romance with you.
I know our married life will be
A paragon of ecstasy
With single bunks and all night drunks I'm through.
But before I claim you as my bride,
There's a question we must both decide:

Who'll close the window in the morning
After we are wed?
It may be as cold as ice,
And it surely would be nice,
If you'd make the sacrifice
And leave our warm warm bed.
Who'll close the window in the morning?
Keep out rain and storm;

I won't ask a lot of you,
But there's one thing you can do,
Please close the window in the morning
And keep our love nest warm.

LOVESICK

There's a pain down deep within my heart,
Medicines will never cure me.
I'm so helpless now that we're apart,
I'm in a critical state!
Help me before it's too late:

Lovesick, I need your kiss to make me well again,
Lovesick, because I fell beneath your spell again;
Like a raging fire, dear, that's burning out my soul,
My love for you mounts higher dear, and passes all control;

Lovesick, without some hope, I'll have to end it all,
Lovesick, one little smile from you would mend it all;
There's just one way to cure me, assure me you'll be:
Lovesick for me.

Marks published my English lyric for *Trink, Bruderlein, Trink*, a German drinking song, and I still get a few dollars in royalties from that. Between 1925 and 1942 Marks Music had some lean years but also such successes as *They'll be Some Changes Made*, *What a Difference a Day Made*, *Say Si Si* and *El Rancho Grande*. My brother Herb joined the company in the 1920s after a few years on *Variety*. On his 1927 honeymoon in Cuba he heard *El Manisero* known as *The Peanut Vendor*, *Mama Inez* and other spritely Cuban music and brought it back to the U.S. to start the rumba craze here. The firm also published the lovely music of Ernesto Lecuona, notably *Malaguena* and *Andalucia*, which became standards through the years. An English lyric made *Andalucia* into a popular hit, *The Breeze and I*. Another outstanding number was *Glow-Worm* by the German composer Paul Lincke. Originally a teaching piece, *Glow-Worm* was recorded in a jazzed up version by the Mills Brothers with an engaging lyric by Johnny Mercer, and became a smash hit.

My father was an early member of ASCAP, but he warred against the organization's self-perpetuating Board of Directors, claiming that he "never received proper consideration from the Society." At that time ASCAPs's payments to authors, composers and publishers were based on three criteria: seniority, availability and uses. They had people with earphones who listened to everything played on radio and television. A song like *Hot Time* was important not for frequent uses but because it became irreplaceable in the portrayal of an election scene. Pop held that the firm's seniority and the availability of such standards as *Hot Time* and *Glow-Worm* should be given more weight in ASCAP distributions.

In 1941 he quit ASCAP in a revolutionary mood and made a deal with Broadcast Music Incorporated (BMI) Performing Rights Society. The five-year arrangement governing the license for 15,000 songs was guaranteed by NBC and CBS.

Then there is the amazing story of *Paper Doll*, written by Johnny Black, the composer of *Dardanella*, a big hit around 1920. One day in 1922 he invited my father to dinner. When E.B. arrived at his home Johnny kept playing songs on his fiddle with a trained canary perched on his shoulder but no sign of food. Among the songs he played, one struck a responsive chord—it was *Paper Doll*. Johnny wanted $25.00 cash as a binder against a contract to be written the next day. When E.B. gave it to him, Johnny promptly sent out for some Chinese food and that was the dinner.

My father liked the song but did not feel it was the moment to publish it, so he "put it in the trunk" as he used to say. It remained there for 22 years until the pin-up craze in World War II brought it to mind. It then became the nation's top favorite, widely recorded and on the Hit Parade for twenty consecutive weeks.

Pop and my brother heard that Black had recently died in a drunken brawl. They found no trace of a widow, so the royalties were sent to Black's father in an old folks' home in upstate New York. *Time Magazine* published the story of the old man's windfall and all hell broke lose. A woman who claimed to have been Johnny's girlfriend said she had inspired the song. What she didn't know was that it had been written 22 years before. Then a woman in Ohio said she had married Johnny a scant week before his death. She was able to establish this and claimed her share of the royalties. But what she really wanted was a chance to enjoy the highlights of New York City. Herb went to Ohio to escort her and a woman friend to the Big Apple. His account of their journey to the city in a Pullman car was unforgettable. After they had been to a few nightspots they were satisfied and went home, but Herb had to catch up on sleep.

In 1944 Marks Music celebrated its 50th anniversary. An honorary committee with many notable individuals was formed with Franklin P. Adams as its chairman. Adams wrote the *Conning Tower* column in the *New York Herald Tribune* under the signature F.P.A. and was a great enthusiast for the old songs. Former Governor Al Smith and Mayor Fiorello LaGuardia were members of the committee as well as many luminaries of the stage and music worlds including Bing Crosby, Aaron Copland, Paul Robeson, Eddie Cantor, Louis Armstrong, Mildred Bailey, The Mills Brothers and leading orchestra leaders including Cab Callaway, Harry James, Guy Lombardo, Vincent Lopez, Jimmy Lunsford, and Xavier Cugat. Among those who attended the event were Maude Nugent, writer of *Sweet Rosie O'Grady*, Harry Armstrong, who composed *Sweet Adeline*, and

Alice Lawlor, daughter of the writer of Sidewalks of New York (East Side, West Side).

When Pop died in 1945 my brother became the firm's President. Herb greatly expanded the educational and classical sides of the catalogue. He published the compositions of Roger Sessions, Norman Dello Joio and William Bolcom. Marks also published Songs to Grow On and other books for children written by Herb's second wife, Beatrice Landeck, an expert in that field. Herb continued the tradition started by Pop of encouraging African-American writers and performers. He published The Banana Boat Song, popularized by Harry Belafonte and two songs not written by but closely identified with Billie Holiday, God Bless the Child and Strange Fruit, a haunting song about lynching in the South.

Herb stuck with BMI for most publications, but he started two subsidiary ASCAP firms, Alameda and Piedmont, in order to be able to publish songs by writers who were ASCAP members. A notable achievement in Herb's time was the 1967 purchase of the George M. Cohan catalogue including Yankee Doodle Dandy, Give my Regards to Broadway and You're a Grand Old Flag. He published the score of George M, a musical about the life of Cohan, which ran on Broadway.

At least 15 Marks' copyrights are now or have been featured extensively in major radio and TV advertising campaigns. Topping the list is What a Difference a Day Made used by NBC, the U.S. Postal Service and several retailers. Popular hits in Herb's era were More, the theme song of an Italian movie Mondo Cane, the music of AC/DC, an import from the Albert group in Australia, and Bat out of Hell featured by Meatloaf, a three hundred plus pound rock star.

Before his death my father had incorporated the business and provided shares of stock for Mimi, his three children and the two half-brothers, Max and Mitch, whom he'd taken into the business. During her lifetime Mimi was trustee for the children's shares, but after her death in 1969 they were turned over to us. I owned about 20 percent of the business and gave my children, Tom and Katie, each about 6 percent of my stock. Stockholder meetings were held about once a quarter and when I was in the U.S. I usually attended. When Herb became ill we hired a general manager and the Board met more frequently. A split developed among the board members. Herb, Alfred Marks, representing his father Mitch, and I generally supported Herb's position as President of the company. Ted Diamond, representing Phyllis, his mother-in-law, and Stephen Marks, representing the interest of his father, Max, felt that many of the valuable Marks copyrights were a "wasting asset" and that we should sell the business. Edgar Simon and his son, Edgar Simon, Jr., were of the same opinion. The proposal hung fire for some time while bids from several companies were considered. But the offer of the Bienstock Brothers and the Oscar Hammerstein estate as co-partners in 1984 was finally accepted. Ten years later we celebrated the 100th anniversary of the E.B. Marks Catalogue at a gala party staged at the Tavern on the Green in New York City.

During the years of negotiation, Herb was in declining health, and at the urging of his wife, Beatrice, moved to Westhampton, Long Island. An inveterate New Yorker, he hung a sign over the door that read West 12th Street and told visitors "If you're not in New York, you're camping out!"

After a lingering illness, Herb died in 1984.

EARLY DAYS IN 65TH STREET

Though I really grew up on the West Side of Manhattan, I was born on the East Side at 53 East 65th Street and lived there until I was about nine. We lived in a brownstone house a couple of doors away from Sara Roosevelt's town house; we sometimes saw her grandsons in their blue caps heading off to school. My earliest memory was when I was about four. I had a mastoid operation at home. Dr. Whiting was the surgeon. I don't remember the operation but I do recall after it, sitting on the floor, my head swathed in bandages, playing with toys given me by a number of relatives who sat around me in a circle.

My brother Herbert's room was on the top floor. He was always inventive, playing games with me, mostly with marbles formed into a regiment, commanded by Colonel Black and Lt. Colonel Brooklyn. Herbert's room contained a curio cabinet with a number of objects that I still cherish. Two are fearsome wooden masks with real whiskers, now in my son's home in Virginia. There was also a lacquered opium pipe together with an embroidered pouch, a pair of handcuffs from the Spanish-American War, several Latin American percussion instruments that make a sound when you scratch them, a pair of ebony castinets, a hunk of petrified wood, several pieces of agate and a bottle of sand in the form of a design. On one side of the bottle the grains of sand delicately illustrated a bunch of flowers and bore my father's name and the date 1890, indicating that it had been given to him or perhaps purchased by him when he was 25 years old. On the reverse side was a nicely designed sailing ship. The bottle has been moved a number of times, from several apartments on Manhattan's West Side, to my homes in Washington, to storage, to my home in Westchester County, and finally to Virginia. As a result, the lower part of the design has been partly obliterated. But enough remains to make the bottle a unique treasure. We have never been able to figure out how the design was imprinted in the loose sand, and beyond that, how the sand containing the design was inserted into the bottle.

We had a dumbwaiter in the 65th Street house, and I remember once making a perilous ride on it, unbeknownst to my parents.

My father arose and left for the office after I left for school, but on weekends we breakfasted together and he always gave me a spoonful of his daily grapefruit. Grapefruit for breakfast became a lifelong habit.

Hunter College was just three blocks away on Park Avenue and 68th Street, and my first schooling was at their Model School. I remember very little about the students, teachers and classes, but one event stands out in my memory. That was the false Armistice in the fall of 1918. I was seven years old. I recall the great surge of jubilation that rocked the school, and being let out of class, only to be called back when the report came that it was premature. The true Armistice came a few days later on November 11th, but it was a distinct anti-climax.

An earlier memory is the election of 1916. Herb and I bet a nickel on the outcome. He bet on Hughes, and until late in the evening it appeared that Hughes had won. But Wilson prevailed in the morning's light. Herb threw my winning nickel at me and I remember retrieving it from under the bureau.

In the summer, we went to Great Neck, leaving after school was over in June and returning to the city in September. Our large, attractive house, called "Cherry Lawn," was on Lakeville Road, near Northern Boulevard and near the Sperry plant which served as UN Headquarters in its early years. I learned tennis on our clay court. My father and sister played, and Herb and my brother-in-law Edgar were good enough to reach the finals of the local tennis tournament. Friends of my father, including Sigmund Spaeth, the Tune Detective, frequently came to play. He was well known in those days as a writer on music, and he also had an entertaining radio program.

My parents never learned to drive. Before I was born, they stabled two horses called Prince and Victor in our big barn located about 100 feet from our Great Neck house. Their first car was a Pierce-Arrow, but that was before my day. I recall the Marmon we had in my childhood. It was driven by a part-time chauffeur named Jack Kelly. He would let me sit in the front seat when he did an errand, and I grew very fond of him. Jack had his own car, a sporty yellow Mercer roadster. Very early one morning, by pre-arrangement, as a special favor, he took me out on the Motor Parkway which had an entrance near Great Neck. I'm vague as to exactly what that Parkway was. I know it wasn't part of the growing public highway system. It's my impression that it was a privately financed road taking well-to-do motorists from the city to their Long Island homes. There was very little traffic on it. Anyway, when we reached the Parkway, Jack let out the throttle and for the first time in my life, I had the thrill of going 60 miles an hour in an open car.

I didn't learn to drive until after college, when I was working in New York. My friend Ralph Elias took me out in his battered Ford. After several lessons, I successfully drove over the Queensborough Bridge and a few days later got my license. When my folks moved to Great Neck year-round, I was their driver in the Mercury my father purchased.

When I was nine, my sister Phyllis was married, and my brother Herb went away to college. As a result, my father decided to sell the 65th Street house, and we moved to an apartment on the West Side of Manhattan at 99th Street and West End Avenue. I began to play with the kids around the block. Al Bleier was a close friend and I formed a bond with the two Coleman brothers, but that all changed when, after a couple of years, we moved back to a floor-through apartment in the renovated 65th Street house. There, for the first time, I shared a room with Herb when he wasn't at college. My mother didn't like it there, so in a year or two we moved again to a West Side apartment in the Rockfall at 111th Street and Broadway. That neighborhood proved a most congenial one. I transferred to P.S. 165 at 109th Street, one of the best public schools in Manhattan, and formed lifelong friendships with Ferd Nauheim, a classmate there, and William Schuman, who lived a couple of blocks away.

My boyhood was filled with happy circumstance. Herb was a thoughtful brother, a great playmate and in some ways more of a mentor than my father. I had good friends in the West Side neighborhoods to which we moved. I played stickball, roller skated, sledded with my companions, engaged at times in mischievous pranks, and was generally content in the public school I attended. I did a piece on my youthful escapades which was bought by Columbia University Magazine. It is called *Upper West Side Story* and follows in the next chapter.

After he left Dartmouth, Herb went to work for *Variety*. One of his jobs there was to write reviews of vaudeville shows. When asked to review the Palace or the Riverside, he would invite a girl friend, but if he drew one of the less reputed theaters in Brooklyn or the Bronx, he would take me. I saw some terrible acts, but also, usually the headliner, some great performers: Ryan & Lee, Lewis & Dody, Bert Williams, Houdini, Thurston and many others.

Herb kindled my interest in modern art. I had visited the Metropolitan Museum on many occasions with my mother, but it was Herb who gave me Sheldon Cheney's book on modern art and took me to exhibitions of the Impressionists and contemporary painters.

I'll never forget an evening when I was nine. After a normal family dinner, I was about to retire when I heard a commotion in the hall. Herb was on the floor, foaming at the mouth, having suffered a grand mal attack of epilepsy. I believe it was his first; certainly it was a great shock to me. Herb continued to have periodic seizures all his life, sometimes in public. With Dilantin and other drugs, he suffered grand mal only occasionally, but he endured petit mal episodes when, in the middle of a conversation, with his eyes still open, he would black out. Herb drank, sometimes too much, and he was accident prone. He could never drive a car, and when he went swimming I was always careful to stay near him. His doctor recommended that Herb have a spinal tap before he was married, in 1927, to insure that the condition was not hereditary. He and Hortense Tyroler had two children. Jean, the quintessential homemaker and mother and grandmother, married Arthur Murphy, a Columbia Law School Professor, and we've remained close friends. Together they have a lively interest in birding, sushi and the arts. Tony, an archeologist who taught at Southern Methodist University, now lives in Santa Fe with his wife Kay. Herb and Hortie's first apartment was on West 96th Street. They were enormously hospitable, not only to their many friends, but also to mine. Bill, Ferd and I were frequent visitors.

In my youth, I always looked forward to summer in Great Neck. I learned baseball on a level, grassy patch in front of the house that was dominated by a large cherry tree said to be a century old. A row of maples on Lakeville Road gave shade. Herb invented a kind of clock golf we played from tree to tree. Behind the house was the clay tennis court that it became my duty to wet down, roll and line. Weekends we usually had family or other guests and as I got older I was admitted to play. During the week I practiced on an inside wall of our barn. The space was too short to develop a proper swing, so I learned to chop the ball, and in eighty years of play, to the despair of my son, I never got beyond a chopping game.

Though she was 12 years my senior, and not a childhood playmate, I adored my sister Phyllis. I used to roller skate across Central Park to meet her when she took out Carol, her first child, in the baby carriage. Phil and her husband, Edgar Simon, with Carol and Edgar Junior, spent a good deal of time with us in Great Neck during the summers. Edgar Simon, from a San Francisco family, was a devoted husband who, during WWI was trained in naval aviation and later became a founder of Composition Materials Company. Carol married Ted Diamond and brought up two sons in Connecticut. She had a successful career in advertising and public relations. Ted, a lawyer and businessman, was a bombardier in World War II. Edgar Junior, at seventeen, was visiting us in Great Neck on December 7, 1941. He was avidly listening to a football game on the radio in the car when we heard the news about Pearl Harbor. When he finally joined us, he expressed annoyance that they kept interrupting the game with bulletins about something to do with the Japanese. Not long afterwards he was in Naval Officer's training and became an Ensign. He married Patty Strassberger who had been an editor at Mademoiselle in New York City, and they moved to her hometown of Montgomery, Alabama and had three daughters. He was a businessman and, with Ted, gradually took over his father's business.

We generally had fish on Friday nights, so Herb, Edgar and I established the Friday Night Fish Club. It had no constitution or rules of order. Its sole purpose was to order rare hamburgers at the Great Neck Village Diner after a fish dinner at home. We were not partial to fish!

I recall the episode of the gray cat. A mangy stray had paid us a chance visit and stayed on for weeks. Mom and Phyllis were convinced that the animal was a cause of allergies and perhaps more ghastly maladies. It came to the point when we were ordered to get rid of it. In memory's haze I can't recall why there was no animal shelter to take it to, but there wasn't one we knew of. Edgar, Herb and I and the cat went off in the car, but the perceptive feline knew what was up and fiercely resisted our efforts to eject him. In Kensington, one of the more affluent sections of the town, we finally got him out of the car. We were just congratulating ourselves when a police car stopped us. "I saw that," said the cop. "That's a major offense!" We were booked for abandoning an animal in a public thoroughfare. We had to pay a stiff fine *and* return home with the damn cat! I can't remember its ultimate fate.

Phyllis went with my Mom and Pop to my Dartmouth graduation, and I always appreciated that. Edgar wasn't much for travel, so a few years later I took Phyllis along when I went as a reporter on the Goodwill Wine Tour of France. I've described that staggering junket elsewhere in this book, but suffice it to say here that Phil and I had a fabulous time. It was her first voyage to Europe in many years and she relished it. When I was in Washington with a three year old, and my wife had to return to the hospital after the delivery of our second child, I felt completely nonplussed. It was wartime (1944) and I had a responsible job. I called Phyllis, who unhesitatingly left her Red Cross work (for which she was later decorated) and came down to relieve us.

Several years after we moved to the West Side, the owner of 53 East 65th Street put a red brick facade over the first two storeys of the brownstone house. This addition probably gave more inside space to the rooms into which the building was being divided. From the street, however, the effect was revolting, and Phyllis who had lived there until she was married was so upset she avoided passing the house from then on. The building remained this way for at least 50 years. In 2002 I was walking with a friend on Park Avenue when we passed 65th Street. "I was born on that block," I said, but when I pointed to the house I was amazed to see the original brownstone front, just as I remembered it from my childhood. A new owner had removed the ugly red brick.

With some encouragement from Vera, I wrote a letter to the present occupants noting that it came from a former occupant. I got a lovely reply from the new owner inviting us to visit and see what they had done to the place. Vera and I made a call and met the Israeli owner and his American wife. Against all advice, he had bought and gutted the structure and completely restored it outside and in. It now has an elevator, a reconstructed floor plan and an attractive roof terrace. I thought of Phyllis and could only regret that she wasn't alive to see it.

UPPER WEST SIDE STORY

By Edward B. Marks for the *Columbia University Magazine*, circa 1960

I retain loving and indestructible memories of the five years I spent on Manhattan's upper West Side as a boy. During the twenties we lived at two addresses in the area bounded by 116th and 96th Streets on the north and south, and Amsterdam Avenue on the east. The western extremity was Riverside Drive and the Hudson, and my friend Ferd and I often headed in that direction after school let out at three.

There were a number of entrances we could take from the Drive into Riverside Park, but cliff-hanging was more adventurous. We knew every handhold and toehold in the gray stone wall that separated the Drive from the Park below. Usually after climbing down we headed for the New York Central railroad tracks. There was no West Side Highway in those days. The Park ended abruptly at a second wall that dropped to the tracks, a wall too smooth to be climbed and far too steep to be jumped. About the only way to make the descent was to leap across a four foot chasm to the roof of a freight car. Empty freights were often side-tracked there for a few hours. When we had made the jump, Ferd and I would climb down the iron ladders and peer or clamber into the empty cars.

The railroad watchmen were not happy about our little peregrinations and sometimes shouted rudely at us. At some point, with or without guards in pursuit, we generally made for the Hudson. There were no wharves or piers in that region of the West Side. The river's edge was full of oil-soaked driftwood, empty bottles, Hudson River "white fish" (condoms), occasional dead fish, and other wretched refuse, but it had the enchantment of forbidden territory. Sometimes we found simple treasures—such as an old inner tube still springy enough to make slingshots—and in mid-stream there were often Navy ships anchored in long file, or Dayliners and smaller river craft to charm our gaze as they steamed by.

When it snowed, we took our Flexible Flyers down to the Drive. This form of amusement also presented its hazards. The most rewarding hill was the famed Gully, just south of the Soldiers and Sailors Monument. This short but steep slope terminated suddenly at the top of the wall leading to the tracks. To avert disaster a la Ethan Frome, one had to brake hard and swerve sharply at the very moment the descent reached its highest point of exhilaration. When the going was icy, not everyone was equal to the display of brinkmanship, with occasional ghastly results.

In those days it either snowed more, or snowplows were less efficient, and snow piles in the gutters used to last for days. They were often taller than we were, and ideally suited for the conduct of trench warfare.

On snowless days, Ferd and I sometimes explored the basements of the apartment houses. The storage and furnace rooms held a particular fascination for us. Sometimes we called on Schimsky, the superintendent of our building. Schimsky was a German with fluctuating moods and a vaudeville accent. He was an early radio buff. In the earphone era when most people were straining at crystal sets or one tube affairs, he had constructed a monumental apparatus with at least eight bulbs and an impressive loud speaker. He experimented with his set for hours when he should have been doing something about the hot water in 4 B or the defective outlet in 7 G. Sometimes he chased us out with a volley of Teutonic imprecations. But, on his more tractable days, Schimsky would suffer us to enter his sanctum, watch him tinker with his masterpiece, and listen to its groans and wails. I suppose he figured that when he had us in sight at least we weren't pushing over trunks or dropping water bombs out of an apartment window.

The water bomb, as any red-blooded city boy knew, was a paper grocery bag filled with water and dropped from a window on a real or imaginary foe in the street below. A successful launching was rarely achieved without eliciting some form of protest. I remember cowering in a hall closet with the lily-livered Coleman brothers while the valiant maid of their household held off a dripping doorman with a torrent of Finnish.

In time we developed a subtler form of missile. The new weapon was not purposed to inflict the physical discomfort of the water bomb, but its psychological impact, especially at night, was satisfyingly lethal. Our research revealed that the common kitchen match, dropped from a height of several stories onto a cement sidewalk, will land head first with a burst of flame and a sharp crackle. Evening strollers were dumbfounded to have the pavement in front of them suddenly pop and flare. When a covey of high school girls presented an especially inviting target we'd let fly with a dozen matches at once. We rigged up an elaborate periscopic device so we could sadistically view the shattering result without revealing the source of the attack.

It wasn't the custom for kids to dress up on Halloween. That annual rite was reserved for Thanksgiving when youthful ragamuffins in old frock coats, discarded ladies' finery or other outlandish disguises canvassed the street chirping, "Anything for Thanksgiving, mister?" We were glad to reap a few pennies. In later years this ritual was moved to Halloween and still later it was consecrated to UNICEF's "Trick or Treat."

Halloween was of course the open season for pranks. We pinned doorbells, planted bricks under old hats for people to kick, rigged up "tappy on the window-pane," and carried on other high jinks. It was before the days of "trick or treat" so there was no incentive to abstain from deviltry. For us Broadway and West End Avenue kids, however, the jack o'lantern season was not one of unalloyed amusement. We annually got our comeuppance when the toughs from Amsterdam and Columbus came over with their flour sacks. These were long stockings, filled at the end with flour and (we suspected) rocks, and whirled like a gaucho's bola. As an implement of street warfare it was not as deadly as a switchblade, but if you happened to come within range you got a resounding whack and a liberal dose of whiting.

The neighborhood seemed more compact in those days, and many of the storekeepers knew us, with or without false moustaches. There was a Japanese store on Broadway selling miniature gardens, goldfish and tiny turtles with painted backs where we spent hours gazing at the wildlife. Woolworth's, a *real* five and dime in that time, had many attractions within our means. Then there were little stationery stores with inviting jars of all-day suckers, licorice sticks, nonpareils, chocolate babies, jaw breakers and other delectable penny trifles for palates which had not yet been numbed by bubble gum.

A stellar attraction of the neighborhood was the stupendous serial change-making system of a local dry goods store. The clerk inserted your dollar and the sales slip into a small metallic container that latched on to a fast-moving wire. You watched the carrier career around sharp corners and curves with the gravity-defying speed of a roller coaster, as it made its upward journey to a cashier's cage located somewhere in outer space. You could also witness its dizzying descent along the same intricate route back to the earthbound counter where you'd made your purchase. It had all the entrancement of a high wire act.

Of course, the silent screen had no serious competitor among the neighborhood attractions. There were half a dozen movies on Broadway between Loew's 86th Street and the Nemo on 110th. I recall especially the Olympia on 107th Street because its classic name is evocative of many misspent hours. If we patronized it more than the others, it was not due to its superior programming but because we possessed the secret of entering it without paying. Some distance from the Broadway entrance, on a side street, a wall of posters advertising the theater's coming attractions cleverly concealed an exit door. There was no way of opening the door from the outside, but we learned to hang about nonchalantly looking at the posters until a patron emerged. A foot deftly inserted before the door closed again was our open sesame. It must have been several weeks before a spoilsport usher spotted us and gave chase.

Another favorite trespassing ground in my youth was the Columbia campus. Many the day we wandered up to Morningside with the object of gaining illegal admittance to South Field where the Columbia teams practiced and played all their home baseball and football games before the construction of Baker Field. Lou Gehrig, an undergraduate in those days, gave convincing evidence of later prowess. I recall a mighty homer from his bat that cleared the 116th Street fence and bounced on the steps of the Low Library, more than two blocks away.

Our own "campus" most of the years I spent on the West Side was P.S. 165, on 109th Street, between Broadway and Amsterdam. I have never met anyone who attended P.S. 165 in this era who does not recall it affectionately. A prime reason for its solid reputation was Jacob Theobald, principal for many years until he became an Assistant Superintendent of Schools. As a boys' school attracting neighborhood youth of diversified family origins and income levels, P.S. 165 had its share of behavior problems, but on the whole discipline was good, with male teachers of unusually high caliber who stood for no nonsense presiding over the upper grades.

Do eighth graders even *attempt* Shakespeare today? I would doubt it, unless counterparts of Celeste Valadon are still coaching them. We put on *Julius Caesar*. Ralph Elias was Brutus, I was Cassius, Ferd was Marc Antony, Dave Rosenberg was Caesar and Dave Strauss played Cinna, the poet. Miss Valadon, despite her French patronymic, was a robust English teacher with a booming voice, bounding energy, and a bombsight eye for detail. She drilled us meticulously in our lines, saw to it our sandals were authentically bound in classic style and our togas had just the right Roman drape. Fortunately for the lad who played Caesar, her passion for verisimilitude did not extend to weapons, and Caesar lived to face later reckonings—in fact, he became a certified public accountant.

When after-school rehearsals or chores confined us to the immediate neighborhood, we were rarely at a loss for company or activity. We went through a perennial cycle of block games, including punchball, stickball, stoopball, boxball, handball, one-a-cat and touch football. In more placid moments, we played and traded marbles, campaign buttons and cigarette pictures. Some days everyone was on the street with marbles. We also did a lot of rollerskating, around the block and in the park; occasionally on weekends we blew our savings at St. Nick's roller rink, then at 66th Street near Central Park West. On balmy Saturdays we'd cross the Hudson by the Fort Lee Ferry at 125th Street, then go hiking and picnicking along the Palisades. We formed boys clubs, mainly to have the exquisite pleasure of blackballing our enemies or putting them through a gruesome initiation ritual.

We were interested in cars, but less obsessed and certainly less well informed on the subject than boys are today. I could recognize most of the makes because of a game I played with my older brother before he went off to college and we moved to the West Side. Pad and pencil in hand, we would sit on a Fifth Avenue bench for an hour or more, checking off the passing vehicles. Today one couldn't keep up with the flow of traffic, but at that time the number of cars was such that there was no difficulty in keeping count. The record of one such competition, preserved in a faded notebook, shows Cadillac led the field with a total of 50. Packard was second with 33, Ford a poor third with 17, Pierce Arrow and

Hudson tallied 14 each, and White, Buick and Dodge trailed with only four each. Chevrolet, Hupmobile and Maxwell barely scored.

We were almost totally oblivious of girls. We had to endure them in Sunday school, and a few of us were compelled by parents to attend dancing school, but for the most part we had no conception of what girls said or thought about or how they spent their after school hours. Even if we had been psychologically and physiologically up to it, dating the opposite sex would have been ruled out by the limited pocket money at our disposal. The weekly allowances we got from our parents were barely sufficient to cover our candy and soda requirements and an occasional movie, let alone other essentials of life. We were forever seeking extra cash.

Before elections we impartially distributed handbills for any candidate who'd pay us. Once, after faithfully carrying out an assignment for the perennially-running Harold Riegelman, his aide tried to pay us off at a fraction of what we thought was the agreed wage. We sought revenge in a particularly insidious manner. Armed with placards, buttons and streamers furnished by the rival party, we paraded up and down in front of Riegelman's headquarters, ostentatiously soliciting support for his opponent. After an hour or so, the exasperated aide succumbed to this counter-offensive and paid us our due.

When the radio craze came along, Ferd and I found it a temporary bonanza. We didn't know a condenser from a grid, but we mastered the technique of putting up aerials. To the despair of the neighborhood janitors we crisscrossed roofs for blocks around with an intricate web of wires. We had to make our installations well above the clotheslines, which meant climbing water towers and escarpments that would have dizzied Harold Lloyd. The heights didn't bother us then, but I go retrospectively green at the thought of myself perched aloft, ten or twelve stories above the street, sometimes in a freezing wind, calmly twisting wires to fasten an insulator to a lead-in. We survived, somehow, and perhaps the city's special hazards may have given us a certain resilience.

As time went by, the West Side area I knew as a boy went into a decline. Housing conditions worsened, and there was a corresponding rise in delinquency and crime. But now, like the fabled Phoenix, the West Side has made a stunning comeback. With the luster of Lincoln Center at one end, the flourishing Parnassus of Morningside Heights on the other, acres of smart boutiques and restaurants in between, and the gentrification of many residential blocks, the outlook is brighter. Indeed, our children may live to see the day when the disappearance of the zip gun and the switch blade from the juvenile arsenal will again make the West Side safe for the water bomb.

GUYS AND DOLLS

MALE FRIENDSHIPS

I followed my brother to DeWitt Clinton, a public high school then located at 59th Street and 10th Avenue, the neighborhood known as Hell's Kitchen. A year or two after my graduation, Clinton moved to the Mosholu area of the Bronx. The 59th Street building today is the John Jay College for Police Training.

The student body at DeWitt Clinton was far too numerous, even then, for the main building, so it spilled over into several annexes in different parts of the City. In my first two high school years I attended two annexes, but finally was admitted to the Hell's Kitchen building. I took the subway in the morning from 110th Street and Broadway to the 59th Street Station and walked over to 10th Avenue. The seedy neighborhood was pretty tough.

I was reasonably popular at Clinton where I was chosen for Arista, the Honor Society; wrote for the *Magpie Magazine*, was elected secretary of the General Organization, and acted in several plays. I played third singles on the tennis team behind Captain Sid Snitkin and Reggie Weir. Reggie was my first African-American friend. He became a successful doctor. We had a good season my senior year, losing only one or two matches.

Established for many years, Clinton had an excellent faculty. Maxwell Naumberg, my English teacher senior year, built on the foundation Herb had given me in English literature. At graduation I received the Alfred Bossom award for excellence in government.

Ferdinand Alan Nauheim

Male friendships were always important to me. In elementary and high school my best buddy was Ferd Nauheim, whose ingenious electioneering won me the post of GO secretary at Clinton. Ferd and I were constantly in each other's homes. Because of his father's business reverses and premature death, Ferd had to go to work directly after high school. He wrote well, spoke well, was a talented artist (people prized his *Ferdoodles*) and became an early, eloquent advocate for mutual funds. He married a Washington girl, Beatrice Strasburger, the daughter of a Judge, and I was best man at their wedding. Ferd enlisted as a Private in WWII, fought in the Battle of the Bulge, and at war's end wrote an appealing war/love novel called *Behold the Upright*. After the war when I worked in Washington I saw a good deal of Ferd and his family. I spoke at Ferd's funeral.

Because I skipped a class somewhere along the line, I graduated from Clinton in January, rather than in June. That gave me almost eight months before college entrance in the fall of 1928. Ferd and I combined our job search efforts and met success at Stern Brothers Department Store at 42nd Street and 6th Avenue (later known as Avenue of the Americas). Ferd got a job in the advertising department and I landed one in the printing shop.

At the princely salary of $20 per week, I spent five months as a printer's devil. That meant I had to clean the ink off the presses first thing in the morning and make myself useful the rest of the day performing simple tasks and running errands. John O'Carroll was a genial boss and I also took to Dalton, Butler and Grant, his three assistants. The shop printed up the various bulletins, forms and internal memoranda required by the store, and set type for most of the ads that Stern's ran in the daily newspapers. Equipment consisted of two linotype machines, a large and a small press, diversified fonts of hand type and a cutting machine. In the interstices of the day I learned a good deal about printing. In addition to inking and cleaning the presses, I had to distribute the handset type in the proper slots, lock up the chases, and operate the cutter. The cutting machine was not in its first youth, and I had to be wary in operating it, but emerged with my fingers intact.

Sometimes Ferd would bring over the ad copy that needed to be set; sometimes I was sent over to fetch it. One day the Furniture Department was advertising a special sale. The banner headline read: "For June brides—Just that Occasional Piece You Wanted!" We caught that in time and the copy was revised. Ferd and I found our duties were sporadic—there were busy hours and some that were slack. Theoretically, we had an hour for lunch, but on slow days we enjoyed a longer interval. Around noon, one of us would go down to the time clock and punch both of us out for lunch. When we actually left for lunch at one, we punched ourselves in and then proceeded to have a leisurely dejeuner, often at the nearby Hotel Wentworth, where you could get a decent three-course meal for fifty cents. When hurried, we would usually head for the Chock Full O'Nuts. The menu there didn't offer much choice, but we were both in love with Ruth Gray, the attractive woman behind the counter. For a fast, cheap and satisfying meal, we patronized the Automat. For fifteen cents you could have a buttered roll and a delicious hot chocolate. If you felt like splurging, a quarter would buy you an appetizing chicken salad sandwich. Something great was lost when the Automats went out of business!

Almost every Friday evening, Ferd and I would go to Grey's Drug Store to buy second balcony tickets for the theater. For fifty cents we saw some fabulous shows. Standouts that I recall were *What Price Glory, The Front Page, They Knew What They Wanted, Journey's End and Street Scene*. To me there was (and is today) nothing like the New York theater, though many years later, working at the American Embassy in London, I was enchanted by the lagniappe of two glorious seasons of the London stage.

I could have worked all summer at Stern's but decided to quit early in June to take a quick typing course. From then on, I typed most of my letters and papers, first on a Remington portable, and later on a succession of machines. Whenever I worked after that, even when I had the most expert secretarial assistance, I always kept a typewriter near my desk to draft on. And one at home. When I was eighty, Vera presented me with a word processor which I at first mistrusted. But in a short time I appreciated its wider scope and subsequently wrote two books on it. I had the same apprehension when I acquired my first computer. It has served me well, despite occasional down periods or loss of memory. But I still keep my trusty word processor in reserve and occasionally resort to it.

Ferd and I developed a puzzling game that netted us a bit of pocket change. We would place a bet with a visitor to one or the other of our two apartments that a doctor we knew was psychic enough to identify any card that he selected from a deck. After his selection, say, of the jack of spades, we would instruct the visitor to telephone a number and ask for Doctor Winchester. He would then make the call (to Ferd's telephone number) and receive the correct answer from Doctor Winchester. The trick was that we each had a list with the name of a different doctor for every card in the deck. This worked out fine until one night my mother, after many such calls, answered the phone and when the caller asked for Doctor Bigelow she answered, "He's out at the delicatessen getting our Sunday night supper." I still chuckle when I think of it.

William Howard Schuman

My other "best" friend was Bill Schuman. We weren't schoolmates but met around the block when we were 10 and 11 and began a close friendship that lasted 70 years until his death in 1992. Bill recruited me for Camp Cobbossee in Winthrop, Maine where we were inseparable comrades and collaborators as campers and later as counselors. Our first song was for a camp show:

WE'RE DRESSED UP FOR THE VISITORS

We're dressed up for the Visitors, the parental inquisitors,
Who snoop around on Wednesdays and Sundays.
Because no people come around, we generally bum around
On Saturdays, Tuesdays, Thursdays, Fridays, Mondays.
On other days we don't have to clean up the campus
Providing that the O.D. doesn't cramp us.
Today we're clothed in purity, with soap as our security,
Since we cleaned up for dear old Cobbossee.

Bill was an extraordinary fellow. He was always bright, talented and funny, but even those who knew him best never imagined the success he would have as a important musical influence and composer, close to Copland, Harris and Bernstein.

With some reluctance my folks agreed to the idea of my going to a sleep-away camp. I embarked on a night train at Grand Central Station and woke up in Maine the next morning. It was my first venture away from home, and I had the usual qualms, but I soon settled in. My friends and tent mates were Bill, Dick Lillienstern and Herb Bloomberg, all from New York, though the largest number of campers hailed from New Jersey. Romulo Marsans, a kindly father figure of Cuban origin, was the camp director; Pop Sawyer, an Amherst graduate and physician, was head counselor. He and Romie Marsans, a 300-pound Dartmouth junior, were the chief administrators.

One of the Newark boys, Bert Steinhardt, took an instant dislike to me, and began to taunt me. He was a shade bigger and something of a bully. He called me "Knock Knees" (which I had) and "Goofus" (which I didn't deserve), and one day in the pine grove I punched him. It was my first fistfight, and I don't recall ever having had another. Anyway, I was beating him when Romie spotted us and broke it up. Bert never bothered me again.

After supper we all went to the recreation hall which had a stage for music and other entertainment. By the third week I was confident enough to get up and recite *Casey at the Bat*. That was the first of my many appearances on the stage. I learned and recited other poems, some of which I still know by heart. They included *Casey's Comeback,* an eloquent ode to *The Ball,* and two parodic gems of Newman Levy: *Hamlet* and *Samson and Delilah.* Hamlet is reprinted in a later chapter.

Bill and I had complementary athletic skills. He caught on the baseball team and was a proficient canoeist. I did creditably at tennis and was a breast stroker on the swim team. Each summer we went off on canoes for several days on the Great Circle trip, taking us from Lake Cobbossee-Contee through Maranacook, Annabessacook and other lakes with Indian names. I also made trips to other camps for tennis tournaments and other athletic events. Our great rival was Camp Kennebec, but I also recall visits to Winnebago, Androscoggin and to the Rangeley Lakes.

As Cobbossee campers, we looked up to several of our counselors. Al Koch, who coached tennis, was a tall angular type with a sense of humor that reminded one of Jimmy Durante. Ros Whytock, our tent counselor, was a gracious, fair-minded graduate student from the Midwest. My favorite was Eddy Gilmore from Talladega, Alabama. Eddy coached baseball, dabbled in theater and helped us put out *The Almanak*, the camp paper. We kept up with Eddy long after we left Cobbossee. He became a reporter, then a foreign correspondent for the Associated Press. From 1941 to 1954 he was assigned to Moscow as a correspondent, and there he met the love of his life. Eddy and Tamara Chemaschova married while he was there, and I remember the cause celebre when he tried to bring her back to the United States. It was the time of Stalin, and many obstacles were set in their path, but he finally succeeded. In 1947 he won the Pulitzer Prize for telegraphic reporting from Moscow.

As camper and counselor, I spent a lot of my camp time writing for and editing the weekly *Almanak*. We collected the news and for a time printed it on a messy, smelly mimeograph machine in *The Almanak* office. At some point, I think we were still junior counselors, Bill had a beat-up car, and would ferry me to Lewiston where we had the sheet printed on a small letterpress. I didn't know how to drive in those days. We would leave camp after breakfast on printing day, deliver the copy to the printer, and enjoy a lazy lunch and convivial afternoon before retrieving the copies and heading back to camp. We met a couple of summer students from Bates College who helped us pass the time agreeably. Mine had the euphonious name of Kay Way.

When my son went to Cobbossee, I revisited the camp. The setting was as I recalled it—from the tented campus, the walk through a pine grove leads to the lake, a grand prospect with two well-remembered green islands in view, Lovers and Spiders. Bill's son Tony also went to Cobbossee. I treasure my camp experience. Among other things, it cemented my friendship with Bill Schuman.

In subsequent years, as we got older, Bill and I wrote songs at camp and produced, directed and acted in several musicals and plays. One was a minstrel show where we blacked up as end men. The show succeeded so well that we gave a second performance for charity at the Winthrop Town Hall. We returned to Cobbossee each year, first as campers, then as junior counselors, and finally as full-fledged counselors. As campers, we paid $300 for the eight week season; as junior counselors we went free and got $100, and as counselors we did a bit better.

Camp was great fun. Sawyer and his successor were disciplinarians, but we enjoyed finding ways to thwart them. Each year we had inter-camp rivalry between the Reds and Whites. The campers were divided into two teams that competed on the athletic field, in the water, on the stage, and in a complicated all-day flag hunt (a kind of treasure hunt). When Bill and I were both on the Red team, we wrote, produced, and acted in a musical called *It's Up to Pa*. It had two performances for the benefit of the Winthrop Community Hospital, one held at Camp Cobbossee Lodge and the second in the Town Hall of Winthrop, Maine. The hit song of the show was *I Want to be Near You*. The chorus follows:

I WANT TO BE NEAR YOU

I want to be near you,
I want to be at your side,
Securely and surely tied to you.
I want to be near you,
I'm aching to take my stand

Where I can be hand in hand with you.
I've been hankering to be anchoring safe in your arms,
Helter-skeltering to be sheltering
Far from alarms, dear;
I want to be near you,
I'm hoping that I can spend
My life to the very end near you.

We borrowed shamelessly from Gilbert and Sullivan and Rodgers and Hart. The Reds won that year, despite formidable opposition from the White team. Meyer Rosenthal, a few years older, and the camp's leading Thespian, was a White. He became a recognized actor on the Broadway stage under the name of Anthony Ross; one of his notable roles was as the Gentleman Caller in Tennessee Williams' *Glass Menagerie.*

When I went off to college, Bill and I resolved to continue writing together, but my attention was distracted by my studies and other pursuits and I disappointed him by being much less productive. For a time, he continued writing popular songs, some with Frank Loesser, another neighborhood friend, but though they had some near misses they never scored a hit. One night Bill's sister Audrey persuaded him to accompany her to his first Philharmonic concert. Symphonic music blew his mind, and beginning the next morning he undertook its serious study, eventually winning the first Pulitzer Prize for Music and Kennedy Center honors. Aside from a few jingles, we rarely collaborated musically again, though the inspiration for his opera, *The Mighty Casey* owed something to my recitation at Cobbossee of *Casey at the Bat.*

Bill was a great raconteur and funster. One of his quips that always amused me is:

FUNEX?
SIFX.
FUNEM?
SIFM.
OKVFMNX *

Bill's wife, Frankie (nee Frances Prince), a formidable achiever in her own right, was also a lifetime friend. She worked prodigiously for Public Television Channel 13. Her capacity for friendship brought together a loyal, small group of people for many of Bill's public events. Margaret and I were at the opening of Lincoln Center and Vera and I were honored to join the Schumans at the Kennedy Center occasion. Coincidentally the Schumans were married the very day Vera was born. It was a sad day in 1994 when, at age 81, lovely bright Frances lost her battle with cancer.

*(Have you any eggs? Yes, I have eggs. Have you any ham? Yes, I have ham. OK, we have ham and eggs.)

Edmund Hall North

My best friend in Great Neck was Ed North. Ed was the son of Bobby North, a retired actor and a friend of my father. Ed and I did a vast amount of exploring the neighborhood. A half-mile beyond our house, it was still fairly wild in those days, and we collected turtles from a meandering stream. One day in 1922, we got up the courage to enter an old abandoned home and had the thrill of finding a document that was then 100 years old. I remember that was the summer my grandfather Marks died.

Sometimes Ed and I would go swimming at the Steamboat Landing on nearby Long Island Sound. Sometimes we went with others on hikes. I enjoyed the Norths' warm hospitality. We often played in a large room above the garage. Once, when we were there, Mr. North brought in a friend, the renowned De Wolf Hopper. Hopper took on a stage persona and, as he had done a thousand times before audiences, gave us a dramatic recitation of *Casey at the Bat*. It made a great impression on me, and I learned the words of the poem.

Ed North went to Culver Military Academy and to college in California and I didn't see him for some years. He became a screenwriter, and when I met him in later life he had written the screen plays for *The Day the Earth Stood Still*, *Patton* and other successful movies.

Ephraim London and Woodrow Wilson Sandler

Other close friends of my youth were Ephraim London, civil libertarian and lawyer for Lillian Hellman in her suit against Mary McCarthy, and Woodrow Sandler, a labor lawyer with the National Labor Relations Board and ultimately a successful arbitrator. Woody was a huge, generous playfellow who could give uproarious imitations of people and sounds. He and I once spent a hilarious week in Bermuda where, among other things, he taught me to ride a bicycle. We stayed at the Gosling guesthouse. Cynthia Dayton, Gosling's wife,was from Bayside, Long Island, and a friend of a friend of mine. We were the only guests. They had a tennis court which was in poor shape. Gosling, a Bermudian, kept saying, "It wants mowing and rolling," so we mowed it and rolled it and played on it. One evening the Goslings invited us to accompany them to a great party. Woody danced with a well-endowed local maiden and returned with stars in his eyes. "You've got to try this," he said, "I couldn't believe my thighs." In the time of Toscanini, Woody and I had a Philharmonic subscription.

Woody, Ephraim, Bill, Ferd and I and a chap named Henry Brandt, formed a poker club which met weekly for two years and had an elaborate set of rules. We called it UMPPA—United Musical Poker Players of America.

LOVE IN ITS MANY FORMS

Male friendships always meant a lot to me, but I have to confess an admiration amounting to a congenital weakness for the opposite sex. It began in Sunday School with my first crush on Audrey, an exotic "bok fish," a term my grandfather used to describe an appetizing young girl. She was a darling youngster, dark and of Panamanian Sephardic background. I remember my prayers at night when I said, "God bless Mommy and Daddy and when I grow up I want to marry Audrey for to her I am sure I will prove a worthy husband."

My first real girlfriend was Lillian. I liked her ample figure. We were both 15 and it was a time of heavy necking. Like girl's basketball in those days that meant a lot of jumping up and down but little scoring. It bothered me unreasonably that Lillian's father had a heavy Jewish accent, but she and I were an "item" for at least two years. At that time Ferd had his Stella (cf. Swift), and Bill had Louise. We featured a song titled *Louise* in one of our camp shows. When we were junior counselors, Bill and I visited a girl's camp, Tripp Lake, to view a performance of *HMS Pinafore* starring Josephine Waterman as Josephine. Jo was from Tampa and fickle me fell for her. When I was a freshman at Dartmouth she was in her first year at Goucher. She was my heartthrob. I had her picture on my desk and we corresponded wildly but never met again until much later (1937) when I saw her, married, in New Orleans.

I lost my virginity, that same freshman year, in Boston with a Radcliffe girl I met through a good friend of Bill's. We met for a date in a Boston hotel and all went well. She was no virgin.

The girl I felt close to most of my college years and whom I invited to several house parties was Fritzie from Alliance, Ohio. We clicked from the start both mentally and physically. She was distantly related to the Warner Brothers. If she had waited, we might have been married, but she was anxious to move ahead, which meant marriage in those days. She had a lot of oomph, was pretty and well built. Art Schlichter, a classmate and a friend since grade school, always admired her and urged me to commit, but I wasn't ready. Fritzie married well, and had a couple of children, but tragically died of cancer in her thirties. In my junior year I met Margery at Smith. She was a cool customer, extremely attractive and I was smitten with her. However an older fraternity brother had the ill grace to snake her once at a house party. They were absent from our dance for about an hour. Ultimately he married her. (I subsequently snaked a girl a fraternity mate brought to Hanover, but had a bad conscience about it.)

After college, Herbert's wife Hortie introduced me to two charming girls. One, Nellie, was virtually untouchable. She was here for a few years with her Dutch parents and saw me off on my first trip to Europe. She was the most beautiful girl I ever went out with. Hortie's other contribution was Joan, from a rich Jewish family, real rich. She invited me to a Smith house party a year or two after my graduation from Dartmouth. She then invited me to spend a weekend at her parents' summer home up the Hudson. I recall a torrid scene in the boat-house. I think she would have married me, but I wasn't ready for that.

Ferd and I made the rounds together. We never paid for it, but had a succession of "easy" girls. Some we met at dance halls in Yorkville. I met Frieda that way, but it was too tough taking her home by subway to Brooklyn. I was also attracted to a very pretty Czech girl named Elizabeth. In my years at the Atlas Publishing Company I had serious romances with two other Dutch girls. One, Charlotte, was the younger sister of friends of Herb and Hortie living at a garden nursery in Huntington, Long Island. I used to borrow the family car to ride out from Great Neck to see her. She gave me a lovely Japanese maple and very good sex, some of the best I ever had. She was lively and always happy to greet me. I also relished Marion, in publishing, a year or two older, who had her own flat in mid-Manhattan. I remember making love to her in front of a roaring fireplace. Then there was Madlyn. A Barnard graduate, she was bright and funny and very well read. The Schumans liked her and Frankie, at least, believed that she would make me a good mate. Madlyn was pretty but on the hefty side and that put me off, though it shouldn't have. More to the point, she was strong willed beyond just being independent and I had a fear of that.

On the light side, I can confess two rather bizarre sexual encounters. I always liked attractive women and had some luck with pickups in museums, libraries and galleries. After working late one evening I was on a Long Island Rail Road train bound for Great Neck. There were very few passengers. I sat behind a young woman reading a magazine. Though other seats were available, a middle-aged man, burly type, sat next to her and began to talk to her, edging closer. She didn't reply to his advances. He was a bit drunk. I sized up the situation and partly out of chivalry and part opportunism, I got up the courage to ask him to lay off. I could have received a punch in the nose, but instead, he took the rebuff and changed his seat. Estella, it turned out, knew very little English but thanked me warmly. She also left the train in Great Neck. I had a car at the station and gave her a ride home. I found she was from the Dominican Republic, living with her sister and brother-in-law who was violently anti-Trujillo, in exile and in danger of his life. His associate in NYC had just been assassinated by one of Trujillo's agents, while shaving, and he had moved out of the city not knowing if *he* was the intended target. Estella was accommodating and passionate and the best thing to happen that summer but, in the fall she returned to the Dominican Republic and though we had a labored correspondence for a while I never saw her again.

While working for the *American Wine and Liquor Journal* I was invited to any number of receptions held to launch a new brand of spirits. On one such occasion I met a voluptuous and rather showy blonde. She was in New York for a week from Oklahoma—I can't remember why. After a few drinks, I took her to dinner and then to the West Side hotel in the mid-forties where she was staying. It was getting late. We headed for the elevator, but were intercepted by the man at the desk who refused me admission. It was the hotel's policy not to admit male escorts of registered female guests after a certain hour. I tried every known ploy to dissuade him but he was firm as a rock, as was I. Wilma and I said "goodnight." It was after midnight, and I had to work the next day, but I was too eager to have the experience die on that note. Back on the street, I perceived that the hotel directly adjoined another hotel that appeared to be the same height. I had a brilliant idea, and phoned Wilma to ascertain her room number. I then peered into the lobby of the adjacent hotel and waited until the man at the desk was otherwise engaged. I nonchalantly took a waiting elevator, and mounted to the top floor. There was no penthouse, but I found a stairway leading to the roof. I had some difficulty making my way in the dark to the roof area nearest the other hotel. On reaching it, I was dismayed to find that the adjacent rooftop was a few feet lower, and there was a gap of several feet between them with a narrow alley below. It was foolhardy, but I was in my twenties with all the ardor of youth. I successfully made the jump. I had a vision of spending the rest of the night under the stars, but was lucky to find an open down stairway. Wilma was pleased with my achievement! I was well rewarded.

This light-hearted portrayal of amorous incidents reflects the impulses and urges of adolescence and early manhood. Even then, I don't believe I ever had a relationship that was purely physical. But as I matured I was attracted to women by something deeper. I found this of course in both my marriages, but also in meaningful friendships with several women. Though sexuality was not a factor, these friendships with the opposite sex had elements not present in my friendships with men. I'm thinking here of long term friendships with Frankie Schuman, Jean Murphy and Jean Nimkin, Jane Moody, Susan Kellermann, Hortie Tyroler Marks Frenkel and Alexandra Joannides.

GILBERT AND SULLIVAN

When I was nine, my brother Herb took me to see a performance of *Ruddigore* at the Park Theater, and I embarked on a life long love affair with the Gilbert and Sullivan operas. Even before I went, I knew a lot of the songs from well-worn recordings. In the years that followed I saw at least three of the operas gloriously produced by the D'Oyly Carte Company that came to America during several seasons. I well remember the *Mikado* of Darrell Fancourt and Martin Green as Ko Ko and Jack Point.

A G&S troupe played in a Maine theater not far from the summer camp I attended. I witnessed several of their productions including the rarely performed *Grand Duke*, the last and least successful of the thirteen operas they wrote. Around that time I fell for my first real girlfriend when I heard her sing the part of Josephine in a girl's camp production of *HMS Pinafore*.

In my teens in New York I took in the splendid productions of Winthrop Ames' *Iolanthe*, *Pirates of Penzance* and one or two others. After college I joined the New York branch of the Gilbert and Sullivan Society. Herb and Hortie were early members and the President was Jerome Meyer, Hortie's brother-in-law. We sang songs and quizzed each other on the esoteric points of the various operas. The cast of the Blue Hill Troupe's productions came to entertain us and we responded by attending their annual performances. For nearly 80 years they have put on professional-quality shows. D'Oyly Carte performers also came around to whet our appetites for their productions.

After a stormy meeting of the Society where the achievements of Gilbert and Sullivan were compared, I wrote a verse that I recited at the next meeting. The *Palace Peeper*, Journal of the Society, published the verse with the following explanatory note: "We do not vouch for the authenticity of the following ballad, which was presented at the June 1938 meeting of the Society as a 'Lost Bab.' It has a very genuine ring about it, and if not penned by Gilbert himself certainly comes from the pen of one who has studied his style." Here's the verse:

THE TWO MISANTHROPES

In a lonely city rooming house, far from the Avenue,
A motley hoard of tenants lived—an ill assorted crew;
No word of cordiality resounded through the halls,
The gloom of years enshrouded deep those desultory walls.

The third floor front was William Spore, a misanthrope for fair,
His share of this world's weary woes almost too great to bear;
Spore had for thirty years or more sold babies' underpinning,
His trade, not highly lucrative, at least kept him from sinning.

Across the hall lived Amos Grife, in solitary quarters,
A man bereft of home and wife, he had five wayward daughters.
But these had married far and wide, from Turkistan to Tampa.
Bad girls! They never dropped a line to comfort aging grandpa.

At close of day each of these men rose to his ivory tower,
Monastically locked his door, withdrew into his bower.
Their bedrooms bleak were side by side, a common bath they shared,
But the two had never spoken, though at times they rudely stared.

A man of habits constant, William always rose at six,
Proceeded then to bathe himself, his thinning hair to fix.
At seven sharp he left the house, his breakfast bent on buying,
While Amos at that hour still in peaceful dreams was lying.

When Grife arose at seven-ten the tub was empty quite.
He could frolic in the soap suds to his lonely heart's delight.

To this daily toilet schedule each rigidly adhered,
And one bathroom was sufficient since they never interfered.

One morning, quite by accident, Grife woke before his time.
Some seconds short of six AM his clock began to chime;
Unwittingly he blinked his eyes, then slowly raised his head,
And, thinking it was seven ten he clambered out of bed.

That morning Spore was following his customary path,
When he heard some water splashing in what sounded like the bath.
In shocked surprise he made his way across the bedroom floor,
And stood a moment listening at the threshold of the door.

Above the water's din he heard a sound that made him start—
A sound that warmed the cockles of his cold embittered heart.
For Grife, from inhibitions free, was singing in the tub,
In accents clear his voice kept time with every rub and scrub.

He started with the Gondoliers, he ran through Pinafore,
He chanted Iolanthe, and he warbled Ruddigore;
He bellowed forth the Pirates with its song about the Foemen,
And with mounting virtuosity, he launched into the Yeoman.

Rhapsodic bliss transported quite the face of William Spore,
As he stood there with his ear glued tight to that celestial door;
He held his peace 'til Grife cried out "I have a song to sing-O"
Then burst inside, as he replied the customary thing-O.

No sooner had he sung the famous line's concluding vowel
Than up sprang dripping Amos (taking refuge in a towel)
They fell about each other's necks, these hardened old recluses
Joined in the holy brotherhood that G & S induces.

From that day forth these comrades fond resolved no more to sever,
They pledged themselves in friendship's name, to leave each other never,
They hurried home from work each day to sing to one another,
Indeed you might have thought that Mrs. Meyer was their mother.

They witnessed all performances of G & S libretti
And greeted all their favorites with bravos and confetti.
They bought all new recordings with unmitigated piety
And soon became star members of our Savoyard Society.

One evening after meeting, overwhelmed with newfound cheer,
They both went out with Katie Etz to get a glass of beer.
They fell to idle talking of the operas and their plots.
Of patter songs and madrigals, of ballads and gavottes.

"Of course, there's not the slightest doubt," said Grife with knowing air
"That Gilbert was the greater of the celebrated pair—
His tender lyric quality, his quips of cutting kind,
The evidence is crystal clear—his was the master mind."

"What ho, my erring comrade!" sputtered Spore "Upon my word,
This is the most outrageous thing that I have ever heard.
You dare compare this montebank to England's great composer,
A gag man to a genius bright—oh fie on you—no no sir!"

The argument waxed hotter and resentment mounted high,
That friendship warm was blighted in the twinkling of an eye,
They slugged each other fiercely, left the place a total wreck;
One took the high road, one the low, and Etz—she paid the check.

Once more each sits in silence in that dismal third floor scene,
Avoiding any meeting in the bathroom in between.
Two more unfriendly critters you won't find in all this cold berg,
One's reading Hesketh Pearson and the other Isaac Goldberg.

And when the Blue Hills do their show they both go every night,
But one sits to the theater's left, the other to the right.
Grife clutches his libretto scanning Gilbert's every rhyme
While Spore pours o'er a tattered score and hums while beating time.

(Note: Mrs. Meyer was the mother of Jerome Meyer, the Society President. Katie Etz was an active member. Hesketh Pearson and Isaac Goldberg wrote books about Gilbert and Sullivan.)

Alas the D'Oyly Carte Company no longer crosses the ocean although it still performs at London's Savoy Theater where Vera and I saw *The Mikado* some years ago. The Village Light Opera Company has filled some of the gap with its popular performances in the Village and at Symphony Space.

Here in Northern California a company, The Lamplighters, holds forth. Vera and I greatly enjoyed their productions of *Patience, Princess Ida* and *Iolanthe* and they can be forgiven for an occasional lapse into syrupy musicals.

DARTMOUTH

In 1928, having completed the typing course, I went once again to Camp Cobbossee for the summer as a junior counselor. That fall I entered Dartmouth and a new chapter of my life began.

In those days you boarded the Montrealer early evening in New York and it dumped you unceremoniously around 4 am in White River Junction, Vermont. From there you took a taxi to Hanover, New Hampshire and got your first look at Dartmouth College. I had never been to Hanover when I arrived that September in 1928, but I felt I knew the place because my brother Herb had gone there.

In my mind there was never any question that I would follow Herb to Dartmouth. It was the only college I applied to and luckily I got in. Herb loved the College and vicariously relived his years there when I was a Dartmouth student. He usually met me in Cambridge for the Harvard game. He was with us one year when we invited some local girls up to a hotel room to celebrate a Dartmouth victory. Herb divulged the fact that our birthdays were a day apart, on April 21 and 22. Said one of the guests, not the brightest of the group, "Gee, it must have been tough on your mother!" Herb and I suffered each year in the Yale Bowl until Dartmouth finally broke the Eli jinx.

I entered Dartmouth with high hopes and never regretted my choice. From Manhattan, I was a reasonably sophisticated kid, but soon found that my sophistication cut little ice with the New Englanders and midwesterners who lived in my dorm. I had the usual freshman qualms on being pitched into a new environment but overcame them reasonably soon and became (and remain) fiercely loyal to Dartmouth. There is no particular logic to my loyalty; it may be the splendid isolation of its setting in the New Hampshire hills that inspires the feeling common to many Dartmouth alumni.

Several indignities were piled on freshmen at that time that happily have vanished with the years. Without exception, we were doomed to wear beanies, silly little caps, throughout the first year. That tradition lasted until 1973. We were also lorded over by sophomores, who hazed us in various ways and could call on us to perform the most menial of tasks, for example, carrying luggage up several flights of stairs to their dormitory rooms.

Another outworn tradition that bred ill will between the two classes was the pushball or football rush, which took place early in the fall before we had really settled into campus life. I forget the object of this senseless struggle in which the two classes battled on the campus. I think the freshman, within a certain time, had to retrieve a number of footballs held by the sophomores. The scrimmage lasted about 20 minutes, at the conclusion of which the freshmen had to run the gauntlet between lines of sophomores who whacked them with paddles, or whatever came to hand. It was rough and tough, and I emerged somewhat the worse for wear. It probably wasn't a direct consequence, but the next day I came down with yellow jaundice, now known as hepatitis, and wound up in Dick's House, the College infirmary. I had barely started my classes, so it got me off to a bad beginning.

There were some compensations. I first shared a room with a junior named Shaw Cole. He was patient and understanding and gave me many valuable insights on what to expect in college. He was on the mend and was soon replaced by a sophomore, Robert Asher, a brilliant student from Chicago, who became a lifelong friend. Bob, from a well-to-do family connected to the Rosenwalds, had been the selected target of Leopold and Loeb, but fortunately for him he was home sick the day of the kidnapping, so they took Bobbie Franks instead. In later years the Ashers were friends of ours in Washington, where Bob worked for the World Bank, and also during a time when we both served in Geneva. I had several dates with Bob's sister, Elise, who later became a recognized artist and the wife of poet Stanley Kunitz, who in his 90s was twice briefly U.S. Poet Laureate.

The food in Dick's House was superior to that served in Freshman Commons, the medical attention was first-rate, and there was a splendid patient library; I read several choice books during my stay. One that I did not read, but noted with interest, was *Have Faith in Massachusetts* by Calvin Coolidge. The former President was a close friend of Edward K. Hall, a prominent Dartmouth alumnus and vice president of AT& T, who gave the Infirmary to the College in memory of his son, Dick, who had died suddenly in Hanover at an early age. Coolidge, who also lost a son prematurely, was moved to inscribe the book as follows: "Dear Ed, In memory of your boy, and my boy, who by God's Grace will be boys throughout eternity." A poignant turn of phrase I wouldn't have expected from Silent Cal.

I was assigned to Richardson Hall, one of the older dorms, where my roommate was J. Rodger Brown of Birmingham, Michigan. He was a joyless chap, and we had little in common. But I made good friends with Ned Disque, from Waterloo, Iowa, and we worked together as "heelers" in the freshman competition to join the staff of *The Dartmouth*, the daily college newspaper of which more anon. Across the hall lived Tom Curtis with whom I had friendly arguments on a wide range of subjects that cost us both a considerable amount of sleep. Tom was already at that age a conservative Republican from Webster Grove, Missouri. He was as cantankerous and unyielding as a Missouri mule, but he was honest. Tom later represented his district in the U.S. Congress and was an important influence in the improvement of our election laws. The Richardson rooms were of ample size and ours was blessed with an open fireplace. We gave it extensive use. It was there that I learned from Joe Truman, the janitor, how to lay a fire and start it with a minimum of kindling.

Ours was the first freshman class to use the new state-of-the-art Baker Library. It had several notable features. The most gratifying of these was free access to the stacks. This meant no waiting around for reserved books and the opportunity to browse for others. There was also the comfortably furnished Tower Room for leisure reading. Finally, we were privileged to observe the creation of an art treasure—the huge mural being painted by Jose Clemente Orozco. It was the era of the great Mexican muralists, Rivera, Orozco and Siqueres. Orozco chose as his overall theme, *An Epic of American Civilization.* He began with the advent of Quetzlcoatl, the Mexican God, moving through the era of the Conquistadores to modern day capitalism. I don't think Orozco's beliefs were as far left as those of Rivera, whose mural at Rockefeller Center in New York was destroyed because he portrayed Lenin and other symbols of communist ideology. But Orozco accented the venality of capitalism by figures symbolizing leaders of business, the military, the church and servile academia. A capitalist type (he could be a Rockefeller) is shown with his mouth agape before a pile of gold.

It was fascinating to watch Orozco, perched on a ladder, creating this vast work in several sections occupying most of the Library's lower floor. He must have had the whole scheme of the mural in mind, but apparently near-sighted, he worked with his face not more than six inches from the wall.

The President of Dartmouth at that time was Ernest Martin Hopkins, a 1900 graduate of the College who had been a successful executive of the Boston & Maine Railroad. During World War I he went frequently to Washington on war-related consultation. Prexy (or Hoppy) as he was called, was a stalwart Republican from New England who was halfway through his incumbency when I entered college in 1928. It seems curious that a conservative would have tolerated the symbolism of this revolutionary artist, but Hoppy was in some way broader than his background indicated, and wanted Dartmouth to experience a wide spectrum of views, even to the point of sometime incongruity. He was a serious man, though on occasion he would light up. One Sunday morning, a stiff-necked professor encountered Hopkins in the college bookstore where he was scanning the Sunday paper he had just bought. Said the professor, "Dr. Hopkins, it surprises me that you first turn to the Sports Section." Hopkins replied, "Yes, I read that before I turn to the Funnies!"

Nelson Rockefeller was a student in Hanover when Orozco was painting his mural. Ironically, it was his father a few years later who destroyed Rivera's mural in New York. In time, Nelson became a founder, benefactor and president of New York's Museum of Modern Art. I knew him only slightly, but in college he was a popular member of his class, played varsity soccer, and was voted "the most likely to succeed."

In contrast to Rockefeller's, was the Dartmouth experience of Walter P. Chrysler, Jr. of the class of 1935. Chrysler disdained the Dartmouth dormitories and rented an apartment on Hanover's Main Street. His supercilious attitude made him an object of ridicule on campus. On one occasion he was the butt of a news story giving a straight-faced account of a social gathering in his home. I've lost the clipping, but it read somewhat as follows: "Walter P. Chrysler, Jr. welcomed friends at tea yesterday in his rooms in the Bridgman Block, Mrs. ---- poured. The decorations were blue and mauve."

As freshmen, we were required to take two broad survey courses covering the social and physical sciences. I much preferred Citizenship, which was taught by Lewis Stilwell and Stacy May, because much of it was relevant to the issues of the day. May, an Amherst graduate, later joined the Rockefeller Brothers Fund, and one summer 20 years later, when I was between jobs, commissioned me to do a paper for the Fund on selected refugee problems. Professor John Poor, an eminent astronomer, taught Evolution, the second survey course. Despite his lofty reputation, I found Poor a boring lecturer, and didn't get much out of the course. Poor also had the bearing and reputation of the absent-minded professor. It was alleged that one day crossing the campus he passed one of his students. On the return trip he passed the student again. "When I passed you before," Poor asked, "Which way was I going?" "You were headed for town," the student replied. "Good" said Poor, "Then I've had my lunch."

Four years of high school Latin were somewhat rewarded by a freshman course where we mostly read Horace, Ovid and Catullus, but if I had it to do again I'd take a modern language to supplement my French and English studies. Except for English, my grades were so-so freshman year. I was putting a lot of time on extra-curricular activities. I got my numerals in freshman tennis, playing doubles and third or fourth singles. We had a passable season but didn't win the Ivy League. My principal quest was to earn a place on the staff of *The Dartmouth*.

A couple of years ago I went to Hanover for a celebration tokening the bicentennial of *The Dartmouth*, lineal descendent of a publication edited by Daniel Webster in the first years of the 19th century. *The Dartmouth* claims to be the oldest college newspaper in America. On this occasion, former editors, managing editors and staffers foregathered. A few celebrities, including Budd Schulberg and Paul Gigot, were present for the occasion.

In my day, freshmen aspiring to be staff members were the lowest of the low, likely to be used as "gofers," but they were given the chance to cover or research a story and sometimes to write headlines or contribute ideas for editorials. It was good training. Some of the other heelers became good friends, notably Joe Boldt and John McLane Clark. Clark was an attractive, charismatic figure. He came from a patrician New England family; his uncle John McLane, a former Governor of New Hampshire, was a college trustee. Clark was literate and quick-witted, and bore himself with easy grace. Boldt, from Connecticut, had a shy, somewhat diffident charm, wrote well, and later became an author and editor. The three of us were among those selected for the staff, and our sophomore year was largely devoted to writing stories and editorials and getting out the paper. Each night a staff member took the copy for the next day's edition to Ed Boyle at the Musgrove Press where it was set in hot linotype. The night editor read proof, made any last minute changes, and the paper went to press about 11 p.m. for distribution on campus and in the town early the next day.

In that era, the Boston papers didn't arrive in Hanover until late morning, so *The Dartmouth* had a clear monopoly on outside breaking news for several hours. We had (and the paper still has) an AP franchise, so we were able to score scoops on important national and international news. Each night about 10, Dave Hovey or someone else who knew shorthand would receive a phone call from AP with the latest news. On the whole, it was well selected but there was a period when we shared the AP wire with a Woonsocket, Rhode Island, paper. We became aware of this when the daily bulletin yielded an annoying plethora of Woonsocket and Rhode Island news. It took a while to resolve that problem.

I and other staffers wrote editorials on various subjects, and for a time I wrote a humor column called "L'Oiseau," but we were no competition for Clark's apt, acerbic pen. In mid-junior year, Clark was elected editor-in-chief by the retiring directorate, I was chosen managing editor, and Joe Boldt became associate editor for the next 12-month period. Russ O'Brien was named business manager and Art Allen, circulation manager.

Despite periodic attempts by the College administration to supervise or even control *The Dartmouth's* editorial policy, the reigning directorate still owns the paper and determines how the year's profits are to be distributed. The split my year yielded $700 each for Clark, O'Brien and myself, and lesser amounts for other editors and staff members. I blew my share on a first trip to Europe, of which more later. Some years after my graduation the editors of the paper supported the striking quarry workers at Proctor, Vermont. The Proctor then running the company was a loyal Dartmouth alumnus and a substantial contributor. A Committee on Student Publications appointed by the President at the request of the Board of Trustees felt that *The Dartmouth's* editorial policy "misrepresented the point of view of student and official college alike." In rebutting this charge, according to *The New York Times* of June 12, 1938, staff members pointed out that the faculty, student, town and clergy sentiment was preponderantly behind the paper. The Committee's report, however, expressed the opinion that *The Dartmouth* "spends too much of its editorial space on large problems of the outside world." It went on to recommend new and improved fiscal policies, approval of salary scales, and general editorial guidance. This was to be provided by appointment of an "alumnus-trustee" who would acquire and hold controlling stock of the publication in trust for the college and have the power "at any time, for reasons that seem good to him to remove any member of the editorial or business boards." O'Brien Boldt, younger brother of my classmate, from the editor's desk, waged a tough campaign, both on and off campus, to maintain a ninety-nine year old policy of complete independence of undergraduate editors. He wrote to former editors and managing editors going back many years and most responses agreed with his point of view.

I retain a three and a half page, single-spaced letter that President Hopkins wrote me on June 14, 1938 in which he says: "It seemed to me then, and seems to me now that as a general principle all projects of this sort which capitalize the College name, its prestige, and its constituency, and especially those which do so for private gain and whose monopoly is protected by the College, should acknowledge and accept responsibility of some kind...I know of no place in life, outside of a college community, where men could operate on the basis upon which editors of *The Dartmouth* contend they are justified in operating without any examination of electoral machinery, without any auditing of accounts, and without any concern as to whether the board in its standards of living and working within a college community represented any conformity in thinking with the ideals which presumably exist in an institution of higher learning."

In a subsequent paragraph he really let himself go: "I do not think that there is anything in the country at the present time which is more endangering liberty than the proponents of the idea that a genuine freedom signifies that one can do just as he damn pleases regardless of any and all effects."

Many words were exchanged on both sides, but in the end, the status quo was retained. A recent editor-in-chief told me in Hanover in June 2002 that another, more recent attempt to impose outside "advisory" control had failed. Over the years, however, self-policing by the incumbent directorate has carried out many of the Committee's recommendations.

Among the beats during the year when we ran the paper were the Pope's first broadcast to a worldwide audience; the merger of the *New York Telegram* and the *New York World*, resulting in the loss of 2,800 jobs; Hindenberg's electoral victory over Hitler by a 7 million vote margin; the German Government's order to Hitler to disband his army of 400,000 Nazi troops; abduction of the Lindbergh baby; assassination of President Doumer of France; Babe Ruth's refusal of a contract for $70,000; Amelia Earhart's return home after her trans-Atlantic solo flight; Garbo's departure from Hollywood; the League of Nations' efforts to make peace between Japan and China over the issue of Manchuria; the deaths of Edison, Sousa, Dwight Morrow, Nicholas Longworth, and David Belasco; Al Smith's attack on the Roosevelt candidacy; Tony Canzoneri's win in a 15-round decision over Kid Chocolate to retain his lightweight title; Democrats taking the House from the Republicans, and Big Bill Thompson's victory in Chicago.

The Dartmouth was heavily involved in two campus stories that made it to the national media. One concerned an exceptionally scheduled football game between Dartmouth and Stanford (both of whom were then dubbed "the Indians"). Harvard graciously made its stadium available for the contest. But before the game was to take place, Mayor James Curley of Boston trumped up some excuse to cancel the arrangement. His concern was that the Dartmouth-Stanford game would outdraw the Holy Cross-Boston College encounter scheduled on the same day. The Mayor's unrelenting stand attracted much media criticism, especially when it became known that Curley's son was attending Boston College. The Dartmouth campus seethed. The dilemma was resolved when a judge issued an injunction ruling against the Mayor. *The Dartmouth* celebrated the decision with a banner headline composed by John Clark. It read: THE CURLEY WORM GETS THE BIRD!

During our stewardship of the paper, in the spring of our junior year, some sartorial genius called for a campus-wide vogue of wearing shorts. We featured the story and it was picked up by the Boston and many national papers. Today, when people wear shorts on planes and in town, even at the theater, such a story would not be newsworthy, but in 1930, it created a good deal of attention. One photo showed Nelson Rockefeller, then a senior, clad in his shorts.

In May of our senior year *The Dartmouth* prepared for its annual Strawberry Festival. I don't recall any strawberries on the menu, but there was a clarion call for good beer, not easy to come by in those Prohibition days. Some students made their own, but others resorted to "near" beer spiked with alcohol, a dubious potion. Joe Pilver, the unofficial college bootlegger, occasionally had beer in supply, but its quality was unpredictable. We sought the real thing, and got a tip from a fellow student that it was obtainable from Slicky Joyce, a purveyor in Mechanicville, in upstate New York, not far from the Vermont border. The student's instructions were to locate a certain alley, near a theater on Main Street, "appear docilely at the door of the bar behind the theater, ring the bell and enter on admittance." I still have the message. John Clark and I set out in his Ford roadster, having first removed the rumble seat. We crossed the Connecticut River and the state of Vermont by way of Rutland Mountain. On finally reaching the supplier, we of course had to sample the brew. It was great, but that indulgence delayed our return journey. The two kegs we bought fit nicely into the enclosed space normally occupied by the rumble seat. We started back to Hanover in the dusk, crossed into Vermont, and were proceeding at a good clip when the dreaded siren of a police car assailed our ears. The cop overtook us and came up alongside. I still remember the moment! We were absolutely petrified. We were sure our last day had come! We could hear the sentence: transporting illegal beverages over a state border. The officer peered at John through the side window. "Hey you guys," he said. "Do you know your left tail light is out? Better get it fixed in the next town." And he sped away. Thanking our lucky stars, we resumed the journey. The Festival was a rousing success.

There is one more incident worth relating. John and I had our own private offices, complete with open fireplaces, in *The Dartmouth* suite in Robinson Hall. We invited a couple of girls to Spring House Party Weekend. They were nice girls, too. One evening we served some beer, soft drinks and a bit of food at *The*

Dartmouth offices. It was all very innocent, but the party was interrupted by the sudden entrance of Spud Bray, the campus cop. He reported us to the College Administration and the next day we were summoned to the office of President Hopkins. Prexy was very angry, and vented his displeasure particularly on John. The fact that John's uncle was a college trustee may have averted a worse fate, but the punishment was bad enough. *The Dartmouth* was summarily turned out of Robinson Hall. With virtually no notice, we had to rent office space at our expense in the Musgrove building on Main Street, and we put out the paper from there for the balance of the academic term. In the fall of 1931 we were reprieved and permitted to return to Robinson. It was a chastening experience.

I had some sophomore lag in my second year, and although I didn't flunk any subjects, my grades suffered. I got very little out of Economics and scored a "D" as a consequence. On the other hand, I took three courses I thoroughly enjoyed. Professor Anderson's history class about World War I was a standout. I was especially fascinated by the description of the arms race. We read *Merchants of Death*, published around that time, which told the grim story of collusion among the armament makers. Anderson, a vigorous red-faced professor with prematurely white hair, was a fiery lecturer. We read Kautsky's transcription of the pitiful Willi-Nikki correspondence—letters between German Kaiser Wilhelm and Czar Nicholas of Russia, who were first cousins, in their last ditch effort to avert war. Royal Nemiah's lucid course on Classical Civilization opened my eyes to the cultural accomplishments of the Greeks and Romans. Herb West's popular course in Comparative Literature similarly presented, in translation, the works of many European writers hitherto unknown to me.

Henderson's Shakespeare aptly presented the Bard's great plays, and in another course I made my first acquaintance with the tales of Chaucer. I did well in both of these classes and was selected to do English Honors work in my junior and senior years. This meant I had no formal classes but, with another classmate, met regularly with a tutor. The classmate was Chuck Owsley from Youngstown, Ohio, a personable and articulate chap who roomed with John Clark. Our tutor junior year was Henry Dargan, a learned but sometimes boring Southerner whose specialty was the 18th century. We usually met in Dargan's apartment where Lullah, his wife, would serve us tea and cookies.

Senior year our tutor was more stimulating. Bill Eddy was a decorated Marine Captain in World War I. He was no militarist, but he was strongly opposed to the pacifist line then preached by so many at Dartmouth and other college campuses. It was a cynical period, barely a decade after World War I, when the venality of the armament makers was revealed, and disarmament was the buzzword of the day. Eddy recognized the fatal flaws in the Versailles Treaty, the troubled state of many European nations, and the illusory nature of "Peace in our Time." He was alive to the moment. He taught an illuminating course on Satire in English Literature, which we sometimes audited. He saw to it that our tutorial sessions contained numerous references to the great satirists of the past and present. We admired Bill Eddy and were pleased when, a year or so after our graduation, at age 39, he was made President of Hobart and William Smith College in upstate New York. In senior year I achieved a 4.0 average, with "A's" in every subject, but my indifferent grades the first two years held me back and I didn't make Phi Bete.

My entering class of 642 at Dartmouth included one African-American, one Native American, and what was said to be the largest number of Jews admitted in any one class. I reckon there were about twenty of us, though we were uncertain of the exact number. Growing up in Manhattan, I never experienced anti-Semitism on the street or in school. Probably half of the students at DeWitt Clinton High School were Jewish. My folks belonged to Temple B'nai Jeshurun, where Rabbi Israel Goldstein held forth. It was there I went to Sunday School and at 13 learned enough Hebrew to get through the Bar Mitzvah ceremony. After that, I never worshipped regularly, though for many years I would spend some time with my folks in shul on Rosh Ha-Shanah and Yom Kippur. And I've always enjoyed Seders. While I've respected the principles of the Jewish creed, I found the ritual repetition boring and have had no interest in religious observance.

Freshman year I didn't quite know how to handle being Jewish. I never denied it, but I didn't advertise it. Sometimes I felt guilty that some of my gentile friends didn't know I was Jewish. Actually my Dartmouth friends freshman year were mainly gentile, though I saw a good deal of Arthur Schlichter and Jerry Altman. I knew Arthur from age ten on. Arthur and I were classmates at P.S. 165, though we went to different high schools. He lived with his mother and two uncles. I was particularly fond of his uncle Arthur who got on very well with E.B. Jerry I met at college. He was an attractive chap with startling blue eyes, a keen wit, and a lively intellectual curiosity.

In the latter part of freshman year I felt increasingly uncertain on the fraternity question. This was compounded when we began to receive invitations to visit fraternity houses. I was aware that many of the best fraternities, under their national charters, were not permitted to pledge Jews. Of course, I was invited several times to visit Pi Lambda Phi which, though founded as a non-sectarian house, had become essentially a Jewish fraternity.

In my brother's day at Dartmouth there were no Jewish fraternities. Herb loathed segregation and prejudice in any form, and strongly advised me not to join Pi Lam. A number of my gentile friends were courted by the smaller houses, and I accompanied them when they went to look them over. The ice was beginning to thaw, and I was reasonably sure of a bid to at least one or two of them. But I felt obliged to make a statement as to where I stood. I fretted about it for some weeks in the spring of my freshman year. I went on solitary walks, often in the Hanover cemetery. Then one day I made up my mind. For once ignoring my brother's advice, I decided to join Pi Lam. In those days, you could not pledge to a fraternity until your sophomore year, you couldn't live in the house until junior year, and fraternities were not permitted to serve meals. As a result, most upperclassmen ate in the town restaurants or in private eating clubs such as Ma Smalley's or Ma Randall's.

Art, Jerry and most of my friends among the Jewish classmates joined Pi Lam with me. They included Irv Kramer, Frank Westheimer and Ralph Elias. Kramer was a husky specimen from Brooklyn. He had promised his folks not to go out for football, but that didn't keep him from becoming a varsity star at basketball and baseball. He was also a formidable touch football player and led Pi Lam to several campus championships. Ralph had been a classmate of mine in elementary school, though we graduated from different high schools. He played Brutus to my Cassius in our P.S. 165 ambitious production of *Julius Caesar* coached by the resolute Miss Valadon.

Born of a petite, delicate Southern belle and her burly tyrannical husband, Ralph was an only child. His family was well off. Ralph was bright and always held strong opinions, but at the same time he was shy in mixed company and something of a loner. I was pleasantly surprised when we met again in Dartmouth's freshman class. We both joined Pi Lam and decided to room together sophomore year. It was an amicable arrangement. I can't say I ever got to know Ralph, but he was a loyal friend. After college he went to medical school and was an intern at Gouverneur Hospital in New York when I was working at the Welfare Council. I vividly recall the sights and sounds experienced when I donned a white coat and rode with him all of one night while he made his ambulance rounds on the Lower East Side. Ralph, for a time, was house doctor at the posh Hotel Madison. World War II came along to rescue him. He became a captain in the medical corps. I saw him infrequently after that. I was in Washington, and then in Europe for six years. By the time I returned to New York in 1954, Ralph was in California. Bored with general practice he had studied psychiatry, and was located first in Ensenada and later in Oakland. My wife, Margaret, and I met him on a western trip and we corresponded. We also met a mutual friend living in California who told us Ralph was highly esteemed as a physician but led a very lonely existence.

One day, without any warning, we had a letter from Ralph informing us that he was homosexual, and that he wanted us to know it. It came as a shock, but yet it seemed, and was, a logical explanation of his repressed behavior over the years. In those days people didn't share such information, even with good friends. Ralph created a mild furor at Dartmouth when he gave $50,000 in support of the nascent Gay and Lesbian Society on campus. Not long before his death, Margaret and I visited Ralph in Oakland. He had retired from practice and was in poor health.

Frank Westheimer, who roomed with Jerry, was one of the bright academic stars of our class. He was a chem major, specializing in organic chemistry, and after taking his Ph.D. taught at Chicago and at Harvard. Dartmouth awarded him an Honorary Degree. We were good friends in college. I went to his wedding in

Philadelphia. In later years when I lived in Cambridge, where he still resides, Vera and I spent many pleasant hours in the company of Frank and his devoted wife Jeanne.

Stan Silverman, '34, active on the *Jack-O-Lantern*, became a lasting friend. He collaborated with Budd Shulberg, '36, on several theatrical ventures.

Pi Lam was no different from other fraternities in submitting new pledges to an initiation ritual. Mine consisted of two parts. The first was a kind of fortune hunt without a fortune. I was taken to White River Junction by car and given a number of chores to perform on my way back to Hanover on foot; one was to count the railway ties from White River to Norwich, across the Connecticut River from Hanover. The second trial took place at night in the fraternity house. I was asked to inspect an oak board on which a number of sharp nails had been implanted with their points up. The board was put on the floor and I was bid to jump on it from a chair that I was helped to mount, barefoot. It was a test of faith. I jumped. Happily, one of the brothers, while I was being blindfolded, substituted a board with rubber spikes.

Once I had joined Pi Lam I felt relieved. I became active in the fraternity, especially in our effort to relocate nearer the other fraternities. We convinced several of our better-heeled alumni of the need to move from the abandoned Catholic Church on South Street which we were temporarily occupying. With their help, we moved to a superior location, and two of them also financed or got us huge discounts on the requisite furnishings. We were still in the old quarters when I started my junior year, so I took a single room there.

I was proud of my accomplishments junior year. I was elected Managing Editor of *The Dartmouth*, Vice President of The Arts, and selected as a member of Green Key, the junior honor society. I was elected Rex of Pi Lam and represented it on the Inter-Fraternity Council. When Dartmouth's three senior honor societies made their pick from the junior class, I was delighted to receive bids from the two best, Sphinx and Casque and Gauntlet (C&G). It was not an easy choice. John Clark was a Sphinx legacy and I was pretty sure that he and other good friends would go that way. The members of Sphinx had a "tomb" where they held meetings and other events, but nobody lived in the tomb. On the other hand, C & G had its own house, ideally situated in a corner of the campus where most of the members lived during their senior year. I knew and highly regarded several of the senior delegation including John B. Martin, the retiring editor-in-chief of *The Dartmouth*. I didn't know who would be in the 1932 Delegation, but very much liked the idea of living at the "Corner," as the house was called, so I accepted their bid.

C & G was founded in 1887 when Tennyson's *Idylls of the King* was all the rage. Its members bore the names of knights; I was Sir Gawain, and our leader was titled King Arthur. The ritual, based largely on the lore of the Round Table, was straightforward and high-principled. There were 20 in our 1932 Delegation, all but four of whom lived at the Corner. I was the only Jew in the delegation.

Each knight with a roommate shared a small study on the first or second floor, and we all slept in a huge dormitory on the third floor, known as the "Poop Deck" or the "Wind Tunnel." It was mighty cold up there on winter nights.

My roommate was Bob Coltman, a serious, extremely bright student from Pennsylvania. Shortly after graduation he married Natalie Walsh, the daughter of publisher Richard Walsh. Walsh's second wife was the writer, Pearl Buck, and I enjoyed meeting them both on visits to Perkasie, in the Pennsylvania Dutch country. Bob became a bank president in Philadelphia, but unfortunately died at a comparatively early age.

My best C & G friend was Carlos Baker, and I spent as much time in his room as in my own. We talked far into the night, and in those pre-*Scrabble* days spent hours playing *Anagrams*. Carlos came from Saco, Maine, had saturnine good looks, and even as an undergraduate was an English scholar of distinction. After graduation, he taught English at several prep schools, and once he earned his Ph.D. became a much beloved and valued professor at Princeton for many years. He wrote the definitive (at the time) biography of Ernest Hemingway, and edited a volume of Hemingway's letters. He never met the writer, but they corresponded. Carlos admired much of Hemingway's writing, but he once told me that the more he knew about Hemingway the less he liked the man. Carlos was polyvalent. He wrote several books about the Romantic poets and some fine poetry, beginning with our class poem, produced extensive criticism, several novels and even polished off a whodunit. He came close to finishing a biography of Emerson, but died of a metastasized melanoma in 1987. I saw him on one of his last days and expressed regret when he said he couldn't finish the book. "Oh, no matter," he said. "Lots of people have written about Emerson." Fortunately, Carlos's family with the aid of an Emerson scholar did the final editing and the book was published in 1996 under the title *Emerson Among the Eccentrics*, to critical acclaim. Carlos's friendship was important to me. He was a rare combination of a sage teacher, a fine writer, and a friend of great sensitivity and compassion. I was privileged to speak at his funeral and I am still in contact with his children.

Other C & G brothers with whom I developed a special bond were Bob Hosmer of Syracuse and John Keller of Cuba, New York. Hosmer had seaman's papers; he had shipped out on freighters and sailed the seven seas before he matriculated at Dartmouth. Later he had a successful business career. Hosmer was movie handsome, invariably friendly and charming. Keller, the funny man in our Delegation, worked for a time with Louis Howe, and together with Joe Boldt wrote a *Saturday Evening Post* story about him called *Franklin's on His Own Now*. Keller's tales of Cuba, N.Y., his hometown, were priceless. I wish he'd collected them in a book. Instead he became a meteorologist. Joe Carleton, a delightful, unassuming chap from Winchester, Massachusetts, confounded everyone by making Phi Bete grades without seeming ever to crack a book. Rod Hatcher, from Lincoln, Virginia, had a razor-sharp mind and devastating wit. He had a gratifying career here and in England for the National City Bank. Bill McCall, star halfback on the Dartmouth eleven, and one of our delegation's few athletes, was a congenial housemate, as was John Sheldon, captain of the varsity tennis team. I was pleased to see John and his wife, Midge, at their home in Longwood, Florida in October 2001. We hadn't met for fifty years. I gave John the sad news that he and I were the only surviving members of the 1932 C & G delegation. About a year prior to that, we had lost Ed Judd, an esteemed surgeon at the Mayo Clinic, who was the Arthur of our delegation.

For me, C & G offered a rare and rich experience in fellowship. Our meetings were serious fun, and we enjoyed the many incidental contacts. I wrote, to the tune of the *Marines' Hymn*, the C & G song for our delegation. At the end of classes, senior year, seven of us drove to Lake Memphromagog in Canada for a memorable last get-together lubricated by welcome draughts of Molson's finc Canadian ale. In 1987 I attended in Hanover C & G's 100th gala birthday party. By that time, Dartmouth had been accepting female students for 15 years, and the knights were complemented by Ladies Guinevere, Elaine and others. Since then several have been elected the Arthurs of their delegation.

Other 1932 classmates meriting special mention include:

Wilbur (Ping) Ferry, center on the football team and president of The Arts. Ping was a rebel from the outset, and never joined a fraternity or senior society. His father was treasurer of the Packard Motor Company. Ping's first job after college was with Labor's Political Action Committee (PAC). He then worked for a time with Nelson Rockefeller's Fund for the Republic. In the sixties he joined Robert Hutchins in the Center for the Study of Democratic Institutions. Margaret and I once visited Ping at the Center's elegant headquarters in Santa Barbara. Ping was half proud, half sardonic as he took us around.

"This represents," he said, "The Leisure of the Theory Class." Ping attended several Pugwash Conferences. As a foundation executive, he and his wife subsidized selected progressive causes. Victor Navarsky, editor of *The Nation*, called him "a radical philanthropist, a free spirit, letter-writer and troublemaker."

Reuel Denney was an author, poet, scholar in American studies and teacher. We were good friends in college and after that in New York. When he was 26, Yale University Press published his first book: *The Connecticut River and Other Poems*. In the 1940s, Reuel collaborated with David Reisman and Nathan Glazer on *The Lonely Crowd*, still regarded a landmark work on American character and society. He also wrote *The Astonished Muse* about American popular culture. Reuel's career included work with *Time* and *Fortune* magazines, and he taught at the Universities of Chicago and Hawaii. He wrote lively, thoughtful commentaries for the 25th and 50th Reunion reports of our Dartmouth class.

Charles Odegaard, a historian of note, taught for some years at the University of Illinois before becoming President of the University of Washington.

Howland Sargeant had an outstanding academic record at Dartmouth and was elected to a term as class president. In later years, he headed Radio Liberty, which broadcast short wave to the Soviet Union, and became an Assistant Secretary of State. He was married for a time to Myrna Loy, the film actress.

Robert (Bob) Ryan, the movie actor, was a particular friend of mine. In college, he was heavyweight boxing champion and the author of a play. After graduation, he worked for a time in his native Chicago, but the stage had allure for him. In 1936, when I was living in Great Neck, I had a call from him. He was to appear in a comedy called *Angel Child* playing in a summer theater in nearby Roslyn, Long Island. Bob's ability and rugged good looks eventually took him to Hollywood. He made 58 films after 1941, including *Clash by Night* with Tallulah Bankhead, *Tender Comrade* with Ginger Rogers, *Crossfire, The Set-Up, Bombardier,* and a great Western, *Bad Day at Black Rock.* Bob's first love was the theater, and he interspersed his movie career with stage appearances. He played opposite Katharine Hepburn in a Stratford, Connecticut, production of *Anthony and Cleopatra* that I witnessed, and also did *Coriolanus* in New York. When I was working in London in the mid-sixties, he accepted an offer from the Nottingham Theater to do *Othello* and *Long Day's Journey into Night.* We went there for the weekend and saw both plays. For a time, Bob and his wife, the mystery writer Jessica Cadwallader, lived at the Dakota Apartment in New York with their three children, and that was the last time I saw them. Returning to Hollywood, they founded a children's school. Jessica and Bob died in 1973. In 2003 at the showing in the Mill Valley Library of a Film Noir in which Bob played a lead, we were happy to meet Bob's daughter, Lisa Ryan, and I was able to give her some memorabilia of her father in his college days.

In my senior year, as vice president of The Arts, I was occasionally called on to entertain and introduce the speakers we invited to Hanover. One was Sherwood Anderson, the author, who spoke about country journalism and the opportunities it holds for the young writer. "I like a small town," he said, "I like people and I enjoy putting out a small town paper." Anderson had bought two papers in Warren County, Virginia, and felt their influence on the lives of his readers was as great as that evoked by his other writings. Others hosted by The Arts included Buckminster Fuller, Will Durant, Salvador de Madariaga, Lewis Mumford, and the poet Edna St. Vincent Millay. Standing out in my memory is the dinner we gave to Millay and her husband, Eugene Boissevein. They had come up by train and had just enough time for a meal before her evening lecture. After we were seated in one of Hanover's restaurants, Edna launched into a long monologue, interrupted only by the waiter's insistence on taking our order. She continued, even after our meal was served. Boissevein looked at her with mounting exasperation and finally said, "For Christ's sake, Edna, stop talking and EAT!" It had the desired effect.

Other literary figures visiting Hanover included Joseph Wood Krutch, later a good friend of Herb's; Joseph Auslander; John Mason Brown and Max Eastman. In the concert series we heard the Don Cossacks and Russian Male Chorus,

Jose Iturbi and Lily Pons. Ted Geisel, (Dr. Seuss), Dartmouth 1925, illustrated the Winter Carnival Program.

I didn't become a very proficient skier at Dartmouth, and in fact rarely put on skis after my freshman year. However, John Clark and some other good friends signed up for the senior Mt. Washington trip, and in a weak moment I was induced to join them. I didn't realize that this involved a physical exam, a conditioning run on Balch Hill, and the inspection of equipment and packs. I didn't have a pack, but borrowed one. We left Hanover by bus Friday afternoon and had a pleasant supper with Ross Hunter, hut-master of Porky Gulch. Next morning after breakfast, our climbing party left for the Old Jackson Road, donned crampons to help us mount the slippery upward trail and reached the summit of Mt. Washington in the afternoon. It was mighty cold and blowy up there, but so far so good. We took off the crampons and prepared for the descent. To avoid interference on the narrow trail, we were dispatched one at a time. I got going rather faster than my expectations. It was getting dark and the visibility was poor. I thought of nothing but the challenge of staying on my feet. About half way down, I heard someone shout at me but I couldn't hear the message. I kept on going doggedly. I finally reached the bottom. By now it was pitch black. In the distance I could see some lights. Nothing looked familiar. I had obviously missed the turn off to Porky Gulch. Alone and cold, I pressed on until I reached a house. I knocked and for a few dollars persuaded the occupant to take me halfway around the mountain to Porky Gulch. The other skiers had all arrived there and were apprehensive about me. Next morning I had to re-enact my arrival by "taxi" for the class movies. Later that day some of the proficient skiers headed for the headwall of the Tuckerman Ravine, but I wisely decided to pass that up. Years later while living in Geneva I became a better and more confident skier.

In a campus-wide poll taken our senior year on the biggest issues of the day, Prohibition got the highest vote with 727, followed by prosperity with 465; war debt cancellation 171; tariff 171;disarmament 97; farm relief 96; reparations 89, and League of Nations 20. Solely on the question of Prohibition, students voted 906 for repeal; 675 for modification; 298 for a national referendum, and 37 to continue it. The faculty voted 186 to 30 to repeal it. In a final poll of 25 seniors, selected faculty, and several town personalities, including Chief of Police Hallissey, beer won the popularity contest, nosing out Serge Rachmaninoff by a single point. Marlene Dietrich trounced Joan Crawford. Al Capone and Grapenuts were the things most to be despised, followed by Bing Crosby and rumble seats.

Despite the high ratings for Repeal of Prohibition and for beer, drinking on campus was far less prevalent in my day than in the last decade or two. A few students mixed grain alcohol, juniper and a product called Peeko to make bathtub gin, or spiked near beer with alcohol. Some bought reputed whiskey or Canadian ale from Joe Pilver. There was some chug-a-lugging of beer at fraternity houses. But if "binge drinking" was going on, I wasn't aware of it. I always liked a saying of John Clark's: "The proof of the bred is in their drinking."

By 1945, the percentage of Jews in the Dartmouth student population had increased, but many well qualified Jewish candidates for admission were turned down. Herman Shumlin, the theatrical producer, wrote to President Hopkins questioning the admissions policy. Hopkins denied that there was a numerical quota for Jews but said that Dartmouth selected its student body so as to achieve a representative cross section of the country. My classmate, Jerry Altman, strongly objected to his reply. In a letter to Hopkins, Jerry protested that "Jewishness of and by itself" should not be "a limiting factor . . . any such policy is evil and must be corrected . . . artificial distinctions in our citizenry are absolutely unjustified and can only be the cause of mischief and grief." In effect, he was arguing for blind admissions. Hopkins was near the end of his tenure, and I'm not aware that the issue arose with any of his successors. Jews are now admitted to most fraternities and, so far as I'm aware, are not disadvantaged. There is no longer a Jewish fraternity on campus. The college now has a policy of "blind admissions" but this refers primarily to need.

The number of African-American students on campus has shown a significant rise over the years. Although they are widely accepted and a number are in leadership positions, they have to some extent retained their racial identity in a campus African-American Society.

Although Dartmouth College was established in 1769, it had its origin in More's Charity School for Indians established by the Rev. Eleazor Wheelock in 1750. Wheelock took Samson Occum, a Mohegan preacher, to England to help him raise money for a larger, more general college. Occum, often wearing his Indian clothing, preached more than 300 sermons during his 2 1/2 years in England and Scotland. The Earl of Dartmouth was the biggest contributor to the new institution, so it was named Dartmouth College.

In time, limited numbers of Native Americans were admitted to Dartmouth. In my class, there was just one, a Sioux named Roland Sundown. Sunny, in Indian regalia, marched at the head of the Dartmouth Band, and he later told us these were his proudest moments. In fact, to create a greater effect, he adorned himself with the more elaborate headdress and regalia of another tribe! Sunny in later years became a teacher on his reservation.

When John Kemeny became President, several alumni, of whom I was one, petitioned him to admit a more representative number of Native Americans, and he made a special effort to do so. In *The Dartmouth Story*, published in 1990, Robert Graham notes that "in the nineteen years between the start of the program in 1970 and 1989, Dartmouth had graduated more than eight hundred Native Americans from some one hundred tribes in North America, compared to the grand total of ten Indians graduated from the college in its last centuries." There is a Native American House on the campus and Native American students are "encouraged to develop their cultural and social programs."

Traditionally, the Dartmouth teams were called the Indians, but that term has become pejorative and is no longer in use. In my day we exhorted the football team with a cheer beginning "Wah Hoo Wah," but a Native American scholar discovered that the phrase means "sodomy" in one of the tribal languages, so it became taboo. (I'm told another scholar found it meant "noble warrior" in another tribal tongue. Be that as it may, the cheer is now obsolete.)

Over the years I've kept close touch with Dartmouth. I've served as an alumni fund agent, reunion chairman, secretary of my class, and am currently its president. With a classmate, I edited class reports for our 25th and 50th Reunions. I was sadly disappointed when an emergency assignment in Yugoslavia prevented my attendance at the 25th. I returned to Hanover in 2002 for my 70th Reunion, probably our last hurrah. I have firm friendships with several of my surviving classmates, though most of my college friends have passed away. I'm closest to our class officers, Marvin Chandler, secretary, and Howdy Pierpont, treasurer. One of my best friends, our vice president Harry Rowe, who successfully planned our record breaking 70th Reunion, died on Christmas Day 2002.

Dartmouth President Wright has invited me as one of 8-10 alumni nationwide to be interviewed for a film celebrating the launch of the public phase of the Campaign for The Dartmouth Experience. The Campaign to be launched in November 2004 will carry a theme from one of Dr. Seuss's books *Oh, the Places You'll Go,* focusing on the paths alumni have pursued since their days at Dartmouth.

TWO AGAINST THE PREPACKS

I wrote this light-hearted account of my summer on Macy's training squad more than 20 years later and sent it to Scott Meredith, a literary agent recommended by a friend. Meredith thanked me for the chance to read "this very professionally-done article," but said that "Life Among the Prepacks" was "not a saleable literary property." He then went on to explain his opinion at considerable length. He said I had "the single most common weakness of first-time article submissions here—an inadequate grasp of the market for fact pieces in today's magazines" and felt there was a "lack of uniqueness in the incidents recounted."

I was disappointed in his findings, but had more faith in the piece, and just before going off on vacation impulsively sent it off cold to *The New Yorker*. On my return I was surprised and gratified to find a letter of acceptance and a check. I couldn't resist sending a note to Mr. Meredith advising him of the sale. I didn't crow. And he sent me a very courteous response. I mention this only to prove the wisdom of the old adage: "Fools rush in where agents fear to tread."

TWO AGAINST THE PREPACKS

As published in *The New Yorker,* November 15, 1958

The hoopla over Macy's centennial has touched off recollections of my own career at that grand old store. In the Depression summer of 1931, about twenty of us between our junior and senior years in college were hired by Personnel, at twenty-five dollars a week. We were known as the summer training squad, and our mission was to learn the business from the ground up, with the expectation that some of us might return after college. In my case, it was from the basement up, since they started me out there, as a contingent. ("Contingent" is—or was—department-store parlance for a kind of seasonal shock trooper. He is sent in where the crowding is heaviest.) I began in Garden Supplies, rapidly graduated to Hardware, then to Electrical Goods, and finally rose to Men's Bathing Suits, on the second floor—bypassing the street floor, which was the only one air-conditioned in those days.

In addition to selling, our little band of collegians was on call at any hour of the day for lectures, conferences, demonstrations, aptitude tests, and other folderol arranged by Personnel as part of our merchandising education. One morning, after an invigorating seminar, our chaperon and mentor, Mrs. Sheppard, asked for volunteers with experience in theatricals. I foolishly raised my hand, and found myself entered in Macy's Sweeps.

The Sweeps were held early in the morning, before the opening of the store. The volunteers were divided into two-man teams, each team dressed up to resemble a horse and labeled with the name of one of the store departments. The departments competed with each other in weekly sales contests, and the Sweeps had been devised as a dramatic way of announcing the results. The horses were supposed to finish in the same order as the departments in the previous week's sales derby, but we were to make the race as authentic as possible, so that the assembled sales clerks could capture the genuine thrill of rooting in a winner. I became the rear end of the filly Garden Supplies, which was in hot sales competition with Small Domestic Rugs and Women's and Misses' Better Dresses. We were slated to finish third, but my front man allowed his competitive instincts to carry him away, with the result that we finished first, in a glorious burst of speed. The surprised clerks in Garden Supplies cheered wildly, but their triumph was cut short by a shrill voice over the PA system announcing that we had been disqualified.

After that humiliating episode, I resolved to do no more volunteering. But the frustration of selling Men's Bathing Suits in July was too much for me, and I yielded to the persuasion of a colleague named Bob when Mrs. Sheppard requested two volunteers for a research project at Macy's Long Island warehouse. I rather fancied myself in the role of researcher. On the appointed day, Bob and I showed up at the warehouse in our best summer suits, sharpened pencils in our pockets.

Along with the Louvre and Chicago's Merchandise Mart, Macy's warehouse in Long Island City must surely be one of the largest structures in the world. Bob and I walked several blocks trying to find the main entrance. Once there, we looked hopefully on the directory under the R's, but no Research was listed. We decided to head for Personnel. No one there seemed to be expecting us, but a man named Davis finally took some interest though he seemed puzzled when we mentioned the word "research." After several calls to 34th Street, he succeeded in reaching Mrs. Sheppard. "It's all right," he reassured us. "You're in the right place." He picked up the phone again. "Is that you, Mulligan?" he said. "Well, I have two research assistants for you. Come and fetch them. Thirty-fourth Street wants us to check the prepacks." In a few moments, Mulligan appeared, a wiry fellow in a gray shirt and workpants. He greeted us laconically, and motioned us to come along. We followed him down a series of interminable aisles and ramps to another part of the building, where, above a stone floor, massive iron shelves held literally acres of sealed cartons, of every size and shape. These were the prepacks. A prepack, we learned, was an article bought at the main store from a floor sample and delivered to the customer from the warehouse, in its original factory-sealed carton. Macy's customers were complaining about the condition of some of the prepacked articles they had received, and Macy's, in its usual zealous manner, was determined to discover the source of the trouble. Mulligan pointed to a shelf, stacked with cartons. "Start here," he said abruptly. "Take down ten or so, open 'em up and make a note of what you find. Then keep going down the aisle, sampling each batch. I'll be back to see how you're making out." He started to turn away, apparently had an afterthought, and looked us up and down, as if seeing us for the first time. "Here," he said in a kindlier tone. "Give me them coats and ties. I'll put 'em in the office. You'll not be needing 'em in this particular work." He headed for a nearby hand truck, stepped nimbly aboard, and off he went.

The first stack proved to be clothes hampers—hundreds of them, mostly made of tin or wicker, with plastic tops. We opened about ten cartons. All seemed in perfect condition. We made a note in our log and moved along to our next lot. More hampers, of a slightly different shade, also perfect. About this time, Mulligan cruised back into view. For a minute, he watched us, critically, and then he stepped off his truck. "No, no," he moaned softly. "Not so gentle. Remember, them prepacks go from here to Delivery, where they put 'em on the trucks. You can bet them drivers won't handle 'em so ladylike. Now, watch."

He climbed a ladder to the top of one of the shelves, reached for the nearest carton, and pushed it over the edge. It plummeted to the stone floor. Stepping down agilely, he pounced on his victim, kicked it, and pushed it savagely across the floor until it hit the wall with a thud. "Now, let's see," he said. He ripped open the carton, snatched out the hamper, and peered at it closely. It wasn't even scratched. "All right," he growled "They packed them Number Fours pretty good—but let's try the Sixes." He moved to the next stack, and in a twinkling had knocked three more cartons to the floor. Getting into the spirit of the thing, Bob and I each claimed a carton for our own and began kicking, punching, and gouging it. "All right, boys," said the panting Mulligan, finally calling a halt.

We began the autopsy in a fever of anticipation. "Aha!" said Mulligan. Sure enough, the side of one hamper had been dented in the melee. "You see," he said triumphantly. "Sloppy packing—Number Six Hundred and Forty Two Green. Get that in the report. Now carry on." And he rode off on his truck.

We took the hint, and after that there was no holding us. We went through an entire Olympic Games with those cartons, including shot-putting, hockey, soccer, and lacrosse. When we had finished with the hampers, we started on lampshades, but they proved disappointedly durable, possibly because of their light weight. We next turned our attention to wastebaskets made of some composition material. They came in sickly pastel colors that did not appeal to us, and they chipped nicely. But our supreme triumph was with enamelware. These attractive pots, pans and casseroles came in smaller cartons better adapted to projection, and we added football, basketball, and volleyball to the athletic repertoire. When we found an easy-to-heft object, we sometimes widened the sampling to insure a more accurate result. During the next several weeks, our passion for research led to the annihilation of some hundreds of dollars' worth of brand-new merchandise. Our technique was completely objective. We played no favorites among the manufacturers. Each day, we would tot up the casualties and move on to the next victims, leaving a pile of bruised objects in our wake. Some cartons and their contents showed stubborn resilience and could be returned to stock. But we were careful not to repeat the whitewash of that first morning, and saw to it that the porters always had plenty of debris to carry off to the special area where the horrible examples of faulty packaging were accumulating.

One day, when we were practicing forward passes with some vitreous china, Mr. Davis, of Personnel appeared on the scene. "Glad to see you're keeping busy, fellows," he said affably. "I came by to tell you that Mrs. Sheppard called from 34th Street. She says that although you're excused from attending the seminars over there, you're expected to turn in a final report on your research project."

The knowledge that we would eventually have to give an accounting placed a mild restrain on our boyish enthusiasm. We reflected more on the results of our mayhem, and even learned something about the elements of good packaging. If an object was too tight in its container, it was highly susceptible to outside shock or jounce; if too loose, it was similarly vulnerable. On the other hand, if it fitted neatly, it could absorb almost any amount of punishment without becoming cracked, chipped or staved in.

It was an active summer. At coffee breaks, we used to race each other down the aisles on hand trucks or rolling ladders, and we relaxed during lunch period by playing in the softball game held daily, weather permitting, on the enormous flat roof. When, in due course, we finished our assignment, turned in our report, and went back to college, our superb physical condition put to shame those athletes who had spent the summer sedentarily roping calves or building roads.

After graduation, neither Bob nor I returned to Macy's. He went to work for a baking company in Cleveland, and I became a reporter for a wine-and-liquor journal. But from time to time I still stalk Macy's basement with a faintly proprietary air, and whenever I see a truck delivering prepacks my fingers start twitching nostalgically.

1932 TRIP TO EUROPE

Before braving the Depression job market in the summer of 1932 I splurged the $700 dollars I'd made on *The Dartmouth* for my first visit to Europe. I had a rather seasick voyage on the "New York," a vessel of the Hamburg-America Line, debarked at Le Havre and went by train to Paris, where I arrived on Bastille Day July 14, 1932. I stayed at the Hotel Vaugirard, and enjoyed the company of a Dartmouth fraternity brother named Randy Valensi who was half French and living with his family in Paris. Randy showed me the highlights of Paris by day and in the evening we enjoyed Lapin Agile and other night spots. We also visited the infamous brothel at 32 rue Blondel not for sex but as voyeurs to watch prostitutes dance around and pick up coins with their genitalia.

Watching the Parisians celebrate Bastille Day was an excitement in itself.

In Paris I had no lack of female companions. I met a Swarthmore girl in the Musee de Cluny who was bored with her tour group and accompanied me to the Rodin Museum, Versailles, and several other joints. One evening we followed Randy's advice and saw a wonderful show at Aux Clochards featuring the singer Lucienne Boyer. I still have her vibrant voice on a record.

I have a letter that I wrote to Bill and Ferd from Paris which they returned to me some years later. It recounts an experience I had in the post office one day when I was trying to make myself understood. In the process, I called over a girl who appeared interested in getting involved. She did understand a bit of English. She was in training for a government position and had to spend some time studying the methods of the post office, telegraph bureau, telephone office and other telecommunications. I walked her over to the telephone office and we found we could understand each other if I talked French and she talked English. It sounds funny but that was the best way. Her father was a French artist and her mother a dancer when they met in Italy. Lucienne, 24, was bright and amusing and attractive to me. She was not fond of the French. She was being vainly pursued by a Russian and an Egyptian but had been in love with a Serb who had returned to Serbia two years before. She lived in a tastefully furnished flat in an elevator apartment. She took me there and we talked for hours. We laughed over letters written to her by her various swains. Finally we drifted into an affair which greatly enlivened my Paris stay.

From Paris I took the train to Brussels. It rained most of the time I was there and it was also a national holiday, but it cleared up that first evening and I walked around with a beautiful but inane Skidmore girl who was traveling with a sister, cousin, aunt and mother and had to be in by eleven o'clock. Next day I saw the majestic Grand Place, the central square whose buildings represent one of the finest groupings of late medieval architecture in Europe. I also visited the curious Wirtz Museum, almost a house of freaks.

From Brussels I went to Cologne where a chap I'd met on shipboard was living. I was greatly impressed by the architecture of the cathedral, though it lacked the beautiful stained glass windows of Notre Dame. My friend Ludwig and I spent a riotous evening at a wine *stube* called Fiesen Kunibert—I wonder if it still exists. After Cologne I passed briefly through Wiesbaden, Frankfurt and Heidelberg and wound up in Munich where I spent a thoroughly enjoyable two days at the art galleries and had a memorable evening at the Hofbrau Haus with Gerhard Gunther, another of my shipmates.

For me the highlight of Bavaria was a visit to the delightful grandmother of a German exchange student named Dieter Schoeller who had spent two years at Dartmouth where we admitted him, exceptionally, to Casque and Gauntlet. (In later years he came to America and I believed him when he said he had not been a Nazi.) When I met his grandmother, Dieter was on a trip to Asia so I didn't see him. Grandma had a chalet in Garmisch-Partenkirschen. I remember the wonderful food: potato salad, sausages and things I am no longer allowed to eat. The mountainous surroundings were breathtaking. Dieter's father was a high officer of the Deutsches Bank where I met him and Dieter's brother.

I then entrained for more sight seeing in Nuremberg, visiting Rotenburg enroute. After a day or two I boarded a train to Leipzig to have dinner and spend the night with Herr Zimmermann, a music publishing colleague of my father.

The railroad car I entered was filled with a lively throng of mostly German youth. They were students of the University of Munich bound for a theater tour of the Soviet Union under the guidance of Professor Docteur Artur Kutscher. Their first destination was Berlin. In the party were a few older people, notably Elsa Naumberg, an American traveling with her daughter Nancy, and Kapila Khanvala, a Brahmin woman of India. I fell in conversation with an attractive *fraulein* who was dying to practice her English. In an hour or so, I felt quite at ease with them all and they proposed that I join them on the trip to Russia. I had no fixed itinerary, I was curious about Russia and I loved the theater, so my impulse was to do it. But when I talked to the tour manager, a man named Venger, he brought me back to reality. It had taken some time for the group to obtain Soviet visas. Since the United States did not even recognize the Soviet Union at that point, getting a visa would be doubly difficult, especially since they would be spending only two days in Berlin. Venger saw no possibility, but said if I still wanted to make a try I could meet him at the Intourist Office in Berlin the next morning at 10 o'clock.

Zimmermann met me when I left the train at Leipzig and we spent a pleasant evening at his home. His English was quite good and by then I had picked up a little German. I felt relaxed when we finished the excellent dinner his housekeeper prepared. In the course of conversation I told him about my encounter on the train. "To Russia!" he said with some excitement, "Russia is part of the future. Whatever happens in this world, good or bad, Russia will be important. If I were a young man I would go to see what it's all about." He went on in that vein. He had been to Russia some years before in the time of the Tsar. He was still importing music from the Soviet Union. He would go again, but in his late 60s did not feel up to the journey. "You must go," he concluded. I explained the difficulties. "You must try," he insisted. He found that a 6 am train would get me to Berlin before 10 and I agreed to take it. There begins at this point, the most extraordinary chain of circumstance that I experienced in a long life.

I arrived at Intourist, on Unter den Linden, a few minutes past ten, but Venger had not yet shown up. A young man was talking in German to the Intourist agent. *Ausgeschlossen* (NO way!) said the agent, "*Soviet visa fuhr Americaner nicht meuglich, ausgeschlossen.*" I got the drift. No chance for a visa. The young man rose and walked towards the door. Somehow he looked familiar. "Are you an American?" I asked. "Hell yes," was the reply. It turned out we had met years before at a tennis tournament between two rival boys camps in Maine. A few years older, Myer Cohen was taking his Ph.D. at Yale. He had hoped to study labor problems in Russia and was bitterly disappointed. I suggested he stick around until Venger arrived, if the idea of a theater tour interested him. When Venger appeared he conferred at some length with the agent but finally turned to us saying, "We can't help you. Intourist says your only chance is at the Soviet Embassy a few blocks from here. We leave tomorrow at noon from the North Station. If you manage to get visas meet us on the train."

Myer and I took off for the Soviet Embassy. The front door was unlocked and we walked in. To our surprise there were no guards on duty. We moved down a long corridor until we reached an open door. Far within, a middle-aged man was seated at a huge desk. He politely waved us in and Myer spoke up in German. At first, the official seemed negative and was directing us to the Soviet Consulate, but when he realized we were Americans, and needed the visas in 24 hours, the sheer lunacy of our quest amused him and he broke into laughter. We had no idea who he was. He could have been the Ambassador. Finally, in a mixture of German and English he spoke, "I can't give you visas: it would be against our rules, but I'm willing to cable Moscow recommending it. If you want to take a chance, go to Intourist with your baggage tomorrow at 10 am and if your visas are granted I'll send you word."

Of course we were there on time, but it was 11 or even a bit later that the Intourist agent got a call saying our visas were granted. We rushed off by taxi to the North Station, caught the train with a few minutes to spare and joined my friends of the previous day on the trip to Stettin in the north of Germany.

I got talking to several men on the train and when we got to Stettin joined them in walking around the town and buying supplies. All the Germans bought supplies, extremely dubious about how the meals would be on shipboard, and thoroughly convinced they wouldn't be able to tolerate the food in Russia. I was more optimistic, but having no desire to be caught short, I stocked up on sardines, cheese, wurst, tea, and Swedish crackers.

We had a most pleasant voyage to Leningrad over the Baltic Sea in a little German vessel. As the ship approached Kronstadt, the Soviet naval base, we had our first look at the Soviet Union. This was prelude to an exciting three-week journey that took us to Leningrad, Moscow, Kharkov and Kiev. I describe the sights and sounds of that experience in a letter written soon after my return to Frank Albert, a longtime business associate of my father's and an old family friend. Uncle Frank had been born in Czarist Russia. He was now deeply rooted in Sydney with an Australian wife and son, but he retained a lively curiosity about the land of his birth. When he learned that I had been there, he asked me to give him an account of my visit to the Soviet Union. What follows in the next chapter are the impressions of a 21 year old American in the summer of 1932.

Journeying out of Russia after a three week stay, we thought the Russian train taking us west from the Ukraine was bound for Warsaw, but instead we were unceremoniously dumped at night at a small sleepy Polish border railroad junction. Protests were of no avail. The train soon departed on its homeward journey back to Russia. There was no town—only a small inn with a few tiny rooms that we gallantly ceded to several of the older women. It was too cold to sleep outdoors. Most of us spent the night stretched out on the floor along the inner walls of the only large room.

Next morning there was a crazy quilt of action. The innkeeper and his wife frantically tried to meet the demand for breakfast. Coarse bread, potatoes, eggs and tea were handed around to sleepy-eyed guests in rumpled clothes. The furniture was sparse. Most of us ate standing in the room where we had slept, or in a barnyard to the accompaniment of clucking chicks. Our theater group had been augmented on the train by several individual travelers. Among them were Kingsley Martin, editor of the *New Statesman*, and Low, the well-known political cartoonist. Among all the clutter, Low patiently shaved with his razor, a cup of water and a bit of soap, but no mirror. No one knew when or ever a train from either the west or east would come to pick us up. Around noon one finally showed up from the west and we were transported to Warsaw and put up at the Dom Akedemitski—a perfect ringer for a YMCA in its accoutrements and especially its welcome shower facilities. We did our best to catch up on sleep.

Warsaw, somewhat like Brussels, has a huge wonderful square of fifteenth century patrician houses, each one a different color with gates and varying facades above the door embellished with marvelous old figurines and animals. It was relaxing and pleasant to be there. We got the impression that the Poles hated both their Western and Eastern neighbors, Germany and Russia. We stopped in at an impressive service in a large Catholic church and it was kind of refreshing after the propagandized Russian churches. I wrote in a letter home that we saw the ghetto "walled in by itself and remarkably independent from the rest of the city." Even though I was traveling with a group, it was naive of me not to want to explore it at the time. I was young and I just didn't have that kind of interest then. I was more impressed by Warsaw at night. In my letter I wrote, "the cafes are new, bright and shiny, the music far more tuneful than we had heard in the Soviet Union, the dancing is positively spectacular and the women are gorgeous. It may have just seemed so after the absence of that sort of thing in Russia. Here was real gaiety and a certain amount of prosperity." We sampled many drinks, among them Polish whiskey, Polish cordials and a delicious cocktail of half cherry brandy and half vodka. I sometimes make and serve a concoction consisting of Cherry Heering, quinine water and lime. It's definitely weaker. We'd had our fill of vodka in Russia where we could buy it for less than a mark a bottle (25 cents). We sometimes drank it on the long night train rides.

Before leaving Eastern Europe, I'd like to describe a serendipitous happening in Russia that I didn't cover in my letter to Uncle Frank. It's our second day in Moscow and the group is a-twitter because this evening we are to witness a performance of the famed Vachtangov production of *Hamlet*. But it turns out there aren't enough tickets to go around. When we draw lots, Myer gets a ticket but I don't. The rest of us are to see a movie. In Manhattan, I can see a Russian movie at the Stanley (in NYC) any time I feel like it, so I decide to take the chance of finding a seat at the theater. No luck at the box office, but I wait in the lobby hoping for a miracle. Curtain time finds me there alone and discouraged. Just then an attractive young woman enters breathlessly. "Are you Mr. Antonov?" she asks in English. I decline the honor. "Oh, dear," she exclaims. "I'm supposed to meet him here. I have a ticket for him." "The curtain's going up," I reply, "take me instead!"

Myer and the others are astonished when I walk out at the first intermission with Elizabeth Elson in tow. After the show, he and I take her to the Hotel Metropole for the evening described in my letter. It turns out that she, too, is at Yale, teaching at Professor Baker's Theater School. Around one o'clock in the morning we escort her back to her hotel. She's leaving early the next morning for Paris.

After my return to the U.S. in October I decided to take in the Yale-Dartmouth football game in New Haven. I phoned Myer to see if he'd accompany me. He couldn't make it, but insisted that we meet after the game—he had a surprise for me. You guessed it. Myer and Elizabeth were to be married. Over 70 years later they were still married when Myer died at age 95 in 2002. Elizabeth is in a retirement home near Philadelphia and was 100 in March 2003. We have kept in touch over the years. When I was writing my Master's thesis on the Federal Theater, Elizabeth was directing its program in Northern California, and she gave me some very helpful information. Some years later, when I was unhappy with my Washington job in public housing, Myer jump-started my UN career by offering me a job in Geneva.

Back in Berlin, it was good to get clean and have laundry done. My cleanest shirt had been worn at least six times and I was pretty tired of my light gray flannel suit, the only one I took to Russia. Elsa Naumberg and her daughter Nancy—friends from the trip to Russia—told me about the Pension Oliva on Kurfurstendamm and I got their room after they sailed for America. In my letter home I wrote, "Everything is clean, the people are nice and their sunken tile bathtub has a grand shower. All I am paying is three marks a day with a good breakfast included. As I look out over the broad expanse of my bedroom I feel I am monarch of all I survey—chairs, bed, three windows, two bureaus, telephone, sink, everything—I cannot help feeling how little the prospect of getting to work appeals to me. But I will. If I get a job I'll work like hell for five years. Then I'll come over again and spend all I've made." I really had no awareness of what was boiling up in Europe at that time that had its climax in the rise of the Nazis and the Second World War.

Myer took off immediately for Yale but I stayed on in Berlin for close to a month. In Berlin I found a letter of introduction from my father to Paul Lincke, composer of *Glow Worm*, one of the staples of the Marks catalogue. Lincke, in his 60s, lived in Wannsee, a Berlin suburb. He gave me a splendid reception! He received me in bathrobe and slippers and we talked for over an hour. He took me to tea at the Bristol Hotel (for him, lunch) bringing with us a pleasant girl of 18, the daughter of Robert Ruhle (a music publisher). She appeared from upstairs just as we were leaving. I never found out what she was doing there but she certainly wasn't his girlfriend. After lunch we drove around the town and at one point we passed a detachment of men in Nazi uniforms. Lincke, who was not Jewish, assured me that the present government—Hindenburg was still President and Walter Reichenau was Chancellor—would remain in power. I think he sincerely believed this, as did a number of other Germans I met in Berlin. It was six months before the Reichstag fire and before Hitler took over as Chancellor. I had no reason to think otherwise.

The next day we dined again at the Bristol and he brought the girl's identical twin sister. I found her more interesting, and as Lincke was busy in the afternoon I took her to Luna Park. The next evening we went to *Katharina*, a musical featuring a popular soprano from Budapest, for which Lincke had given me a couple of tickets. I liked Linke very much. He died a few years after I was there. I wrote my folks "He has an amazing amount of savoir faire, natural grace and nonchalance. On Sunday he will take me to a country inn where he took Herb for a wonderful steak."

At the recommendation of my shipboard friend, Gerhard Gunther, I telephoned Ika von Mengersen, who turned out to be a congenial playmate during my days in Berlin. Ika was the daughter of a German captain who was killed in the war. She was a graduate teacher in gymnastics and a Mary Wigman dancer.

(Mary Wigman was the Martha Graham of Germany.) Ika came from a *junker* (noble) family that had an estate in Neustralitz am Schliersee to which she invited me. The estate, called a *gut*, was kind of a vestigial feudal village dominated by one family. The shop keepers, artisans, even the local farmers were somehow bound together under the pervading influence, if not direction, of the family. It was quite an experience for me to visit such a place.

Ika had friends in the film business, and for a time I had hopes of finding a job dubbing English subtitles into German films, but it didn't work out. She showed me quite a bit of Berlin. We saw Max Reinhardt's noted production of *The Miracle* and that delightful musical called *The White Horse Inn*. We visited the Wild West Room and several of the others at Kempinski's, a cafe with intercommunicating telephones at each table. We also took in the Kabaret de Komicker, a swell joint, and the Zigeuner Keller, a Gypsy boite where we listened to Gypsy music and drank Tokay.

Berlin had a fascination for me, but my money was running out and I had to head home. I had $200 left out of the original $700, when I got to Berlin, but had practically nothing left at the end of the month.

Before I left New York, my cousin Steve had counseled me to buy rail tickets for my intended European destinations from the Swiss National Railroads. I followed this itinerary up to the Soviet diversion. I now wished to travel home directly from Berlin but there were complications. My return tickets routed me through most of Switzerland. In good weather, and with ample cash, I would have enjoyed that, but it was mid-October, damp and chilly, and I had no money left for hotel rooms. Fifteen years later, on assignment to Geneva, I came to appreciate the beauties of Switzerland, but endlessly winding in and out of its lakes and mountains, nursing a bad cold, and subsisting for the most part on sandwiches snatched at railroad buffets, I leaned to hate day and night third class coach travel on Swiss trains. I was fatigued, dirty and hungry when we pulled into Le Havre but savored my return ocean passage to New York. You can imagine what a relief it was.

Ahead of me was the need to find a job—in the depths of the Depression.

I didn't feel I was brainwashed after a three-week visit to the Soviet Union, but I couldn't help being affected by the new ideas and surge of hope I observed even during that short stay. I recalled the comment of a young man we met in Moscow's Park of Culture and Rest. He was fingering the cloth of my coat. He spoke no English, but as he stepped back, admiringly, he raised his hand with five fingers extended. I didn't get it at once, but soon realized what he was trying to convey: "In five years we will have this." He was referring to Stalin's Five-Year Plan.

In later years I thought that he and many others of his generation must have been cruelly disillusioned. But when I returned to the U.S. in the fall of 1932 we were in the depths of Hooverism and the Depression. So I was, for several years at least, a cautious champion of Soviet attempts to break away from the old capitalist mold and start something new. I wasn't then and never did become a political partisan. However my interest in the goals of Socialism was fanned by my brother's wife. I don't think Hortie ever joined the Communist Party, but in the early 1930s at least she was a doctrinaire exponent of the Party line. Hortie persuaded me to enroll with her in a course given by an organization named *Pen and Hammer*. I don't recall how long she stayed with it, but after one or two meetings I got fed up with their positivist jargon and dropped out. I could not accept the infallibility of their judgments.

I kept up an interest in what was going on in the Soviet Union and was more or less sympathetic to the dispatches of Walter Duranty, *The New York Times* correspondent in Moscow who won a Pulitzer Prize in 1932. Duranty was criticized in later years because of his optimism about the Stalinist future. As he put it on June 14, 1931, "Stalin is giving the Russian people—the Russian masses, not westernized landlords, industrialists, bankers and intellectuals, but Russia's 150 million peasants and workers—what they really want, namely, joint efforts, communal effort. And communal life is as acceptable to them as it is repugnant to a Westerner." About that time I read Lincoln Steffens' autobiography in which he says, after a visit to the Soviet Union, "I've seen the future and it works."

In March 1933, I went with Bill and Ferd to President Roosevelt's inauguration in Washington and was soon caught up in the enthusiasm of the New Deal. I was delighted when the U.S. recognized the Soviet Union shortly thereafter. A year or two later a friend of my brother's, Mick Uris, who knew I had been to Russia, took me aside at a party and tried to recruit me for the Communist Party. I told him I had no interest in joining, and, as time went on, especially after the Nazi-Soviet Pact, I lost interest entirely. Mick became a successful screenwriter in Hollywood but was eventually blacklisted.

LETTER TO UNCLE FRANK

Here is the letter I wrote to Frank Albert, a music publisher and our family friend in Australia who had been born in Russia and asked me to send him an account of my travel there. This is printed as I wrote it.

124 West 79th Street
New York City, N.Y.
March 23, 1933

Dear Uncle Frank:

I don't see how, in a few hundred words, I can give you any sort of an idea as to what I saw in Russia. In the first place, it wasn't all seeing—a lot of it was tasting, smelling, hearing, even sensing. And then I was there so short a time, no doubt some of my impressions were incomplete, possibly false. But one thing I do know. Germany and the Germans are my pleasantest memory of Europe; Italy was the most beautiful country I saw; but Soviet Russia was far and away the most interesting, and the one I am anxious to see when I re-visit Europe in years to come.

In one respect, I'm very glad that I came into Russia knowing practically nothing about it. I had no axe to grind for or against communism. I could look around without thinking at all times of the political "significance" of this or that. I went there on a lark, with twenty-four hours notice, merely because I was curious.

Perhaps I should begin at the beginning. After a couple of delightful weeks in Bavaria, I was on a train going from Nuremberg to Leipzig. My intention was to stop off at Leipzig for a few days, spend the weekend at a villa in the Harz Mountains in Thuringia with some friends, and then head for Berlin. On the train I fell in with this German group that were expecting to go to Russia in two days. I didn't know much German, but several of them spoke English quite fluently, and there were a few Americans among them, so the upshot was that I became interested. They were a group studying drama at the University of Munich, and that was to be their special study during their stay in Russia, although they were also to include other things. The price of the trip was ridiculously cheap—250 marks for about three weeks including everything.

By the time the train neared Leipzig, I was almost sold on the idea, but at the last minute I was discouraged by Venger, the man in charge of the travel arrangements. "You can't possibly get a visa in time," he said to me. "These people had to apply weeks ago." I pretty well banished the idea from my mind as the train neared Leipzig and I was just leaving the platform when he yelled to me, "If you want to have a try, meet me at the Intourist office in Berlin tomorrow at 10, but I doubt it."

I took the chance and went to Berlin on a 6 o'clock train the next morning. Venger had not yet arrived. When he did, the Intourist Agent said it was very unlikely that I could obtain a Soviet visa in time. They agreed that I could make a try at the nearby Soviet Embassy which I did. A return wire granting me permission arrived the next day forty five minutes before the train bearing the party was to leave. But it all worked out, somewhat miraculously, in one of those mad rushes that half worry you to death when you are in the midst of them, but are a pleasure to look back on.

The little German boat on which we made the trip over the Baltic Sea to Leningrad looked woefully small, but we all managed to fit on it somehow. All the men slept on berths in one big cabin, and all the women in another. The food was surprisingly good. And the trip was --- beautiful. We were on the water three nights and two days—out of sight of land from Swinemunde to Revel—and the weather was perfect all the time. It was a swell beginning to the trip, because it afforded us a fine opportunity to get acquainted. The group was much larger than I thought. There were three Americans besides myself—a young man, and a young girl and her mother; there were two Swiss; there was an Englishman and there was a Swede; there were two East Indians, one of whom was a charming young woman from Bombay who had studied in America and England, wore her native dress, subsisted on fruit and nuts which she brought along, and told fortunes with her tongue in her cheek. Altogether, there must have been over eighty Germans from every part of Germany, men and women, young and old, interesting and dull. We had several professors, an engineer, a Presbyterian minister, two lawyers, a doctor, a theater critic---and various others of every type.

The morning we arrived in Leningrad was particularly thrilling. The weather was lovely, and we all stood on the deck, eager for the first glimpse. We passed Kronstadt, and we began to see little boats here and there—each bearing a (red) flag with the hammer and sickle. The pilot, grizzled and picturesque, clambered on board, and everybody on the boat craned his neck to get a look at the first live Soviet citizen. The entrance by sea to Leningrad is through a canal, part natural, part artificial, and it requires pretty ticklish navigation at some of the bends. Signs giving directions on both banks were in Russian and English. The English looked good, if a little archaic at some points.

The harbor at Stettin had been filled with many idle ships, but here things were different, and in every shipyard we saw men at work—painting, scraping, loading cargo. There were a few foreign boats there, mainly English and German. Slowly we steamed up the Neva River, past the shipyards, up to the New Admiralty building, in front of which the Customs office was to be found.

I can well understand how the old St. Petersburg must indeed have been a city for the Tsar. It still carries something of the imperial atmosphere about it when you see it at first glance, but when you look around you see how changed it all has been. I don't know if you were in this city in the days before the war—but in any case you must surely have heard of the Nevski Prospect, the famous avenue which runs through the center of the city. Now it is called the Prospect of the 25th of October, in commemoration of that famous date in the revolution, but it still seems to be the main artery through which courses the life-blood of the city. Day and night it is packed with people walking to and fro, in the sidewalks and in the streets. They are dressed very much the same, crudely, but not shabbily. Their clothes are workmen's clothes, made of coarse materials and totally lacking in style, but they are not dressed in rags. Practically all walk; although the trams that rush through the streets are also overcrowded. They are bright red, these trams, and they move along very swiftly, stopping only at certain points, not at every block. The passengers enter at the rear and get out at the front—we hear there is a fine if they do otherwise. The fare is 10 kopecks, practically nothing for a Russian, and only 5 cents for the foreigner who has to buy rubles at the full rate. I will explain about the money later.

There are many horse-drawn carts going to and fro, especially in the day time, all equipped with the ponderous wishbone wooden harness, but practically no automobiles. Only fairly battered-looking cars once in awhile, which are supposed to be granted to Commissars of a certain rank who need them in their work. The only exception to this is the fleet of beautiful new Lincolns, maintained in each of the cities we visited by Intourist (the Soviet travel bureau). Just why Intourist possesses these cars, which are totally out of place in their surroundings, is something of a mystery, but I suppose it is pretty much a matter of "front." They must have acquired them at the same time they received permission to build the Ford factory at Nizhni Novgorod, since the two cars are made by the same company. But there are only a few of these in each city, and the total effect is one of horses and people walking. There are a few motorbuses, both for citizens and for sightseers.

We stayed in the October Hotel (I am not attempting the Russian names), a hotel at one end of October Avenue, near the Lt. Schmidt Bridge. It looked wonderful from the outside—all newly done we thought. On the inside, it was not quite so fine, although it was a thousand times better than what we had expected to find. We found a curious mixture of old and new, especially in the lobby. Much of the general outline had been reconstructed in a definitely modernistic style, but standing around everywhere were heavy gold framed mirrors and imperial looking chairs from the old days which made the whole thing very incongruous. The rooms were decent enough—in Leningrad four of us had a nice large room with single beds. Furthermore the food was good—the bread, the eggs, the vegetables, the famous tea, and the borscht. The borscht was especially marvelous. Not just beet soup—which I had an idea it was, but a wonderful rich brown stew with cabbage and carrots and meat and various trimmings that was plentiful, and had a delicious flavor, and was almost a meal in itself. We were given tickets for each day's meals, and the tickets were collected by the waiter each time.

Some of the people were troubled by bedbugs during the three nights we spent in Leningrad. I fortunately was not and I think a lot of it may have been imaginary, although some of them had welts to show. However, we were traveling what is called "second category" and were *not* staying at the best hotel. Our rate, as figured in our 250 marks, was about $5 per day while those in "first category" paid $10 per day per room.

I cannot of course recapitulate all we saw in Leningrad, but we saw plenty. Everyone's first remark is always "I hear they show you just what they want to show you in Russia." That is partially true. If you leave it up to them they will route you through only the best things. But we saw plenty of other things too on our own, walking around during the day, and even more particularly at night. Of course, we saw plenty of holdovers from the old culture, and in general it amazed us how well kept up the old things were. For example, we naturally went through the Hermitage, the famous museum, and it looked to be in fine shape. Of course, it was weird seeing people in workmen's clothes—women who looked like scrub women—trudging through the halls of the former palace, wide-eyed, curious, definitely trying their best to learn. The museum itself is wonderful, truly one of the most important in the world, what with thirty-nine Rembrandts and a marvelous Spanish collection. Perhaps you have seen it.

The famous Cathedral of St. Isaak, the biggest church in the city, is now an anti-religious museum, and although the exterior is the same, and the mosaics are retained by the altar, the entire inside is a display of propaganda against the Church. Huge posters with huge lettering and vivid pictures show how the Russian church exacted money from the poor people, forced the country into war, and things of that kind. Others show what the money spent on churches would have meant in terms of industry and education. I never saw such propaganda anywhere as I saw in Russia—not only religious, all kinds—the greatest advertising campaign in the world. Other posters in the church show how churchmen were burned for discovering scientific fact contrary to the teachings. The whole purpose is to blast superstition out of the minds of these people. We went into another, smaller church on Sunday to see what it was like. There was a service going on (they are not prohibited, except for children under 16 who are not allowed to attend). All the people were old people, however. The young walked by outside with heads held high.

We went to a marriage bureau in Leningrad. You can be married any time you like, so long as both parties present a certificate of health. You can be divorced when you like, the next day if necessary. In fact, if only one of the couple wants a divorce, he or she can go to the court alone and get it. The next day the other one gets a postcard in the mail telling the news. Despite this fact, however, divorce is not as prevalent as it was at first, it having been found that a man who cannot make up his mind about marriage, is naturally indecisive and shiftless, and hence does not deserve as good a job. Since a man's position, and in a manner of speaking, his wealth, up to a certain point, depend on the job he holds, that would seem to provide a very neat check.

In Leningrad we went to a very interesting place outside the city where a nobleman formerly had his chateau. Now that chateau has been converted, practically as it was, into a "rest house" for workers, where they can get a week's vacation when they feel the strain. The people there seem quite healthy and cheerful. Again, the irony of the thing. It is, as someone has said, almost a case of the janitor with his feet on the boss's desk when the boss is out.

We rode out to Peterhof in probably the dirtiest day train I've ever been in to see the Tsar's summer palace. The palace is now open for inspection to the public, and the grounds have been converted into a park, where workers can go on their day off with their families. The place is beautiful—something like Sans Souci, but infinitely handsomer, because it looks out on the Gulf of Finland. Incidentally, we went swimming in the gulf and it was fine.

We went to the theater only once in Leningrad and saw a bitter satiric play by Astrovsky. The audience was really half the play. They enjoyed it tremendously. I didn't enjoy it as well, although some parts were very funny. It was the most merciless comedy I ever saw. But more later about the theater in Moscow.

All our rides between cities were night rides on trains, and it was in prospect of these, chiefly, that we had provided ourselves with food before leaving Germany. The rides were long, from twelve to eighteen hours each, and because of our category we were to travel "hard" instead of "soft." As a matter of fact it wasn't so bad. Each of us had a wooden shelf, and they provided us with a reasonably clean straw mattress encased with some material, one sheet, one straw pillow, and a kind of peculiar cover. On the rides we usually sat up late, sitting on the bottom shelves, talking and eating our food. At every station, we would go out and get hot water for our tea. On the rides between Moscow and Kharkov and Kharkov and Kiev, we were warned against bandits who might climb up on the roofs of cars and hook things out through the windows. The men in each car had to alternate on guard duty. But nothing ever happened to frighten us. Besides, it was terribly dusty even if we kept the windows closed. We were filthy during and after the end of each of the three rides, and only cleaned up after we got to our hotels, and sometimes not so well then. We didn't strike any hot water until we got to Kiev. That is, enough for a hot bath. You could get a pitcher of hot water for shaving if you asked for it and if you could make them understand it.

Usually the Intourist guides were ready and willing to help us whenever they could. They are really very high type people. They arranged all our meals and baggage transportation, and personally escorted us wherever we went, except if we skipped out alone. They would explain all the Russian in the parks and museums, and act as interpreters in the theater, etc. We found a few English speaking people, and a few German-speaking people. That was about all. Some of the guides went right through with us from Leningrad to Kiev.

It is probably Moscow in which you are chiefly interested. We were there the longest time—about a week all told, I think. I did not think the city was as pretty as Leningrad. It looks to be terribly crowded for one thing. Another thing it lacks is an avenue with the color of the October Avenue. But on the other hand, it is far more picturesque, oriental, teeming with action, patriotic, polyglot, and awesome than any of the other cities. This is partly because of its size, partly because it is the capital of the Soviet, and partly because it just naturally has a sprawling, seething, curiously scrambled appearance.

We stayed at the Novo Moskovskaya (New Moscow), which is certainly not one of the best hotels by a long shot, and yet we had no real cause for complaint. There are some really first class hotels. Notably the Savoy and Metropole, the latter the center of about the only nightlife the town affords. However, our hotel was in a swell location, right on the Moscow River with the Kremlin directly on the opposite bank, making it about a five minute walk across the bridge and up the hill along the Kremlin wall to the Red Square.

The houses in Moscow, or at least many of them, have been whitewashed, but they are not in good condition and it is easy to see through most of the attempt that has been made to keep them presentable. On the street, as in Leningrad, one sees hundreds of people all the time, wandering to and fro, especially at night. There are quite a few movies, and they are well attended. We went to one in Leningrad, and another in Moscow, and another later in Kharkov. We also visited the studios where they are made in Moscow. They have little in the way of elaborate equipment, but they are very conscientious and some of their pictures are good, though there is nothing worse than a bad one. In general their theater is much better.

We went to theater four times in Moscow and I was genuinely thrilled by what we saw. After the cheap piece we had seen put on by the traveling company in Leningrad, I did not expect much of the Soviet theater, but believe me there is a manifestation of the hand of genius in the sort of work that is done on the stage in Moscow. The height of the stage is used in addition to its width and depth, and that height is used with terrific effect, very often to show class struggle, sometimes just for artistic effect. We saw Shakespeare's Hamlet, Schiller's Kabale und Liebe, and two Russian plays, one pre-revolutionary by Ostrovsky (but considerably amended, I imagine), and the other post-revolutionary. We saw them training young actors one morning at the Meyerhold Theater. They go through regular routine exercises to develop grace and suppleness of motion.

The Hamlet of the Vachtangov Theater is especially interesting, and I will wager like no Hamlet you have ever seen on any stage. Perhaps you have heard about the production. The Soviets cannot allow the supernatural, therefore the play is played without a ghost. More than that, Hamlet himself plays the part of the ghost by putting on and taking off a ghost's disguise to suit his convenience, and blowing his words into a conch shell when he wants to simulate his father's deeper tones. Instead of being a lean, philosophic, melancholy Dane, Hamlet is represented as a short, ugly, pot-bellied little man who is scheming for the throne, who employs the "ghost" deceit as a stratagem. The whole play through, he plans, and his famous soliloquies take the form of conferences with Horatio. Even the famed "To be or not to be" speech is interpreted not as Shakespeare intended it. It is given when Hamlet takes the puppet crown and sets it on his own head—"To be or not to be *King*" is the thought. Not Hamlet, you will say. Right. But farce though it is (and it is farce most of the way through), the production is mounted magnificently, and the cast is superb. That, at least, cannot be denied.

The theaters are very nice, and we understand that workers obtain seats through their "trusts" (i.e., where they work) for the performances. They are entitled to so many per season for practically nothing. In much the same way they gain admission to concerts, opera, moving pictures and things of that kind. In fact, if we were convinced of nothing else in Russia, we did come away with the idea that on the cultural side at least, the Soviets are doing a masterful job.

The system of parks alone bears ample testimony to this. Perhaps the best example of a park is the famous one in Moscow, the Central Park of Culture and Rest. It is truly that, in both senses of the word. There is plenty of opportunity to loll around or play, and there is plenty of opportunity for learning. I cannot hope to remember half the things we saw in the park, but some of them were a regular movie theater; a second movie theater showing only films of mechanical and engineering interest; a huge exhibit of workers' art of all kinds—painting, sculpture, etc.; swimming facilities; a splendidly-equipped nursery for children of workers, where they are kept all day, fed and instructed; a public lecture hall in the open air; several reading rooms with libraries of books and newspapers; a football field where a match was in progress between Turkey and Russia, in addition to various other games indulged in by a great many, and a group singing songs under the direction of an energetic song leader. And all over, in the paths between the buildings and in every building, propaganda of all sorts. Sometimes it takes the form of busts or pictures of Lenin and Stalin (never Trotsky, whom Stalin forced out of the picture). More often it is seen in huge signs in big red letters which show how Russia's production of some product has increased during the last five years, whereas everywhere else in the world (in the capitalistic countries, of course) it has decreased. Another very amusing manifestation of this is seen in a type of amusement booth they have in the park at odd points, not dissimilar to those in Coney Island or the Prater, where the object is to throw balls at something to attempt to hit it. In this country, it usually takes the form of a Negro's head, the common expression being usually "Hit the nigger in the eye and get a glass of beer."

In Russia, however, they order things somewhat differently. The objects of punishment are none other than small puppet caricatures of Lloyd George, John D. Rockefeller, Clemenceau, and others of that genre. Quite a game! They are the targets.

These parks seem to play an important part in the life of the people. Each one is provided with a band, and at night it is quite fine watching hundreds of people strolling around. Since there are practically no cafes and the prices at these are beyond the reach of many; since their living quarters are usually not of the best; and since the theaters cannot yet accommodate all who would like to go, it provides about the best way there is of spending an evening. There are restaurants of course. We visited a few that were connected with hotels, although we could hardly spend any money there. They seemed to be crowded with reasonably happy people. And there was plenty of drinking. In addition to the amount of *pivo* (beer) that is allowed each man, (you see them standing around in the street waiting for it), there is also other liquor available. On the whole, the cities we saw seemed quite temperate, but we ran across a few drunks, all kindly disposed toward us fortunately.

Perhaps this is as good a time as any to clear up any mistaken ideas you may have about the money. People come back from Russia and say that everything is frightfully expensive—that meals are $10.00 and that it costs a dollar to buy an apple. Well, they are *partially* right. Russia *is* expensive for those foreigners who are foolish enough to change any appreciable amount of their money into rubles.

When you enter the country, you must register all your money. Then you can change as much as you like into rubles, at their rate of exchange, 50 cents a ruble. This is what the ruble was worth before the war, I believe. The only trouble with the system is this—the ruble in Russia today is worth about 5 cents. It is hard to place its value at any point because there is so little one can buy with it even when one has rubles, but the fact remains that anyone who pays 50 cents for a ruble is paying ten times what it is really worth.

There are two ways of getting around this. One way is to buy rubles cheap outside of Russia, e.g., they sell for about 30 pfenning in Germany. Or you can perhaps get a Russian to sell you some rubles cheap in return for some of your valuta (foreign money) which is very precious to him. But these ways are dangerous. First of all, you are not supposed to bring rubles in or out of the country, and it will go hard with you if you are caught. Secondly, there are damned few Russians who will sell you rubles, partly because of their own scruples about the ethics of the thing, partly because of their great fear of being caught.

The alternative is to change into rubles only what you absolutely need and keep the rest of your money in valuta. This is what we did. We each bought about three dollars worth of rubles for carfare, emergencies of any kind, etc., and we kept the rest of our money in good German marks.

Under this arrangement, we could not shop in stores in the towns where we went. But as I said before, there is practically nothing to buy in those stores, even if you did have the money in rubles and were willing to spend it. There is no idea of merchandising, as we know it elsewhere in the world. Only the simplest of necessities are stocked in those stores where trading is done in rubles. And they look as if they are doing practically no business at all.

This is, of course, because of the way the thing functions. A man gets his allowance for food, clothing, in fact all necessities, from his trust, and he presents tickets at his factory for that merchandise. No money passes hands at all. In time they hope to be able to do away with money, but at present they still need it for street car fares, etc. If a man wants something beyond what he is allowed, he must pay for it, and pay somewhat dearly. For example, in order to economize, certain vegetables are rationed to all on certain days of the week. Let us say that on Tuesday, the vegetables chosen are cabbage and cucumbers. All right. Tuesday comes along and Smolenkovitch decides he wants beets instead. Does he get it through his trust? He does not. He has to pay extra, and plenty! Sugar, butter, etc. are very dear.

Now, here is the other side of the picture. The Soviet government, too smart to waste the tourist money that comes in each year, has devised a rather neat plan. In each city it has established so called *Torgsin* stores, where the foreigner may deal, may select regular food stuffs, or the fancy things he would like to bring home to show people he's been to Russia. In these places, the ruble is not accepted. Only valuta is valid currency, and marks, pounds, francs, dollars, yen, anything that has a standing in the world's financial market is acceptable. Furthermore, they will make change for you, although you often have a hell of a wait until they figure out just what is coming to you. In your change, you may get a little Swedish, or Turkish, or Dutch money thrown in if you're not careful. The prices are in rubles, you see, so it is rather difficult to figure things out. However, things are priced at rubles considered much more equitably—in fact at their 50 cent value, so that you are paying just about what the things are worth. Thus a handsomely hand embroidered shirt cost me three dollars, a little embroidered cap about 75 cents and a bottle of vodka about 80 cents. Arrangements have recently been made that Russians can also deal in the Torgsin stores, if they are sent money by relatives in other countries. Since they can buy things there that they cannot possibly buy outside, they are anxious to spend the foreign money there, and of course the government is glad to pile in just that much more good solid currency, in contrast to their own dubious ruble. Torgsin stores do a good business selling extra food to these people.

A funny thing happened one night when we were in Moscow. We went to the theater about 8—(we used to breakfast at 10, lunch at 4 and have supper at 11 or so). After the theater we thought we would try the Hotel Metropole, about which we had heard so much, instead of going back to our own hotel for supper. It would mean wasting one of our tickets but we thought for once we would see what the nightlife of Moscow had to offer. We went there, entered the dining room, and were ceremoniously ushered to a table. Many people were around at other tables, and all in all it was a lot swankier than any other place we encountered in Russia.

On second glance, we noticed a few shortcomings. Our waiter's white coat was a bit soiled, and he did not seem to have on much in the way of a shirt. There was a ten-piece orchestra, of which only three members had on coats. Their favorite tune was "Thanks for the Buggy Ride" which we had some difficult recalling. The diners looked to be chiefly foreigners of one sort and another, Russians of the Commissar grade, and various nondescripts that might have been anything. There were also two Negroes (who looked suspiciously like American Negroes) dancing with two rather handsome, though quaintly dressed white girls.

We asked for a menu and received one that was in French and Russian, with the prices given in terms of Russian money. We felt like having steak, but when we saw that steak was down for 16 rubles per portion, we decided that we would have to get along on something else—8 dollars was a little too high. But the other prices were very little lower. Finally somebody had a bright idea and asked the waiter for the valuta menu. He bowed, took away the menus we had and brought us others in which the prices were given in German marks. Steak was 3 marks! Imagine, a difference of about $7.25 for one portion if we had paid in Russian money. We had the steaks. They were good. We paid in marks.

In Leningrad we had met a boy who had been a year in America working in a Ford factory in Michigan. He had shown us all around, proud to show off the best things. He was curious about America and things that had happened there since he left. He said life in Russia was fine except that you could buy nothing except what was imperatively needed. He envied us our shirts and ties and offered to get us anything within his power if we would sell him some of our clothing. We each gave him a shirt and a tie, and he was tickled to death, though he did not dare to walk out of our hotel with them, and we had to wait until we were outside, in a deserted alley before he would accept them from us. He stuffed them in carefully under his clothes, afraid to be caught with them.

In Moscow we met a man who had been born in Russia, gone to America as a young man, worked there for over twenty years, married and raised a family in America, and then come back to Russia with his family to live. He was one of the foremen in the big electrical factory we visited in Moscow, and he was possessed of a really amazing enthusiasm for the Soviets. His only interest in America was to know who had won in baseball the previous season.

We saw many other things in Moscow which I shall have to pass over briefly. There is a wonderful Museum of Western Art containing matchless examples of Matisse, van Gogh, Cezanne, Picasso, etc., probably the finest individual collection in the world. There is a fine Museum of the Revolution, where the entire history of the revolution is traced from its earliest beginnings and brought up to the present in striking pictorial form. Ironically enough, this is housed in the former English Club of Moscow. In another museum, the Tretyakov Galleries, pictures by Russian artists are hung. Here you see the whole history of Russian art—from the 12th and 13th century icons to the 17th, 18th and 19th century pictures of the court, and finally the 20th century pictures and posters of the workers. The contrast is really quite striking. I particularly remember one picture showing workers learning the operation of tractors in the fields at night by illustration of a motion picture film. You can see the workers, eager, bent forward—anxious to gain every possible glimpse of the film bringing them this newfound knowledge.

We visited a hospital—clean and well equipped but lacking in screens so that there were flies everywhere inside. They also had special buildings for special contagion cases. These buildings looked solid enough, but they were made of wood . . . "just made to last 25 years or so," one of the guides at the hospital told us. "At the end of that time we won't have any more contagious disease. Then we'll burn them down." It sounds ridiculous to say so but I believe he really meant it when he said it.

We also went through a prophylacterium where former prostitutes are cared for. The Russians claim to have reduced prostitution to practically nothing, and in the cities I visited it certainly appears as if they have. Whereas cities like Vienna and Berlin are infested with them, we saw none the whole time we were in Russia, although we were told there were certain pathological cases which cannot be cured. At the prophylacterium, they told us that there is no direct legislation against prostitution. There the women are simply cared for, they are taught a trade, and they are given a job before they are discharged. We had the yellow ticket system of the old regime explained to us, and saw these horrible passports that the women used to have to show wherever they went. We heard from another source (an engineer) that the real reason prostitution has declined to almost nothing is not so much because of the state care or because of laxity of morals in the people and ease of divorce. He said it was simply because prostitution did not pay. If a woman was a prostitute, and not allied with any trade, her food, clothing and shelter become intolerably expensive—so much so that she could not possibly afford it. Some of the higher commissars, as might be expected, keep women, but that does not present much of a problem.

Of course the high point of Moscow, and indeed of the whole trip was the famous Red Square and the tomb of Lenin. Nothing I can say can give you any idea of its terrific power and splendor. When you were in Moscow, it had ceased to be the seat of the government, and the walls of the Kremlin must have been lacking in significance to a certain extent, but today, when so much is going on behind those walls they have an added mystery and awesomeness about them. We were escorted through the chief parts of the Kremlin, and saw a collection of jewels and precious metals and ivories of which I had never seen the like. We also went through the churches in the Kremlin where the Tsars were baptized, married and buried. The Russians are attempting to restore these to their former beauty; they were being rehabilitated while we were there. But, as I say, the real thing is the Red Square, and especially the tomb itself. The Square you probably remember. It is about a five minute walk from the Metropole and Grand Hotels down in the direction of the river. On one side is the Kremlin wall and the tomb; on the other is a huge, empty department store; on one end is the historical museum, once inhabited by the bishop of Moscow; on the other end is the Cathedral of St. Basil, a building so curious that Peter who had it built is alleged to have put out the architect's eyes so that he could never build another so beautiful. At night the Square is all lit up, and above the wall, over the tomb, flutters a bright red flag. By day, you can still see the imperial double eagle on the Kremlin towers: it may represent an era that is dead but it is very handsome and the Russians are conscious enough of that fact not to be rash and pull it down just because it is a symbol of the old empire. The tomb itself is made of marble— marble of all colors, with the different slabs coming from all the different republics of Russia. It is a curious building—modernistic in its conception, and yet blending marvelously with the Kremlin wall. There are two soldiers on guard at the entrance, night and day, and others within. The line forms early in the morning and by the time the entrance is open at 2 PM it stretches down past the cathedral. Slowly they are allowed to file in. We were allowed in too, mixing in among the Russians.

You go down a dimly lighted ramp, with a soldier at every turning, and you suddenly enter the room itself where the body lies. It catches your eye from the moment you enter, and holds you fast. You file all the way around the body, so close that you could put your hand out and touch it were it not for the glass case which surrounds it. Lenin lies there as if asleep, his hands folded naturally across his chest. You walk completely around him once and then you file out slowly.

It is really uncanny, and yet I am sure that the figure is real. People told me they had heard it was wax, and I went in half expecting to think so myself, but after passing as close to it as we were allowed to I don't see how it could be. If it is a secret process of embalming (as they say) it certainly is the most remarkable thing you have ever seen. And it is not horrible or ghastly or repellent in any way at all. And the paradoxical part of it is this. In the Soviet they claim to have dispensed with gods and images of all kinds. But if this reverence of Lenin is not idol worship or hero worship or whatever you want to call it—I don't know what is!

There was much more in Moscow that I cannot relate now. We next went to the Ukraine, where it was noticeably warmer; where the costumes and people were a little more picturesque and where the influence of agriculture began to show itself.

The first city we went to was Kharkov. This is really the newest big city, and has the advantage that they can plan it as it grows—not like Moscow for example where they must first displace the old. In Kharkov is the biggest building in Soviet Russia—a tremendous building called The Palace of Industry which is to house all the chief divisions of the government. Though only thirteen stories high, it covers a vast portion of ground. The building is not finished yet by any means, though the actual construction is finished. We went up in an elevator, and that seemed to be all right. We looked over the entire city from the roof. But inside the building they say things are not yet in shape. The Russians have great trouble getting such things as door knobs, for example. Their heavy industry plan does not provide for that sort of thing. Kharkov also has a gigantic tractor factory, supposedly the biggest in the world, and we saw the initial construction of what is planned as the world's biggest opera house. There is also a fine park packed with propaganda like all the rest, but also offering many cultural and recreational facilities. There are also new homes for workers, apartments similar to those we saw rising in Moscow, which look very promising. Kharkov has a fine new hospital, much more modern than the one we saw in Moscow.

There is no question, this is the city that may step out and show its heels to all of them yet. The Ukrainians are talented and industrious people, and if they can be whipped into the Union like some of the other cities further north, they will probably go far. Till now, however, the government seems to have antagonized them in their dealing with the grain situation, etc., and they are one of the weakest and more rebellious links in the Soviet chain. But watch Kharkov.

Kiev was the last city we visited, and in some ways the loveliest. It did not have the bustling harbor and main thoroughfare of Leningrad; it did not have the official air and general congestion and activity of Moscow; it did not have the ambitious projects of Kharkov; but it seemed lazier, greener, warmer than the others. Perhaps (I hesitate to say it), it was a little more European. I think I feel this way about it for a number of reasons. First of all, we had been rushing madly through the other cities and were due for a little rest; and secondly, it was warm and pleasant while we were there; and thirdly, the hotel was the best we struck in Russia -with excellent food, *warm* water, and a maid who actually understood what we wanted and got it in something under an hour's time. This last is simply amazing—the Russians, despite their activity of recent years, are the most delightfully lazy people imaginable when it comes to getting things done. Most of them. But this maid had lived 16 years in Philadelphia and that may account in part for her efficiency.

At any rate, we took our time in Kiev. We spent hours just walking around the streets and loafing around the park. We took a fine ride up and down the

Dnieper River in a steam launch. We did very little in the way of intensive sight-seeing, and it was just as well. We did go to see the famous Lavra Monastery, the oldest in Europe. Here we were shown the various tricks of the trade as exposed by the Soviet. How indulgences were bought by all manner of people who wanted blessing, and how the effectiveness of the indulgence varied with the price paid. A donation of so much meant the blessing afforded by a bishop's finger, a little more, by the bishop's whole mummy. The last of the monks were driven out in 1928, when two women of the town came to blows in a fight for the love of the youngest monk—then aged 73!

We saw a fine "ballet" (vaudeville show) in Kiev with some good dancing—especially one number in which, oddly enough, the girls were dressed up as Charlie Chaplins. We also attended an open air concert given by the Kiev Symphony Orchestra at which an all Rimski Korsakov concert was played. This time I think all the men had on coats.

We were in Kiev about three days, and the last day it was so warm and sunny that in the morning a few of us went down to the river with our bathing suits under our arms. There was a swell beach on the other bank that we wanted to get to, but we didn't know just how. Finally we reached a little pier where there was a man with a boat. After wild gesticulations of every kind, and frantic attempts at every language we knew, we managed to get him to understand that we wanted him to take us across and call for us again in two hours. When we got to the other side we had a grand swim. A group of soldiers from the Red Army were swimming at the same time. Some of them spoke a little German and they were very nice to us, showing us where to leave our clothes etc., although if truth must be told it wasn't a very ceremonious sort of thing—we just left them where we took them off. They seemed like a fine bunch of fellows—young, clean, and good sports all of them. They were playing on the beach, running up and down, exercising, tripping each other up, and that sort of thing. We liked them.

As you can see I have run out of white paper. I have also pretty much run out of thoughts. I have not written this letter all at once—I preferred to take my time on it and write a longer letter than I originally intended so you must forgive me for being so tardy in sending it to you.

The tone of the letter is pretty optimistic. You probably must think me a 100 percent Communist myself by now. This is not the case. I'm a lot more sold on things than before I went to Russia. I am more convinced now than when I left. Since my return I have seen how depressed conditions are here. In other words, it has been something of a steady progression to a point where I am about half convinced. Of one thing I am certain—that we too often get the wrong side of the picture from the newspapers, which look upon the Soviet Union as if it had been going two hundred years instead of fifteen. Considering its youth, and considering what life in Russia *for the average man* must have been before I think there must be a vast improvement. Of course, there are a many great inconsistencies. The government has mismanaged the farm situation and embittered a great many of the peasants, with the result that the food supply is nowhere near what it should be. Another thing is that the untutored Russians have made a botch of numerous factories and mechanical processes. Under the guidance of American, English and German engineers for example they can make tractors that are satisfactory but they haven't the ability to fix these tractors, or even operate them the way they should be, once they get out to the farms and away from foreign supervision.

But there seems to be a great and growing spirit among the people, and that, after all is the important thing. They have been willing to take the chance, and they should be allowed, if not encouraged to carry it through. Whether it would work in any other country is not the question at hand and I think you would find comparatively few Russians who think it is. They are primarily interested in building up their own country at this time.

So much for that. For the rest, beer is back (as you have probably heard from my father) and during the first week, at least, it has been a great success. Everybody is naturally anxious to try every brand, and the first few days every restaurant was practically a madhouse. Now the thing has settled down a bit. The new beer is tasty, but it is non-intoxicating. For once the Congress is right— the beer is really non-intoxicating. Oh, I suppose a couple of quick cold glasses on an empty stomach might give one a gentle glow, but nothing really more than that. Now it remains to be seen whether we can get over the last hurdle, and have the Prohibition amendment repealed. Two states have voted for Repeal already, but thirty four more are necessary to get a three quarters majority.

George Bernard Shaw spoke here yesterday. On his world cruise, he stopped only one day in New York (his only visit here) and talked for an hour and forty minutes. He has been having great fun for years insulting Americans and America. Yesterday they had their first, and probably last look at him. His speech was received with varying comments: some said that he was getting old and his speech was all muddled: others that his speech was witty, thoughtful and provocative. I share with the latter group, and even my father, who has grumbled about Shaw and his wisecracks for years, had to admit that he said some things which were excellent.

I am sorry again not to be able to tell you about certain other places I visited, but I think I've said enough. The rest can wait. All I can say is that six months in New York have convinced me that I would give my eye teeth to be on the briny once more, bound for anywhere. Travel is great until you get back.

My very best to Aunt Minna, Lex and yourself, fondly, Eddie

BEER, WINE AND LIQUOR

THE END OF PROHIBITION

When I returned from Europe in November 1932 I had no clear idea of what I wanted to do. Before I left, Jesse Butcher, another friend of Herb's and a big wheel at CBS Radio, had offered me a job in public relations, but over the summer he was a Depression casualty and lost his job. The thought of returning to Macy's didn't allure me. I had little to offer an employer except some skill in writing and editing mainly acquired as Managing Editor of *The Dartmouth*. Through a friend, I was given an interview at the Atlas Publishing Company, which produced a dozen trade papers in various fields.

Prohibition was finally on its way out. It would be another year before liquor was legalized, but beer was back. At first, there was a 3.2% alcoholic limit, but soon full strength brew was reintroduced to the market. Atlas Publishing, headed by a canny publisher named Charles Lipsett, decided to launch a magazine in the field, and *The Brewing Industry* made its appearance. Joe Zimmerman, editor-in-chief of all the Atlas publications, hired me at $20 weekly to be associate editor of the new magazine. That was fun for a while. I visited the old New York breweries starting up again, and some of the new crop. In Brooklyn I interviewed Rudy Schaefer, up and coming scion of F. and M. Schaefer, for one of my first articles. I also inspected the revived Liebmann Brewery in Brooklyn and regarded with wonder the huge vats of the Jacob Ruppert Brewery in Yorkville, Manhattan. I did stories about companies producing brewing machinery. I learned about hops, an essential ingredient of beer. There was early brisk competition between the domestic growers, mainly in Oregon and the famed product imported from Czechoslovakia. Another good source of copy (and advertising revenue for the nascent magazine) was the struggle for supremacy between the can and the bottle. Both had advantages, though diehards resisted the idea of drinking beer out of a can. Similarly, metal kegs began their inroads on the traditional use of wooden barrels.

Domestic beers dominated the market. Under the new laws, brewers could no longer own saloons which, in the pre-Prohibition era, flourished as "tied houses." Their pernicious influence was widely seen as an important factor in making the country dry. In the old song: *Father, dear Father, Come Home with me now, the Clock in the Steeple Strikes Ten*, the child has come to the saloon to persuade her father to leave. Under the Raines Law, saloons were required to serve food, but in many cases their observance took the form of one perpetual sandwich kept under glass, widely known as the Raines Law Sandwich.

A few brewers had been able to hang on during Prohibition by selling near beer (without alcohol) and other malt products. Now that beer was legal again the beer barons weighed in with extensive, highly sensitized advertising campaigns. Foreign beers also found a place in the market. Americans knew the Canadian brands, such as Labatt's and Molson's, which had trickled in during Prohibition, but Bass from England, Heineken from Holland and Beck's from Germany soon gained favor. My father was particularly pleased when one evening I brought home a case of Guinness Stout.

In 1933 the Volstead Act was repealed and John Barleycorn reappeared in an avalanche of wines and hard liquor. Some states had local option: counties could vote themselves dry or wet. The entire state of Kansas for a time was dry. This meant a fair amount of border crossing of state and county lines by people who wanted a drink. Some ex-bootleggers were able to obtain licenses to operate bars or package stores. In a number of states, still today, you can only buy off-premises liquor in state-operated package stores. There were abuses right from the beginning, and the Drys kept up a steady drumbeat for reform. The Women's Christian Temperance Union (WCTU) showed unexpected lasting strength. There was never again the threat of National Prohibition, but in many areas the Drys fought a formidable rear guard action. I could see the impact of this, and wrote a piece called The *Drys Crusade Again but with New Tactics* that appeared in an issue of the *The New York Times Magazine* on October 25th, 1936, reprinted in a later chapter.

Atlas Publishing decided there was gold in the rush of distillers, importers and wine makers to claim their share of the burgeoning market, and started a new magazine called *The American Wine and Liquor Journal*. I got a five dollar raise and became its associate editor. It led to a wide variety of experience in what at first was an exciting field. Those were dizzying days. I wrote stories about distillers, wine makers, importers, distributors, and aspiring retail dealers. Many of the retailers were ex-bootleggers who had obtained licenses and were now "legit." I especially savored the interviews with European producers who came to the United States to re-establish their brands. There was Charles Sichel, whose vineyards in France and Germany made fine table wines. The Domecqs of Spain and the Crofts of Portugal looked for a revival of interest in sherry and port. And of course, many distillers of Scotch vied for the market.

I can't recall his name, but an American recruited by Johnnie Walker to promote their product told me of his orientation visit to the venerable Walker distillery at Kilmarnock. After a tour of the premises, he was taken to the firm's sanctum sanctorum and offered a dram of very ancient malt Scotch. "I'll have it on the rocks," he said. The host firmly demurred. "You must na' bruise the whisky," he retorted.

I got a good story from Fred Myers, purveyor of Myers' Jamaica Rum, one of our leading advertisers. In making a rum drink, I still follow the recipe Fred gave me: one of sour (lemon); two of sweet (sugar); three of strong (Myers rum, of course), and four of weak (water).

In March 1934 I rode Schenley's "Prosperity Special" train to visit distilleries in Pittsburgh, Pennsylvania, Lexington and Frankfort, Kentucky, and Lawrenceburg, Indiana. It was a deluxe trip. The dinner menu on the train included fresh shrimp cocktail, broiled Delaware River shad roe, chicken pie (a favorite of mine), and braised sirloin of beef with mushrooms. And, of course, complementary beverages. I was invited to tastings of the International Wine & Food Society. I visited wineries in Brooklyn, New Jersey and upstate New York. I wrote articles recommending changes in our wine laws.

I did my best to keep the stories for the *Journal* newsworthy and objective, but had a running battle with Bill Margolis, the business manager, who bombarded me with requests to write puff stories about the firms and products illustrated in the magazine. Fortunately, my editorial resolve was shared by our managing editor, Lou Lightfoot, of whom I grew very fond. Lightfoot had worked on a New York daily and other periodicals and was highly professional—when he was sober. Unfortunately he was a slave to the bottle, and his job on the *American Wine & Liquor Journal* offered too many temptations. At least once a week he came in roaring drunk after lunch. Another reporter and I did our best to cover for him. We generally escorted him to the print shop where the noise of rolling presses drowned out his mutterings and he could sleep it off.

As time went on, I found my job at the *Journal* less and less interesting. It was hard work, and I was continually fighting with the business manager. The business itself became less glamorous. Many of the new brands, especially in the whiskey trade, were swallowed up by National Distillers, Schenley, Seagram and the other big companies. Trade practices took on a dog-eat-dog format and a fair amount of corruption came in. The wine trade in those days was not much better. Cheap wines abounded, and there was much adulteration of the product. America's wine consumption was very low, and there was little appreciation of domestic vintners intent on making a quality vintage.

Meanwhile, Charlie Lipsett poured on new assignments. The *Journal* gave birth to a second publication, the *Wine and Liquor Retailer,* that took more and more of my time. And in 1936, with very little assistance, I was set to work on *The Red Book of the Wine and Liquor Trades* in addition to my duties on the two magazines. Compiling *The Red Book* was no mean feat. I worked a good deal of uncompensated overtime. Its 602 pages was a vast compendium of every aspect of the trade—Producers, Distributors, Retailers and Dispensers. It was, of course, liberally larded with advertising. I've wondered sometimes, over 65 years later, how many of *The Red Book* entries are still valid.

By 1937 I felt exploited, and was losing interest in the job, when temporary relief came from an unexpected source. For some months, its promoters had advertised The Goodwill Tour of France in the pages of the *Journal*. They had chartered the Ile de France, one of the great trans-Atlantic liners of the day, and persuaded the French Government, wine producers and distillers to play host to a boatload of American wine and liquor dealers. Atlas had a "due bill" (instead of paying for the ad in our magazine they provided free boat passage) and Bill Margolis planned to go. But a few days before the sailing his wife became desperately ill. I got to go instead, and I was off on a rollicking adventure. I wrote an account of the journey—*Through a Wine Glass Hazily*—which appeared in *Playboy* magazine and is reprinted here.

THROUGH A WINE GLASS HAZILY: A STAGGERING ACCOUNT OF ONE OF THE WETTEST JUNKETS IN HISTORY,

By Edward B. Marks as published in *Playboy*, February 1965

In that still-Depression year of 1937 my salary as associate editor of the *American Wine and Liquor Journal* was a pittance, but attractive fringe benefits went with the job.

I particularly enjoyed the time spent around the town interviewing the greats and near greats of the trade that was being re-established in the United States following the Repeal of Prohibition in 1933. Many of these were the representatives of foreign wine and liquor concerns seeking to restore the name and fame of their brands. I remember several talks with Charles Martell and Maurice Hennessy, who were striving gamely to kindle a taste for fine cognac in palates deadened by bootleg rye. And I recall an especially lively session with the Right Honorable Andrew Jameson, then 81 years old, who told me he had once shot buffalo on the plains with Teddy Roosevelt. A man not easily daunted, Jameson cherished the notion that quality whiskey-drinkers would prefer John Jameson's Irish to Scotch. In this hope, alas, he was deceived. Irish got off to a slow start in the post-Repeal market, though the invention of Irish coffee has since helped make up some of the lost ground.

In those days, Andre Simon, doyen of the world's gourmets, came from abroad to preside at the tastings of the Wine & Food Society, which generally took place at the Plaza. I hardly qualified as a gourmet, but my crass connection with the trade got me in. I succeeded in impressing an up-to-then skeptical young woman by escorting her to a superb tasting of oysters and champagnes. A trial of port wines and cheeses greased the way to another romantic triumph.

I also recall, through a haze for which the interval of years can only partly be held accountable, the graduation exercises of the first bartenders' school to function in the post-Prohibition era. Behind a brightly burnished bar that had been bountifully provisioned by a thoughtful distiller stood a dozen confident young men. The exercises differed from most commencements in that the graduation ceremony and final examinations took place simultaneously. In their gleaming white uniforms, the graduates awaited your drink order and your critique of their performance. The guests rose to the challenge. In a freeloading session, probably unmatched in academic history, they then conscientiously tested the virtuosity and versatility of the fledgling barkeeps, recording their judgments (for as long as they could) on the official rating forms.

My work took me to all forms of distilling, rectifying and winemaking establishments, including those whose hasty veneer of respectability thinly concealed their more dubious status in Prohibition days. By way of encouragement, I was usually invited to sample the newly legitimized products, and what I have referred to as fringe benefits came perilously close at times to being occupational hazards. One languorous spring afternoon, after a morning visit to a Brooklyn winery topped off by a heavy Italian lunch, I was interviewing an important distilling executive. I asked him a provocative question, leaned back expectantly for his reply and immediately dropped off to sleep.

Lest the reader be misled by these bibulous accounts, let me hasten to say that most of my days were grubby ones, spent in the business publication's dirty, drafty office on Lafayette Street. There I wrote up my interviews, phoned trade sources for market quotations, edited correspondents' copy, shamelessly cribbed relevant news items from the dailies, and spent long, lugubrious hours compiling entries and reading proofs for *The Red Book of the Wine and Liquor Trades,* first directory of the resurgent industry. Our business manager had an idea a minute. I badly needed a holiday but saw no chance of a respite until summer. Suddenly, deliverance came from an unexpected source.

For some months, our advertising columns had carried advance notice of the Good Will Tour to France. The basic idea for the tour was a sound one. The French wine and liquor interests were anxious to extend their market in the United States. Americans traditionally crave to visit France. Why not charter the *Ile de France,* take over a shipload of American wine and liquor dealers to see the sights of Paris, visit the vineyards and distilleries and sample the goods at the source? The enterprising American promoters went the next step and persuaded the French to pick up most of the tab. The tourists' outlay would be limited to the round-trip ship passage at minimum rates. All living expenses in France—hotels, meals, transportation, Paris entertainments—were to be defrayed by the French.

I began to salivate when the first ad for the three-week tour appeared in our magazine, but there seemed little hope of making the trip. Our business manager had staked it out for his very own. But the winds of chance changed his plans shortly before the take-off date and I fell heir to a first-class cabin for the journey.

In a burst of generosity, I invited my sister along, at her expense. I gave her my cabin and she put down the minimum fare for a tourist accommodation which I occupied. On a glorious April morning our friends and relatives came to see us off, my brother brandishing a *bon voyage* bottle which proved wholly surplus, since one of the importers had ordered up drinks for all hands.

As the sleek, immaculate ship churned out of its berth and made for the harbor, Phyllis and I joined the throng on deck. Though my own transatlantic travel had been limited to a low-budget trip, I sensed, early in the game, that this was going to be different from most luxury voyages. The passengers somehow lacked the *soigne* look of characters shown in the cruise-ship ads or depicted by Noel Coward in *Private Lives*. The bulk of the 700 on board were wine and liquor wholesalers, retail storeowners and tavern keepers making their first crossing. In dress and deportment they fell somewhere between an Atlantic City convention crowd and the Appalachian mob. First class did contain a few affluent importers and industry leaders, but most of those in the better cabins had landed there because an indulgent distiller had ponied up the higher fare to accommodate a favored customer.

In addition to the *Ile's* superb cuisine, passengers were offered gratis an aperitif and a choice of fine vintage wines at luncheon on the first day. We took this as a commendable initial gesture on the part of one of the better-known importers, and were agreeably surprised when selected beverages of another importer made their appearance at dinner. Imagine our pleasure when still another merchant played host for the evening's gala, with all drinks on the house. Besides all this, expensive favors were distributed. The following day three different firms gratuitously stocked the beverage side of the menu. And so it went for each of the six days of the voyage. The ship was afloat in more senses than one. I rode the tide happily until the evening Chauvenet's Sparkling Red Cap and a rolling sea did me in.

But even in the privacy of a stateroom, one was exposed to the temptations of the bottle and other sybaritic enticements. Each cabin received daily injections of miniature and not-so-miniature gift bottles of brandies and liqueurs, cigarettes and cigars, chocolates, flowers and perfume for the ladies, and other lavish souvenirs.

We reached Le Havre in a comatose state, and looked forward to a few relaxing days in Paris before visiting the wine districts. But any hopes of resting up were dashed when our tireless leaders plunged us into the daily schedule. In addition to large doses of the usual sightseeing, we previewed the Paris Exposition of 1937, lost our francs at the greyhound races at Courbevoie, and took in the Folies-Bergeres and several fashion shows.

Conditioned by their shipboard experiences, many of our group enthusiastically pursued their new penchant for collecting souvenirs. If no souvenirs were provided, they carried off what was portable, and for some of our more acquisitive types not even the Louvre and the Palais de Versailles were off limits. The log for the three-day stay also included an official reception and banquet, a lunch at which the growers of Burgundy uncorked some of their best bottles for our pleasure and on our last night, a gay but exhausting finale offered by Cinzano at the Bal Tabarin.

Slit-eyed and bone-weary, we left Paris early the following morning in a fleet of buses headed for champagne country. At a brief ceremonial stop at Chateau-Thierry, we split up for visits to the leading champagne *etablissements*. Phyllis and I went with a group of about 30 to the Bollinger *caves* at Ay. A tour through the cellars was followed by an exquisite luncheon catered by Prunier of Paris, which included *Le Jambon de Bayonne, Le Brochet de la Loire dans sa Gelee* and a *Sauce Gribiche,* and *Le Caneton Lamberty,* washed down with copious draughts of Bollinger's Extra Quality Brut (1914 and 1920) and topped off with a masterful Marc de Champagne, 1917. As a special souvenir of the visit, each guest was presented with a graceful shallow silver tasting cup engraved with the date.

We remounted our bus in a pleasant haze. Next stop was Reims, where we rejoined the main party for a tour of the cathedral and a reception and dinner tendered by the Syndicat du Commerce des Vins de Champagne. The Hotel de Ville was adorned with French and American flags, the tables were piled high with all manner of delicacies for those who still cared about eating. I couldn't tell you what food was served, but I do have an indelible recollection of champagne, more champagne and still more champagne—the most, surely, that was ever gathered in one place for consumption at one time. The black-frocked dignitaries of the town and Syndicat never got off their prolix phrases on Franco-American friendship. There was no audience to hear them. The rivers of champagne, pouring forth in such ceaseless abundance, had carried away with them all remaining inhibitions. I hold the memory of a swilling, swaying, swinging, singing, dancing, prancing throng of my fellow-travelers—their glasses long since discarded—who drank from their bottles and waved them about. Some left the hall with their bottles and wandered noisily up and down the streets. Some sang questionable ditties on the cathedral steps. An obstinate few perched atop one of the buses and kept spurning the driver's entreaties to climb down. I don't suppose it was more disorderly than some of our classic conventions, but imagine a convention with champagne in prodigal amounts served absolutely free!

Before the effects had fully worn off, we entrained for Bordeaux, where more goodies were in store. Again, our formidable company was broken up into smaller groups that were theoretically more manageable. Our visit to the old house of Cruse & Fils Freres was a happily uneventful afternoon of wine and sunshine. I found most appealing the lovely vistas of vineyards showing the first blooms of early spring. That evening the Bordeaux Syndicat des Vins, not to be outdone by its competitors of Burgundy and Champagne, produced a magnificent feast to the accompaniment of a glorious succession of Bordeaux greats that climaxed with a classic Latour '21.

The next day we staggered on to Cognac, a busy town of 16,000, for a visit to its famed brandy distilleries and, heaven help us, another sumptuous banquet. The higher proof of the local liquor posed a new challenge to our tosspots. The

French did not appreciate it when one of our number in a sudden fit of chauvinism, pulled out a bottle of Old Taylor and loudly acclaimed its virtues.

France's liqueur and cordial makers were our hosts on the final day. Phyllis and I were in a party of 100 or more who headed for Fecamp, on the Normandy coast between Le Havre and Dieppe, where the Benedictine Distillery is located. Although it had been a commercial enterprise for some years, the plant retained the lugubrious air of the monastery it once was. In one room—possibly a vestigial link with its religious past—pallid teenaged orphans were patiently wrapping each bottle in its tissue enclosure. We dutifully went the rounds and were about to leave with the inevitable gift bottles when an officer of the firm that imports Benedictine to the United States beckoned to us. Mme. Le Grand, truly *la grande dame* of the establishment, had invited a privileged few to join her for a commemorative glass in the family's private chamber.

About a dozen of us were guided to a high vaulted room heavy with rich tapestries and massive oak furniture. In this setting, flanked by two of her sons, Mme Le Grande looked frail and tiny, but she carried herself with surpassing dignity. At her command, a flunky opened a huge cabinet, bringing forth an ancient bottle and a set of magnificent fluted glasses. Mme Le Grande filled the glasses, pouring with a steady hand, and handed them to the guests. The venerable lady spoke briefly in French, then, in English that was quaint but lucid, she offered a toast to the company, imparting a special warmth to her words. It was a sentient moment, and we all stood silent. I was standing next to a beret-clad New Jersey retailer who had wandered in by mistake. He seemed awed by the occasion, but was the first to break the silence. "Bottoms up!" he shouted, drained the liqueur at a gulp—and put the glass in his pocket.

That evening a jaded, droopy, souvenir-laden band boarded the lovely *Ile* at Le Havre for the return voyage. Again, the daily schedule called for the wine and liquor firms to play host on every possible occasion, but the sauce had lost its savor. The more durable passengers went through the motions of party going. They were joined by replacements for a few members of our original group who had fallen by the wayside somewhere in France. These fresh recruits had been unaware, at the time of booking passage, that their crossing to New York was to be other than routine; they were wide-eyed at the wonderment of it all. Meanwhile, some of our seasoned drinkers, bored with conviviality en masse, sought solace in the ship's bar, where it was actually possible to pay for a drink.

Throughout the trip the ship's gym and steam room were crowded with penitents frantically trying to get themselves back in shape. Morning and evening the decks were crowded with determined walkers. Some of our shipmates released their energies in a last burst of uninhibited souvenir collecting, silverware, ashtrays, demitasse cups—almost anything that wasn't tied or welded down—disappeared from view. The situation got so bad that the day before our arrival in New York the passengers were warned by the Line that unless pilfered items were returned, there would be an intensive search of each cabin. A rumor also went around that a certain French museum had cabled the ship demanding the return of *objets d'art* which had vanished the day our hoard of locusts had swept through the premises. The threats were never publicly carried out. Perhaps some of the missing loot was returned. But the Customs men at the New York pier were confronted with a conglomeration of curios rivaling those of Citizen Kane, not to mention a stupefying amassment of bottles ranging from miniatures to jeroboams.

When we finally stepped from the pier into Manhattan's spring sunshine, there was an added meaning to the old cliche "to set foot on dry land." I can't honestly say that my days of wine and liquor made a teetotaler out of me, but they did help to keep me out of the gutter. The next year a second shipload set sail on the Good Will Tour to Italy. When I heard about it I had twinges of nostalgia, not to mention nausea. But by that time I had put the *American Wine & Liquor Journal* and its temptations behind me.

A TASTE FOR WINE

I'm old enough to have vivid memories of Prohibition, during which I certainly imbibed my share of beer smuggled from Canada, and bathtub gin. Enough genuine Scotch continued to trickle into the States to sustain its rise to favor, despite the bootleg sale of many spurious bottles.

A "cordial shop" was the retail equivalent of a speakeasy bar. In the window, bottles of soft drinks such as soda, tonic or ginger ale were innocently displayed. When you placed your order, the sales clerk would produce the desired bottle from under the counter. A Marx Brothers movie showed Chico serving a customer who orders a bottle each of Scotch and rye. Chico dives below and is seen filling the two bottles from the same jug.

I retain the price list of Rainbow Cordials and Beverages on West 74th Street in Manhattan, where I was a customer. Service was impeccable. One could buy Johnnie Walker for $3 a quart, $30 a case. White Horse was $4, $42 a case. American whiskey ranged from $1 to $4 a pint, Gordon's gin was 75 cents a bottle, and a case of Bacardi rum sold for $30.

Bootleggers varied in their claims of authenticity. "Right off the boat," some would say. After one swig the customer might testily reply: "Yeah, they must have scraped it off."

I've included many of the highlights of the Goodwill Tour of France in the *Playboy* article "Through a Wine Glass Darkly." I've mentioned in that article that my dear sister Phyllis accompanied me on the round trip voyage on the Ile de France and the French vineyard tour. I also got a ticket for a friend of mine, Felix Fertig. I gave Phil the first class cabin I was entitled to, and Felix and I bunked together in 3rd class. That had its complications the first night out. Felix and I tried to visit Phil in her cabin but found the door to first class was locked. We could communicate only by phone. But the next day Felix managed to wheedle a key from the steward so we could get together. We had a fabulous trip. I quote from a letter Phil wrote her husband, Edgar Simon, April 11, 1937 when we were on the train from Paris to Bordeaux:

"I last wrote you as we were going out two nights ago. We had dinner at a very elegant place, Cafe de Paris, having their specialties, veal with wine sauce, mushrooms and truffles. Very fine! We then went to the Bal Tabarin which the entire tour filled to overflowing. We got there at 11.45, only intending to stay a short while, but as the show was the best the three of us has ever seen, we stayed until the end, 1.30 A.M. Champagne flowed like water, as usual, and we met the manager of the place who asked us to his table and kept pouring until we cried: "Stop." He told us about the girls in the show, as he picked them out; there were all kinds including many Americans. Herbert's guide had waited for us since 11, and we left with him. He first took us to a place called Resurrection, where you have a drink on a coffin. Then, in another room, someone standing in a shroud, through some illusion, is made slowly to become a skeleton. And so on. We then went to 32 rue Blondell, of which you've heard, I'm sure, and still another place after. We ended with onion soup at Les Halles, getting back to the hotel after 5. As we had to leave very early that morning for the whole day, Felix didn't go to bed at all, but Eddie and I got an hour's sleep.

"As you can guess, we were not too peppy all day yesterday. We left the hotel at eight, and rode through the most beautiful rural districts and small towns that I have ever seen. We stopped at Belleau Wood and Chateau Thierry to see the graves and two large memorials, and stayed in Chateau Thierry, a lovely little town, long enough to have three or four glasses of champagne (this is the morning, remember) at the town hall. We then drove to the Bollinger champagne plant, where we had a marvelous lunch, catered by Prunier of Paris."

I still like a glass of beer and occasionally a bit of Scotch, a Bloody Mary or a rum drink, but in my own vintage years I've come to a greater appreciation of wine. Some of this harks back to my three years as an Associate Editor of the *American Wine and Liquor Journal*, during which I sampled both European and American wines being introduced, or reintroduced, to the U.S. market. I went to tastings sponsored by the International Wine and Food Society and others, and the occasional dinner at which wines were featured. One such was given by the American Wine Institute at New York's Hotel Lexington the day following my 24th birthday. A resplendent banquet of oysters, mock turtle soup with sherry, filet of sole, filet mignon, grapefruit salad and meringue glacee was accompanied by choice California Reisling, Chablis, Sauterne, Burgundy, Claret, Chianti, Zinfandel, Moselle, Port, Sherry, Muscatel and Angelika. I don't remember what Angelika was or how it tasted. It was doubtless sweet.

In my years abroad I had ample opportunity to enjoy fine wines, first in Geneva where I came to savor several varieties of Beaujolais as well as the delightful Swiss white wines. It took me a while to appreciate Greek wine, but I favorably recall Camba and Domestica and occasionally still order a bottle when dining in a Greek restaurant. Retsina is something else again—definitely an acquired taste (like Nuoc Mam sauce in Vietnam).

Some years after my return to the United States I bought a house in Leesburg, Loudoun County, Virginia. On a thousand-foot ridge, four miles from the town, it has a commanding view of the Loudoun Valley, and some miles to the West, the Blue Ridge Mountains. Descending from my house, on Mount Gilead, is a sloping field. I never cultivated it, but for some years allowed a local farmer to plant feed corn, with his agreement to sow a couple of rows of sweet corn for our table.

But one summer evening, when we were having a glass of wine on his porch, my Australian neighbor and I decided to plant vineyards on our respective fields. We called the Virginia State Viticultural Office in Blacksberg, and they dispatched an expert who tested the soil and found in each case it was conducive to the growth of white wine grapes. We heard that Lew Parker, a chemist living quite near us, was starting a farm winery on his property, so we struck a deal with him: he would provide the labor to plant and supervise our vineyards, buy our grapes at the market price, and sell us the resulting wine at a substantial discount. The wine would be sold under the Willowcroft label.

I decided to plant mainly Chardonnay and Reisling vines on my plot of a bit more than an acre, and added a few rows of Seyval Blanc, an indigenous grape producing a very dry wine delicious with seafood. It takes about three years before the young vines produce grapes. The Virginia State Tax laws are very understanding in this regard: they allow you to offset your initial costs with the income derived from the first productive years.

That was twenty years ago. The vineyard has never been much of a moneymaker, but it generally yields a small profit or at least breaks even, unless there's an untimely frost or insect blight. In the early days our nemesis was deer. I always loved those gentle creatures until they began raiding our vineyard. We tried all manner of remedies. Someone told us that human hair repels the inroads of deer. We harvested the sweepings of local barbershops and decorated the vines, but that didn't prove much of a deterrent. Neither did scarecrows. Finally we circumnavigated the area with a fence. It wasn't high enough, and the deer either vaulted it or burrowed their way inside. It wasn't until we electrified the fence that deer were discouraged from foraging. But every year Lew, with special permission, shoots one or more invaders with a hunting rifle.

My son's family now live in the house and own the vineyard. But I still savor the wines, which have won prizes in Texas and Orange County, California. And when I visit, it's a pleasure to watch the sun sink to the West over the vineyard and the Blue Ridge Mountains.

I made passing reference in my *Playboy* piece to the International Wine and Food Society. It deserves additional mention, especially the efforts of its founder, Andre Simon, to instill a love of wine in American palates.

While most Americans preferred whiskey and beer, there had always been, before Prohibition, a discerning minority of wine lovers. My father was not a connoisseur, but he kept a small cellar which he was legally permitted to carry over into the Prohibition era. He published a popular song of the first dry days, plaintively sung by Bert Williams, called "Everybody Wants the Key to My Cellar."

Except in the big hotels and cabarets and among foreign-born residents, quality wines were not widely consumed in the United States. Wineries existed in California, New York, Ohio and a few other states. A few had licenses to continue making wine for sacramental purposes after passage of the Volstead Act.

Andre Simon had succeeded before the country went dry to establish a few branches of the Society in the United States. With Repeal, he revisited the U.S. with the determination to promote quality wine consumption. But in the 1930s and succeeding decades, wine importers and domestic producers fought an uphill battle to achieve any significant sales volume.

Simon and his wife made a voyage to the U.S. in December 1934, laying the ground for revival or creation of American branches of the Society. They met with wine lovers in New York, Boston, Chicago, San Francisco, Los Angeles and New Orleans. He returned alone in 1935, visiting a dozen or more cities, including Kansas City and Baltimore, where durable branches of the Society took root.

In his second volume of autobiography, *In the Twilight*, published in 1969, Simon recalled the high expectations of French growers when Prohibition came to an end. "The proprietors of many famous vineyards," he writes, "and the heads or senior members of important wine firms from Champagne and Burgundy, and many more from Bordeaux . . . sailed for the U.S.A. full of hope and joy. They all came back full of gloom; they had lost their time, their money, and their illusions: the Americans showed little interest, and certainly no enthusiasm, for wine."

The interest in wine grew slowly. It wasn't for lack of effort.

In the push to promote wine sales, veteran U.S. producers such as the Italian Swiss Colony, Beaulieu and Wente Brothers of California and Great Western and Korbel's in New York sought to recapture their pre-prohibition markets. And of course many new vintners entered the field. The California Wine Institute helped by sponsoring institutional advertising. Such was the interest in the American market that just two years after Prohibition Repeal, our Wine and Liquor Directory listed 79 imported port wines, although port has never been a widely popular drink in the United States. It was not until the 1970s, however, that all these efforts really paid off, when a new generation suddenly took to wine, and sales soared.

I attended several of the early tastings sponsored by the newly launched New York Wine and Food Society. Three of them stand out in my memory. One featured a variety of delicious cheeses and a choice of no less than 17 port wines, ranging from $14 to $50 per case. The second tasting, staged at midnight in the great ballroom of the Ritz-Carlton Hotel, studied the merits of 26 champagnes. Most of the renowned brands were served in the 1928, '26, '23 and '21 vintages, along with a few non-vintage and private *cuvees* as well as two still champagnes.

The Society tasting I most vividly recall was of oysters and white wines. It was held at the St. Regis Hotel in March 1936 with the enthusiastic cooperation of the Oyster Institute of North America. Eighteen varieties of oysters were served to the accompaniment of 20 white wines. The oysters came from Florida, North Carolina, the Chesapeake Bay region of Virginia and Maryland, Delaware Bay, Long Island and Rhode Island. They included Bluepoints, Gardiners Island Salts, Narragansett and mammoth specimens from Chincoteague Bay. (When the English novelist Thackeray, on a visit to America, tasted a Chincoteague, he said the experience was akin to swallowing a baby.)

The oysters were complemented by choice Alsatian, Pouilly Fuisse, Chablis, Graves and Rhone wines from France; Moselle and Rhine bottles from Germany; some from Hungary, Italy and Spain.

In the first five years after Repeal, the New York Society arranged a total of 27 tastings. The first held in May 1935 featured French still white wines. Others displayed sherries, Madeira, American wines, light wines for summer, red burgundies, cognacs, armagnacs, Spanish brandies and marc; and as a year-ender, punches, cups, eggnogs and kindred drinks.

During this period, the Society also staged a number of dinners, including some dedicated to Russian, Viennese, New Orleans and American cuisine. The very first dinner, held at the Savoy-Plaza Hotel on 14 November 1935, was attended by 280 diners who "sat down to a perfectly cooked meal, and not a single one of the diners broke the no-smoking-during-dinner rule."

Many outstanding events followed, but the Escoffier dinner, the first of the 1936-37 season, deserves special mention. It was held at the Hotel Pierre, and the attendance of 357 diners was the largest number ever to meet together under the banner of the New York Wine and Food Society. One of the glories on the menu was Mousse de Sole Escoffier, prepared by Charles Scotto, a former pupil of the great master.

It is regrettable that Andre Simon was unable to attend many of these gala events in New York and other American branches whose establishment he had fostered. I met him after a talk he gave on his 1935 visit to America. I was much taken by his knowledge, courtliness and authority. Other members of the New York Society I knew in those years were Bob Misch (who became the secretary), Charles Sichel, Harold Grossman and Harold Wile.

A persevering missionary, Simon made four more visits to the U.S. before World War II, the last time in May 1939. Returning to the States in 1946 at the invitation of Crosby Gaige, Simon and Frank Schoonmaker made an extensive tour "to get people interested in wine . . . We were given introductions, met some nice people, had some good meals, but did no good at all."

The last time Andre visited the United States was in May 1966 for a convention of the Wine and Food Society in Chicago. At that time there were some 20 American branches of his brainchild, 12 of them in California. The South had a dedicated membership, but its influence was limited. It would still be some years before America developed a real taste for wine. Were he to visit the U.S. today, the Founder would be astonished and gratified by its mounting popularity.

Simon, in his *First American Impressions*, wrote: "The tragedy is that in a country where there is more cattle, grain and vegetables than in any other, as well as an enormous variety of fish . . . the standard of feeding should be so low, or it would be more exact to say so utterly wrong . . . The average American does not trouble to think about the value, taste, preparation and effects of food any more than children do in the nursery." He would be surprised, perhaps flabbergasted, by the widening appreciation of gourmet cooking today and the lively interest in preparation of everyday cuisine.

Discriminating buyers of wine can choose now from amazing selections in retail stores and in the formidable wine lists of many hotels and restaurants. With our increased knowledge has come the recognition that choice American wines can compete with the best that Europe can offer.

I drink very little hard liquor these days, but enjoy a glass of wine, be it imported or domestic. We have come a long way in the 60-odd years since Prohibition's Repeal. Andre Simon would be mightily pleased. His steadfast efforts have finally paid off.

THE STRIKE AT ATLAS PUBLISHING COMPANY

The welcome distractions of the Good Will Tour didn't allay my desire to move on from Atlas Publishing. I cast my net in several directions with the object of widening my horizon. I felt stuck where I was, and determined to find work that fed the soul a bit more. But before I cut loose, I wanted to improve the working conditions at Atlas. In the spirit of the times, it seemed to me the place was ripe for union organization. I talked with several of my co-workers and found they agreed.

The Newspaper Guild was still young, but it was gaining in prominence. Atlas publications weren't exactly newspapers but maybe the Guild would be interested in moving into the trade paper field. I queried them, found they were receptive, and within a very short time, Jack Ryan was assigned to us as our organizer.

The Guild unit was formed in July 1937 and consisted from the very first of a majority of the editorial staff and representative workers from other departments. Four of us were principally concerned in negotiations with the Guild, Tom Feigenbaum, Adolph J. Bourrienne, Jon Gregg and myself. The unit held several meetings during the summer and fall. In January 1938 we asked the Guild to write a letter to the management asking them to meet with authorized representatives from the Guild office to discuss bargaining terms. The letter was sent out but never acknowledged by the Atlas management.

At this point Fate stepped in. The Printer's Union, Typographical Union No. 6, known in the trade as "Big Six," called a strike against Atlas Publishing on February 2, 1938. Atlas had a print shop called Bardeen Press in Stamford, Connecticut, and a smaller crew consisting of a linotype operator, pressman and two make-up men at its New York office. On the day the strike was called in Stamford, and it looked as if the New York printers were also going out, I conferred with Ryan, relaying news of the development. During the next few days I was in close touch with the Guild office, acting as a clearinghouse for Guild information. Ryan instructed me to tell the others that because of the "Big Six" situation, it would be necessary for us to go through the picket lines for a few days. He asked me to get as many signatures as possible to a paper authorizing the Guild to act as bargaining agent. The editors signed first, then other employees, and at a meeting held Friday night, February 4th, the paper containing 22 signatures was turned over to the Guild. We also decided that if there were layoffs the next day we would strike. As it turned out, there were six layoffs. At a meeting after work in union headquarters across the street we decided not to come in Monday, February 7th. Jon Gregg and I were named joint strike chairmen.

On Monday, Ryan and Milton Kaufman of the Guild met us early in the morning and advised us that certain conditions with respect to the "Big Six" strike made it inadvisable for us to strike Atlas at that time. We never fully learned what the "certain conditions" were. Instead, a committee of six editors went into Lipsett's office with Ryan, and the latter presented our demands. That afternoon, Zimmerman came into my office while Feigenbaum and I were talking and exacted a promise from us not to discuss Guild matters during business hours.

It was most unfortunate that a question of inter-union jurisdiction persuaded the Guild not to move ahead with our strike while the issue of the "Big Six" strike was pending. It nipped our effort in the bud, and gave the management time to recover. The situation was described in the February 28 issue of *The Guild Reporter* under the headline: "Big Six Strike Accord Sought." It read:

"Clarification of the Typographical Union's stand in regard to joint cooperation with the Guild in the strike at the Atlas Publishing Company in New York was sought last week by the New York Guild in a letter sent to the Executive Committee of Typographical Union No. 6. The Guild has 22 members on the 12 trade publications handled by the company. The Typographical Union called the strike on February 2."

The Guild's letter reviewed the efforts of the Guild to reach an agreement with the printers which would protect Guildsmen refraining from walking through picket lines against the possibility of being left out on the street when the printers settled their strike. It was pointed out that the situation "was intolerable for Guild members," and that the Guild was offering support to "Big Six" and not seeking help.

On February 9, the Executive Committee of "Big Six" in its reply, took the position "that it will instruct the union to attend any conference the Guild may call of all the unions interested."

The Executive Committee of the Guild, in studying this reply, noted "that its proposal is neither rejected nor accepted. Indeed, it finds the Typographical Union suggesting that the Guild initiate a conference of seven unions in a strike which it has not called. We are frankly puzzled. In the current Atlas situation, the Guild sought assurances from Typographical Union No. 6, even prior to the actual calling of the strike. A review of the circumstances will make this plain.

"The editorial department has been organized for six months, and the Guild learning of the efforts of Typographical Union No. 6 to bring Atlas into the fold of union shops, conferred in September of last year with Mr. Wright (Ralph Wright, ITU organizer) in an effort to map out a joint program.

"The actual calling of the strike was coincidental with the action of the Stamford local of the ITU in whose jurisdiction is located the out-of-town print shop of Atlas. Almost a week before, the Guild learned that a strike of the Lafayette St. plant was scheduled, but "Big Six" representatives did not furnish the Guild with any definite information. On the very eve of the strike, President William Ward, when pressed by a Guild officer, disavowed any specific knowledge of the impending strike.

"On Feb 6 six Guild members were discharged, including three women who had refused to read proof; that is, refused to scab on the striking compositors. Since then, another has been discharged. The Guild charges that the publisher fired them in order to discourage further Guild organization and specifically, to discourage, through intimidation, any support in the editorial and business departments for the striking mechanical department men."

The article goes on to say that "The Guild immediately filed a complaint with the National Labor Relation Board," but if anything came of it, we never heard the result. In the succeeding weeks, the management pursued a relentless harassment and denigration of a number of the Guild members of whom I was one.

I had always had independence in the selection of the stories I wrote and the appointments I made to obtain and confirm the facts in the stories. Joe Zimmerman, editor of all the Atlas papers, called me in to say that henceforth I would require advance clearance to do my work. The *Journal* editorial office was moved to a less desirable location, presumably because it would be more difficult there to discuss union matters. I was no longer to dial my own phone numbers, and my outgoing letters were subject to scrutiny. I was then sent to Baltimore and Washington on an editorial assignment clearly intended to get me out of the way.

Shortly after my return Joe Zimmerman called me in and verbally dismissed me (several other staffers met the same fate). Zimmerman said the reason for my dismissal was a fall-off in *Retailer* advertising, but on researching the matter I found that advertising for March actually doubled the February total. Moreover the management announced in the March issue that it would soon publish regional editions of the magazine for the Eastern, New England, Midwestern and

Pacific States. This didn't sound like retrenchment! In answer to my question, Zimmerman said I was perfectly competent; that was not the cause of dismissal. I asked him for a written notice of dismissal, but he said it was not his practice to give one. There is no question in my mind that I was fired for my union activity.

I thought for a time I had a case, but the NLRB kept postponing action. Meanwhile, Lipsett sold the liquor papers to the business manager, Bill Margolis. On July 12, 1938 I received the following letter from Jack Ryan:

> Dear Ed:
>   We have discussed your case again and it is the opinion of Kaufman and Isserman that in view of the sale of the paper on which you worked, there is little chance of actually getting anywhere with the charge now before the Labor Board.
>   The most we could hope for is the back pay, and in hoping for this, we are being really optimistic. It is suggested that we drop the case and wait for another opportunity to deal with Mr. Lipsett.
>   Will you drop me a note, or step in the office and let me know how you feel about it?
>   Sincerely,
>   John F. Ryan, Organizer

Needless to say, it was a bitter, disillusioning experience. Up to then, I had admired the Guild's effectiveness in improving the lot of newsmen, but in this instance they fell far short of the mark. Was it their reluctance to cross swords with "Big Six," a much more powerful union? Or was it, as rumor had it, that they were about to strike *The New York Times* and had to marshal all their resources to that objective?

I didn't lose my faith in unions. In a later job with the National Refugee Service, I joined the Social Service Employees Union (SSEU). I don't recall any startling issues that came up. I was content to be an inactive, dues-paying member.

THE DRYS CRUSADE AGAIN BUT WITH NEW TACTICS

By Edward B. Marks, *The New York Times Magazine*, October 25, 1936

The liquor question, overshadowed since repeal by more pressing national problems, is by no means a dead issue. Encouraged by the growing resentment against drunken driving, drys all over the country have launched a new crusade for the reclamation of wet territory by local-option vote. In California and in Massachusetts, Statewide polls on local-option will be taken on election day, and in a large number of towns and counties in other States the wet-dry issue will play an important role, with indications that the drys will do better than hold their own.

Prohibition has always been cyclical in American history. At the conclusion of the Volstead era it was thought by many that the prohibitionist of familiar cartoon portraiture would never again be revived, yet recent months have shown that the old gentleman is again a public figure of significance, and he is a changed man. No longer are the battered topper, the black frock coat, the brandished umbrella so much in evidence.

There was madness in the methods of the old-time drys. The individual drunkard was pilloried. The saloon was cursed as an unholy abomination and the saloon-keeper labeled as the "recruiting sergeant for the army of crime."

Today, instead of generalizing about the evils of alcohol, as exemplified by the remote case of the drunkard who beats his wife, prohibitionists are stressing intemperate weaknesses which directly affect the community. They point to what they call the pernicious effect of the cocktail hour on women and the younger generation and cite the presence of women in bars. They charge that the increase in liquor sales has brought, in certain areas, a corresponding decrease in sales of milk and food. They deplore the squandering of relief checks for liquor. They mourn the alcoholic as an additional burden upon the sober taxpayer.

The chief pre-prohibition dry agencies are back in the field with renewed militance, and cash contributions to carry on the fight are pouring into dry headquarters in liberal amounts. The Woman's Christian Temperance Union has adopted a program for raising a million dollars within the next five years to re-establish national prohibition. Moreover, the W.C.T.U. has inaugurated an educational campaign, national in scope, which is intended to discredit the results of repeal by advertising and through an extensive lecture network. Radio broadcasting is to be used when possible.

The Anti-Saloon League with branches in 44 States is actively aiding the local-option cause in many towns and counties. To this end F. Scott McBride, veteran dry leader, recently resigned as general superintendent to head Pennsylvania's active unit. Through its anti-saloon campaign committee the League helps to finance dry candidates, of whom there are an increasing number.

Many church groups are displaying a revival of interest in the dry cause, including the Methodist Board of Temperance, Prohibition and Public Morals, which is again issuing its familiar clip sheet from Washington.

Harry Emerson Fosdick and Christian Reisner are among ministers who have recently inveighed against the liquor traffic.

New secular dry groups are coming to the fore. In Chicago the American Businessman's Research Foundation disseminates propaganda designed to appeal chiefly to business executives. It deals with such practical considerations as the effects of alcohol on industrial efficiency.

All of these organizations are concrete manifestations of dry purposefulness; the drys mean business. Though proceeding cautiously, they are constantly working to prevent the repeal of State and local prohibition laws still in effect, and are concentrating their support in vulnerable areas, petitioning for local option wherever the opportunity presents itself. National prohibition by 1945 is their announced objective.

A statement of policy in this regard was recently made by O.G.Christgau, assistant general superintendent of the Anti-Saloon League. Mr. Christgau said: "the situation is varied; each State is a separate problem.. . . Our attack may be like football with forward passing where possible, or bucking the line; it will probably be mostly 'straight football' for a while." That the straight football tactics have already resulted in substantial gains in some States is evidenced by the fact that 1935 saw an increase of 94 percent over the previous year in the number of dry counties, and 149 percent in dry towns.

For a year or more after repeal the wets were still converting dry territory, but now the tide has turned. In recent months where a dry electorate has voted wet it has been chiefly because some other issue of social concern hinged on the outcome of the ballot.

Sale of liquor is at the present time unlawful in 7 States, while 28 wet states have dry areas, including New York with 36 dry towns. On election day eyes will be focused on the returns in Massachusetts and particularly those in California, where the drys won the first skirmish in a local-option battle by obtaining 199,327 signatures to the petition calling for a State-wide vote.

In the national election the prohibition question remains in the background, but in view of the fact that there are borderline States in which a small group may hold the balance between one major party and the other, it may play at least a minor role, for the Prohibition Party has, in the words of Edward W. Blake of

Chicago, national committee chairman, "hit the come-back trail on the broken promises of the wets." Its Presidential candidate is D.Leigh Colvin of New York, a veteran dry campaigner. In line with the new dry position there is a social security plank in the party's platform as well as the main plank attacking the liquor traffic.

Perhaps the drys' most persuasive argument today is drunken driving. Whether or not the figures supplied as evidence of its increase have been reliable, newspapers and magazines have devoted considerable attention to them, and the question is not one which can be dismissed by a mere wave of the hand.

In the old days an occasional drunk drove a horse and wagon through a plate-glass store window and some people thought it was funny. Today drunken driving involves the safety of many. It is pointed out that drinking at football games and roadside bars, and even at private parties where the guests are returning home by car, may have serious consequences.

Although the drys continue their traditional blows at Demon Rum, their tendency today is to glove the punching hand.

The anti-alcohol drive is carried on in hygiene textbooks, school essay contests, lectures to women's clubs, youth conference work, church meetings and in many other quarters. The evils of alcohol are dramatized in one-act plays and presented in motion-picture form. Beginning in New York and gradually extending westward, W.C.T.U. billboards dot the main highways, warning the motorist that there is "Poison in Beer, Wine and Whisky."

The drys cite figures purporting to show that drinking is more widespread than ever and that there is an increase in the number of alcoholics, especially among women. They assert that increased drinking must inevitably result in a larger number of "addicts, defectives and dependents to be dealt with in the future."

According to the drys, the $500,000,000 received by the government last year for liquor taxes was "tainted money." "Only a short-sighted view will regard these receipts as an asset to the government and the people," they say. The prohibitionist does not spare the trade in his denunciation but is firm in his belief and fervent in his declaration that "the liquor traffic has used every possible means of trade promotion." Before prohibition, the distiller and brewer were attacked for their part in encouraging the growth of the saloon. They were represented as being the insidious force behind this institution, which was itself branded as the chief cause of the nation's woes. Today the attack is somewhat different.

While the drys make no secret of their disgust at the saloon's return, the producing industry is criticized primarily for its direct influence on the consuming habits of the public through the medium of advertising. They charge that there have been advertisements published which frankly had as their purpose the attraction of new drinkers.

Despite the best efforts of the brewers to sell beer to the public as a temperance drink, the drys draw no distinction between hard and soft liquor. Beer contains alcohol, and that is enough to condemn it in their sight. There was a famous old dry chant immortalizing an American institution which went:

The brewer's big horses, coming down the road
All loaded down with Old Lucifer's load.
They step so high and they step so free
But those brewer's big horses can't run over me.

Now there is a counterpart, written to the tune of *Maryland, My Maryland*:

I will not eat my waffles brown
Alongside one who gulps beer down;
I'll take my patronage away
And hunt me up a new café.
The grocer where I used to buy
Sells beer on tap while I stand by;
I'll not go back though I go far;
I'll buy no groceries over a bar.

The wine producers have thus far been relatively ignored by the drys, partly because wine is still a negligible factor in the market compared with beer and liquor, and because wine drinkers are seldom encountered in rural areas, where the dry movement has its greatest strength.

Sentiment against drinking is said to have been aroused in many homes during the three years since repeal. Surveys by State liquor boards and social research groups have shown opinion on repeal to be about evenly divided. It is the disgruntled half which is giving loudest expression to its views. Many of these people want prohibition restored. They are not in sympathy with the serious efforts being made to restore to the word "temperance" its original meaning. They are not satisfied with half-way measures which seek to discourage but not outlaw drinking.

Because the temperance objective is so vague in character, it is said, the vast numbers of those who cherish the temperance ideal cannot be recruited for active service until the battle lines are more clearly drawn. Prohibitionists, on the other hand, have a definite objective to which all their energies can be devoted. With the vigorous tactics of extremists, they are enlisting not only moral but financial support.

COLUMBIA AND THE FEDERAL THEATRE

Though Atlas Publishing fired me during the Depression, I wasn't too worried about being jobless. Summer was coming on and I looked forward to some tennis and travel. I was part way through a Master's program in Sociology at Columbia University. I had enrolled in 1935 for two courses, one in Victorian literature and one in Sociology, which I much preferred. It was a great hour for Sociology then at Columbia. Robert Lynd, Casey and Merton were on the faculty, and I decided to go that way. Two or three evenings a week, after work, I would pile into the Canal Street subway station for the 40-minute ride to ll6th Street at Broadway. My immediate mentor was a Canadian chap, an instructor named John Innes. He helped me round out a program that ultimately led to an M.A. in 1938. The Lynd and Casey courses were fascinating, and I suffered through a required course in Statistics.

In my second year I decided to write my thesis on the Federal Theatre, and Innes supported the decision. From earliest years, I was always a theater buff, but beyond that, I was greatly attracted by the range and power of their productions as a vital element of the Works Progress Administration. While designed primarily to give work to unemployed actors and other theater people, the Federal Theatre Project (FTP) had inspired leaders who recognized and fostered its potential as an interpreter of the contemporary scene. Some of its productions were mundane and lifeless but others were noteworthy. Among these were Shakespeare and classical drama, dramatic satires, such as *The Cradle Will Rock*, and the on-target *Living Newspapers*.

The director of the Federal Theatre was Hallie Flanagan. A Vassar College drama professor, Flanagan was a real hero in the way she tackled the job. There was considerable opposition in Congress, not only to the idea of a federal theater but also to some of the productions that they felt were critical of government policy. The very existence of FTP was threatened from the beginning. Flanagan proved an ardent and eloquent witness at hearings held on the Hill. The FTP was not only a temporary harbor of safety for unemployed theater folk. It also attracted some of the best talents and brains, including such people as John Houseman, Orson Welles and Marc Blitzstein. To some, the FTP was a step toward the creation of a national theater. With adequate funding and a friendly government climate, it might have moved in that direction. Flanagan's book *Arena* chronicles the story.

In the summer of 1937 I decided to devote my two week vacation to a field trip exploring FTP's structure and productions outside of New York. I borrowed a friend's car and visited several FTPs in New England and upper New York State. Some of the performances were routine "stock" potboilers and rather boring vaudeville and circus acts. But the audiences were, on the whole, enthusiastic about the first live staging many of them had ever witnessed. On the return journey to New York, I stopped off at Poughkeepsie to see a special premiere of *One Third of a Nation* before it opened in New York City.

Further thoughts about the FTP are contained in *Star Spangled Showmen,* a summary of my Columbia Master's thesis which follows. The thesis clearly reflects the uncertainty of the Project's future and the opposition its continuance faced in Congress. Those who hoped that the positive elements of the program would become the basis for a government-supported national theater were doomed to disappointment when Congress withdrew its support for the Project in 1939. (Original spellings and punctuation have been retained.)

STAR SPANGLED SHOWMEN
The Dilemma of Federal Theatre

I.

In the closing days of the last session, Representative Short of Missouri executed a toe dance on the House floor before a sniggering group of Congressmen. "We are asked to teach people to do this," he jeered, "at a time when twelve million go hungry and unemployed."

Thus it was that despite earnest efforts made in its behalf, the Coffee-Sirovich bill providing for a permanent government subsidy of the Fine Arts was heartlessly laughed down this June (1939).

The summary rejection of the bill was a grave disappointment to some people who expected at least that the measure would receive serious consideration. To others who had never given the bill a chance, it was merely typical of legislators' reactions during the warm season when they are impatiently yearning for trout streams.

The significance of the bill was that it was the first measure to reach Congressional halls to make some definite proposal for the perpetuation of the Federal Arts Projects. Over a three year period, these projects, in the opinion of many, have rendered valuable service. But even their most ardent proponents cannot visualize their indefinite continuance under the Works Progress Administration.

Federal Theatre can be thought of in two ways. It can be looked upon as giving temporary relief checks to broken-down performers until they can find jobs again in private entertainment channels. It can, on the other hand, be construed as the first effort on the part of the Government to recognize the value of the theatre as a social and cultural force by granting to deserving actors salaries from the Treasury of the United States.

That these two views are not, in many respects, reconcilable, is indicated by the difficulties which Federal Theatre has encountered in achieving the results it has shown to date.

The position of the Federal Theatre is not widely different from that of a stock company required to put on *Hamlet* with an *Uncle Tom's Cabin* set. For almost three years the Project has been forced to operate under rules and regulations designed primarily for engineering. The tireless energy and infinite resourcefulness of its directors have succeeded in cutting through some of the red tape, but it has been an uphill battle all the way. As it progresses, Federal Theatre is finding it more and more difficult to reconcile its artistic and intellectual aims within the limitations of the organizational plan under which it was created and from which it derives its support. The gap from relief drama to national theatre has not been bridged. There are no pat answers on Federal Theatre. Since its inception was authorized by a grant of WPA funds in August, 1935, it has led a precarious existence. Its continuance over a period longer than six months has never been positively assured. Actors under WPA have been granted week-to-week security in their profession to a degree never previously known. At the same time, their future has been purely provisional with any serious curtailment in WPA funds almost certain to result in the detruncation or complete elimination of the existing set-up.

The continuity and direction achieved by Mrs. Hallie Flanagan and the other directors of the Project have been won in the face of the obstacle of unpromising material, outside opposition and administrative difficulties. Of these, the last have been the most persistent and the most serious.

These stumbling blocks evolved from the very nature of the administrative premise. While its directors were never willing to accept Federal Theatre at its face value as a relief project, they were soon forced to recognize the very serious handicap in working with a personnel subject to many restrictions. When practically every other adjustment has been made it is this adherence to the WPA regimen and working plan that still impedes the Project's directors at every turn. Although vast audience support has been gained, newspaper antagonism for the most part overcome, and the essential aims of the Project have become part and parcel of the cultural program of many communities, it is still impossible for the furtherance, or even maintenance of these advantages to be assured because of the Project's unique political dependency.

II.

As early as 1833 William Dunlap called in vain for "one great theatre in each great city of the Union, supported and guided by the State." In succeeding years there were similar proposals. But it was not until a century later that Federal subsidy for support of the stage became an actuality. Its ultimate realization was due, not to any sudden recognition by the government of the artistic and educational possibilities of such a program, but simply because actors, like plasterers and seamstresses, were out of work and hungry. The government's entrance into show business was totally different from the usual form taken by such participation abroad, where subsidies take the form of an outright grant of funds to an existing, privately-managed theatre company.

Instead, using unemployed actors on relief rolls as its nucleus, the Government organized its own troupes wherever a sufficient number of qualified applicants appeared. In the Metropolitan centers, such as New York, Chicago, Boston and Los Angeles, there was no dearth of available talent, and this was similarly true in a number of smaller towns.

The depression in the theatre industry antedated the 1929 crash by a number of years. There was, traditionally, a lack of continuity in the type of patronage and haphazard management under which the commercial stage existed in the United States. Even in the so-called good old days, when there were five and six touring companies of every New York success, existence in the theatre world was precarious for many of those engaged in the profession.

The technological displacement of actors and other stage workers by the movies and radio was the final crushing blow, but even before that time the stage had almost entirely fallen prey to a commercialism which made any sort of artistic experiment and planning difficult.

Despite the colorful reputation of the theatre, show business is hardheaded and concerned primarily with box office profits. Acting as a profession may be picturesque and it cannot be denied that there are occasional quick flights to stardom, but by and large it is probably as uncertain as any line of work could possibly be. Even the box office draws are "at liberty" a goodly percentage of the time and for performers less in demand engagements are often widely spaced out, even in good years.

In the old days, a run of a hundred performances in New York was accepted arbitrarily as the line dividing a success from either a moderate or complete failure. Examination reveals that in the ten-year span from 1924 to 1934 the annual number of New York productions achieving that distinction fell from 58 to 26. The total for 1929, a midway point, was 44, evidence that the crash itself was not the sole factor in the decline. A comparable drop can be noted in such theatrical centers as Chicago and San Francisco, and in the number of stock companies and road shows the country over. The conditions around New York were aggravated by several additional factors: Even in "boom" times there was consistent failure, year after year, of over 80 percent of the shows actually produced. When the consumer purse strings tightened as the depression came on, the supply of "angels" with money to back shows became sadly depleted. Hollywood, which had also contributed heavily to the expansion, all but dropped out of the picture. It quickly became evident that Times Square was vastly overbuilt from a theatre standpoint. Most of the playhouses passed into the "absentee" ownership of banks and insurance companies with no intention of risking such capital as was available, and the great majority of the houses were soon "dark."

There is little question that the rigidity of union wage scales in the many theatrical unions, coupled with shop restrictions on Broadway and on the road, contributed to the curtailment. As the depression came on, maintenance of wage costs when net profits were shrinking made this especially true. But the high cost of play production originally came about as a result of abuses stemming from long years of managerial extravagance, with every theatre salary, whether of an actor or a stage hand, including unemployment insurance.

At the outset of the depression certain other amusement forms employing large numbers in their heyday were defunct, or on the way out. In the former category was minstrelsy, the glamour of its appeal outmoded. Puppetry was a lost art, and the foreign language theatre had fallen away to practically nothing. Vaudeville still survived, though dealt a mortal blow by movies and radio. Burlesque could not keep pace with the times, and its famed "wheels," like the great vaudeville circuits of former days, became atrophied. Even the circuses, despite perennial appeal to many, folded up one by one until only a few of the largest remained.

III.

It was somewhat ironic that actors, who had always been among the first to come to the assistance of public causes, should finally succumb to hard times. A long period elapsed before actors were willing to concede that an emergency really existed. Accustomed by long usage to seasonal unemployment, they struggled along for months hoping for engagements. Stop-gap measures, including a cooperative revue, actors' dinner club and a stage relief fund stemmed the tide for awhile, but by 1933 stage folk were turning to the United States for relief in increasing numbers. That summer, New York State, through local boards of education, gave aid to professional actors through the formation of acting companies in Nassau and Westchester counties. However, it was not until early in 1934 that the Federal Government first gave evidence of its interest in utilizing the talents of actors on relief rolls. Emily Holt, associate counsel of Equity, worked out a plan with Mrs. Charles H. Sabin which won the approval of Equity executives in New York and was proposed to the Civil Works Administration. On January 12, 1934, a CWA appropriation of $28,000 was granted to finance a project sponsored by Equity and the Board of Education. The plan was to put twelve plays into rehearsal for early presentation in schools, museums, auditoriums and hospitals throughout New York City. Similar plans evolved in several other cities.

In its relief sense at least, CWA drama was a direct antecedent of later WPA explorations in this field. There was no special virtuosity in CWA performances: entertainment was the sole end in view. CWA was clearly relief theatre: no attempts were made to merchandise it or sell it; none to attract attention by the production of provocative plays or the use of arresting stage techniques. Federal

Theatre's resources were greater; its immediate scope broader and deeper; its philosophy more progressive.

IV.

In 1935, a total of $6,784,000, or approximately one-fourth of the total WPA funds set apart for the establishment of four arts projects, was designated to provide employment for 12,000 theatre people for a period of six months. Hallie Flanagan, director of Vassar's experimental theatre, was selected as national director, largely on the basis of her program submitted to the WPA Administrator Harry Hopkins.

While she acknowledged that the immediate aim of the project was to put back to work those theatre workers in all branches of the industry who had been on relief rolls, she hinted at broader objectives. At an early stage she pointed out that to regard the theatre only in terms of what had been hitherto experienced was the "timid wasting of an unprecedented chance."

Her regional assistants and advisors consisted, for the most part, of community and college drama people, and a smattering of commercial producers with an interest in the theatre beyond the box office returns. Much of the progressive and liberal impetus given the project at its inception may be ascribed to the zeal of these officials, none of whom seemingly took a "official" view of his job. The patient and sympathetic cooperation of WPA higher-ups in Washington was also an early attribute.

During its first year the Project was concerned largely with the solution of internal problems. In this dramatic undertaking without historic precedent there were countless administrative, technical, financial, legal and union questions which had to be settled, locally and nationally, so that the Project could proceed. In a number of instances there was conflict between the local Project supervisor and the WPA administrator who controlled the purse strings for the unit. All too frequently, the administrator with no real knowledge of show business would impede needed action.

Lack of funds frequently hampered and is still impeding FTP progress. Because all but a small percentage of available money is set apart for salary use, the budget for technical equipment and props is limited. A story is told of Paris the Great, strong man for the WPA circus in New York, and formerly known in the profession as Ivan the Terrible. Ivan was told by the manager of the circus unit that economies had become so necessary that he would have to unbend nightly all the iron bars and rods he twisted like pretzels during the performances, so that they could be used again the following day.

This incident, despite its humorous aspect, is illustrative of the type of financial stress that has consistently deviled the Project. The percentage devoted to non-labor costs has been shaved to less than 10 per cent. Today the Project employs only two-thirds of its peak personnel load of 13,000, operates in 22 states instead of 28.

The Project workers did not submit to these personnel cuts without a struggle. This was particularly true in New York, where the original leadership of Elmer Rice and the experimental character of the Project attracted a large left-wing group. When the first wholesale WPA cuts were announced late in 1936, the New York Project workers together with those in other Arts Projects literally resisted tooth and nail. On subsequent occasions they displayed similar tactics to the great embarrassment of Washington officials. The main interest of those protesting may have been their jobs, but the desire to keep the Project alive was a secondary factor of no mean significance. Federal Theatre, they had come to feel, represented something worth saving.

The primary consideration of the FTP directors at the outset was the rehabilitation of its personnel. Many of the applicants were old actors whose response to the idea of work relief was far from immediate. Because Federal Theatre had no mechanism to deal with the delicate problems related to this type of psychological adjustment, many were proud, condescending, even non-cooperative in the Project's earliest days, but as their interest in its varied activity grew they lost their reluctance to take part. As in the CWA period, it was generally found at first that actors on relief were afraid of being identified, but as time went on they evinced a greater interest and feeling of participation. Actors became competitively interested in new parts and vied with each other for publicity. A sense of "belonging" had been engendered.

As evidence of their desire to keep before the public, a troupe of colored actors who had been rehearsing a show for the best part of a year became so exasperated that they picketed Project headquarters in an effort to force its production. The impromptu performances of *The Cradle Will Rock*, despite its official censorship, also manifested the insistence of the actors to be heard.

One of the Project's most difficult jobs has been the reworking of usefulness in talents turned rusty, or transference of skills from outmoded entertainment forms. In New York a re-training school for Project actors was set in the Old Provincetown Playhouse. In California, experiments to heighten the timeliness of vaudeville were inaugurated. In New England, conservatism is the keynote, and actors who are growing too old to study, are given radio scripts to play over the air. Others are given walk-on parts, or occasionally "bits" are written for them.

With the cooperation of supervisors, FTP actors are constantly rehearsing new material in the hope that someone will see their work and offer professional engagement. Interesting in this connection is the attitude of New England vaudeville troupers to performances at the English High School of Boston. This auditorium gets regular weekly vaudeville from the Project, and is similar to other free shows given by the Project save in this one respect. The hall is located near the city's theatrical section and performers know that regular booking agents occasionally "catch" the shows. Although the audience consists of poor people from the community, the actors play as if the top were $1.50 or more.

They jockey for good "spots" on the bill, and some to refer to this hall as the "Palace."

Project directors are generally liberal in their attitude toward private bookings, and will release Project acts for private entertainment for any reasonable period. The run of *On the Rocks*, Shaw's play in New York, was recently interrupted for the summer so that relief actors might accept engagements in what *Variety* terms "strawhats," or summer theatres.

During 1937 the rate of "absorption into private industry" was quickening. According to a statement made by Mrs. Flanagan, about a thousand Federal Theatre workers left the national Project for jobs during the year. However, in the first six months of 1938 there was a resurgence of actors who wanted their FTP jobs back again. A Federal Theatre ruling now guarantees recidivism for the relief actor whose private engagement ends within a three-month period. This provides an incentive for the Project workers to seek outside employment. Before the ruling, there was no assurance that a man would be taken back on WPA, and many were afraid to accept short term jobs.

The compensation of Project workers was determined at the outset by agreements reached with the heads of all theatre unions. For actors, the relief wage finally agreed upon was $23.86 for New York as measured against a prevailing Equity scale of $40 a week. Recent WPA cuts reduced this wage to $22.78 for a 24-hour work week for all actors whether they are in vaudeville, circus, puppetry, or legitimate. Non-relief actors (there is a small complement) get exactly the same wage. There is no such thing as a "star" salary, the lowliest walk-on receiving the same payment as the lead. Outside of New York the salaries are slightly lower but in line with prevailing regional union scales.

Under the agreement with Equity, Project members are permitted to give six performances a week, but the period each day is limited to four hours, which is said to be a handicap when a new play is being rehearsed. This also explains why shows giving a Saturday matinee dispense with one evening performance. A performance, or service may consist of a bit or lead in a play, or simply in reporting for rehearsal. If the actor is a vaudeville or circus man he gets credit for a full service, even though his act may take only five or ten minutes to perform.

The sum of $98.70 monthly is the standard security wage for others besides actors, though the rates and hours vary in accordance with the union's prevailing scale. For the same security wage as that received by actors, stage hands are required to work only half this time, or two weeks a month, so that their pay is in line with a union scale which has always been among the highest. Consequently, the cost of stage hands is one of the Project's highest expenses because two crews weekly are necessary for each play. From time to time there have been readjustments required on the mechanical end. In the case of actors, Equity on several occasions has complained about the number of "amateurs" on the Project, and indeed whenever the Federal Theatre has been under fire this charge has been aired. Mrs. Flanagan and her staff have held at all times that young people are essential to keep the Project fresh and pliable and have retained youngsters who had relief status, in many cases giving them responsible jobs. For the most part, people who have emerged from the Project to make good outside have been from this younger element.

In consideration of the many difficulties attending the administration of the largest theatrical troupe in the world, the Project has been surprisingly free of serious criticism, or even accusation which might have been expected. Partly because the stakes are low, and partly because of the caliber of people attracted, there has been a minimum of graft. On the West Coast it was charged that ambitious actresses were gaining admission to the Project on false pretenses so that their work might attract favorable Hollywood notice. More recently New York headlines called attention to widespread embezzlement in WPA box offices, but as it turned out, the front page "sensation" involved but a dozen people and a few thousand dollars. Generally speaking, however, imputations of this sort in the Project's history have been few and far between.

V.

Although the letters W-P-A are still anathema in certain parts of the country, the Federal Theatre has won whole-hearted acceptance by large sectors of the population. The Project's attempts to bring back the stage by broadening the base of the American theatre is succeeding at the rate of a million new faces in the audience for each million dollars spent. Thus far, it is estimated, over 30,000,000 people have witnessed Federal Theatre productions of whom 65 per cent have never before seen a play with living actors.

The Federal Theatre has provided entertainment indoors and outdoors, in rain and in fair weather, on holiday mornings and on Saturday nights. It has produced plays for veteran theatre goers in Chicago and San Francisco; old stock audiences in Indianapolis and Bridgeport; farmers in Maine and the Dakotas. It can speak French in New Orleans, Spanish in Tampa, Yiddish in New York and Los Angeles. For millions of kids it has performed Shakespeare in high schools, vaudeville in orphan asylums; puppet shows in playgrounds; mystery drama in CCC camps; circuses in empty lots. It has amused soldiers and sailors, lunatics and jailbirds, inmates of hospitals and homes for the aged, and thousands on street corners in under-privileged neighborhoods.

For many citizens, even in Metropolitan New York, main stem of the American theatre, the role of playgoer was a strange one. Questionnaires distributed by Federal Theatre early in its history disclosed that only twenty per cent of those in its audiences who answered had been to the theatre within the past five years, the majority attributing their non-attendance to financial reasons. Broadway is geared to high box office prices, and the demands of New York's literate millions with less than $3.30 or $2.20 to spend are not solved by a few rows in the rear of the balcony at $1.10. The New York audience survey showed a large percentage of lower middle class occupations, with 21 per cent teachers and students. Many school and labor union groups attend en masse, these party blocs comprising over 40 per cent of the paying audiences.

By its own proud boast, Federal Theatre has consistently directed its attention to the four million, rather than the four hundred. During the first year of its operation, a total of 87 per cent of all FTP shows were free. More recently it has been the Project's policy to charge something, if only a nickel or a dime, which could help to defray the non-labor costs of these productions. Of course, the performances in parks and public squares, such as the Caravan shows given in New York, Chicago and San Francisco for the past three summers, are necessarily free, but where town halls, granges and schools are played, the Project is now attempting to exact some sort of subsidy. This may take the form of an outright guarantee, or, in line with practice developed by New England's thrifty Project, it may consist of supper or transportation. For example, a Maine town "hires" the Federal troupe of vaudevillians to play during its Home Week celebration. The show is given on Main Street, with the local fire department and American Legion Post sharing the expense of bus transportation and other incidentals. The two circuses in New York and New England are sponsored for many of their engagements by civic organizations and veterans' groups, who provide the lot, give the show its advance billing, and get out the crowd in return for a certain percentage of the "take."

Today, admission ranging from 10 cents to $1.10 is charged for about 30 percent of Federal Theatre's productions. A 55-cent top is fairly general for dramatic and musical shows, although the Project has recently upped its orchestra charge to $1.00 in the case of several metropolitan productions. During the six month period from September 1937 through February 1938, there were 1,200,000 paid admissions to 2,108 performances in all parts of the country.

At the Project's inception, it was thought necessary to prepare the ground, especially in regions where the living theatre had fallen into disuse, by the presentation of simple, homely plays of the family comedy genre. Manchester opened with *Your Uncle Dudley*; Indianapolis began with Tarkington's *Clarence*; Omaha's opener was *Three Wise Fools*, and Bridgeport played *The Shannons of Broadway*.

Save for its value as entertainment, there was perhaps little to justify the production of this type of play. This was doubly true in view of Federal Theatre's announced aim to bring to outlying regions plays of greater social relevance. But the going was tough, at the outset particularly. There was a definite problem involved in warming up audiences—indeed, of getting past the box office window an audience that had not been going to the theatre, at least for several years. This was characteristically true in the smaller cities where the movie had such a strangle-hold that a number of instances were reported where patrons were astonished to find the "show" that they were attending was not a talking picture.

In some cases, casting difficulties and curtailment of local production expense made the one-set potboiler the most desirable vehicle. It remains almost the sole dish on the bill of fare in several New England and middle western towns where Federal Theatre is gaining much of its support from old stock audiences accustomed to this type of presentation. In certain sections supervisors are constantly laboring to overcome a background of intense political resentment and have consciously veered away from controversial plays.

While there have been exceptions, it is becoming more and more evident that success for Federal Theatre plays in the larger urban communities is in almost direct proportion to their artistic merit or the effectiveness of their social message. This has been true right along in New York and Los Angeles, twin spearheads of FTP, and is fast becoming an actuality in such towns as Hartford, Seattle and Atlanta. It would be stretching a point to say that every Federal Theatre production in these towns satisfies one or the other of these basic requirements. But it is evident in all parts of the country that scripts of a cheap, outworn, trivial or vulgar nature are disappearing from the lists.

"Our Federal Theatre," said Mrs. Flanagan, "born of an economic fear, built by and for people who have faced terrific privation, cannot content itself with easy, pretty or insignificant plays." The trend has been to encourage native playwrights to contribute to a planned program, national in scope, regional in emphasis, and American in its democratic attitude.

In New York as in other parts of the country there have been an increasing number of plays authored by native Americans, especially for the Project. During the past six months this has been notably true in New York, where *Haiti* and *Prologue to Glory*, both original scripts, were given their premieres by WPA. Apparently the time has not yet come when the established American playwright will forego the prestige of a Broadway production with "name" direction and stars in the cast for a presentation by Federal Theatre, but the Project is fast winning over many writers who like its policies and freedom from restraint.

It is significant, moreover, that America's two winners of the Nobel Prize for Literature have displayed more than a passing interest in Federal Theatre. One of the Project's earliest sensations was the simultaneous production in eighteen cities of Sinclair Lewis's *It Can't Happen Here*. While the play itself was disappointing to some people, evoking a variety of responses, its anti-Fascist theme was timely and it was seen by close to 300,000 people paying an average admission price of about 30 cents. Of particular interest were the two Yiddish productions in Los Angeles and New York, and a Negro version in Seattle, in which the theme of oppression of racial minorities was made especially poignant. It is an interesting sidelight that Hollywood, which at first rejected the opportunity to make this film, is now planning its production.

As early as November 1936 Eugene O'Neill spoke of the "thrilling possibilities" possessed by Federal Theatre, which he said had the "opportunity to bring legitimate stage productions to every community in America, whether that community be rural or urban."

Another dramatist who early manifested an interest in Federal Theatre is George Bernard Shaw, whose plays, together with O'Neill's, are now being done in repertory in many of the Project's leading units. When Shaw concluded his arrangement with Federal Theatre, granting presentation rights, one of his conditions was that at no time could any of the series be produced at higher than a fifty cent top. Shaw cabled America last year when Project personnel cuts were impending. "Of course, the first thing they curtail is American culture," said the Irish dramatist. "Congress needs drastic lynching. Those who voted for barbarism should perish by it."

VI.

In line with a Project trend emphasized during FTP's second year there has been an elevation of production standards, with a corresponding improvement in the calibre of plays presented.

A visitor to the "provinces" during the first six months of 1938 might have seen *Ah Wilderness* in Salem, Mass., Miami, Newark, San Diego, New Orleans and Chicago. He could have witnessed *Porgy* in Hartford, *Hell Bent for Heaven* in Atlanta, *Boy Meets Girl* in Louisville, *The Weavers* in Los Angeles, *Awake and Sing* in Pasadena, *Excursion* in Cincinnati, *Everyman* in Jacksonville, *Councillor at Law* in Seattle, *Judgment Day* in San Francisco, *The Left Bank* in Manchester, *Anna Christie* in Denver, *Pygmalion* in Roslyn, Long Island.

It is true, of course, that the endeavor of Federal Theatre to bring to smaller towns the best of the classics and stimulating new American plays of relevance has not in every case been successful. In some instances even the plays of O'Neill, Shaw and Elmer Rice have fallen wide of the mark, either because they were over the heads of the audience, or because the available cast, ofttimes consisting of old vaudevillians, was not able to cope with their subtleties.

In New York, and several other larger cities, the preparedness of the audience and the diversity of the available talent are such that the production of some genuinely exciting shows has resulted—exciting both from the standpoint of virtuosity of production technique, and aptness of social theme.

Here a strenuous effort was made from the first to give playgoers a type of production which they might not readily expect to find on the commercial stage, even if they had the price of a ticket. Notable illustrations of this trend were such Federal Theatre successes as the Negro *Macbeth*, *Murder in the Cathedral, Dr. Faustus* and the Living Newspaper shows. In addition, Federal Theatre supplied a long-felt need for marionette and children's theatre productions, dance dramas, foreign language plays, and Gilbert and Sullivan at a price within reach of all.

The education of audiences to new plays and new stage techniques has had encouraging reward in the Project's most distinctive accomplishment to date— the creation and development of the Living Newspaper. Written from actual source material, these plays present the facts on contemporary social themes. Part of the technique's resourcefulness is shown in the rich variety of ways in which the informational, sometimes statistical material is made vivid and exciting. There is the further advantage of complete flexibility furnished by the episodic form of the play. As events occur, entire scenes may be inserted or deleted, and Living Newspaper endings can be adjusted to conform with Supreme Court decisions or the passage of new legislation. The plays have been generally representative of the viewpoint of the present Administration, in that *Triple-A Plowed Under* is an analysis of the farm problem; *Injunction Granted* of collective bargaining; *Power* of the TVA and the Government's entrance in the utilities field, and *One Third of a Nation* of Government-sponsored housing.

While confined chiefly to New York during the first two years of the Project's existence, the pages of the Living Newspaper are now being spread in other cities. Chicago this year pioneered *Spirochete*, a Living Newspaper on syphilis. Oregon produced *Flax*, New Orleans offered *Flood Control*. Productions of *One Third of a Nation* are being readied for such cities as Seattle, Philadelphia, New Orleans, Detroit and Cincinnati, with the play altered slightly in each case to accommodate the local housing problem. Hartford is planning three Living Newspaper productions for next season, including one on the Negro, and another on the consumer problem entitled *Behind the Label*.

No description of a Living Newspaper show can approximate its potency on stage. There are two reasons immediately evident for the extraordinary effectiveness of the type of presentation. In the first place, there is its dramatic form. Although the facts depicted in Living Newspapers are available in any public library; although the conclusions reached are rarely startling per se to any informed person, the sharp incisiveness of action in the theatre, coupled with shrewd timing, produce a vivid impression that is moving far beyond the power of the printed page.

The second outstanding characteristic of Living Newspapers is the *entente cordiale*, one might almost say solidarity of interest prevailing between actor and audience. While especially noticeable in Living Newspaper productions, this also applies to other Project dramas. Federal Theatre's audiences appear to many reviewers as immediately more interested and participant than an economically comparable group of movie-goers.

Let me illustrate this by quoting some of the dialogue from *Power*. Whereas in *Triple-A* the consumer is militant and remote, in *Power* he is highly personalized, familiar to everyone in the audience.

The curtain rises to show two electricians and a stage manager at a switchboard on the stage.

LOUDSPEAKER: This is the switchboard of the Ritz Theatre. Through this board flows the electric power that amplifies my voice, the power that ventilates the theatre and the power that lights this show.

STAGE MANAGER: (picking up a fat cable) It all comes through here.

There follows a scene showing the many home and industrial uses of light, with a crisis arising throwing an entire city in darkness. Next a carefully-documented scene sketching electric invention, the private sale of power and the combination of private companies to end rate wars.

In the next scene the consumer makes his entrance, or rather he is discovered after a searching arc has been played all over the stage. Described as a "meek looking little man," he is sitting on a chair in one little corner.

LOUDSPEAKER: Ah, there he is!

(Consumer gets up and comes downstage)

LOUDSPEAKER: What do you pay for electricity, Mister?

CONSUMER: Too much. (Reading bill) Seventeen cents a kilowatt hour.

LOUDSPEAKER: What's a kilowatt hour?

CONSUMER: I don't know.

An electrician explains that when a 1000-watt bulb, obligingly lowered to the stage, has burned an hour, that's a kilowatt hour.

CONSUMER: Now that I know what that is I still think I'm paying too much.

LOUDSPEAKER: The company that services you is only making a fair profit.

CONSUMER: What's a fair profit?

LOUDSPEAKER: Six to nine percent.

CONSUMER: Who said so?

LOUDSPEAKER: The Courts.

CONSUMER: And the bank only gives me three. What do they do with all that money?

LOUDSPEAKER: It goes back to the stockholder in dividends.

(Consumer picks up his shopping bag and starts off)

Where are you going?

CONSUMER: I've got some shopping and I'm going to stop in at the company. I'll tell those people something! Seventeen cents a kilowatt hour!

(He goes out and immediately returns. Overhead spot picks out two grocery clerks. Consumer crosses to first clerk.)

CONSUMER: How much are your potatoes?

FIRST CLERK: Fifteen pounds for a quarter.

CONSUMER: Too high. I'll go some place else.

(Crosses to second clerk)

How much are your potatoes?

SECOND CLERK: Twenty pounds for a quarter.

CONSUMER: Fine, I'll take 'em.

The same is repeated at two butcher shops with pork chops. Finally consumer goes to call on Manager of electric company. One man this time.

CONSUMER: How much are you charging me for electricity?
MANAGER: Seventeen cents a kilowatt hour.
CONSUMER: Too high. I'll go some place else.
(He crosses and looks around, walks in circles, sees no one)
Where's the other fellow?
MANAGER: There is no other fellow.
(Projection changes to "M is for Monopoly")
CONSUMER: You the only one selling electricity in this city?
MANAGER: That's right.
CONSUMER: And if I don't get it from you I have to do without it?
MANAGER: That's right. Would you like to discontinue service?
CONSUMER: (Apologetically) Er...no...never mind.

BLACKOUT

Carrying this point further, there is a possibility for sympathy across foot-lights in a Federal Theatre show that rarely presents itself in the case of a regular Broadway production. At a $3.30 top the audience may warmly applaud the cast, but there is a certain decorum in the relationship of actor and patron which is rarely broken. The patron does not identify himself with the actor, except insofar as he closely follows the action of the play. On his side, the actor is often inclined to be aloof and in any case rarely identifies himself with the audience.

In Federal Theatre there is a somewhat closer tie existing between patron and artist. The audience, as a matter of fact, does not consist of "patrons" in the same sense as that applied to a Broadway audience

Further evidence of the difference between audiences is seen in the reception accorded to various plays. Federal Theatre took a number of shows which had never succeeded on Broadway, and did surprisingly well with them, especially on the road. Conversely, Broadway came to grief when it tried to reproduce in "private enterprise" the success scored by the Project with *Murder in the Cathedral* and *Censored*.

To be sure Federal Theatre with its obligation to cover only non-labor costs has a tremendous advantage, and an FTP hit show is not a hit show by Broadway standards. Late in March, the New York Project broke its own record, taking in $7,792 in one week for its current productions which included *Haiti, One Third of a Nation* and *Prologue to Glory*. This represented virtual capacity. Yet the box office total was less than half the weekly receipts for one successful commercial show.

Broadway's own reactions to the Project have undergone an interesting evolution. FTP at the outset did not occasion anything more than mild curiosity in

Times Square. At the end of the first year Lee Shubert could say: "So far, the Federal Theatre Project has not been competition. The prices have been low. They have not been able to afford high-priced actors." Federal Theatre's meticulous observance of Broadway union standards; its avoidance of the conventional Broadway play, and its early agreement to occupy theatres on the fringe of the theatre belt, helped to establish its position.

In *Variety's* review of 1937, the writer on Federal Theatre cited its value as a builder of audiences which "the commercial theatre business has done nothing to develop during the entire last decade."

However, a number of factors this spring contributed to a cooling off of Broadway's enthusiasm. An administrative shakeup of the New York Project brought in new executives definitely "Broadway-minded" in comparison with the visionaries who formerly directed production in Manhattan. In a somewhat meager Broadway season, managers objected to the Project's presentation of three "hits," at least two of which bore a closer resemblance to typical Broadway shows than anything previously attempted by the Project in New York. The feeling of FTP's encroachment was further aggravated by the Project's excursion into display newspaper advertising to publicize its productions. Although these ads appeared only once-a-week in line with tight budgetary limitations, Broadway was visibly disturbed.

Variety said on May 4, "Showmen intend to secure a showdown on the policy of the Theatre Project and hope to get a clear indication whether WPA intends outright competition with the commercial theatre." This protest took the form of a petition distributed for signature to Broadway producers, charging that the Project, "subsidized by the Government" was offering "unfair competition to an industry sorely pressed by high taxes, also costs of production and operation." Managers admitted that they were in sympathy with the aims of WPA as a relief organization, but felt that it had overstepped the bounds.

The vast majority of managers, including Jed Harris, Guthrie McClintic and the Theatre Guild, signed the petition. George Abbott and the Mercury Theatre were outstanding among those who refused to sign.

The Mercury owes to the Federal Theatre much of the credit for the success of its initial year. It was a direct offshoot of the Project. Its directors, Orson Welles and John Houseman, while employed on the Project, were chiefly responsible for *Macbeth* and *Dr. Faustus*. The Mercury launched *The Cradle Will Rock* with practically the identical cast that was to have been used by the FTP.

As expressed by its national director, Federal Theatre's aim is not to compete with privately sponsored drama, but "by building new audiences, by introducing new dramatic forms, and by stimulating new dramatists, to afford the commercial theatre a form of competition which is the life and not the death of trade." After her recent return from a vastly successful road tour, the manager of Helen Hayes was quoted as saying that the Federal Theatre was helping to restore interest in the road.

VII.

There remains a strong tendency to regard Federal Theatre as something apart from the regular Broadway stage. But as production standards have improved, this difference has been less pronounced. Lately Federal Theatre has been accorded several distinctions. Its *Prologue to Glory*, given a coveted four-star rating by the New York Daily News, was awarded honorable mention for the 1938 Critics Circle prize. Arthur Arent, writer of *One Third of a Nation, Power* and several of the previous Living Newspapers, was given a Guggenheim fellowship for the further exercise of his talents. Announcement was recently made by Random House that two volumes containing six plays produced by the Project would shortly be published in book form with a preface by Mrs. Flanagan. The script of *One Third of a Nation* was bought for the movies.

As it rounds its third year, Federal Theatre has reopened many of the nation's stages and contributed new American plays to their sustenance at many points. It has, in addition, performed highly acceptable functions in its intelligent revival of classics; in its development of a theatre for and by Negroes; in its insistent emphasis on a "Theatre of Youth"; in its restoration of a foreign language drama; in its creation of a new audience for the dance, and in its morale-building entertainments for the physically and socially handicapped.

The future of the Project is problematic. There is some likelihood that if times improve, the Federal Theatre may eventually be liquidated as "unnecessary." If times grow progressively worse, FTP on its present scale may be viewed as a luxury, and there will be a demand among certain groups to convert the work relief program, including Federal Theatre, to a less expensive home relief status.

VIII.

Project history shows that when personnel cuts impend, the smaller and more outlying units are the most severely affected. On June 30, 1937, the New York project was reduced from 5,725 to 4,016, California from 2,205 to 1,596, Illinois from 1,207 to 807, and Massachusetts from 960 to 682. These cuts, while drastic, in no case amounted to more than 33 ½ percent. At the same time Alabama was cut from 108 to 24; Colorado from 170 to 35; Ohio from 212 to 99 and Washington from 193 to 75, cuts averaging well over 50 per cent. In addition, the state projects of Rhode Island, Texas, Delaware and Nebraska were completely wiped out, even though their combined personnel roster was only 254. Iowa's unit, reduced from 60 to 30 at the time of the cut, has since been entirely liquidated. Thus it appears that further curtailment of the Project, if it follows the course of previous reductions, may mean the elimination of all but the largest units.

If the Government were to abandon Federal Theatre, there would be vehement protests from highly vocal groups, but there is small likelihood that concerted effort from any other quarter would come forward to keep it alive. It is possible that in a few cities municipal support might be granted, or that individual units might form cooperative companies and tour around for a time, but of FTP's present roster of 8,739, of whom about 50 per cent are actors, relatively few would be absorbed.

Efforts on the part of a large number of people to create a permanent Federal arts program took concrete form in two Congressional bills, later fused into one. Led by Senator Pepper, and Representatives Coffee and Sirovich, the groundwork for this legislative attempt occupied a large number of people this winter and spring. Many notables of the literary, artistic and theatre worlds attended Washington hearings in its behalf, the list taking in such diversified talents as Burgess Meredith, Lillian Gish, Jane Cowl, Orson Welles, Theodore Dreiser, Rockwell Kent, Roy Harris and others.

The bill as finally presented proposed to lift Federal Theatre and the other arts projects out of the WPA, setting them up independently under a permanent Bureau of Fine Arts. It provided for a Commissioner appointed by the President; absorption of existing WPA personnel, with an expansion of 20 per cent, and wage minimums of $30 weekly. Artists were to be given the right to organize and bargain collectively.

Brooks Atkinson of the New York Times voiced his demurrer to the proposal to absorb Federal Theatre intact, saying that it meant, "consolidating permanently the original blunder of taking people onto the Project uncritically. It is urgent that some standards of competence be specifically incorporated into the bill. A Federal Bureau of Fine Arts can never be anything but a headache unless the people it employs are genuine artists."

The Coffee, Pepper, Sirovich bill, sunk in committee for most of the last session, came up in the last few days of the session. It never had a chance. Congressman Short, in whose own state of Missouri municipal opera has flourished for years, snuffed out its chances with one clumsily executed *pas seul* on the House floor.

Federal Theatre directors refused to be drawn very deeply into any discussion involving its possible future as a national theatre. They have consistently endeavored to cut their cloth to fit the existing needs of the various locales within the present set-up. Under capable guidance, the Project has shown evidence of very purposeful direction in a number of ways.

Many observers agree with critic Burns Mantle that "at least a start has been made, and a more promising start than ever has been made before, toward the eventual founding of such a national theatre as we have been dreaming about for years."

It is obvious that at this time there is no cure-all for Federal Theatre's dilemma—that until some feasible plan can be evolved, it will continue to operate in pragmatic fashion along present lines. One day it may very likely gain enough community support to attain its desired legislative ends. In the meantime, the following suggestions are put forward as ways to increase the Project's social effectiveness:

1. Release of the Project from the impermanence and fear of cessation which has occupied its attention at every move thus far.
2. Discontinuance of the system wherein Federal Theatre is subjected to regulations designed primarily for engineering projects.
3. Selection of administrative personnel for their understanding of theatre problems and people.
4. Autonomous administration of Federal Theatre as part of a program including all the Arts.
5. Flexibility in Project controls and personnel selection to avoid "hardening of the arteries" from too much institutionalism.
6. Selection of personnel by standards of competence other than relief.
7. Administration of the Project with wide latitude given to regional controls; in practice a centralization of services, a decentralization of authority.
8. Organization of regional direction in such a way that infiltration of ideas will be possible from the bottom up as well as from the top down.
9. Encouragement of state, municipal and community participation and support, with a view to making the Project as self-sustaining as possible.
10. Extension of the Project's sphere of activity to rural areas in generally wider circles throughout the country, with amplified touring whenever possible.
11. Continuance of the present program of community services for the handicapped.
12. Cultivation and extension of the Project's play production policy, laying stress on the introduction of indigenous material by native playwrights presented in new dramatic forms.

THE WELFARE COUNCIL OF NEW YORK CITY

In the spring of 1938, I got a job as managing editor of *Better Times*, the publication of the Welfare Council of New York City. The Welfare Council, which no longer exists, was a loose federation of the voluntary social and health organizations in the city. It was headed by Robert P. Lane, with Leonard Mayo as his deputy; both had distinguished careers in the field of social work administration. *Better Times* was a fortnightly bulletin of welfare news with four illustrated quarterly magazine issues. The editor was Hiram Motherwell.

Motherwell was a wonderfully literate man with a serious drinking problem. He had been editor of *Stage Magazine* and later held two important posts in the Federal Theatre as Regional Director for New England and head of its Play Policy Board. I never did understand how he came to the Welfare Council, where he was a fish out of water. I think it was a result of some family connection with Bob Lane.

I liked Motherwell enormously, and in his best moments he was a superb editor. A Federal Theatre colleague spoke of his "warm humanity and understanding" and it was a fair characterization. I did some of my best work under his auspices. He stretched me—that is to say, he stimulated my imagination to undertake projects far beyond the routine. He gave me my head; rarely interfered with my daily work. But he came in at the right moment with fresh ideas. The little that he wrote himself was simple and eloquent, and he provided editorial touches that greatly enhanced the pieces he enlivened.

The news bulletin was a handy reference sheet containing timely articles and a welfare calendar. But the quarterly issues covered, in a colorful manner, a wide variety of lively subjects. In June 1938 I wrote the lead story for the issue on *Our City's Schools*. This was followed in December by an issue on New York's burgeoning low-rent housing program. A feature of that issue was a nine-photo takeout of the shifting welfare problems of the city by Lewis W. Hine, titled *A Famous Camera Does Thirty Years of Case Work.*

Our issue of February 1939 on *Child Adrift in New York* was extremely popular, with requests for reprints from many parts of the country. On its cover was the reproduction of an 1812 steel engraving titled *The Foundling*. We hit the jackpot with the April 1939 issue called *Metropolitan Diary*. I got thirteen men and women of the thousands actually on the job to reveal their typical day as a probation officer, visiting nurse, blind placement worker, vocational counselor, legal aid practitioner, worker with the homeless, health station worker, worker with the aged and others. We called it *Four Horsemen of the Metropolis*—the *Daily Record of New York City's Defense against Poverty, Disease, Demoralization and Crime.* It was especially gratifying to have the comment of Paul Kellogg, editor of the prestigious *Survey Magazine*, who said: "Your April number of *Better Times* is a humdinger. Hats off to that scheme of yours for portraying the day's work on the job of the social workers of the city. And you have played it up so tellingly with pictures, old and new. Over the years, we have had occasional single articles of this sort, but I am covetous of your imagination in bunching them together in a smash hit."

In the April 1939 issue we also had a piece called *The Refugees—Their Chances in America*, which told about efforts to place pre-war refugees in flight from Hitler. I interviewed William Haber, Director of the National Refugee Service, established to coordinate the activities of the cooperating agencies. Haber liked the story and offered me a job. I was reluctant to quit *Better Times*, but sensed that the Council's future was uncertain. In fact, it did not survive World War II. Another consideration was economic. The job with NRS meant a slight raise in salary, and I was engaged to be married. I took it.

Before leaving the subject of the Welfare Council I want to mention a few of the staff who, in one way or another, served as mentors and encouraged my progress. They were specialists in various fields. Outstanding was Moe Beckleman, who came from the Jewish Welfare Board and headed Group Work. A big man in mental and physical stature, he later became a leading official of the American Joint Jewish Refugee Committee which saved thousands of Jews from extermination. Another star was Marie Lane, with whom I worked after the war when she was Chief of Welfare for the International Refugee Organization. I don't recall Sophia Robison's exact title, but in and out of the office she was an important influence and guidepost. Sophia lived in a large apartment on 110th Street and Broadway and invited many friends, young and old, to her Sunday night suppers. Sometimes twenty or thirty people would drift in during the evening. At a certain moment, Sophia, or one of her children, would call for quiet, and she would introduce everyone there, asking them to say a few words about what they were doing. This was a bit painful, but edifying as she had interesting and provocative friends.

A very vocal participant was Jimmy Wechsler who later became the editor of *The New York Post*. The ambiance and food were always most enjoyable.

Over the years, between and during other assignments, I did consultancies and writing jobs. The first of these was a paper I reasoned and drafted for Mary Boretz. Mary directed the Foster Home Bureau of the Hebrew Shelter and Guardian Society and was also a friend. I think I met her during my stint as managing editor of *Better Times* magazine. She was then in a kind of war with a much older and better endowed organization called the Hebrew Orphan Asylum.

It was Mary's strong contention that orphans or children temporarily deprived of a parent's care would do better in a foster home than in a huge multiple facility. She could make the case eloquently on her feet, but wanted to marshal her arguments in a paper she was going to present. She had collected a good deal of evidence supporting her cause. She convinced me, which made the job easier. I took on the assignment when I left the Council and she was well satisfied with the result. I didn't follow events closely after that, but understand that the efforts of Mary and others led to a gradual erosion of support for the huge congregate asylum and the acceptance of more individual care for a child in limbo in a foster family or at least in a smaller, cottage-type facility. Mary wrote to me in September 1939 when I finished the job, "I am grateful to you for having organized the material and got me started again on something that I had found impossible to undertake."

Another mentor I knew from the Welfare Council was Lester B. Granger, a 1918 graduate of Dartmouth. Granger was Secretary of the Council's Exploratory Committee on Negro Welfare. At a Harlem meeting in January 1939 called by the New York State Temporary Commission on the Condition of the Urban Colored Population, Granger urged the State to take the initiative in the employment for Negroes. He cited figures showing that of 9,000 laborers employed by the State Highway Department, only 11 were Negroes, and that of 20,000 State Hospital employees, only six were Negroes. After World War II, Granger served for ten years as President of the Urban League, and was an active teacher and positive force for African-American welfare. In 2002, the Tucker Foundation at Dartmouth decided to offer a Lester Granger Award to "a graduate who has exhibited leadership and innovation while meeting community needs and benefiting an under-served population." I was honored by my selection as one of the first two recipients of this award. I spoke at the award dinner attended by President Wright, the Trustees of the college, the Officers of the Tucker Foundation, members of the Granger family and other members of the college community.

I've been asked what I thought of the Depression. I can't honestly say it had any great effect on where I lived, what I ate or wore or even what I thought, beyond a distinct feeling that something needed to be repaired. I was lucky to find a job, but of course I was aware of and disturbed by long lines of job seekers, squatters in the Central Park Reservoir, the Bonus Marchers and other evidence of economic misery. I was captivated by the promise of reforms offered by the New Deal and had faith they would somehow remedy the situation.

In the late 1930s my job at the Welfare Council opened my eyes to appalling needs in education, health, sanitation and housing, but with the influence and accomplishments of Mayor LaGuardia and Robert Moses there was a forward thrust at least so far as New York was concerned. The 1939 World's Fair gave the buoyant illusion of progress. Working on *Better Times* magazine entitled me to a press pass for the Fair, and I made full use of it. In the course of half a dozen visits I was greatly impressed by the exhibits at the French, Swedish and General Motors pavilions. At the New York Telephone exhibit you could make long distance calls without charge and I took advantage of that.

MARGARET AND KATHARINE

Three days a week, at the end of the working day, I would take the subway from Canal Street to the Morningside Station at 116th Street and Broadway. After a class or two at Columbia I would grab a bite to eat and head home. Invited to a party one evening, tired as I was, I decided to take it in. I spotted a tall, dark, attractive girl named Margaret Laurens and we talked for some time until eventually I walked her home. She lived in an apartment in the East 70s, and after a couple of more dates we became lovers. From the first, I was struck by Margaret's good looks, her intelligence and her lively spirit. Her beloved father, Carl Levi, had died during a family trip to Europe when she was 17. Her mother, Florence Levi, was living with Margaret's younger sister, Helen, in a Park Avenue apartment. Margaret stayed on good terms with them, but wanted her own living space and she had the means to afford it. She had also changed her name to Laurens. She quit Wellesley in the middle of her junior year, never finished college, but studied at the Art Students League and with a number of teachers. She first studied sculpture with Archipenko and Jose de Creeft (of whom more later) but switched to painting. I joined her for a week in Provincetown where she was studying abstract expressionism with Hans Hofmann.

Margaret and I found we had a great deal in common, including tennis (she was an excellent player), fondness for travel, love of the theater, and a penchant for word games and whimsicality. She was warm, friendly and fun in a group. I was anxious for her to meet my family and friends. On one of our first dates, we went up to New Haven for the Dartmouth-Yale football game with Herb and Hortie. Bill and Frankie Schuman took to her at once, and so did Ferd, Woody and several of my Dartmouth friends. Their approval was important to me.

Not long after we decided to be married, she moved back into her mother's apartment. Florence, who came from a Brooklyn brewing family named Liebmann, had a bachelor brother named George, of whom I grew quite fond. Margaret's older brother, named Harold, was running the London branch of the family's sausage casing business, and I didn't meet him for some time. (As a child, Margaret was embarrassed by the nature of her father's business; when asked about it she would say he made overcoats for little dogs!) Margaret's father was born in Germany but had emigrated to London where the family lived in Hampstead Heath when Margaret was born in 1911. Her older sister, Eleanor, was married to a creative dress designer named Sylvan Rich.

My parents met Margaret on several occasions. They liked her, and the feeling was mutual. I kept putting off their inevitable meeting with Florence, but when we decided to get married, it had to happen. Florence had something of the bearing and character of a grande dame. She had an unpleasant voice and was not especially winning or gracious, but I got along pretty well with her. My folks went to her apartment to meet her, and my father completely charmed her. After that, it was smooth sailing.

Margaret and I were engaged something less than a year and were married on June 20, 1940, at the Hotel Pierre in New York. Florence gave us a lovely wedding. It was a lively occasion with most of our friends on hand, and we hated to break away. It was not the happiest time to be wed. On that day France fell to the Nazis! It was also a hectic period at NRS, so we took off for a long weekend but deferred our honeymoon for a couple of months. We took a small apartment in a building owned by the Sailors' Snug Harbor on East 10th Street, near Wanamaker's store, Grace Church and Washington Square. Our first rental was $65 a month. In August, we bought a new Plymouth for $700 and drove to Mexico on our honeymoon. En route, we stopped in San Antonio where we visited a good friend, George Baumann. We crossed the border at Laredo and stopped again at Monterrey. We finally reached Mexico City and were typical tourists there, visiting Chapultepec, strolling on the Reforma, viewing the murals of Rivera, Orozco and others, and marveling at the exhibits in the great Museum of Anthropology. During our stay there was a bit of excitement—Trotsky was murdered! This was of particular interest to Margaret because at the outbreak of the Spanish Civil War, when she was in Spain, she was immediately sympathetic to the Loyalists but later withdrew her allegiance when she realized that their valiant cause was being subverted by Trotskyites.

We visited Cuernavaca and Taxco, where we bought a silver tea and coffee service, a wedding present from my Uncle Max and Aunt Lulu. We took a boat on the floating gardens of Xochimilco, saw the myriad churches of Puebla and the picturesque ruins of Teotihuacan. We then headed south for Oaxaca, much more Indian in character and not to be missed. The orthography was quaint: on the menu one day we found "salad-mixed, tossed and thrown" and also "dreaded veal chops." Our last excursion took us west through heavy jungle country to Orizaba. Before leaving its tropical charm, we bought a huge bouquet of gardenias from a roadside vendor and put it behind us in the car. Some miles from the city, I stopped the car and we looked at each other. The flowers were gorgeous, but their odor was completely cloying. By common consent, we threw them out the window, but their suffusing aroma stank up the car all the way back to Mexico City.

Margaret was extremely healthy and a fine athlete—she had played basketball and was a good swimmer and tennis player. But she developed a fever and had to stay in hospital some extra days after our second child Tommy was born in 1944. Later, in Geneva, she had a bout of hepatitis. She kept well until 1978 when she was astonished to find that she had ovarian cancer. We were in New York then, and she underwent treatment at Lenox Hill Hospital. She had a brief remission early in 1980, and was able to arrange for a SoHo showing of her art. When her condition worsened in the spring, and she told me she wanted to spend her last days in Leesburg. I drove her down and she held court for the weeks before her death. She even held a fashion show when she gave to our daughter Katie, daughter-in-law Lucky, niece Carla and a few intimates, including Trudy Brown, some of her clothing, jewelry and other prized possessions. There, with the devoted care of family and friends, and with the exceptional support provided by the Northern Virginia Hospice, she died peacefully at home on June 30, 1980. I was immeasurably saddened. We had shared so many experiences together. We were good friends as well as husband and wife. We were able to celebrate our 40th wedding anniversary ten days before she died. The children and a few good friends were with us on that poignant occasion.

In her last months, Margaret developed some interest and even belief in an afterlife. But she was philosophical about it. "If nothing happens," she said, "I won't know the difference anyway." We had a well-attended memorial service on Mount Gilead a few days after Margaret's death. My brother and sister came, as well as Margaret's siblings, and many friends were there to pay tribute. I have a tape of the proceedings.

ARTISTS I'VE KNOWN

Through Margaret, I met three of the outstanding figures in the art world of the 20th century. Two were Spaniards she had befriended during sojourns in Europe before we met. Jose de Creeft, with whom she had studied, achieved considerable success as a sculptor after his immigration to the United States. "Pepe," as he was called, did a sculptured head of Margaret which is in the collection of the Brooklyn Museum. Perhaps his best-known work is the large bronze statue depicting a number of the images in *Alice in Wonderland*. Children playing in Central Park near the East 72nd Street pond are frequently seen freely clambering over it. I remember Pepe as a small, wiry, witty and mercurial character. I possess a lovely olive wood sculpture of mother and child that he fashioned and a signed handmade greeting card he once sent to Margaret. Pepe lived from 1884 until 1982.

Margaret never studied with Esteban Vicente, but he and his wife were good friends until he died in 2001 at the age of 97. Esteban studied sculpture in Madrid but by 1928 abandoned it for painting. He had his first exhibition in Paris. He met Picasso there, but according to his *New York Times* obituary, "did not embrace the modern styles proliferating in the city." In 1936, Vicente relocated to New York where he established himself in a career that ended only with his death. I have two small paintings he did soon after his arrival in the U.S. One is of refugees from the Spanish Civil War; the second, in a lighter mood, is of a bacchanalia. It was hard scratch for Vicente in those first years in New York, but when he "arrived at abstraction after a prolonged process of trial and error in the late 1940s," he became extremely successful. The critic Harold Rosenberg described him as "one of the leaders in creating and disseminating" abstract expressionism. By then he was painting on large canvasses selling well into five figures. Vicente and his third wife, Harriet, lived in the Beaux Arts apartment on West 57th Street in New York, although many of his later paintings were produced at their home in the Hamptons. Several years ago I unearthed an oil painting of a bearded man among Margaret's early paintings. I thought it resembled Esteban and took it up to his studio. It was a portrait Margaret had done of him in the thirties, and he received it graciously. He also signed for me one of the small paintings which I brought up with me. Esteban was a large, genial fellow. Vera and I attended a number of the last exhibits of his work at the Berry-Hill Galleries in New York which represented him after 1989.

Vicente was a founding member of the New York Studio School in 1964. He also taught at Black Mountain College, Yale, Princeton, NYU and the University of California. His former students included Chuck Close and Susan Crile. In 1998, the Spanish Government honored him by opening the Esteban Vicente Museum of Contemporary Art in Segovia, where he was born. He and Harriet invited Vera and me to the inaugural ceremony but we were unable to travel at that time.

Margaret studied with Hans Hofmann both at the Art Students League in New York and in Provincetown. I met him in the summer of 1938, when we visited him and his wife in their colorful Provincetown house decorated with examples of his exuberant work. Born in Bavaria in 1886, Hofmann moved to Paris in 1904, but returned to Munich at the outbreak of World War I. He opened his own art school in 1915 which had an international flavor, attracting such American students as Louise Nevelson.

When I met him in Provincetown, Hofmann was known primarily as a teacher. Among his students were the painters Helen Frankenthaler, Lee Krasner, Larry Rivers and Red Grooms. Relatively few of his paintings were then on public display, except at the University of California at Berkeley where as early as 1931 his work was first exhibited. In 1934 a space for the regular presentation of art exhibitions on campus opened in a former steam-heating plant. Some thirty years later, Hofmann made possible the realization of President Clark Kerr's dream for a university art center by offering a gift of 47 paintings and a quarter of a million dollars on the condition that the university construct a proper art museum to house the collection. (After an irksome conflict with the Board of Trustees in the 60s, Kerr was asked to resign. A reporter asked him how he felt about that. "Oh!" he replied, "The same as when I came in—fired with enthusiasm!") The new museum was completed in 1970. By then Hofmann's paintings were in the collections of an increasing number of museums around the country. As stated by Peter Selz, Professor Emeritus at Berkeley, "Having absorbed the structural lessons of Cezanne and Cubism, Hofmann "loosens form to let color determine structure." The review of a June 2001 exhibit of his work in the *New York Observer* called him "Lovable Hans Hofmann." The reviewer wondered "whether we're likely to see a painter of similar stature—of similar optimism, ambition, and authority—in our own time." I vividly recall his sunny personality, the way he punctuated his rich German dialect with the word *"Niche?"* signifying, "Isn't that true?" and what has been called his "affirmation of the joy of existence."

My other contacts with artists have been casual. When I was interim President of the U.S. Committee for UNICEF in 1985, Keith Haring came to the office for the launch of first day stamp covers he had embellished with his characteristic figures. We talked for a bit about his work, and he very quickly tossed off a couple of small drawings I later framed with the stamp covers issued on that occasion. Haring, who started as a graffiti artist in the New York subways, was widely known by the late 1980s for his whimsical, innovative portrayal of babies and other creatures. In one of his diaries he said: "I am now 28 years old on the outside and nearly 12 years old on the inside. I always want to stay 12 years old on the inside." Tragically, he died of AIDS in 1990 at the age of 31.

I'll insert at this point several real-life incidents of serendipity relating to the arts. When my father died in 1945, my brother, sister and I divided his extensive library because my mother had no place for the books in the small apartment to which she moved. In my brother's lot was an illustrated edition of Tennyson's *Idylls of the King*. He didn't highly prize the volume, and as a birthday gift decided to present it to Lewis Landa, a friend of his and mine then teaching English at Princeton. A day or so later, Landa called to say he couldn't accept the gift—it was too valuable. It was illustrated by early photographs of the British photographer Julia Cameron; the Princeton library valued it at several thousand dollars. Herb convinced Lewis that they should split the proceeds.

Though divorced and remarried in 1950, Herb remained friendly with his first wife who had married an old family friend. In fact, he called Leo Frenkel his husband-in-law. The Frenkels had a number of paintings, including a work by a mediocre Dutch painter that Leo had inherited from his father. They didn't particularly like the dark painting and decided to sell it. They took it to Christie's without stipulating a price, but said they would like to keep the frame. A week or two later, Christie's called to say that that the painting might be by one of the Breughels and they were researching the matter. The Frenkels lived in some suspense until they finally got a call that it was confirmed as a Breughel. They traveled around the world on the proceeds—and they retrieved the frame!

The third incident relates to my friend Alexander Squadrilli, whom I first met when he was European Coordinator of the U.S. Displaced Persons Commission in Frankfurt after the war. Squad later became Representative in Egypt and

Director of Operations in the Gaza Strip for UNRWA, the United Nations Relief and Works Agency for Palestine Refugees. His father had been a restorer of paintings, and Squad knew something of the craft. While in Egypt, he met a Greek-Egyptian dealer named Aeschylus Stavridis who bought paintings in Europe to sell to well-to-do foreigners and affluent Egyptians. In anticipation of his eventual retirement from the UN, Squad had recently revived an interest dormant for thirty years in the collection, authentication, and restoration of old paintings. While visiting Stavrides, Squad eyed on the wall a large painting in poor condition which his host had acquired along with several others at an auction sale in Edinburgh in 1949. It was identified as a possible Claude Lorrain, but sold anonymously with no information as to its provenance or authenticity. Stavridis wanted $15,000 for it, which was far more than Squad was willing to pay, but he agreed to do what he could to arrest the deterioration for the painting's sake and without obligation. In the process, he uncovered strips of paper pasted on the edges of the canvas which came from a French Almanac of 1804/5, which confirmed his belief that the painting was, indeed, a Lorrain.

In 1965 Stavridis decided to move to Lebanon with his family and paintings. He informed Squad he was now willing to sell the painting for less, and they agreed on a price of $4,000. Two years passed without dramatic incident. Squad moved the painting to Gaza when he was put in charge of relief operations there; it was holding up well after its treatment. On June 5, 1967, the Israeli forces attacked Gaza, raking it by their artillery fire. Squad had put the Claude away in a closet protected by some walls, but he feared for its safety. When it was clear that Gaza would remain under Israeli military occupation for the indefinite future, he packed the Claude with other paintings, rugs and books and left them with a forwarding agent in Ashdod to await further instructions. After a family reunion in Rome (Renata, Squad's wife, was Italian), the family moved to an apartment in London's Eaton Square, and Squad pursued his efforts to authenticate the painting. I was then working at the American Embassy, and Squad kept me informed of his progress. He did trace the early provenance of the painting—it was twice sold at Christie's in 1812 and 1815 but had been out of sight for more than 120 years.

One day an elated Squad called me. Marcel Roethlisberger, Professor of Art History at the University of California at Los Angeles, and author in 1965 of the first catalogue raisonne on Claude Lorrain, after close examination of the photos Squad had sent him, proclaimed the painting a genuine Claude Lorrain.

The word got around London, and many came to see the Claude. The possession of so valuable a property became a preoccupation. Insurers required that Squad's home never be left unattended by an adult. So the Squadrillis had to have "Claude sitters" when they were out of the house. We and other friends were occasionally called on to provide this service. The painting was on loan to the Arts Council of Great Britain for a Claude Exhibition in 1969, after which it was left on loan with the Ashmolean Museum in Oxford for four years. During this time, Squad moved to a new assignment in Geneva, but he kept negotiating with several interested museums. It was finally sold to the Houston Museum of Fine Arts in February 1973 for $135,000. Philippe de Montebello, who later became Director of New York's Metropolitan Museum of Art, considered this pastoral landscape the most important purchase he made for the Houston Museum. The title of the painting is *Pastoral Landscape with a Rock Arch and a River* and it was painted circa 1630. An oil on canvas, it's 37 1/2 by 52 1/2 inches.

Margaret did a fair number of representational watercolors, pastels and oil paintings, but she was essentially an abstract expressionist, and that's what she was pursuing as Hofmann's pupil. In our 40 years together she exhibited her works in Washington, Virginia, New York and Europe, and sold quite a few paintings. A most successful exhibit and sale was held in SoHo a few months before she died in 1980. She contributed a lot to my interest and knowledge of art, building on a foundation which Herb and Mimi had initiated. One of our friends in Washington was Eleanor Ullman, the niece of Etta and Clarabell Cone who in the 1940s lived in a Baltimore apartment. One day Eleanor took us there to meet the sisters and view the fabulous collection of French paintings they had acquired during their years in Paris with Gertrude Stein. These precious works are now properly on display at the Baltimore Museum of Art, but when I saw them they filled every nook and cranny of the Cone apartment, including the bathroom. Etta took me around to see the wonders. As we walked into a room containing several Ingres and Seurat paintings she asked if I was interested in the works of these two artists. I got off an inspired reply, "More in Seurat than in Ingres."

Margaret and I collected naive paintings. Before we were married, we ventured into Bucks County, Pennsylvania, to purchase a few examples and some old furniture. Once, in a junk shop, we spied a painting on glass of the sinking of the Titanic, and bought it, though it was cracked. Some years later we showed it to Selden Rodman, the critic and writer. He fell in love with it and in a swap gave us the choice of one of his fine, early Haitian paintings. The *Masonic Funeral* by Seneque Obin is one of our prized possessions. Vera developed her own enthusiasm for primitives and we continued to pick up a few in our travels.

When we moved to California, Vera began painting again after a thirty-year hiatus and has been turning out some very creditable seascapes and other acrylic works. My stepdaughter Vivian Barad, from her earliest years, exhibited an unusual skill in all forms of visual expression. She is on her way to a career as an industrial designer. My daughter Katie has also produced some quite attractive watercolors. Two of my grandchildren have shown marked artistic talent. Theo is currently studying printmaking at the University of Utrecht in the Netherlands.

KATHARINE

The birth of our first child, Katharine, on August 27, 1941, brought much joy to Margaret and me. She was healthy and beautiful. Her birth occasioned a certain amount of celebration on the part of our friends. I had written an acrostic verse for the birth of Bracken Charles O'Neill, son of my Dartmouth friend Charlie O'Neill:

FOR BRACKEN

Bonaparte conquered the world in his folly;
Rasputin bedeviled the Russian Czarina;
Abdul Amir was a stranger to fear;
Cellini wooed many a sleek signorina;
Krupp is a character easy to blacken;
Edward of England stepped down for his Wally.
None of these guys is the size of young **BRACKEN**.

Child of sweet Constance and sapient Chas,
Here's to your triumphs in life's grim arena.
Artisan, baker or petticoat-maker,
Resist aggression and scarletina!
Live with a scantling of snafu and snarls,
Enjoy the new grass and the amorous lass,
Savor good wine like your genitor **CHARLES**.

O'er all that's worthy set your seal.
Notch your gun, but shun the subpoena.
Ease your climb with a ready spiel;
Interest yourself in the concertina.
Lend your back to the commonweal.
Luck to you, Bracken Charles **O'NEILL**.

By way of retaliation Charlie wrote a charming ode wishing "all milk and silk and tickled toes for Katie Marks, the 8 pound rose." I was less charmed by the visit of another college friend, Ping Ferry, also a new father. He took one look at my child and said, "You should see *my* baby!"

After Katie was born, we moved to a slightly larger apartment in the same building for $75 a month. We had the part time help of a pleasant, efficient woman named Dora Jones. Dora received a good many phone calls and occasionally absented herself to attend "meetings." We learned that Dora in her other life was quite a personage. To wit, she was the General Secretary of the Domestic Workers Union. We liked and respected Dora. She adored Katie, and her union responsibilities rarely interfered with her work for us. We once attended a gala reception in Harlem given by the union in her honor.

Katie was two when we moved to Washington, and lived there until she was six. Katie was an enchanting child with an early, original turn of mind. She quickly became friends with the Ryan children who lived opposite the house we rented on McKinley Street. Mrs. Ryan once asked Katie if she went to synagogue. "Oh, no," Kate replied. "We're not fancy Jews." On her way to school, Katie went by a church with a statue depicting Jesus extended on the cross. Passing it, she said, "Look, that girl's doing a swan dive." One day at age three or four, Katie was missing. Margaret was frantic until she received a call from a woman who had met Katie on a bus leaving Chevy Chase Circle. She apparently wished to explore the town, had walked to the Circle, and boarded the bus, quite alone.

We flew to Europe when Katie was six, and spent the next six years in Geneva and Athens. On our return to the United States, Katie resumed her schooling in the Westchester public schools.

After graduating from Mamaroneck High in Westchester, Katie spent a couple of years at the University of Wisconsin, and her junior year abroad in Geneva, but when we returned for a second incarnation in Washington, she decided to live at home and finish her degree at George Washington University. She then went to Berkeley and earned an M.S.W. at the University of California. She was there during the contagious sixties, and it profoundly affected her life. She became a proficient therapist but was strongly influenced by the prevailing drift toward an alternative lifestyle. She calls herself "an expressive arts therapist," gives workshops on meditation, womanpower, and how to overcome stress. She believes that freeing the voice can help people heal the body. Her book *Circle of Song,* a collection of ritual music and chants gathered from many parts of the world, is in its third edition. Earlier in New York, Katie had expressed her interest in dance by organizing several free range "dance jams."

Kate has enjoyed being a wanderer most of her adult life. At different times she has lived in Europe, Asia, Hawaii, Colorado and California. In recent years she has bought a home and lived in Amherst, Massachusetts. She's been an attentive daughter, always checking in by telephone and visiting us as she moves about the country.

LEESBURG

In 1962 I had just returned to Washington to work for USAID, and we wanted a weekend place. My friend Helen Wilson spotted an ad in the Georgetown paper offering a house for sale on Mount Gilead, Leesburg VA. We fell in love with the place at once, and bought it for $20,000 from a retired Navy Captain. He and his wife were sad to relinquish it, but had reached a time in life when this seemed imperative.

The structure we bought was a log cabin built in 1763, supplemented by a stucco/stone addition some years later. It included a kitchen/dining room, small living room, two bedrooms upstairs and a bath and a half. The house was supported on huge beams with a crude basement underneath. The log room had been a school house in the Colonial era and then a small church, before it became a residence. The logs were incised with Roman numerals from I to X. We think the original log structure was moved from another location and reassembled at the present site.

When I went to London for a two-year tour in 1966, I rented the house to a friend. One day I was surprised to find a letter from Captain Swanson, the former owner, entreating me to sell the house back to him, his health and circumstances having improved. I regretfully declined to do so.

During our Leesburg years, the area became quite a center for artists. Margaret worked fairly steadily and sold quite a number of her paintings. Alfred and June McAdams, our nearest neighbors, both painted professionally; Dagmar Wilson, whose house adjoined the McAdams', had considerable success with her literal landscapes. Dagmar was also a political activist, having founded Women Strike for Peace in her previous Georgetown era. Bob and Ruth Sivard, whom I first met in Geneva in the late forties, sought to buy my house after they rented it. I didn't want to part with it, but sold them adjoining land on which they built a house. Bob was an asset to the growing Mount Gilead art colony. He painted extensively in France and the U.S. I especially prize a Sivard I own that depicts a nun rising from the Paris Metro. Her wimple in its outline resembles the frame of the Metro's art deco subway entrance.

I well remember the Mount Gilead Art Show that took place one Saturday and Sunday in the early sixties. It was well publicized in the *Loudoun Times Mirror* and hordes of visitors toured the display of paintings, pottery and other objets d'art in the Marks, Wilson, McAdams and Sivard homes. Parking was a horrendous problem, but the venture resulted in brisk sales.

Margaret and I added a downstairs art studio, bedroom and bathroom and a swimming pool to the house. Several years after her death my son acquired the place and subsequently added a large room and kitchen that greatly enhanced its value. Looking west from the house one has a spectacular view of the Loudoun Valley and the Blue Ridge Mountains.

THE FOURTH REICH

The victims of Hitler found few doors open to them in the years prior to World War II. The St. Louis, a mercy ship freighted with refugee cargo was turned away at Cuban, U.S. and other ports. At an international conference held at Evian, France, in 1938 only one country offered hope of refuge for a small number. With an eye to the economic development of his island, President Trujillo, in an unaccustomed gesture, offered a haven for several hundred Jewish refugees at Sosua in the Dominican Republic. It is a tough jungle area for only the most rugged settlers, but this doesn't discourage a white-bearded patriarch in a temporary refugee camp in Europe who is keen to make a fresh start. "You're in your seventies, Grandpa," he is told by the worker for the American Jewish Joint Distribution Committee, "too old to make it as a pioneer."

"I'm going" he replies, "I'm tough. I'll work hard."

"But the heat," they tell him. "You'll never stand it. It's 110 degrees in the shade."

"So I won't go in the shade," is the undaunted reply.

Many refugees craved immigration to the United States, but under our rigid quota laws only limited numbers with close relatives or other claims to preference were able to qualify. In that era, there was no special legislation for refugee admissions. Those who came had to fit under the prevailing national origins quotas. Fortunately the quota for German-born was relatively high and not fully utilized so that German Jews could fit under it if they had the requisite sponsorship. Actually, only 4000 of the 13,000 people who entered the U.S. under the German quota in the fiscal year 1941 left directly from Germany; the majority came from transit countries, such as Portugal and France.

There were no schemes for mass resettlement of refugees. The U.S. Government gave visas, one by one, to refugees presented by the religious and nonsectarian voluntary agencies. If there was a close relative, potential employer or other logical sponsor, that person was called upon to provide an affidavit of support. If the applicant had no natural sponsor, the agency obtained an affidavit through one of its local affiliates. The affidavit guaranteed that the refugee would be employed, or have other means of support, that he would be housed, and, most important, that he would not become a public charge. In soliciting affidavits from its affiliated groups, the agency agreed to take over the responsibility for the family if the sponsorship broke down.

While covering the news of the New York's social agencies for the Welfare Council's *Better Times* I decided to do a story on the refugees leaving Europe for the U.S.A. William Haber, Executive Director of the National Refugee Service (NRS), liked the story and offered me a job at NRS.

The NRS was an amalgamation of a number of organizations helping the reception and placement in the U.S. of refugees escaping from Hitler's Germany before and as a result of World War II. They were mostly Jewish refugees, so the principal agencies involved were the Hebrew Immigrant Aid Society (HIAS) and the National Council of Jewish Women. HIAS, established in the late 19th century, had helped thousands of Jewish immigrants to enter the U.S. Now it was working closely with the American Jewish Joint Distribution Committee (AJDC) whose efforts brought to safety victims of the Nazis in all parts of Europe and some who had fled to China.

The NRS shared the premises at 165 West 46th Street with smaller agencies assisting Catholic and Protestant emigres, of whom there was a liberal sprinkling, especially in mixed marriages. The Quakers also played a helpful role in the integration of the newcomers as did committees set up to meet the special needs of doctors, musicians, lawyers and other professionals. The refugees founded their own organization, known as Self-Help, which also gave assistance within its limited resources.

Haber, a dynamic, assertive Professor of Economics at the University of Michigan, was brought in early in 1939 to become the executive director of the NRS. (Vintage Michigan alumni recall his famous course at Ann Arbor, dubbed "Haber's Labor"). He had been at NRS only a few months when he hired me in June of 1939 to direct the Division of Social and Cultural Adjustment. At NRS I met Henry J. Kellermann, who was to become a lifelong friend. A refugee from Germany, Heinz (as I first knew him) served his adopted country most capably in a number of posts. The son of a rabbi, Henry first came to Baltimore where he met his future wife, Mignon Pauli, in the home of Rabbi Lazeron. I met him two years later, in 1939, when I was brought in to supervise him as acting Director of the Division of Social and Cultural Adjustment. It could have been an awkward situation but it all worked out. We cooperated amicably on the job and became close friends. Henry died a few years ago, but I remain in touch with his widow. I'm the godfather of one of his sons and have always been a friend and admirer of his daughter, Susan. Mignon, now 97, lives in Maryland.

At the outset of the war, when I was in Washington, Henry sought to enter government service and I referred him to my friend, Jerry Spingarn, through whom he landed a job with the Office of Strategic Services (OSS). This led after the war to a distinguished career. Henry made an important contribution to the post-war reeducation of Germany, first serving as an aide to General Lucius Clay, then working with Adenauer and others to promote the reeducation of

German youth. He was also on the delegation of U.S. specialists at the Nuremberg trials. Kellermann then carried out several key assignments as a State Department official, beginning with service in Paris as U.S. Representative to UNESCO (later an Ambassadorial post). This was followed by more than five years as deputy chief of mission and Charge d'Affaires of the U.S. Embassy in Berne, Switzerland. His final service with State was as the first Environmental Officer. In the course of his effective career he received a State Department Superior Award. After his retirement from the government, Henry taught classes on the environment and other subjects at Georgetown University.

Kellermann was one of the last Jews to receive a law degree from Humboldt University in his native Berlin. In 1989 Vera and I joined him and Mignon there when he was given a deferred Golden Diploma from the University Law School. On this occasion we listened to him lecture in German to the students on the accomplishments of the Weimar Republic, a different Germany of which they were largely unaware. The wall had just come down and we were thrilled to tour East Berlin and see through his eyes the way he remembered it. A warm friend for 60 years, Dr. Kellermann exemplified in an outstanding way the vital contribution an exile can make to his new country.

In our division at NRS we referred the refugees to English classes, housing possibilities and other community resources. We were in constant touch with scores of voluntary organizations offering free or low cost services for the newcomers. Ability to speak some English was a prime requisite. The early refugees were mainly business and professional people with a higher degree of education who knew some English and were generally able to bring out some money. The more resourceful ones got out first. Later arrivals were less well prepared for life in a new country, and due to severe, restrictive laws passed in Germany in 1938, had to leave with less resources. But as virtually all were literate, it was essential to find ways to teach English as a second language to the educated foreigner. This became known as ESL.

At first, the refugees were enrolled in classes throughout the city offered by the Works Progress Administration, but in 1939 the Government suspended the WPA classes. We had to find alternative instruction, especially for groups such as emigre doctors who needed English to pass Board examinations permitting them to practice in the U.S. Ministers could preach, professors could teach only if they knew or learned English. Musicians were the luckiest, as they spoke a lingua franca. For lawyers the path was more arduous—the whole basis of European law is different from ours. In general, it was best to train them for business, accounting or tax work.

Fortunately many settlement houses, agencies, temples, clubs and individual volunteers rose to the challenge. We even arranged for volunteer-taught English classes at the NRS office. In addition to English classes, we sought free or low-cost resources to meet a variety of requests from the 50 or 60 emigres who came to the office daily. They sought housing, day and nursery care for their children, information about recreational resources, where to swim, hike or fish, meet friends, find free or cheap camp vacations for their children, enroll for vocational training, obtain seats in temples for the High Holy Days, and how to meet other emigre needs. Our services supplemented the case work administered by social workers assisting the newcomers, many of whom experienced trauma in their flight.

We relied heavily on volunteers to help our limited staff. In 1940, NRS had 56 volunteers on its rolls, some working in the office handling referrals and clerical work, and others on call for special assignments. One volunteer got free tickets for emigres to attend lectures, film shows and theatrical performances. The voluntary services of a pharmacist were enlisted to give a course in pharmaceutical terminology so that European pharmacists could brush up on American lingo and doctors could acquire a knowledge of these needed terms. Volunteers greatly assisted in the evaluation of musicians, though we found there were restrictions on the numbers taken into the union.

In the late 19th century's floodtide of immigration, the agencies then assisting Jewish immigrants arranged for many of them to arrive by ship directly to Galveston and other ports far from New York. NRS similarly sought in various ways to encourage dispersal to the hinterlands of as many as possible of those docking in Manhattan. Local committees were exhorted to step up their sponsorships. If a specific job could be offered, so much the better, but when this was not feasible, refugees were encouraged to accept "community invitations." This meant guaranteed support for those who ventured forth until the breadwinner, with local assistance, was able to find employment.

New York as the first port of asylum still attracted the vast majority. To avoid the formation of new ghettoes, we urged the newcomers to "go west" where they would find more *lebensraum*, more chances for successful adaptation. The Quakers helped by providing temporary shelter in hostels they established in Indiana, Iowa and elsewhere in the Midwest.

Our division at NRS informed new arrivals in New York of the wonders of other localities. We maintained a library of economic and social data about communities in all parts of the United States. We organized a "This is America" daily showing of films and slides. At that time I had never been west of Albany, but I was soon able to describe with rising conviction the glories of the American West and South. In a number of cases where refugees with no connection in New York or valid reason to stay there turned down an offer of sponsorship in another city, the agency went to the extreme of denying relief in New York. This hard-nosed policy usually had the desired effect, though some families decided to stay in New York regardless. "Relief" in this sense was temporary support provided by the private agency. At that time it was a condition of the refugees' immigration to the U.S. that none should become a charge on public welfare. Though the sanction was seldom invoked, aliens receiving public funds were subject to deportation.

Many refugees had family connections and other valid reasons to settle in New York and of those who headed elsewhere a certain number found their way back to the Big City.

How to convince a new refugee that Omaha offered a better prospect for living than Washington Heights or the West Bronx? The best way was to avoid the issue by having the family proceed immediately from dockside to an Omaha, Chicago or Atlanta train, without lingering in New York. If the family stopped over in New York, even for a few days to break the journey, it was often fatal. It was partly the allure of the big town, partly the comforting presence of other refugees. In New York the refugees lived in the same neighborhoods, formed or re-established their own clubs and societies and read the same newspaper, a weekly in the German language called *Aufbau* (meaning "reconstruction") which was launched by an enterprising emigre journalist. *Aufbau* chronicled the lives of the new arrivals and carried the advertising of merchants and services catering to their needs. So many refugees clustered in Washington Heights that people began calling that area of Manhattan "The Fourth Reich."

We had our best results with refugees who were just off the boat, had no anchor relatives in New York, and had not yet been sucked into the vortex of the Fourth Reich. Once they became even partly acclimated, despite the offer of incentives, it was difficult to dislodge them.

We argued, with some effect, that a draftsman, accountant or piano teacher would find a warmer welcome, better housing and more meaningful employment in another setting. We maintained contact with federations of Jewish social agencies, synagogues and even families offering homes, jobs and community facilities in Cleveland, Atlanta, Seattle and other American cities, and informed the newcomers of such opportunities. We passed on success stories of refugees who had "made it" in Kansas City, Denver and Duluth.

The general economic situation was somewhat better, but traces of the Depression remained. We had to contend with a certain amount of anti-refugee feeling. The humanitarian argument was probably our best line of defense, but our interpretation of the program also included the following:

1. The actual number of immigrants arriving in the 1931-40 decade was small, in fact the smallest number (526,000) admitted to the U.S. in more than a century. The immigration quota for Germans was filled for the first time in 1939.

2. The refugee flow affected all faiths, creeds, and an increasing number of nationalities.

3. Most of the newcomers were rapidly finding adjustment in the United States. Some were even successful in establishing new businesses. NRS made a survey of refugee enterprises in 1939. In over 300 businesses responding to the questionnaire over 70% of the 3700 employees were American citizens.

4. Refugees were enriching our cultural and scientific life. The roster of distinguished arrivals included Albert Einstein, Thomas Mann, Kurt Weill, James Franck, Bela Bartok, Enrico Fermi, Walter Gropius, Lion Feuchtwanger and Louise Rainer.

Some of the professional people, entrepreneurs and educated white collar workers found it difficult to adjust to a more demeaning job and less pocket money. Inevitably a reaction set in, the *bei uns* syndrome, a comparison of their former opulence with their present reduced state. American relatives and friends soon tired of accounts of how wonderful everything was *bei uns* in the old country. There was the story of the refugee's poodle. Back in Germany he was a Great Dane! The refugees commiserated with each other. One complained to another at the lack of attention he was getting. "I'm surprised to hear you say that," said the other, "people are very attentive. They take you out to dinner, buy you fancy clothes, find you a good job, install you in a nice apartment." Exclaimed the first refugee, incredulous, "This happened to YOU?" Slight pause. "No, not to ME. To my sister."

One of the agencies promoting the refugee cause was the Central Good Neighbor Committee. It was headed by Dr. John Lovejoy Elliott, then Leader of the Ethical Culture Society, and Eleanor Roosevelt was one of the members. In 1941, she invited us to Hyde Park. I wrote to my folks at the time: "Spent a pleasant day at Hyde Park. Perhaps you saw the *New York Times* picture of Mrs. Roosevelt dishing out hot dogs. It rained during the morning, so that the meeting and lunch were held not outside her cottage, as anticipated, but right in the big Hyde Park home itself. Mrs. R. served all of the guests, and, we understand, even buttered the hot dog rolls herself!"

Having a considerable interest in the stage, Margaret and I entertained some of the theater people and did our best to make contacts for them. We were especially drawn to a middle-aged Viennese actress named Lilia Skala, who had had a successful career in her own country. Her charm and talent prevailed, and after several Broadway engagements she went to Hollywood and got more important roles. She was nominated for an Oscar as Best Supporting Actress for the Mother Superior in *Lilies of the Field*. In was in this picture that Sidney Poitier won the first Oscar for a leading man ever awarded to an African-American. Lilia later played in *Roseland, House of Games* and as late as 1991, at the age of 94, in *Men of Respect*. I kept in touch with Lilia over the years. She and her husband lived modestly in Queens and we dined in their home.

There was a good deal of political ferment among the NRS staff in those days. It was before the 1941 Nazi-Soviet pact, and quite a few staffers had pro-Soviet sympathies. Some of this carried over to the Social Service Employees Union. I joined SSEU but took no active part in it.

After Pearl Harbor there was an immediate slackening of refugee arrivals. Psychologically, too, there was a change at NRS. The work continued, but it had a new complexion. I became restless and sought a job more closely related to the war effort. Some of my friends had enlisted; others were drawn into war mobilization efforts. America's entrance to the war brought other complications. Refugees from Europe were subject to a bewildering barrage of government regulations affecting enemy aliens. Example: a militant antifascist emigre was hired to broadcast twice a week from New York over the short-wave to Europe. But because enemy aliens were not permitted to have short-wave radios, his wife was unable to listen to his broadcasts.

Early in 1942 I spoke to Bill Haber and found him sympathetic to my desire for a change. There was agitation on the West Coast to evacuate persons of Japanese ancestry, despite the fact that two-thirds of them were American citizens. The Hearst and McClatchy newspapers were sowing suspicion and distrust. Many citizens were envious of the prosperity of Japanese-American farmers and entrepreneurs. It was rumored that a Japanese submarine had been sighted near a California shore. Lt. General DeWitt, commandant of the Presidio, recommended the evacuation of the Japanese-Americans from the West Coast, and the Pentagon issued orders to round up 110,000 living in California, Oregon and Washington. They were herded into temporary assembly centers including the Tanforan and Santa Anita Race Tracks. The plan was to move them all inland to relocation centers where they would be confined until the war's end. A civilian agency, the War Relocation Authority, was created in March 1942 to manage the centers.

Milton Eisenhower, Ike's younger brother, who was Coordinator of Land Use in the Department of Agriculture, was selected to run the new agency. Haber knew Eisenhower and agreed to give me an introduction to him. He interviewed me and I got the job. Margaret and I set out for Washington and a new life. We left New York in February of 1942, little knowing that it would be more than a decade before we would again reside in the States, and 34 years would pass before we'd return to Manhattan.

RELOCATION OF JAPANESE-AMERICANS— WRA'S ROLE

In the early months of World War II, largely as the result of hysteria and hostility, nearly 120,000 persons of Japanese ancestry, of whom two-thirds were native-born American citizens, were summarily evacuated from the three West Coast states in an unprecedented military mass exclusion order. They were first herded by the Army into racetracks, fairgrounds and other temporary assembly centers, then moved inland to ten barracks cities known as relocation centers hastily erected by Army Engineers. The job of administering the program was handed to a newly created civilian agency, the War Relocation Authority (WRA), and Milton Eisenhower, Ike's younger brother, was named its first director. I joined the Washington staff of WRA in April 1942, and assisted in drafting the first policy statement for management of the centers.

The task we were called on to accomplish was controversial and complex. On the one hand we would be attacked for being "too soft on Japs." On the other hand, there were Americans, and not just in the Civil Liberties Union, who believed that a great wrong had been done by the mass incarceration, without trial, of a large group of U.S. citizens. I'll always remember a letter that was sent to my boss not long after he had been given the assignment. "Well, Milton," read the letter, "they certainly have handed you a poker that is cherry red with heat!"

I was fortunate to get in near the beginning. This happened to me several times in my working life and I savored the fresh impetus of a new program. Some of this is reflected in a letter I wrote to my folks on May 7, 1942: "Mr. Eisenhower is back and things are beginning to hum at the War Relocation Authority. I talked to him briefly today just after the Governor of Arkansas had left his office, and he asked me to attend the first staff conference on policy—which will be this Saturday afternoon beginning at 2 pm and should be very interesting. In addition to the specific short-term job that the Authority is doing in resettling 120,000 Japanese in new homes and finding them work, there are certain long-term aspects of planning that appeal to me very much. It is community planning from the ground up, since the Authority will be managing ten new cities built out of raw land—each with a population of 10,000 to 20,000- and must plan every detail in connection with them—work, education, health, recreation, housing, community self government and so on. Although these relocation centers will be under military guard—for the protection of the Japanese, as much as for anything else—they will not be "concentration camps" in any way, shape or form. They will be an American answer to what has unfortunately become a wartime necessary."

I knew nothing of the Japanese-Americans before I took the job with WRA. I had never even been on the West Coast. I learned that a Japanese-American family generally consisted of an Issei (first generation) father, his considerably younger wife, whom he had sent for, probably as a "picture" bride, and their Nisei (second generation) children. The Issei parents, despite long residence in the United States, were aliens because our laws at that time excluded them (and many other Asians) from becoming American citizens. The Nisei were U.S. citizens and proud of it. Many of the young men had sought to join the United States Army. Nisei in Honolulu, Chicago and New York were accepted. A combat team recruited in Hawaii became a highly decorated unit. Nisei from the West Coast states were detained at the relocation centers. They were not subject to the draft and only much later in the war were permitted to enlist.

Early in 1942 Army trucks rounded up Japanese ethnic families in the three states and bore them off to the assembly centers. These were administered by the Wartime Civil Control Administration (WCCA), a branch of the military charged with carrying out the first phase of the evacuation program. Many evacuees had to leave their homes on very short notice, and were permitted to take with them only a hand-carried suitcase or two. Like vultures, some opportunists approached Japanese whose names they had looked up in the telephone book in quest of property the evacuees might be willing to sell at sacrifice prices. Many in the panic of the moment sustained huge losses in the sale of homes, stores, farms and other worldly goods. In August 1942, the Farm Security Administration turned over to WRA's Evacuee Property Division 6,644 pieces of agricultural property totaling 258,000 acres, with an evaluation of more than $100 million. The Federal Reserve Bank turned over 5,300 pieces of commercial property and residences worth over $100 million, including 413 hotels in San Francisco, Portland and Seattle. These and other properties— everything from apartment houses to curio shops—were to be managed by that Division and returned to the evacuees at war's end.

Norman Y. Mineta, a former member of Congress and George W. Bush's Secretary of Transportation, was among the evacuees. His father lost his insurance business in San Jose. He recalled the evacuation experience in later years: "It was the 29th of May, and I was wearing my Cub Scout uniform. My friends from the troop came down to see me off." Other Californians were not so considerate. One suggested that a response to the question: "Any known physical defects?" should be merely: "Just tell them you're a Jap." Another commented: "We've won the war as far as California is concerned—we got rid of the Japs." Galen M. Fisher of the Institute of Foreign Relations, in an article titled *Japanese Evacuation from the Pacific Coast* published June 29, 1942, said "People who have never known a Japanese are advocating that they all be kept in concentration camps and in no case be allowed to settle, even temporarily, in their communities. Evidence of this attitude has appeared not only in the press but also in the signed statements of all but one of the fifteen western state governors to the Tolan Congressional Committee." The exception was Governor Ralph L. Carr of Colorado. Governor Chase Clark of Idaho was quoted as follows in the newspaper report of a speech he made May 22, 1942: "A good solution to the Jap problem in Idaho—and the Nation—would be to send them all back to Japan, then sink the island. They live like rats, breed like rats and act like rats. We don't want them buying or leasing land and becoming permanently located in our State."

Conditions in the tar-papered barrack rooms of the assembly centers were minimal. Each room housed a family. Privacy was practically impossible and furnishings were minimum. Eating and bathing were in mass facilities. The evacuees were generally submissive, though one night 1,200 walked out of the mess hall at the Santa Anita racetrack assembly center when sauerkraut was served to them. Quoted in the newspaper was a crack that "the only race at Santa Anita these days is the Japs."

Several months passed before the evacuees were moved to the ten relocation centers erected by the Corps of Engineers. From the standpoint of amenities, they were no great improvement over the assembly centers. Each family had a room that was 20 by 24 feet. Children missed school for a few months, but were in classrooms by fall. WRA was interested in sites "which had possibilities for extensive agricultural development or for year-round employment opportunities of other types." The Army insisted that all sites be located "at a safe distance" from strategic installations. In the end, most were constructed on Federal land, two in Arizona on unused portions of Indian reservations. One in southeastern Colorado was on privately owned land purchased by the Army. And Manzanar, near Death Valley, was on land controlled by the City of Los Angeles as protection for its municipal water supply.

By the summer of 1942, approximately 33,000 out of 86,000 people then in residence at the centers were employed at $12 a month for unskilled labor and those undergoing vocational training; $16 a month for skilled labor and the more responsible clerical and community service jobs, and $19 a month for highly skilled and professional employees. In addition, cash allowances ranging from $1.50 to $4.75 a month were provided to cover the cost of clothing for each employed evacuee and each of his or her dependents. My salary then was about $500 a month, a little better than what I got at NRS but it was a low federal grade.

In the early phase of WRA's stewardship I visited all ten of the centers which were located inland in California (2), Arizona (2), Arkansas (2), and Colorado, Idaho, Utah and Wyoming (one each). The average center population was 10,000 but Poston, on an Arizona Indian reservation, had 20,000 inhabitants. My job was to develop a community activities program with American voluntary and religious agencies that was intended to provide the evacuees, cut off as they were, some continuing access and relation to American institutions and pursuits. We found a ready response from most church groups and such voluntary bodies as the Boy and Girl Scouts, YMCA and YWCA, Future Farmers of America, National Parents and Teachers Association, American Association of University Women, Rotary, Kiwanis and the Lions, etc. Some organizations established congregations and chapters or branches at the centers. However we soon recognized that at best, life at a relocation center was no substitute for normal existence and at worst could be a discouraging and debilitating experience. The centers were fenced by barbed wire, the exterior guarded by the Army, but there was no charge against any of the individuals living within. While the centers were managed by a civilian agency, to the evacuees living behind the fence it must have seemed very little different from internment.

Paradoxically, center life both strengthened and weakened relationships between parents and children. The fact that the evacuees lived a family to a room threw together the first and second generations and in some cases had a "Japanizing" effect on families well on their way toward assimilation in the American community. There was even some lessening of the ability of some of the young people to speak correct English. On the other hand, congregate living and the breakdown of normal household arrangements tended to diminish the respect of children for their parents. Children were quick to sense the demoralization affecting many families. Work habits were allowed to slip. The communities were artificial. There were schools, hospitals, police stations, recreational facilities, scout troops and churches, but it was distinctly not a setting in which to bring up children.

My boss in the Division of Community Management was John Provinse. A native of Red Lodge, Montana, he had received his Ph.D. in Anthropology from the University of Chicago and taught at the University of Arizona before joining the Dept. of Agriculture as a specialist in rural development. Milton Eisenhower brought him over into WRA, where he and John Embree, who headed Community Analysis, stressed the importance of interpreting the actions of the evacuees in the light of their culture and experience. This at times irritated the center directors more likely to think in terms of engineering, agriculture and administration. John was a unique combination of a freethinking westerner and a thoroughgoing academic. He was an ideal boss—someone I could look up to. He was thoughtful, immensely perceptive, soft spoken and gentle in manner. He counseled me to continue my studies and earn a Ph. D. Sometimes I regret not having taken his advice. After he left WRA, John became Assistant Commissioner for American Indian Affairs.

The evacuees produced most of the food consumed at the relocation centers, staffed the schools and clinics and took care of internal security. Considering the provocation, the behavior of most residents was exemplary. The Japanese-

Americans are enterprising and creative people. They made the desert bloom with the works of art they fashioned from crude local materials. A book by Allen Eaton titled *Beauty Behind Barbed Wire* is a testimony to this. Poignant images of daily life at the centers were captured by Mine Okube, a talented Nisei, in *#13660*, a book illustrating her years at the Topaz Relocation Center in the Utah desert.

WRA took seriously its responsibility for the welfare of the Japanese-Americans. It made a real effort to administer the centers fairly and provide community services to meet essential needs. But the residents, living in crude, ill-furnished barracks cities under military guard, were far from content. As Carey McWilliams put it in his carefully documented book *Prejudice— Japanese-Americans, Symbol of Racial Intolerance* "they were compelled to live in semi-communal fashion under the most exasperating conditions. Facilities were primitive; overcrowding was common; and the enforced intimacy created literally limitless possibilities for friction and irritation." McWilliams quotes from several of the evacuees. Hanna Kozasa said: "The shock that we sustained, and the bitterness that overwhelmed us was most trying. The barbed wire fences, the armed sentries, the observation towers, increased our sense of frustration to the point that many have not been able to regain a proper perspective. The most alarming aspect of life in the centers is the demoralization it is working on the people. It is sapping their initiative in a frightening manner."

Frank Watanabe said: "The most terrible factor concerning camp life is the havoc this uneasy, restricted and enclosed life is working upon the young people's character and personality. Many of the youngsters are growing up in this environment knowing very little about the outside."

Franklyn Sugiyama put it most dramatically when he said: "In the relocation centers, the people are like fish dynamited—they are helplessly stunned, floating belly up on the stream of life."

The low wages paid for community service and agricultural work were another source of discontent. Shortly after WRA had assumed administrative control of the centers, in the fall of 1942, problems arose at Poston and Manzanar. At Poston, the evacuees went on strike for ten days, and the following month a riot occurred at Manzanar. The Community Analyst at Poston was Lt. Commander Alexander H. Leighton, an MD and anthropologist, who believed from the outset that social anthropology should be an integral feature of the administrative process. In such crises as the Poston strike he counseled understanding and restraint in dealing with individuals under stress. In his book *The Governing of Men*, based on his Poston experience, Leighton makes the following recommendations:

"Consider aggression as a human reaction to circumstances, not merely as innate cussedness, the work of evil men, or a racial peculiarity.

"Recognize rumors, suspicions, scapegoat tendencies, gang activities and crime increase as symptoms of aggression arising out of stress.

"Never make threats or pass laws that cannot be enforced; there is no quicker way to undermine the power of an administration."

Leighton attributes the title of his book to words uttered by Danton before his execution: "Oh, it were better to be a poor fisherman that to meddle with the governing of men."

After three months at WRA, Milton Eisenhower was drafted by Elmer Davis to be his deputy at the Office of War Information. Dillon S. Myer, who began his career as a County Agricultural Agent in Ohio, came to the WRA job from the Department of Agriculture where he headed the Soil Conservation Service. A tall, kindly man, Dillon was a great educator and a gifted leader. The heart of his work lay in trying to conserve—in soil conservation and in human conservation. Dillon immediately saw the importance of having the nation recognize that the Japanese-Americans were as much American as were the rest of us. Within his first two months on the job, he decided that WRA's mission was not just to make the centers reasonably habitable, but to help the evacuees leave the centers for relocation as widely as possible outside the evacuated area.

Before the final contingent of evacuees entered the centers, circumstances made it possible for two groups to avoid detention and re-enter the outer world. The special problem of Nisei college students was noted as early as March 1942 and brought into focus by the preliminary report of the Tolan Committee and the creation of a Student Relocation Committee on the Berkeley campus of the University of California. In May, WRA Director Eisenhower asked Clarence Pickett of the American Friends Service Committee to form a non-governmental agency to deal with the problem. The resulting National Student Relocation Council, formed at a meeting in Chicago, enlisted the cooperation of colleges and universities so that hundreds of students were able to resume their studies as early as autumn 1942 at institutions east of the exclusion zone. Eisenhower designated me to attend Council meetings which were held in Philadelphia. Over 5,000 evacuee students ultimately benefited from this program.

The second group exempted from residence at the relocation centers were seasonal farm workers. In May 1942, the sugar beet producers, citing a critical shortage of workers, convinced the WRA and the WCCA to permit immediate recruitment at the assembly centers. The first group of 15 from the Portland Assembly Center went to work on farm lands in the extreme eastern part of Oregon. During the year, approximately 10,000 evacuees left WCCA or WRA centers for seasonal work in Idaho, Utah, Montana, Colorado and eastern Oregon. According to the WRA report, although "many had occasional unpleasant experiences . . . none reported any bodily harm or any really serious difficulties."

The work was hard but the seasonal workers rejoiced in their freedom. Tom wrote his family September 21, 1942 from Emmett, Idaho: "How's everybody? Don't worry about me. Because I'm sitting pretty good out here in Idaho. We had a four hundred and fifty mile drive to here on bus. Pretty good ride. We reached here that night at ten. That is up to Ontario which is on the borderline. From there beet contractors took us to Emmett. Picking prunes is just about all over now so we are going to pick apples instead . . . The people here so far have been very nice to us." On Sept. 27, Tom writes: "Yesterday I made seven dollars and sixty-three cents. Some days a little below seven dollars. The apples here are very small, otherwise we could pick a whole lot more. We put in about nine and a half hours of work each day so I am doing better than seventy cents an hour . . . Boy we six young fellows can eat and since we are making enough we sure eat good foods too. The atmosphere of being out of camp makes it taste that much better."

In contrast was the experience of Ted Shigeno in a letter written Sept. 27, 1942 from Corvallis, Montana: "Thought you would like to know some thing about Montana and beets. Briefly—very sad. We've been working since Tuesday and only averaged about couple of dollars a day . . . I thought we simply top beets directly from the ground but here beets must be pulled and shaked, piled in a row and then topped. Double work . . . Our grand abode looks something brought over from the Kentucky hills or the Oklahoma dust bowl . . . No electricity—we expected that, and no running water . . . no bathing facilities of any sort. Take our daily cleansing in a washtub!" Ted had mixed comments on community acceptance. On the one hand: "We were very well received at church with all the old ladies and gents greeting us that they're glad to see us here." But when they left the church to have lunch, two places refused service and a third made them wait "for a heck of a long time." It's not too surprising he ends the letter by saying: "We are looking forward for the return to Tule Lake."

But most seasonal workers and virtually all college students were pleased to be out of the centers. The WRA Director and General Counsel sought ways to grant leave to others wishing to settle on the outside. Return to the West Coast was denied for the duration of the war, but, with the consent of the War Department, the way was finally cleared for evacuees to head east, first to the intermountain and midwest states, and ultimately to the eastern and southern states. Certain conditions had to be met before an evacuee was granted "indefinite leave." These included security clearance, and a guarantee of employment and housing. In some cases, the offer of community acceptance by a reputable religious or non-sectarian agency was deemed sufficient. Thus the Quakers, the Brethren, and certain other religious groups developed hostels where evacuees could find temporary refuge pending location of housing and placement in jobs.

This aspect of the program—helping evacuees return to a more normal life—had greater appeal for me than the community activities program at the relocation centers, so I applied for a change in status and became a resettlement officer. I went off to a variety of urban centers where I enlisted the cooperation of Federal, state and local officials, non-governmental agencies, religious bodies, prospective employers and labor unions. An early field trip in my new capacity included visits to Chicago, Milwaukee, Madison, Cleveland and Des Moines. In general, I found people receptive to the notion of welcoming the Japanese-Americans.

There were problems and pitfalls, but many Japanese-Americans, especially the Nisei, found an acceptance and new lifestyle more satisfactory than they had known on the West Coast. The challenge to WRA was to develop a favorable climate of opinion in wartime America for the reception, placement and integration of Japanese-Americans. This was achieved largely through the creation of local committees which undertook to provide the necessary auspices and assurances. To accomplish the resettlement of larger numbers, WRA established a chain of relocation offices from Billings, Montana, to Boston where its relocation officers worked with the local citizenry and the voluntary agencies to help evacuees re-establish themselves. The first such office was opened in Chicago in February 1943, and by the fall of 1944 a total of 33,000 evacuees had been resettled, most of them in communities where the pre-Pearl Harbor population of persons of Japanese ancestry was negligible.

Despite opposition from many newspapers and the House Un-American Activities Committee (HUAC), Dillon pursued his objective of permitting the evacuees to leave the centers, never yielding an inch. He won the support of Secretary Harold Ickes and of courageous Congressional leaders. He kept saying in effect, "You can trust these people. The overwhelming majority are loyal Americans that we can vouch for. You need them and they need you." Myer demanded the return to uniform of evacuees who had been dismissed from the Armed Forces, urged the acceptance of Army enlistments from the evacuees. He foresaw the favorable impact that would be created by the recruitment of a Regimental Combat Team of Japanese-Americans. Later, as the war neared its end, he pressed for the re-opening of the evacuated area permitting the return of evacuees to their homes before the war's end in the Pacific. He then set a target date for closing each of the relocation centers. He had to fight to persuade many of the evacuees and their long-time liberal supporters, to accept the idea that the centers must not be allowed to become a new type of American Indian reservation. When the final report of WRA was issued, its subtitle appropriately read: *A Story of Human Conservation.*

National community acceptance of the evacuees was given a boost when the War Department announced in January 1943 that "a substantial number of American citizens of Japanese ancestry would be admitted to the Army of the United States." Nisei from Hawaii already constituted a unit that had fought with conspicuous bravery. Dillon Myer succeeded in convincing John J. McCloy, Assistant Secretary of War, that it was desirable to recruit from the centers as well. The resulting military unit, known as the 442nd Combat Team, fought bravely in Europe, and by war's end was the most highly decorated unit in the Army. Their service was limited to the Atlantic theater, but individual Japanese-Americans with a requisite knowledge of the Japanese language were assigned to intelligence work in the Pacific areas.

Despite the War Department's decision to recruit a military unit from the centers it is of interest that Lt. General John L. DeWitt, Commanding General of the Western Defense Command at the Presidio, was still unrelenting. A few random statements from testimony he submitted to a sub-committee of the House Committee on Naval Affairs, sitting in San Francisco in April 1943, will serve to illustrate the point. " . . . (there) is the development of the false sentiment on the part of certain individuals and some organizations to get the Japanese back on the west coast. I don't want any of them here. They are a dangerous element. There is no way to determine their loyalty. . . . It makes no difference whether he is an American citizen, he is still a Japanese. . . . You needn't worry about the Italians at all except in certain cases. Also, the same for the Germans except in individual cases. But we must worry about the Japanese all the time until he is wiped off the map."

In connection with the recruitment of evacuees for the combat team, WRA early in 1943 decided to undertake a general registration of all persons seventeen years of age and older. The evacuees were at first asked to "swear unqualified allegiance to the United States of America and foreswear any form of allegiance or obedience to the Japanese emperor." While the wording was subsequently modified, there was insufficient recognition that "loyalty" is a complex concept. This was particularly the case for aliens who, under the law at that time, could not become American citizens. Disloyal elements created disturbances and taunted Nisei on the deprivation of their civil rights. "So you're an American citizen? Well, let's see you walk out of this center."

Among the dissidents, a large number were Kibei. These were American-born Nisei, mostly young men, who had been sent to Japan for their education and then returned to the United States. When a considerable number of this disaffected group as well as some Issei and Nisei asked to be repatriated to Japan, it was decided to segregate them in one relocation center at Tule Lake, California. Loyal residents of Tule Lake were distributed to the other centers. For a time, protests continued at Tule Lake, but as there was a shift in the tide of war, and a Japanese victory became a less likely outcome, most of its residents recanted. Hearings were held and the dossiers prepared as a consequence were sent to Washington for review by the WRA staff. For some weeks, each of us, in addition to our normal duties, was charged with the review of a growing number of dossiers. We had to decide, on the basis of the evidence, whether an evacuee's change of heart was genuine, and whether he or she was worthy of reprieve. I came home each night with a bulging brief case of these dossiers and conscientiously reviewed them to determine the good faith of the appellants. It was a bit like playing God. In most cases I sensed that the recantation was, indeed, genuine.

The third phase of the program, which began even before the war in the Pacific ended, was the closure of the centers. As victory approached, war-induced hysteria died down. On January 1, 1945, the War Department announced that the West Coast was open for those evacuees who wished to return. WRA announced simultaneously that it would maintain the relocation centers for a maximum of one year. Tule Lake was not included in that decision. By August 1945, two-thirds of the people at Tule Lake had been cleared by the military, but the status of some of the others was still in doubt.

We in WRA didn't see the necessity for it but the Administration decided that WRA should not continue as an independent agency but should be incorporated under the Department of the Interior. Secretary Ickes did not interfere with Dillon Myer's able administration of the program but as a civil libertarian he gave needed support vis a vis the Pentagon and the Department of Justice.

By January 1945, about half of the 112,000 Japanese-Americans evacuated from the West Coast had been resettled in other parts of the country. There were 17,000 at Tule Lake, and 35,000 remaining at the other relocation centers. Virtually all of the evacuees remaining at the centers returned to their West Coast homes. An indeterminate number of those who resettled elsewhere in the country also elected to return. However, one result of the evacuation experience was the wider dispersal of the Japanese-American population throughout the United States.

In the final stage of the WRA operation, I and other staff members made several trips to the West Coast, consulting with state and local officials and citizen groups. The object, of course, was to test the climate and ensure, to the extent possible, that the evacuees would have a reasonably trouble-free return. Some vestiges of vigilantism were encountered, but, with the end of the Pacific war in sight, we found people willing, if not eager, to have the evacuees return to their homes. Those who had not sold out in panic were able to recover the farms, stores, homes and other property held for them by WRA's Evacuee Property Division.

The outstanding record of the Japanese-American Combat team quieted all but the most rabid racists. Local committees helped to smooth the path, but the successful reestablishment of the Japanese-Americans was due above all to the courage, faith and resilience they displayed under conditions which sorely tested their loyalty to the United States.

Because of its significance in this country's struggles to promote civil liberty and because it represented for me a test of my own values, I want to add some background about the evacuation experience and what led up to it.

Many books and articles have been written about the wartime evacuation of the West Coast Japanese-Americans. Was it, as alleged at the time, a "military necessity" or was it an unnecessary violation of the civil rights of a minority, based largely on racial prejudice?

Immediately following Pearl Harbor, the Department of Justice interned the Germans, Italians and Japanese whose loyalty was suspect. Of this number 2,192 were Japanese. But rumors of sabotage and fifth column activity were widely circulated, including reports of signaling from shore to Japanese submarines. While none of these rumors were ever substantiated, the inflammatory columns of the Hearst and McClatchy newspapers, a column by Walter Lippmann, nationally known and widely respected columnist, in which he said "The Pacific Coast is in imminent danger of a combined attack from within and from without," a letter written to FDR by seven members of Congress from California, Oregon and Washington, and a strong recommendation from Lt. Gen. DeWitt, all had their effect. On February 19, 1942, President Roosevelt signed Executive Order 9066 authorizing the Secretary of War "to exclude any and all persons, citizens and aliens, from designated areas in order to provide security against sabotage, espionage and fifth column activity."

In June 1945, Eugene V. Rostow, then Professor of Law at Yale, wrote in the Yale Law Journal that in the U.S. during World War II, "100,000 persons were sent to concentration camps on a record which wouldn't support a conviction for stealing a dog."

A Commission on Wartime Relocation and Internment of Civilians established by President Jimmy Carter concluded in 1983 that Roosevelt signed the executive order "without any careful or thorough review of the situation." McCloy called the report's conclusions "well and good in hindsight, but none of us had that at the time." This may have been true at the War Department, but it's known that Attorney General Francis Biddle opposed the evacuation.

The Commission's report stated that "the exclusion and removal were attacks on the ethnic Japanese which followed a long and ugly history of West Coast anti-Japanese agitation and legislation." This was unquestionably true. Although ethnic Japanese never exceeded three percent of the population of California, the state of greatest concentration, the War Relocation Authority, in its final report, said that "after 1905, the West Coast has never been without at least one powerful, zealous and single-minded group devoted wholly to the purpose of preventing Japanese immigration and dispossessing as many as possible of the Japanese residents already established on this side of the Pacific." The most powerful was the California Joint Immigration Committee established in 1921 under the leadership of V.C.McClatchy, publisher of the *Sacramento Bee*, which included the Attorney General of the State of California and representatives of the American Legion, the State Federation of Labor, the State Grange and the Native Sons of the Golden West.

After Pearl Harbor, these groups beat a steady drumfire for exclusion, as did formidable interests competing with the Japanese in the production or marketing of fruits and vegetables. At the outset of World War II, 42 percent of all truck crops grown in the state were produced by persons of Japanese ancestry, and competitors were jealous of their success.

Few voices were raised in protest at the exclusion order. An elderly Issei's reaction was poignant. "Surely this doesn't apply to me," he said. "I'm an American, with a certificate of honor received for bravery in World War I." The next day, he was found dead, with poison in one hand, and the certificate in the other. The evacuation affected 106 Japanese-American veterans of World War I in American Legion posts.

The Japanese American Citizens League (JACL), the principal organization of the Nisei, claimed to have a membership of approximately 20,000 by the spring of 1942 in nearly 300 communities. It was urgent for JACL to take a stand when evacuation loomed. The national JACL secretary testified on February 23 before a Congressional committee exploring the problem in San Francisco. He said, "If, in the judgment of military and Federal authorities, evacuation of Japanese residents from the west coast is a primary step toward insuring the safety of the Nation, we will have no hesitation in complying with the necessities implicit in that judgment. But if, on the other hand, such evacuation is primarily a measure whose surface urgency cloaks the desires of political or other pressure groups who want us to leave merely from motives of self-interest, we feel we have every right to protest and to demand equitable judgment on our merits as American citizens."

On the whole, as noted in the final WRA report, "the Army had the advantage of a surprisingly docile and cooperative spirit on the part of the Japanese affected." However, several individuals brought suit against the Government, and on June 23, 1943, the Supreme Court handed down its decision in the case of Gordon Hirabayashi vs. United States. In his book Carey McWilliams notes that Hirabayashi had been convicted of violating both the curfew and the evacuation orders. "While the court held that the curfew regulation was a valid exercise of the war power, it pointedly refused to pass on the question of the constitutionality of the evacuation order. From language contained in the various opinions filed in the matter, it is quite apparent that the Supreme Court entertains the gravest doubts as to the constitutionality of evacuation insofar as the Nisei are concerned. Mr. Justice Murphy, for example, said that the curfew order 'goes to the very brink of constitutional power', and Mr. Justice Douglas, in a significant concurring opinion, said 'detention for reasonable cause is one thing, detention on account of ancestry is another.'"

The other landmark case concerned Fred T. Korematsu, who was jailed for failing to report to a San Francisco assembly center for evacuation in 1942. His conviction was upheld by the Supreme Court which ruled unanimously in 1943 that the Government was justified by "military necessity" in its blanket exclusion of Japanese-Americans from California, Washington and Oregon. In a second case decided the following year, the Court by a vote of 6 to 3 confirmed the decision. Koramatsu was sentenced to five years' probation. Hirabayashi served two years in prison after his arrest in Seattle.

In January 1983, petitions were filed on behalf of Korematsu, Hirabayashi and a third Japanese American, Minoru Yasui, who spent nine months in solitary confinement after being arrested in Portland for curfew violation. In their petitions, the three asked that their convictions be overturned on the basis of documents that they maintained showed that Government officials knowingly presented false evidence that there was a "military necessity." In October, the Department of Justice filed a brief motion in the Korematsu case agreeing that the conviction should be set aside as "an unfortunate episode in our nation's history." In her ruling, Federal District Judge Marilyn H. Patel called the government's response "tantamount to a confession of error." Arthur J. Goldberg, former Supreme Court Justice, and a member of the Carter Commission, called Korematsu "one of the most ill-conceived decisions handed down by the Supreme Court, perhaps second only to Dred Scott vs. Sanford."

The Commission in June 1983 recommended payment of $1.5 billion in compensation to the evacuees. Under the Civil Liberties Act of 1988, Congress paid $1.6 billion in reparations to more than 81,000 Americans of Japanese ancestry, an estimated 98 percent of those eligible. The final reparations payments of $20,000 per individual were made in 1998. The payments were welcome as a belated acknowledgement of the injustice done to American citizens and a racial group numbering less than one tenth of one percent of the U.S. population. But they would never be enough to obliterate the stain left on the American escutcheon. There was something terribly wrong about the evacuation, and most of us who worked with WRA empathized deeply with the people affected.

TOKEN SHIPMENT OF REFUGEES
FROM EUROPE

One morning in June 1944 my WRA boss, Dillon Myer, read in the *Washington Post* that the President had given our agency a new responsibility, the care in a "temporary haven" of nearly a thousand European refugees. They were to be transported from Southern Italy to America on the return voyage of the Henry Gibbons, an army vessel, and would travel by train to Fort Ontario, a disused Army camp in Oswego, N.Y. which would be hastily refurbished for their arrival. The fiction was to be maintained that the refugees were not actually in the United States. They were, if you like, being kept on ice with the understanding that at the war's end they would return to their homes. Before leaving Europe they had signed a pledge to do so.

The Oswego project was the brainchild of Franklin D. Roosevelt, or it may have been suggested to him by Henry Morganthau, Jr., Secretary of the Treasury, whose father directed resettlement of Greek refugees in the 1920s. Morganthau, Jr. supervised the War Refugee Board, established to set the overall policy for the project, though the Shelter was to be administered by WRA. Only a thousand, mostly Jewish refugees out of the hundreds of thousands in Europe at that time were affected by this wartime gesture of the President. For the most part, the United States, with its restrictive immigration laws and isolationist mood, in the words of the historian Arthur Schlesinger, Jr., "had shrugged off the plight of European Jews." However it was the first time that a group of unsponsored refugees were given asylum in the United States and, in a sense, it paved the way for the admission of much larger numbers under special post-war refugee legislation.

Because of my experience with refugees from Europe, Myer put me in charge of a new "War Refugee Division" in Washington. We recruited a staff to man the Emergency Refugee Shelter at Oswego. One of WRA's seasoned project directors, Joseph H. Smart, was appointed Director.

The largest single group among the refugees were Jews from Yugoslavia. Actually the population included persons of eighteen nationalities. Of 918 Shelter residents in October 1945, 304 were classed as Yugoslav, 239 as Austrian, 167 as Polish, 92 as German and 38 as Czech. Others came from Russia, Bulgaria, Rumania, Danzig, Hungary and Turkey. The Jewish refugees included representatives of the three major religious groups, the Orthodox, the Sephardic and the Reformed. To aid the administrative staff, WRA's Community Analysis Section prepared a paper reviewing briefly the principal Jewish holidays and customs. This compendium would prove valuable interpreting the requests and actions of the residents not normally encountered in Federal administration. About 10 percent of the population were Catholic or Protestant.

The new residents of Fort Ontario were a sophisticated group, wise in the ways of camp life from their European experience. Some were pathetic, but many were people of spirit and talent. They grumbled, as well they might, at the bitter cold of Lake Ontario's winter, but they sang, painted pictures, put on theatrical performances. The children went to the town schools. Some of the adults mingled with residents of the town. A few marriages took place. Twenty-three babies were born at the Shelter on American soil. Some of the residents had sons in the American Army. Could it really be said that these people were not in the United States?

The camp residents published the first issue of their newspaper, *Ontario Chronicle*, in November 1944, just three months after their arrival at the Shelter. In his word of greeting, Dillon Myer called the launching of this venture "one of the best indications of your community's stability. The hectic days of 'moving in' and 'settling down' are over, your children are in school; men and women are at work; your Advisory Council is functioning; many of you have beautified your simple dwellings with a rare touch of artistry. You can now think in broader community terms . . . to take the next step for a fuller community life: the publication of a newspaper."

There were daily problems, of course. Even when weather conditions were favorable, the administration had difficulty in recruiting sufficient workers for the roads and grounds crew and other units performing outdoor tasks. When winter came and the snowdrifts were piled high, the problems of getting the heavy work done were magnified a hundredfold. The consumption of fuel went up, requiring large quantities of coal to be unloaded from freight cars and hauled to the various buildings. This also necessitated removal of large quantities of ashes. In addition, there was the vast problem of snow removal, as the presence of huge drifts impeded other routine project chores such as the orderly disposal of garbage.

The Shelter population lacked a sufficient number of men able-bodied enough to perform arduous tasks in severe weather. Of those who had the physical stamina, many were from professions, trades and totally unrelated kinds of work. Some had the European notion that hard physical labor was demeaning, and this played a part in their reluctance to perform the heavy tasks.

The Shelter administration made countless pleas for the recruitment of workers. Meetings were held with the Shelter's Advisory Council, the house leaders, the heads of the nationality groups, and a refugee labor committee. When attempts to recruit enough full-time labor failed, the administration fell back on a plan by which the heavy work was shared on a rotation basis, but the results were never really satisfactory.

Fortunately, the work situation had its lighter side. One rotation worker wrote a piece called "I Have Removed Garbage" for the *Ontario Chronicle*.

"Last Friday," he wrote, "was my D-Day, excuse me, G-day, since I was requested to help in removing garbage. Coal or garbage, that is the question, and I prefer garbage. We are five, all fine fellows from 54 to 36 who handle the heavy cans as if they were tennis balls. My job is to take the cans and empty them in the truck. Sometimes the stuff is frozen and you have to make several times boum-boum, it is to knock the cans vigorously on the floor before garbage kindly agrees to leave its container. The garbage is an interesting material, reflecting the spirit of our residents . . . In the afternoon the principal material which we remove is ashes, a step-brother of garbage and a family member of coal.

"Centuries ago ashes were a symbol of sadness, but I doubt if the ashes which our forefathers spread on their heads were of the good Ontario quality which is a bit heavy. The work in the furnace room makes us thirsty but the canteen is near and the beer is fresh. And so 'All's well that ends well' and beer, beautiful Yugoslav songs, and a nice chatter with the American driver who is a fine guy terminate my historical day. I have removed garbage."

It was hard to keep one step ahead of the resourceful refugees, and the Administration trying conscientiously to follow Federal regulations occasionally came a-cropper. Because most of the residents were Jewish, many of them orthodox, there were frequent occasions when regulations had to be modified to permit strict religious observance. Mostly it was a question of special diet or arrangements for the appropriate service of food. Joe Smart would get on the telephone and with the zeal of a new convert to the faith defend the necessity for two sets of dishes—one for meat and one for dairy so that everything would be properly kosher.

One day a delegation came to Joe's office requesting the installation of a *mikvah*. A *mikvah*, it seemed, was an absolute requirement, though the Shelter had been running for some months without one. What was a *mikvah*, I asked Joe?

He explained it was a ceremonial bath used by orthodox women during their period when they were not supposed to use other bathing facilities. I asked Joe why several of the normal baths couldn't be set aside for this purpose. Joe said he had tried that, but according to Jewish ritual law a *mikvah* had to be built under rigid specifications. I was reasonably sympathetic but I found our administrative people adamant on the subject. They challenged me to find a precedent

for constructing a *mikvah* in a Federal installation. I finally called a friend at one
of the Jewish agencies assisting the refugees at the Shelter and explained the
situation. They rose to the emergency and the *mikvah* was duly installed. The
dedication of the *mikvah* was one of the high points in Shelter history. I was curious to know what a *mikvah* dedication consisted of, but unfortunately I wasn't
able to make the occasion. For all I know the ritual bath may still be found in
one of the abandoned buildings of Fort Ontario.

The arts flourished at Fort Ontario. Some of the work produced at a painting
class won prizes at an exhibit in Syracuse. Though Syracuse was only 35 miles
away the winning artists were not permitted to travel there. A writer who had
been a Viennese playwright did an article on his refugee experience in Italy that
was accepted in *The Commonweal*. Several of the singers and musicians performed in Oswego and there were some outstanding theatrical productions. Performances were staged in two Shelter theaters by Austro-German, Russian, Zi-
onist, youth and children's groups.

As time went on the refugees developed more and more contacts with the
outside. Some were visited by relatives living in the United States. The daily
presence of many representatives of voluntary agencies also offered a window to
the world. As the war in Europe neared its close an underlay of uncertainty as to
their future made the camp residents a restless group. With few exceptions they
yearned to remain in the U.S.

Joe Smart became closely identified with the refugees and supported their
ardent desire to be admitted to the United States. He felt so strongly, that after
22 years of government service, he resigned his job as Director of the Fort Ontario Emergency Refugee Shelter on May 15, 1945 "to be free to lead the fight
for freedom for the refugees."

In his response to Smart's letter of resignation, Dillon Myer expressed his
appreciation "for the leadership you displayed at the Shelter since its inception
in carrying through a program beset by so many inherent difficulties outside of
your control. I feel that WRA and the residents of the Shelter owe you a debt in
recognizing at a very early stage, the paradox of maintaining, under such
restricted conditions, a refuge within a democracy for victims of Fascist
aggression."

Smart was succeeded by Malcolm Pitts, a veteran administrator who acted
for a time as interim Shelter Director. Pitts introduced a new system devised to
bring about the accomplishment of necessary maintenance operations. This
variation of the earlier "rotation" system was called the redistribution plan. Priorities were set up for Shelter workers, and those not working or assigned to
lighter tasks were required to take turns on the roads and ground crews or in
other essential duties.

With the end of World War II in sight, the Government needed to address
the question of the refugees' future. Were they to be held to the pledge made before their departure from Italy that they would return to Europe at the war's end?

A Congressional Committee on Immigration and Naturalization, chaired by Samuel Dickstein, was authorized "to make an overall study . . . to determine just what should be done with regard to the number of people in this camp, from the standpoint of some humane justice for them." When the six Congressmen of a sub-committee reached Fort Ontario on June 25, 1945, Pitts and I met them. We took them on a tour to show them the classrooms where the refugees were learning English, the exhibition hall with various works of art, the workshops and other features of the camp.

As the first witness called before the Committee, I reviewed the history of the project, steps taken by the Government to administer it, and the principal activities of the residents. The subcommittee heard testimony from General William O'Dwyer of the War Refugee Board, who flew up from New York and spoke movingly in the refugees' behalf. He argued that they should be permitted to leave the Shelter under adequate sponsorship, pending a solution of their problem that would be in keeping with United Nations repatriation policy. Pitts and other WRA officials told of the expense and difficulty of operating a plant far in excess of the population's needs. The citizens of Oswego were represented by officials of the school system and State Teachers College, the police chief, the publisher of the Oswego Palladium-Times, and a local attorney, who was Chairman of the town's Advisory Committee on Fort Ontario. All praised the talent and deportment of the Shelter population, young and old. The Superintendent of Schools said the children's scholastic performance had been "superior" and their achievement "amazing." The High School Principal called attention to the fact that eight of about 40 high school students from the Shelter had qualified for the National Honor Society.

But the most impressive witnesses were the refugees themselves. Among those called were Mrs. Rosa Mosauer, a widow with two sons, a staff sergeant and a lieutenant in the U.S. Army overseas; Jacob Ernest Kahn, whose wife and two children lived in Minneapolis; Mrs. Regina Loewit, whose husband worked in a New York war plant; Josef Langas, age 14, who was President of his class in the Oswego Junior High School; Prince Peter Ouroussoff, who said he had no further use for his Czarist title but wanted to join his sister, director of a ballet school in New York; Jakob Charasch, whose two sons were in the U.S. Merchant Marine, and several members of the Fort Ontario Boy Scout Troop.

The sub-committee did not get to hear Alfred Thewett, a 65-year-old Viennese fashion designer. Mr. Thewett was scheduled to be called, but died of a heart attack the night before the hearings began, a scant three months after his wife arrived in the United States on an immigration visa.

Spirits were high while the Congressmen were at the Shelter. The refugees put on a special performance for the honored guests. During the summer, though rumors flew wildly in the Shelter, and no decision was reached about their future, the residents were somewhat more relaxed.

By July 1945, Joe Smart formed a blue ribbon committee with impressive membership known as the Sponsors' Committee of the Friends of Fort Ontario Guest-Refugees. Eleanor Roosevelt (who had visited the Shelter), Thomas E. Dewey, Roger Baldwin, Ernst P. Boas, John Dewey, W.E.B. DuBois, David Dubinsky, Albert Einstein, John Haynes Holmes, Herbert H. Lehman, Reinhold Niebuhr, William O'Dwyer, Katherine Anne Porter, Raymond Gram Swing and Norman Thomas were among its members signing a statement urging that the refugees be given "their immediate freedom to live and work wherever they choose in the United States." Many of us, in Government and outside, strongly supported this view. Joe Smart ceaselessly put forward the case in Washington.

The Committee's efforts were bolstered when 27 leading residents of Oswego drew up and signed a petition to the President and Congress recommending that the refugees be permitted to leave the Shelter, "reside at places of their own choice," accept gainful employment, and qualify for admission to the United States.

It's my understanding that the Dickstein sub-committee voted to close the camp but could not agree on the disposition of the population. In any case, the full House Immigration and Naturalization Committee in July 1945 asked the State and Justice Departments to "determine the practicality of return and requested that the Attorney General ...declare those unable to do so to be illegal aliens subject to immediate deportation proceedings, and make disposition of them in accordance with the provisions of existing laws and procedures."

Shortly after the Dickstein sub-committee made its report to the full Committee on Immigration and Naturalization, it was decided that a panel representing the three concerned Government agencies would review the dossiers of all camp residents to determine their fate. The panel consisted of Joseph P. Savoretti, a long experienced immigration officer, Marshall P. Vance of the State Department, and yours truly, representing the WRA/Department of the Interior. We met for several days in September 1945. As anticipated, we found that the overwhelming majority sought to remain in the United States. I took the view that none should be returned to a devastated Europe against their will, but my colleagues from State and Justice outvoted me in case after case, recommending U.S. residence only for those who could qualify for admission under preference categories of the U.S. Immigration Law.

The panel found that 32 persons desired repatriation, 72 sought admission to other countries and the balance of 814 wished to remain in the United States. We unanimously agreed that 119 individuals in the last group should be classed as "not practical to return." I dissented on 90 percent of the remaining 695 cases, holding that in view of conditions in Europe and the policy of UNRRA and the U.S. Army not to force involuntary repatriation, the refugees should be permitted to stay in the United States.

When Pitts departed on July 1, 1945, I moved to the Shelter with my family to serve for a month as its acting director. I had visited the Shelter on several occasions, but living there gave me the chance to become better acquainted with the general situation and with a number of the residents. It was a pleasant experience. I was there during the summer when morale was higher, and I was struck by the positive attitude and creativity of quite a number of the refugees. I relished their sometime gaiety, expressed on occasions when they danced the Holky Polky, a dance they had learned in Europe from the liberating British 8th Army.

From early December, 1944, when the Refugee Advisory Council resigned because of a labor dispute, no group of residents represented the Shelter population in its dealings with the administration. This meant that as Shelter Director I had to spend a good part of every day meeting with groups representing the workers, the nationality committees, the Freedom Committee, the house leaders and individuals whose problems really did not merit my attention. Recognizing the desirability of having a channel of communication, the refugees, with my encouragement, formed a new organization called the National Board of Fort Ontario Residents. Nine members of its 30-member board met as an Executive Committee with the administration. This Committee, composed of two Yugoslavs, two Austrians, two Poles, two Germans and a Czech, first met with me on July 18, 1945, and continued to function for the last six months of the Shelter operation.

In late July Clyde H. Powers came in as Shelter Director and served in that capacity until the Shelter's close. Powers had been with the Bureau of Indian Affairs for a number of years before joining the staff of WRA in 1942 as Chief Engineer. His impartial and understanding direction of the project was a stabilizing influence in a difficult period of uncertainty as to the future of the refugees.

In August 1945, 53 Yugoslav refugees sailed on the Gripsholm for voluntary repatriation. A party of 13 Yugoslavs had departed on the same vessel in May. Two Shelter residents left for South Africa and Uruguay and a third was destined to leave for Czechoslovakia in October. These 69 persons were all who left the country during the life of the Shelter.

All during the final months, the administration was faced with the question of whether desirable changes of policy, personnel and program should be made, in light of the fact that a decision regarding the future was expected at any time. As they awaited the Christmas holiday season most of the refugees were discouraged by the seeming fruitlessness of their own efforts and those of their relatives, friends and interested committees to obtain their freedom. Month after month of delay and uncertainty had worn them to a ragged edge.

The final report of the WRA Medical Social Consultant who served at the Shelter from November 1945 until its close contains the following paragraph: "The type of emotional problems existing among the residents which related to family life as well as to individual adults and children and reflected on the general health were essentially the same as those found by the medical social worker among patients in a hospital in any average community, particularly during a crisis period. Here there was a concentration and intensification of these problems, however, brought about by the traumatic experiences from which this entire selected group had suffered for several years immediately preceding their arrival in this county and from the abnormal ingrown conditions under which they had to live in the Shelter. Separation and loss of parents, children, husbands or wives, family disharmony, sexual incompatibility and insecurity about the future were some of the causes which led to emotional problems and physical breakdown."

Just before Christmas, the decline in morale was reflected in *The Golden Cage*, an opera written and composed by two Shelter residents, which was given a concert performance. The libretto traced the history of the group from their refugee days abroad to the present, and poignantly reflected their hatred of confinement. In a scene at Fort Ontario, reminiscent of the days immediately following the group's arrival, "elegantly dressed American ladies" hear the "poorly clad refugees" singing behind the fence:

"We are in a cage without reason,
We are in a cage, a golden cage;
We're missing nothing but our freedom."

While the show was in rehearsal the joyous news reached the cast that President Truman had signed an Executive Order on December 22, 1945, granting freedom and the right to apply for immigration status for the refugees. The show's ending was modified accordingly: a messenger comes in with the news of President Truman's reprieve, and the refugees laugh, dance and sing.

In his Executive Order, the President said that a careful study by the State Department and INS showed that most of the Shelter residents would upon application be admissible under the Immigration laws. He added: "It would be inhumane and wasteful to require these people to go all the way back to Europe merely for the purpose of applying there for immigration visas and returning to the United States."

If it had been left to the Committee on Immigration and Naturalization or the State and Justice Departments, most of the refugees would have been returned to Europe. But, in the end, the efforts of Joe Smart and his blue ribbon committee, the residents of Oswego and the Jewish organizations prevailed.

The first contingent of 95 refugees left the Shelter for Niagara Falls, Canada, on January 17, 1946, to change their status and return. The last group left on February 5. Their destinations were more than 70 communities in 21 states. Nineteen for various reasons were found inadmissable. The Shelter was closed on February 6, 1946.

I wrote the official history of the Fort Ontario Shelter for the Department of the Interior. This 106 page account is titled "Token Shipment—the Story of

America's War Refugee Shelter." The dramatic plight and rescue of 1,000 refugees inspired Ruth Gruber to tell their tale in a book called *Haven: The Unknown Story of 1,000 World War II Refugees*. *Haven* was made into a four-hour mini-series starring Natasha Richardson which was broadcast by CBS in February 2001. Others featured in the cast were Anne Bancroft and Hal Holbrook. Joe Smart found time to write his account of how the Fort Ontario Refugees won their freedom. This documented chronicle, under the title *Don't Fence Me In*, was published by Heritage Arts in Salt Lake City, Utah in 1991. An earlier book by Sharon R. Lowenstein under the title *Token Refuge—The Story of the Jewish Refugee Shelter at Oswego, 1944-1946* was published by the Indiana University Press in June 1986.

Gruber, an American journalist assigned by Interior Secretary Ickes to accompany the refugees on their original voyage from Italy, visited the Shelter on several occasions and was an eloquent spokesman on their behalf. Over the years, she has kept in touch with many of them, and was the keynote speaker in October 1981 when 25 of the survivors attended the dedication of a Fort Ontario monument erected by the Syracuse branch of Pioneer Women/Na'amat and the Jewish Community of Central New York. Joseph Papp and Gov. Mario Cuomo spoke at a 40-year reunion of Shelter residents held at the Public Theater in New York on August 3, 1984. In the first edition of the *Oswego Reunion Newsletter* published in September 1984, Gruber hailed the achievements of former Shelter residents. She said: "Among us are a vice president of the American Stock Exchange, a composer of classical music, a pathologist, an anthropologist, film makers, psychologists, artists and owners of large and thriving businesses."

Nostalgia for the Oswego experience has led to the creation of Safe Haven, Inc., a non-profit group dedicated to hold in memory what happened at Fort Ontario during World War II. Its members meet periodically, have made videotapes based on interviews of the families of camp residents, publish a newsletter, and have sponsored the establishment of an Oswego Safe Haven Museum in Fort Ontario Park.

FAIR EXCHANGE

(Housing was very tight in Washington during and immediately following World War II. The incident described in the following vignette that I wrote never happened but it almost could have. This vignette was republished in several languages in foreign magazines but first appeared in *The American Magazine*, June 1946.)

Max and Leila Mudge capitalized on the housing shortage by renting out their extra room at an exorbitant rate. The location was good, and even at the price they charged they never had difficulty in finding lodgers. But the turnover was high. The room was tiny, uncomfortably hot in summer and cold in winter, and Leila did nothing about keeping it clean.

One day Max's boss decided that he was just the man for their office in Brazil. Leila was aghast. "It's so far away! And we don't know any Spanish!"

"You don't have to," said Max. "They speak Portuguese and we can learn some before we go if it doesn't cost too much."

Leila had an idea. "The room," she said "It's empty again. Why not offer it to someone in exchange for lessons?"

So they put an ad in the Sunday paper, and, sure enough, a prospect shortly appeared. "Good day," he said with a charming accent. "Are you the people who wish to learn Portuguese?"

"Yes, please come in," said Leila.

"My name is Baru. Happy to make your acquaintance. Are you going to Brazil?"

Max nodded.

The visitor went on, "Have you ever studied the language?"

"We don't know a word," said Leila.

Mr. Baru smiled. "My language is a difficult one," he said, "But you will be surprised how quickly you can learn it."

"This is the room," said Leila.

"Oh," said Mr. Baru. He was plainly disappointed. But in Washington a room is a room.

The next three months were a nightmare for Mr. Baru. The rent was free, but he had to pay for everything else, even the soap. Though they were stingy hosts, the Mudges wanted full value when it came to the language lessons. They resented every minute he devoted to his own affairs. If he took an evening off for a movie, they would greet him with savage reproaches when he came in, then insist on a lesson that would last until early morning hours. They studied with dogged tenacity. When the time came for them to depart, their ability to converse was amazing.

The wearied Baru returned to New York. He went to his favorite restaurant, where he was greeted by an old friend:

"Well! Where have you been?"

"Oh, hello, Anton," said Baru. "I've been in Washington the last few months. Just got back."

"Washington? Where did you stay? They say it's impossible to find a room."

"I had great difficulty. But I finally got a small room, rent-free, with a couple who wanted to learn Portuguese."

"But, my dear Baru, you don't know any Portuguese!"

"True enough," the other replied with a faint smile. "They'll be in for a surprise when they reach Brazil. They speak fluent Rumanian."

TOM

My son, Tom, was born in Washington, March 25, 1944, but was only three when the family moved to Geneva after I accepted a job there with the United Nations. We landed in London where I took possession of a small Standard car I'd ordered in advance, and we drove to Geneva.

While we were house hunting and getting settled, we put the children for a few weeks in a home d'enfants in Villars, a lovely mountain resort. It started them on the road to French, but in retrospect I'm not sure it was wise to separate them from us in that transitional period. We found an attractive house in Carouge, a Geneva suburb near the French border, and the children continued their education at the nearby school run by M. and Madame Hodel. That was a pleasant experience, and they got a solid foundation in French. We became close friends with our nearest neighbors, the Meyers, and their four young sons became playmates of our kids. Tom and Francois Meyer were especially close, and used to wander along the Drize and climb the Wellingtonia Sequoia tree in our front yard.

When we moved to Greece three years later, Tom and Katie went to the Anglo-American School where, in addition to the usual subjects, they had some instruction in Greek. When we asked Tom if he was interested in piano lessons, he said he wanted to learn the violin. He persevered with it, and at Dartmouth, after graduating from Mamaroneck High, he was a member of a quartet and symphony orchestra. After college graduation in 1965, he worked for a year with my brother, Herb, in the music publishing business, but opted for a more direct musical career.

About that time Tom was married to Judy Brister, the daughter of a Dartmouth classmate of mine. Judy had been brought up in Latin America and was bi-lingual. They moved to San Francisco but in a year or so parted. Judy returned to Latin America. She and Margaret were bonded closely and traveled together in South America in 1969. There Judy was caught up in a political morass and had to leave without any notice. She had a son with her Chilean husband but the marriage ended and she now lives and works at the UN in NYC. We have maintained a warm relationship.

Some years ago Tom told me that after his marriage ended he met Yvette Branczyck, a French woman living in San Francisco. Together they produced a son, Thomas Branczyck, who was brought up by his mother and maternal family in France. When he was thirty, Thomas decided to find Tom. Yvette helped him find his father in Leesburg and since that time Thomas has been warmly accepted as a son and grandson. He lives in London with Keiko Takatani and works in finance.

In the summer of 1970, Nigeria's war with Biafra was winding down, and Margaret and I decided to take a long deferred safari vacation. Tom joined us in Lagos and after a few days there we took off for Uganda in an Ethiopian Airlines plane. It was a Uganda before the era of Idi Amin. We spent the night in Kampala and the next day we visited the source of the Nile and the spectacular Murchison Falls. We flew from there to Nairobi where we spent the first night at Tree Tops where Princess Elizabeth, on her honeymoon, first heard she was Queen of England. Seeing the animals highlighted from our bedroom window whetted our appetite for a safari, which was satisfied the next two days at Amboselli, a comfortably tented camp in a wildlife preserve. It was an odd feeling to be inside a window-walled jeep wandering the plains while gazelles, wildebeests, giraffes and other game were glimpsed running or sauntering by. We felt we were in a cage in the zoo.

Tom, who always loved climbing, told us that while in Africa he wanted to scale Mount Kilimanjaro. He had ascertained that climbing gear could be rented there at the base of the almost 20,000 foot-mountain. The climb would take the best part of three days. We stayed to watch him take off with a climbing party of about a dozen, half U.S. Peace Corps volunteers, half a group of German youths and two guides. We then drove east to Mombasa on the coast where we found a hotel and spent the night. Next morning we went out on a boat to explore the harbor and have a swim. Unfortunately, Margaret stepped on a sea urchin, an agonizing experience. The boat captain and I took her to a clinic to have the sharp needles removed from the bottom of her foot. Before she could be treated she had to be registered. The clerk asked a series of questions. Margaret was writhing in pain but when the inquiring clerk asked her "Tribe?" without looking up, Margaret couldn't help laughing. Happily relief followed soon after.

We returned to Kilimanjaro in time to see Tom and one of the Peace Corps stalwarts triumphantly return to base. They were the only two who had reached the summit; the others had bowed out at the midway hut or nearer the summit. Tom said he had never before experienced the exertion required to negotiate the last thousand feet before the summit. It wasn't so much the grade but the difficulty in traversing the scree (boulders and other stones) strewn along the path. All of this with the air getting thinner and thinner—they had no oxygen supply. Tom descended on a high. They gave him and the volunteer laurel wreaths for their achievement. Tom savored the experience all his life and periodically referred to it.

We flew from Nairobi to Dar es-Salaam, and after an exotic day in Zanzibar went to Serengeti where we were lucky and stunned to see hyenas attacking and devouring a wildebeest, and two lions mating and many other large animals. We then flew to Addis Ababa before taking off in rainy weather on visits to Gondar, Lalibela and Axum. We visited the villages of Falasha Jews still clinging to their ancient beliefs. Some years later most of the Falasha immigrated to Israel.

We three finished our tour in Asmara, a port on the Red Sea, now the capital of Eritrea, but in those days an Ethiopian province. An Italian colony for many years, Asmara more than any place we saw in Ethiopia had the appearance of a modern city. We found a huge American PX there where we stocked up on items unavailable in Lagos, and Tom bought a suit, several shirts and other articles of apparel. At that point we split. Margaret and I returned to Nigeria while Tom flew back to the U.S.A.

Through a friend, he auditioned and gained a seat in the Vancouver Symphony Orchestra. Early in his eight-year stay in Canada, Tom married a Dutch woman, named Lucretia Niehe, a nurse by profession. Four sons, Jethro, Paolo, David and Theo, were born in Vancouver and a fifth, Vincent, after they moved to Tucson where Tom played in the local orchestra and earned a Master's Degree in speech therapy at the University of Arizona. Several years after Margaret's death, Tom and his wife, Lucky, decided to move East into our house in Leesburg, Virginia. Lucky, a talented *bricoleur*, has enlarged and made many improvements in the property over the years.

Tom pursued an active career as a violinist in the Maryland Symphony Orchestra and as first chair in the rising Loudoun County Symphony. He also taught violin and viola to adults and children in his Leesburg studio. Several years ago he produced *The Disciplined Bow*, a 90-page, new practical approach to learning violin technique. He worked part-time with the Loudoun County Public Schools teaching Spanish, math and other subjects to homebound students. He had a way with difficult adolescents.

Tom's sons have all profited by his initial instruction in strings. Two specialize in the viola, two in cello, and one in violin. Under Tom's leadership they established the Marks Family Strings which performs at weddings, fairs, and on other occasions.

In the early morning of May 6, 2003, Tom was driving his youngest son Vincent, to school. He had braked at a stoplight but as he again moved forward he was sideswiped by an advancing car and killed instantly. Vincent was badly shaken up, but aside from whiplash, and the horror of the experience was not injured.

Tom's death was a cruel blow, not just to his immediate family and friends but to all who knew him. He was recognized as a leader in the social, cultural and especially in the musical life of Northern Virginia. Tributes came from far and wide, and over a hundred relatives, fellow musicians and friends joined Lucky and their sons at a musical memorial after his death. I was unable to cross the country to grieve with my daughter-in-law and grandchildren but sent the following message read by our dear friend Susan Kellermann:

"How quietly he would sift among the records we had brought to Greece until he found the one he wanted to hear. There were others he liked, but he was especially drawn to one of them, and he would play it again and again.

"He was six or seven at the time. Margaret and I asked him if he would like to take music lessons. We'd heard of someone who was a fine piano teacher.

"'No,' he said quite firmly. 'I want to learn to play the violin.' The record was Mendelssohn's Violin Concerto.

"We didn't know then we were launching a legend—one might almost say a dynasty of fine music, exemplified by what you are hearing today. I long to be with you at Mount Gilead, among so many of the people I love best in this world, celebrating the life of a worthy son. Tom was an exemplary blend of mentor, artist, loyal family man, and friend of the community. He was a conscientious, creative worker, an articulate commentator, a serious citizen and he had an infectious zest for fun and games, especially word games. He was a well-rounded, thoroughly intelligent man.

"In close and loving partnership with Tom for thirty years was Lucky, a woman of remarkable strength and wisdom. She and Tom lovingly created and cultivated these five young men. In the depths of her own grief Lucky found the words to comfort me in our phone conversations this week.

"From California, Vera and I send to all of you our warm affection and appreciation for your touching messages of condolence."

The local press was extravagant in its praise of Tom's accomplishments. The *Washington Post* in its obituary said:

"The Loudon Symphony nearly canceled rehearsal last week to mourn the death of Tom Marks, a beloved violinist who was among the group's founding members...Marks, 59, who was killed in a car crash Tuesday morning, was a teacher to many of the musicians and a mentor to others. Over the years, he used his gentle manner and humor to persuade discouraged players to stay with the group by helping them tackle particularly challenging pieces."

The *Post* quoted several colleagues: "I just can't believe he's gone," said Kathy Crabill, a violinist who was one of Marks's students. "I felt more at peace when I started playing because I felt that in spirit he was there and would have wanted us there." Mark Dalrymple, the Symphony's webmaster and a contrabassoon player, recalled how Marks' contribution to the group went far beyond his own talent. "Every week, Tom was there for rehearsals, working with the string workshop, teaching lessons, leading the string section by example...I watched the Loudoun string section mature into a professional-caliber organization over the years, and a great deal of that credit goes to Tom." Michael Rohrer, a bass player and long time friend, said, "He seemed to revel in every moment, no matter what he was doing...how is it possible that such a life force could be simply snuffed out in an instant?"

The Loudoun Symphony Orchestra honored Tom at a concert where his chair was left vacant. Several of my musical grandchildren performed on that occasion. The Maryland Symphony Orchestra, of which he was a long time member, dedicated a concert to him in the fall of 2003.

I know now what people mean when they say there is no happening so sorrowful as losing a child. It took me quite a while to recover from the shock. My only consolation is the remarkable legacy he has left in five stalwart sons of marked musical ability.

After thirty years of a happy marriage, Tom's death meant, for Lucky, the unbearable deprivation of a loving relationship and the irretrievable loss of so much she and Tom had built up together. Fortunately his sons have been most supportive, spending days at their Mount Gilead home together in a display of family solidarity.

The last time I saw Tom was when he and Lucky made a special trip to visit and comfort me while I was hospitalized in NYC just two months before the tragic day.

TENNIS

From my earliest years, I have been fascinated by tennis and have followed the game all my life as both a player and spectator/fan. My father, brother, sister and brother-in-law played. As low man on the totem pole, I was responsible at an early age for dampening, rolling and marking with lime the clay court we had in Great Neck. Also for pulling the weeds. I was a passable player, but no star. I made the tennis team at Camp Cobbossee and DeWitt Clinton High School, and won most of my matches on the Dartmouth Freshman team. I was an enthusiastic member of Geneva's International Tennis Club and made many friends there.

Margaret was a strong player, a southpaw. She played a good deal in our Geneva years and we joined a tennis club fairly soon after our arrival in Athens. All the courts were outdoors, and it was often too hot to play. Margaret bravely entered the national tournament in Greece which attracted international players. She unluckily drew Margaret Court Smith, then British champion, as her first round opponent. My Margaret got one game, I think probably as a courtesy. After the first set, Smith offered Margaret one of her rackets. "This might be helpful," she said. "You've been playing with a couple of broken strings." Margaret looked at her racket. "Migosh," she said, "I was so nervous I never noticed it."

There was no Sunday meeting of the Organization of African Unity Conference I attended in the former Belgian Congo in 1963. A USAID officer posted in Kinshasa asked me if I would like to play some tennis. It sounded like a great idea but I told him I had no tennis clothes with me. "Don't worry," he said, "We'll fit you out with something." They found socks and sneakers that were my size and produced a dark T-shirt and a pair of gaily colored shorts. We started the game, but a tiny man dressed in white came over almost immediately to tell me I couldn't play because I was not appropriately dressed. The other players, in white garb, remonstrated, asked the club manager to make an exception, but rules were rules, and I had to get off the court. It seemed ironic in the extreme that club rules prevailing in Colonial times were still slavishly observed in a highly unstable nation riven by civil war following the threatened cessation of Katanga.

A few years after my return from Greece, I was running ICEM's New York office, receiving refugees bound for the U.S., mainly those of European origin, in flight from Communism. It was 1956, and refugees from the aborted Hungarian revolution were streaming into Austria. By a quirk of fate, about 20,000 of those fleeing Hungary were given asylum in Yugoslavia. I received a cable from Geneva to proceed at once to Geneva, and then to Belgrade where I was to head an international ICEM mission to resettle the refugees in other countries.

I thought immediately of Myer Cohen, with whom I went to Russia in 1932 and who was later my boss in Geneva. Myer had recently returned from Yugoslavia where he had been the resident representative of the United Nations. I called Myer to ask if he had any special suggestions; I had never worked in a Communist country. Could he give me the names of a few Yugoslavs that he trusted? He gave me the names, then said, "Take your tennis racket." I remonstrated, saying I couldn't arrive in an emergency situation swinging a racket. Myer said, "Stick it somewhere in your luggage. And take an early opportunity to join the tennis club. I found it was the best, perhaps the only place where I could talk informally with the government people. Their homes and offices are mostly bugged." I took his advice, and he was right!

When I lived in Mamaroneck I had a regular weekend game at Harbor Island with Bill Nimkin, Ben O' Sullivan and others. In 2003 I was interested to learn that this public area had become a tournament site where Boris Becker would oppose John McEnroe in a veteran's match and other featured players were scheduled to perform. Washington is an active tennis town and I enjoyed playing with friends there in each of my three incarnations in that city. I taught the children to play tennis when they were quite young. Kate always enjoyed the game but Tom showed a particular aptitude for it. When we were living in Mamaroneck, Ben O'Sullivan and I decided to send our sons to a tennis camp in Hamtramck, Michigan. They were fairly cocky kids until they were pitted against Peaches Barkowicz who was considerably younger and smaller than they were. She easily polished them off one at a time. Be it said, Peaches grew up to be a ranking player.

Tom's game soon surpassed mine but we always enjoyed playing together. He was infinitely patient on the court and invented several variants of the game for short term play. Over the years he taught each of his sons who in turn made the tennis team at their high school. Today they are all excellent players.

Back in the U.S., Margaret and I spent a fair amount of time in our Leesburg house, especially in Washington's torrid summer. We found tennis-playing friends who regularly entered the annual tournament played on the Chamberlain court in nearby Waterford. I was then in my early 50s; Margaret the same age. We fared pretty well: one year my partner and I won the men's doubles, and Margaret and I took the mixed doubles. Then the competition got too strong.

In Saigon, I had little time for anything but work. However Sundays were usually free, and I decided to join Le Cercle Sportif, an ancient but well-maintained facility with a pool and probably a dozen courts. Once a club for the French and expatriates, it now had some Vietnamese members. There were some excellent players, and it was fun and relaxing in the Saigon heat, to have scampering ball boys. One Sunday morning I played at another Saigon court. It was a time of local unrest, and after we'd played a few games, an unfriendly wind blew tear gas generated by a Buddhist demonstration our way and we had to leave the court with smarting eyes. A last note. When I revisited Saigon—now Ho Chi Minh City—with Vera in 1998, I wondered what had become of Le Cercle Sportif. Everything looked different and we had trouble locating the site. It was now an open Vietnamese recreation park, teeming with lively people of all ages on this Sunday afternoon. The courts looked very much the same. There were no ball boys. But the principal change was in the numbers of players. On all but one or two courts, there were *three* on a side—generally two at net and one in the back court. That was a surprise!

When I left Vietnam in 1966 I got the plum USAID job in London that I had previously sought. I was based at the American Embassy in Grosvenor Square. The Embassy wanted to promote social contacts between the U.S. officials and the Brits, and consequently paid most of the dues for Americans willing to join British clubs. I could have joined one of the Pall Mall clubs, such as the Reform, but I chose instead to become a member of Hurlingham. Situated about a half hour from London, the venerable Hurlingham Club was one of the earliest venues for polo. It also has about ten perfectly manicured grass tennis courts. For the first time I (and my feet) had the utterly delightful experience of playing on grass. There was a pool at Hurlingham, one could play at lawn bowls, and croquet was in high favor. In fact, the 100th anniversary of croquet, a game allegedly created at Hurlingham, was celebrated at a grand occasion attended by Margaret, at which the Queen made an appearance. At Hurlingham they also set a decent table. But the tennis was sublime. The combined efforts of Hurlingham and the Embassy got us tickets for Wimbledon, which was a great treat. During my time in London I won the U.S. Embassy tennis tournament staged at the Residence Court in Regent Park.

In Nigeria, Peter Bloom, my deputy, who already belonged, persuaded me to join the downtown Lagos Club with an over 90 percent Nigerian membership, and I never regretted it. A highlight of that experience occurred in 1969 when Arthur Ashe and Stan Smith came out on an officially sponsored U.S. visit. Ashe impressed everyone with his courteous manner and fine array of strokes, but the Nigerians took special delight from the whimsical on-court antics of the towering Smith. Later we joined the mostly expatriate Ikoyi Tennis Club, near our home, and played in several tournaments there, but it lacked the exuberant charm of the Lagos Club.

Shortly before our marriage Vera and I joined the Mount Auburn Club near our home in Cambridge, Massachusetts, which was originally started as a tennis club and had excellent outdoor clay courts and air-conditioned indoor courts. Vera was a beginner and showed a real aptitude for the game. However, she found time scarce since she was still working full time and derived greater rewards from other forms of exercise. She never enjoyed the competitive aspects of club team tennis though together we were able to play a fairly well matched game as she improved and I aged!

In 2001, when we moved to California, I attended a tennis clinic and played some easy senior doubles at the public Mill Valley Boyle Park courts, but reluctantly had to concede that my active playing days were over. I turned to milder exercises and joined a gym where I work out with a trainer.

(upper left) Grandpa Bennett and Grandma Hannah Marks when they celebrated their Golden Anniversary on November 5, 1921.

(lower left) A view of East 65th Street in Manhattan showing brownstone house at extreme right (No. 53) where EBM was born April 22, 1911. The home of Sara Delano Roosevelt, mother of FDR, is shown at the left.

(right side) My Pop and Mom, Edward B. Marks and Miriam Chuck Marks.

(top) A family picture, circa 1950. Surname is Marks unless otherwise indicated: Top row: Stephen, Gloria, Robert, Bernice, Herb, Margaret, Beatrice Landeck, EBM; Middle row: Unidentified, Barbara, Mimi, Mitch, Lulu; Bottom row: Tom, Katie, Alfred, Victoria, Barbara.

(bottom) The 1927 tennis team at DeWitt Clinton High School. EBM is at extreme right, bottom row. At extreme left, same row, is Reginald Weir. Fourth from left is team captain, Sid Snitkin.

(upper left) William Schuman, American composer who won the first Pulitzer Prize for Music. A lifelong friend of EBM, Bill was President of the Juilliard School of Music and President of Lincoln Center.

(upper right) Dr. Henry Kellermann, close friend and colleague of EBM. Kellermann had a distinguished career in the rehabilitation of post-war Germany and as a U.S. Foreign Service Officer.

(bottom) Ferdinand Allan Nauheim, one of EBM's closest friends from age 11 until Ferd's death in 1986. Ferd had a successful business career and was also know for his Ferdoodles, of which one is shown here.

(top) John McLane Clark, Dartmouth friend, with Kim. Clark was Editor-in-Chief of The Dartmouth when EBM was Managing Editor.

(bottom) Seven members of the 1932 delegation of Casque and Gauntlet, a Dartmouth Senior Society, are shown in a post-graduation frolic at Lake Memphromagog in Canada. EBM is at extreme right, bottom row. Behind him is Carlos Baker, later head of the English Department at Princeton and the author of the definitive biography of Ernest Hemenway and other books. Top row: Hazen, Judd, Hatcher, Baker; Bottom row: Hosmer, Keller, EBM.

(top) Herbert Edward Marks, brother, Phyllis Marks Simon, sister and EBM at the 85th birthday party of Phyllis in 1982.

(bottom) Margaret Levi Marks, first wife of EBM.

EBM and four executives of the Hiram Walker distillery in 1935.
We are posed in front of the control panel of one of the giant stills at
the world's largest distillery in Peoria, IL.

(upper left) Katharine Marks, daughter of Margaret and EBM.

(upper right) Thomas Marks and Lucky Niehe Marks,
son and daughter-in-law of EBM.

(bottom left) Marks grandchildren with their mother attending
David's wedding to Fanny Bray in France.
Left to right: Theo, Lucky, David, Vincent, Jethro, Paolo.

(bottom right) EBM and grandson Thomas Branczyk.

EBM, Chief of Mission, UN International Refugee Organization,
Athens, Greece, 1950-53.

(top) EBM in Vietnam, 1965. At left is John Thomas, a colleague and friend of many years, who later headed the U.S. program for Cuban Refugees and the International Migration Organization. Between us is Lt. Hai of the South Vietnam Government's Secretariat for Refugee Affairs.

(bottom) Saigon scene. After twenty-three years, EBM is reunited with foster child Xoi and her Vietnamese family.

(top) On his retirement from the Agency for International Development (USAID) in 1976, EBM receives the first Distinguished Career Award offered by the Agency. The Award is being presented by Dan Parker, USAID Administrator, while Margaret Marks looks on.

(bottom) EBM with Mike Adler, Mission Director of USAID Nigeria during the war with Biafra in 1968-1970, when EBM was Assistant Director for Relief and Rehabilitation.

(top) EBM with second wife, Vera J. Barad.

(bottom) The Barad Family: Standing: Vivian, Jason, Amelia, Todd with Wyatt, Vera, Michael; Seated: Desmond and Ed.

(top) Hugh Downs, broadcaster who still holds the world's record
for the most hours on the air, served for ten years as
Chairman of the U.S. Fund for UNICEF.

(bottom) Henry Labouisse, former Executive Director of UNICEF.
Labouisse earlier headed UN Relief and Works Agency
for Palestine Refugees and was U.S. Ambassador to Greece.

United Nations Secretary-General Kofi Annan and EBM cut the tape opening
the exhibit at UN Headquarters of United Nations Posters based on the book,
For a Better World. The exhibit opened in New York in December 2000
prior to a world tour. Mrs. Nane Annan can be seen at left of photo.

AN INTERLUDE IN HOUSING

As an American I was assailed by twinges of patriotism after Pearl Harbor. With a wife and a three-month- old baby, I didn't feel called on to enlist, though I was prepared to enter the service if drafted. The mission of the War Relocation Authority satisfied my urge to be active in the war effort and was also related to my experience at National Refugee Service (NRS). The job was a constant challenge. But early in 1944, finding that Ferd, Woody, John Clark and many of my friends were in uniform, I began to have second thoughts. These came to a head when Leland Barrows, one of the top WRA officials, resigned to enter the Coast Guard. (I admired Leland. After the war he entered the diplomatic service and it was my pleasure to stay at his Yaounde residence in the sixties when he was U.S. Ambassador to Cameroon.) When Leland enlisted, I was sorely tempted to notify my draft board that I no longer wished the exemption to which my WRA job entitled me.

Before taking this step, I had a word with Dillon Myer, WRA Director. In quiet, persuasive tone he convinced me that in my present job I was accomplishing much more than I would be likely to achieve in a service assignment. At 33, with a second child on the way, I allowed myself to become convinced he was right.

Shortly after the war's end, the Oswego Shelter closed. By that time, the Japanese-American evacuees had left the camps. Most had returned to their former homes on the West Coast, though a fair number of those who had resettled in other parts of the country decided to stay there. (I was pleased to hear this; the diaspora meant that there would no longer be such a concentration on the Pacific Coast.)

In my work at the Welfare Council, I had become acquainted with the efforts made to promote more livable housing conditions. I was especially fascinated by the promise of low-rent public housing. As WRA was leaving the scene, I joined a new government agency created to meet the rising demand for veterans' housing. I found myself in a lively outfit called the Office of the Housing Expediter. During 1946 and 1947, the Office worked with nearly 800 mayors' emergency housing committees to promote home building through community action. Veterans, labor, the building industry, state and local governments, merchants and manufacturers and civic groups were encouraged to pool their efforts to produce low-cost homes or apartments for purchase or rental. For example, the city of Rochester, NY, provided land without cost, and eight banks formed a non-profit corporation to provide 152 apartments for veterans at moderate rentals. In Reading, PA, following the mayor's initiative, large homes were remodeled to furnish 178 additional apartments.

Part of my job was to gather and publicize examples of successful actions undertaken by voluntary community cooperation. We put out a series of Community Action Bulletins. One that stands out in my memory was "Conversions Provide Homes Faster."

About a year after I joined the Veteran's Housing Agency, Dillon Myer was put in charge of the Federal Public Housing Authority. That had greater appeal for me, and I told Dillon I wanted to transfer over to his agency. He agreed, and I entered on the new assignment with high hopes and ideals. It didn't take long before I was disillusioned. The main reason for my disappointment was the lack of interest shown by Congress, which mutilated the agency by its budget cuts. Dillon was a savvy government executive, but his efforts to stem the corrosive tide were fruitless. The fact that he was not one of the public housing cognoscenti didn't help. The experts in the field have their own uncompromising administrative techniques. They had, for instance, developed an irritating, off-putting jargon that in my judgment limited our efforts to interpret the program. It reminded me of a saying voiced by a former boss of mine in a similar type of situation: "I see the bridle and the bit all right, but where's the bloody horse?" While I was with the FPHA, it was threatened with extinction. I stuck with it about as long as Dillon did, but I yearned for a job that would get me back to refugee work.

Myer Cohen, with whom I had traveled in the Soviet Union, was now assistant director of UNRRA—the United Nations Relief and Rehabilitation Administration—which had been established near the end of the war to care for the refugees in Europe's displaced persons camps in Germany, Austria and Italy. UNRRA maintained the refugee camps and helped those refugees wishing to be repatriated to Eastern Europe, but because the Soviet Union was one of its members, UNRRA was constrained from resettling the refugees who wished to emigrate to the United States, Canada, Australia and other receiving countries. I was aware that a new international body, the International Refugee Organization, was to be formed. Since the Soviet Union would not be a member, IRO would be able to assist the many refugees desiring resettlement. I was immediately interested and wrote to Myer, who was slated to be IRO's Assistant Director for Care and Maintenance. He offered me a job at IRO's Geneva Headquarters as Deputy Director of IRO's Division for Liaison with Voluntary Agencies. Margaret liked the idea of living in Europe, so I accepted the offer and we were soon off to Geneva.

INTERNATIONAL FILM ASSOCIATES

In 1946 I was in Washington, working for a time in the Veterans' Housing Program and then in the Public Housing Agency. We lived in a rented house on McKinley Street, near the Chevy Chase Circle. We vacationed in Capon Springs, West Virginia, and on the Eastern Shore of Maryland at Bethany Beach. Margaret and I had a five-year old and a two-year old. We had many friends, including the Timburgs, Barths, Ashers, Spingarns, Gilberts, Kaplans and Mapeses. We had met Spencer Mapes and Mary Losey Mapes through the Schumans. Mapes, as he was known, had been a colleague of Frankie Schuman's in the New York State Employment Service and Mary had taught at Sarah Lawrence while Bill Schuman was on the music faculty there. Mary was deep in documentary films, and with several other specialists in that field came up with the idea for International Film Associates (IFA), a business organization devoted to increasing the sponsorship of documentary films. The magazine *TIDE* for April 5, 1946, featured an article about the venture saying that "for a client, IFA would work out a project of films, recruit talent and supervise all productions."

John Grierson, who pioneered in documentaries for the British government and during the war headed Canada's National Film Board, was IFA Chairman, and Board members included Jean Benoit Levy, French director and educator who became Director of Films for the United Nations, and Robert J. Flaherty, ex-Arctic explorer, known as "the grand old man of documentary films," who made one of the first ones, *Nanook of the North.* Mary was secretary-treasurer, and I was flattered to be asked to serve on the Board. IFA provided research, production and distribution plans for UNRRA, the Intercultural Education Bureau, the Children's Bureau and the American Library Association. However, because Grierson's commitments to Standard Oil and others limited his availability, IFA for a time continued principally as a base for the exchange of information and as a source of reports on specific aspects of documentary film developments.

Mary and Mapes had twin boys about the same age as my daughter, Katie. On a particularly hot summer day, Mary took the twins and Katie and her maid for a drink at the soda fountain of a Peoples' Drug Store. After waiting a long time, it became clear they were not going to be served. When Mary remonstrated, she was told by the clerk and the store manager that they could not serve a "nigger." Mary was not one to take such things lightly, and she protested strongly then and in later correspondence, but it was to no avail in the Washington of that day.

Having seen *The River, The City* and other great documentaries of that era I was always regretful that IFA never achieved its primary purpose. But I left the U.S. the following year to resume refugee work with the UN's International Refugee Organization in Geneva, and Mary eventually followed to take a responsible post in WHO's Film Division. On the ski slopes of Megeve, Mary introduced us to her brother, the film director Joe Losey, who was there with Robert Capa, the famed photographer. Capa was shooting a winter sports story for *Holiday Magazine*, and took a picture of my daughter, Katie, making a clenched-teeth descent, which appeared in the magazine.

OFF TO GENEVA—AND THE IRO

It was with rare excitement that we packed up the essentials and left Foggy Bottom in August 1947 to start a new life abroad. Our friends, the Spingarns, moved into the house we were renting on McKinley Street. They subsequently bought it for $20,000.

We embarked for London on a BOAC two-deck airplane operated by British Airways. Katie by then was a sensible six, but Tom at three was unpredictable, so Margaret dosed him up with paregoric so he would be tranquil on the overnight flight to London. Unfortunately, it had the opposite effect, and despite our efforts to control him, he marched noisily down the aisle of the plane. En route, he was fascinated by the ear trumpet of an ancient Brit and woke him up by blowing into it. We did our best to rein him in for the balance of the voyage.

We stopped in London on the way because I had ordered a small gray Standard we were taking to Geneva. We were late landing at Heathrow that Saturday morning, and although I was able to take possession of the car, we needed papers from the Bank of England before we could take it out of the country. On the phone, the Old Lady of Needle Street was obdurate: the Bank closed promptly at noon. But in response to my impassioned plea that we couldn't wait until Monday, the reluctant office stayed open an extra half hour, we got the papers, and were triumphantly on our way.

In Geneva, we put up at the Champel pension of M and Mme Jordan. Except for a venerable pensioner, we were their only guests. We had a comfortable downstairs suite, and every evening Mme Jordan served us a reasonably good dinner. The breakfasts were choice. Neither of the Jordans had any English, but Margaret's French was quite good and mine improved each day. M. Jordan was a small, dark man with flashing eyes. He was almost excessively polite, but he did relish correcting our French. One evening he came in with a telegram for Margaret. He stood there while she opened and read it. Her face blanched a bit. "Mauvaises nouvelles, madame?" he asked her. "Oui," she replied, "Ma mere est mort." His response was entirely in character, "*Morte*, madame," he said.

Shortly after our arrival in Geneva, we installed Tom and Katie in a home d'enfants in Villars, an attractive mountain resort a few miles east of Lake Geneva. We thought the cool mountain air would benefit them in hot August, and the exposure to French would be an asset when they started school in a few weeks. In retrospect, they were perhaps too young for the experience and felt lonely, even though we visited them on the weekends. By the time they returned, we had found a comfortable house in Carouge, a suburb of Geneva, located within a few miles of the French border. Carouge, we learned, had an interesting history and tradition in the arts. In the opinion of some Carougeois, Geneva was a suburb of Carouge. We lived on the Route de Drize, named for a lazy stream soon discovered by my children who played along its banks with their Swiss neighbors. Our house was located on a good-sized plot dominated by a huge Wellingtonia Sequoia tree. When he was a bit older, Tom would terrify us by climbing to its upper reaches.

The Monday after our arrival in Geneva, I drove to the Palais des Nations, where the headquarters of the International Refugee Organization (IRO) was temporarily situated. The Palais, a large, ungainly white building, was built to house the League of Nations, but was taken over by the United Nations after World War II. The large park on which it is sited, with its commanding view of Lake Geneva, had been given to the League by a Swiss family with the understanding that three conditions would always apply: 1) the family burial plot would remain undisturbed; 2) the park would be open to the public, and 3) peacocks would be allowed to roam there unmolested. To this day, one is charmed by the gorgeous plumage of these lordly creatures, if not by their weird, cacophonous honk.

The interior of the Palais, with its long winding corridors, is a labyrinth. My stay there as an IRO official was fairly brief—we moved to the Palais Wilson, then to a temporary building on the rue des Paquis, but 25 years later, when UNICEF moved its Paris office to the Palais des Nations, I spent almost two years trying to find my way around the ungainly building. At some point in its past, in tribute to its maze-like character, some wit decided that one of the corridors should be called La Salle des Pieds Perdus—the Corridor of Lost Steps. An apt characterization!

Working for the IRO was my first experience in an international organization. Our first Director was William Tuck, a superannuated U.S. diplomat, contemporary and friend of Herbert Hoover, but I had very little contact with him. However, I had a high regard for his successor, J. Donald Kingsley, a much younger, more appealing, and more imaginative executive. Myer Cohen as Assistant Director for Care and Maintenance supervised the bureau to which I was assigned, and we were able to continue our friendship of some years in a cordial and effective working relationship. Myer was a genial, creative spirit and a good boss.

I worked in Myer's office under a redoubtable Canadian woman named Marjorie Bradford, Chief of the Division of Voluntary Agencies. Marjorie had had the same responsibility in UNRRA. Well into her fifties, she had rather set ideas about things, but was a decent person, well versed in the capabilities and liabilities of the forty-odd national and international agencies we worked with. I was Deputy Chief of the Division. The Non-Governmental Organizations (NGOs) provided valuable supplementary assistance to in-camp or free-living refugees. Some found sponsors, jobs, housing and other forms of aid for resettlers. The Quakers offered orientation to the U.S.-bound migrants. The Unitarians conducted classes where doctors could catch up on recent developments in the medical field. I knew quite a few of these agencies from my previous work—among them Catholic Relief Services, Church World Service, AJDC, the Boy Scouts and Girl Guides and the YM/YWCA, but found there were many others in the picture including the Lutherans, the World Council of Churches, the Mennonites, the American National Committee in Aid of Homeless Armenians, and the British, French, Polish, Italian, American and Yugoslav Red Cross Societies. There was also the Jewish Agency for Palestine, not really an NGO, but the quasi-governmental body we dealt with prior to establishment of the State of Israel.

In post-war Europe, especially in Germany, where the largest number were located, the agencies needed billets, gas for their vehicles, identity papers, shipment of supplies, and other forms of logistical support. IRO signed agreements with most of them to facilitate their work. Altogether we staked the agencies to more than a million dollars in cash and kind. But this was many times repaid by the services they performed.

I found in this job, as well as in prior and subsequent assignments, that while NGOs can sometimes be a nuisance, they can make an important contribution—give you a bigger bang for your buck—if they are guided in constructive channels and given reasonable logistical support. They generally have more flexibility, and can often provide a personal touch, too often lacking in the performance of a governmental or intergovernmental agency.

Marjorie had brought over from UNRRA a young Welshman named Trevor Pierce, and he and his Norwegian wife became friends. Another member of our staff was Daniel Clouzot, a Frenchman with long residence in Geneva, who had published several books of whimsical children's stories. We worked together quite well as a unit; periodically, one or another of us would make a trip to the field, usually to visit refugee camps in Germany, Austria or Italy and consult with the volags (voluntary agencies or NGOs) working there.

In our Division of Care and Maintenance I re-encountered Marie Lane, Welfare Chief, whom I had known at New York's Welfare Council. I also worked closely at times with IRO's medical staff headed by Rudolphe Coigny, a Frenchman, assisted by Jimmy Petrie, a Scot and Pat Kennedy from Ireland.

Not long after our arrival in Geneva I was invited to join a group of officials and NGOs who were going to visit Dachau. In the party were two old friends of mine, Walter Bieringer and Martha Biehle. By the time of our visit, the last imprisoned residents had been moved and the premises scrubbed and sanitized, including the shower room and other lethal facilities. That should have made the visit more tolerable, but instead it accentuated the stark precision of the horrors that took place there. My subsequent visits to the Holocaust Museums in Washington, Paris and Israel gave a more realistic but somehow less ghastly image of these designer death machines.

At the end of World War II, an estimated eight million displaced persons (DPs) were liberated from prisoner of war enclosures, concentration and slave labor camps. Most desired to return to their homes. To accomplish this, the victorious armies and UNRRA, working with repatriation missions from countries of origin, organized transport by truck, train and boat to France, Belgium and Holland, to the Scandinavian countries, to the Baltic states, and to Russia, Poland, Yugoslavia and other countries in Eastern Europe.

But with the descent of the Iron Curtain, many refugees proved unwilling to return to communist regimes in Eastern Europe. The UN's Economic and Social Council decreed that repatriation should be carried out only with the consent of the individual refugee. UNRRA continued to give legal protection and assistance to more than one and a half million refugees in German, Austrian and Italian camps or living precariously in the local economy. It could also aid the diminishing number of those wishing to repatriate. But its mandate did not permit aid to refugees wanting to resettle in a third country.

The Economic and Social Council early in 1946 recommended that UNRRA and the Intergovernmental Committee in London should be succeeded by a non-permanent specialized agency of the United Nations which would be responsible for all work done on behalf of refugees. But in the discussions leading to the creation of the International Refugee Organization (IRO), there was clearly a difference in the views of the Western countries and those of Eastern Europe. The former regarded the rights of the individual as paramount, but the latter felt the state should be the sole determinant of individual interests. This breach became most evident in differing views of repatriation, The West held it should be voluntary; the East, compulsory. Soviet Russia, Poland, Ukraine, Byelorussia and Yugoslavia opposed the draft when it came up for a vote in the General Assembly later in the year, and eighteen nations abstained.

It was decided that IRO should have a budget of $155,860,550 for administrative and operational costs and that the United States should be assessed 45.75 percent of the operational budget of $151,060,500. By February 1947, eight countries had notified their accession and a Preparatory Commission was set up which became operational on July 1, 1947, by which time 13 states had become parties to the Constitution. I joined the IRO Secretariat the following month, but it remained a provisional body for an additional year until Denmark and Luxemburg joined in August 1948. In all, 18 nations joined IRO.

The new international body carried on UNRRA's responsibilities for identification, registration, classification, legal protection and voluntary repatriation, but in addition it provided resettlement and transport services. IRO took over a caseload of 720,000 persons in camps, who still required material assistance, and another 900,000 stateless persons requiring legal and political protection and aid in completing their reintegration into society.

Over 300,000 of the camp dwellers were Polish; 155,000 came from the three Baltic states, 100,000 hailed from the Ukraine and 30,000 were Yugoslavs. Slightly more than a third were Roman Catholic; the balance were mainly Greek Catholic, Greek Orthodox, Protestant and Jewish.

During more than four and a half years of activity, IRO resettled close to a million refugees, mostly to such countries as Australia, Canada and the United States. IRO furnished travel documents to the stateless refugees and maintained the world's largest civilian fleet of 40 ships, transporting an average of 30,000 refugees per month to overseas destinations. To enable candidates to qualify for a particular immigration scheme and to accelerate their integration, IRO provided vocational training and/or language training. At the height of the program, in mid-1949, a total of 10,000 attended vocational training classes for a variety of occupations. In the same period 38,000 were receiving language training; the majority were learning English, but many persons were enrolled in Spanish, Portuguese and Hebrew classes. Voluntary agencies cooperated with IRO in providing vocational and language instruction. Their input was also important in health and rehabilitation programs, counseling, and individual resettlement, as distinct from mass resettlement.

At first, the rigid immigration laws of the United States severely limited the admission of Europe's residual refugees. The U.S. quotas for Hungary, Yugoslavia, Rumania and other countries of Eastern Europe were woefully small. A wave of public sympathy aided the sponsors of special legislation to open the floodgates, and two acts were passed in 1948 and 1950 which eventually resulted in the acceptance of about 400,000 DP's.

Only 5,600 were admitted to Australia in IRO's first year, but in 1949 the increase in mass movements brought the rate of acceptance to almost 100,000 a year. In three years some 87,000 refugees were accepted in Canada, consisting mainly of agricultural workers, domestic servants, lumbermen and specialists in various trades. Argentina, Brazil and Venezuela were among the Latin American countries accepting significant numbers of refugees. The majority of the Jewish refugees in IRO care opted to migrate to Israel, though others with family connections wound up in the U.S., Argentina or other countries.

In IRO's first year, the rate of repatriation was about 4,000 per month, but in the second, it dropped to barely 1,000 per month. In 1949, with the acceleration in resettlement, the number of refugees receiving care and maintenance fell for the first time below 500,000. The United States was the most insistent of the countries urging an early termination of IRO because of its high operational cost. The IRO's 18-member General Council decided that the Organization would be phased out June 30, 1950. This gave rise to the need for a realistic inventory of remaining problems and their eventual solution. The receiving countries were constantly draining off the younger and stronger refugees. Repatriation was down to a trickle. Some of the remaining camp residents would doubtless qualify for resettlement opportunities. But it was increasingly apparent that arrangements would need to be made for long-term care of at least 160,000 "hard core."

The Council recommended to ECOSOC that "international assistance in the protection of refugees should continue unbroken." It then authorized IRO Director Kingsley to negotiate directly with governments, occupying authorities and institutions to arrange for permanent care of persons denied resettlement opportunities because of physical, social or economic hardships. Thus began what we irreverently dubbed "Operation Handout." IRO allocated $22 million to assist local governments and voluntary agencies in providing long-term care for the "hard core."

As a cog in the machine, I made a trip to Germany, where 75 percent of the hard core cases were living in the limbo of DP camps to consult with various cooperating volags and denominational welfare agencies. I was accompanied by Helen Wilson, a social worker and friend of mine.

The refugees chiefly affected were people with health problems, unattached men over 45 and women over 40. Professionals with skills difficult to adapt were another vulnerable category. And there were a substantial number of cases where the nuclear family was too large. Typical of these was the family of a 53-year-old widow with four children. The oldest, a 21 year-old son working as a camp policeman, might have made it on his own, but the family was determined to stay together. A 16 year-old daughter was in training to become a dressmaker, and two younger children, 15 and 11, were still in school. The family had been turned down for several mass schemes and had no relatives abroad who might sponsor them for individual resettlement.

The major receiving countries took some hard core individuals on mass schemes if they were part of an otherwise viable family. However, Australia required that parents of migrants accepted for mass labor schemes wait at least two years before being called forward. Western European countries, especially the Scandinavians, took more than their fair share. Israel took a larger number than any other country; as a result, the percentage of Jews remaining in the hard core category was lower than that for other groups.

The Survey Magazine, edited by Paul Kellogg, ran in its September 1949 issue, an article I wrote about *The Hard Core DP's*. I termed their fate "a challenge to the world's conscience" and described the situation outlined above. Fortunately, IRO was extended until December 31, 1951, and before it finally left the scene, the German Land (State) governments and the principal church organizations found place for virtually all those unable to qualify for other solutions.

In the summer of 1949 I spent a month in Pasing, near Munich, where Funk Caserne, the largest of the camps in Germany, was located. I went there as a temporary replacement for Bill Boe, who headed the Voluntary Agencies Division for the U.S. Zone of Germany. Bill had been in the Norwegian Underground during the war, and was in poor health due to his confinement in the Mauthausen concentration camp. He was a likeable, enthusiastic chap and I looked forward to seeing him and his colleague Knut Okkenhaug on my visits to the U.S. Zone. I recall a particularly wild evening when I joined Bill and his colleagues in a celebration of Norway's national holiday.

Funk Caserne was one of the better organized refugee camps. At the time of my stay, there was a highly volatile atmosphere, with frequent visits by country selection missions and trainloads of resettlers leaving almost daily. Paul Edwards, from the American West, was one of the top executives of the refugee operation in the U.S. Zone. A hearty, picturesque character, he later went with UNICEF. One of Paul's associates was John Thomas who came to his job in the U.S. Zone from the army, later went into IRO Headquarters, and subsequently had a brilliant career in refugee work. I don't believe I ever visited Wildflecken, a smaller camp inhabited mainly by Polish refugees. But I knew Kathryn Hulme who worked there for several years and wrote a great book about the experience called *The Wild Place*. I commend it as a great read. In later years, Kate wrote *The Nun's Story*, widely read and translated to the screen.

I made several visits to Lemgo, seat of the refugee operation in the British Zone of Germany. It was under the command of Major General Fanshawe, who in my perception exemplified the essence of the British military. Working with him was a lively Scotsman named Tom Jameson, an American named Mike Thomas, and Jeanne Vickers, a young British woman who later joined UNICEF. Being in Lemgo was like being in England: British military vehicles abounded, and you could shop at NAAFI, the British equivalent of a PX.

Just prior to the creation of Israel, the Jewish Agency arranged for the registration, processing and transport of refugees to Palestine. They discouraged—one could say interdicted—the resettlement of Jews desiring other destinations. Sometimes Jewish refugees would surreptitiously come to our office to press their claim to go to the U.S. or another overseas country where they might or might not have a relative willing to sponsor them.

A phase of IRO's work that particularly interested me was the Resettlement Office, headed by Pierre Jacobsen, a Danish-born, young, handsome, charismatic, and extremely able Frenchman. It was said that he was the youngest major general in the French army in World War II. PJ (as he was known to most of us) was fluent in French, English, German, the Scandinavian languages, and had good knowledge of several Asian tongues. He didn't suffer fools lightly and could be bitterly incisive, but I always found him fair. His main aides in Geneva included an Italian count, Robert Rossi-Longhi; Henryk Van Loon, a Dutchman in charge of shipping with Cliff Wyatt as his assistant, and Hans Citroen, Chief of Individual Resettlement. Rossi-Longhi was an affable aide-de-camp. Van Loon was an expert in his field. Wyatt was a big, genial Brit with a remarkable flair for entertainment. He was one of three people I met in my lifetime who could play anything on the piano by ear.

Hans Citroen and I hit it off well and became firm friends. In his job, Hans helped scores of refugees find resettlement opportunities suited to their talents. Hans and his wife, Ruth, were born in Berlin, but as prescient Jews left for Holland soon after Hitler took power. They became Dutch citizens but subsequently had to flee to France and, I think, several other countries in Western Europe, ending up in Switzerland. Hans spoke idiomatic English and his knowledge of other European languages was comparable to PJ's. The two Citroen children migrated to Israel, where Dolly in time became a member of the Knesset. At the close of IRO, Hans and Ruth decided to join their children in Israel. When I visited them in 1953, Hans (now Hanan Cidor) had a job with the Ministry of Foreign Affairs. He told me the most difficult task he'd ever accomplished was learning Hebrew. He learned it well enough to come full circle and served for some years as Israel's Ambassador to The Hague.

Though the deadline for IRO's existence was extended several times, the staff at Geneva Headquarters felt increasingly threatened. Morale was low. What could be done to restore our flagging spirits? I sought out Gene Lyons, a young American in the Budget Office. At a sandwich lunch we decided to write and produce a musical revue. We wrote relevant words to some of the popular songs of the day. Instead of *We Ain't Got Dames*, we wrote *We Ain't Got Jobs!* Instead of *I've Got Sixpence*, we offered *We've Got Generals.* signaling the fact that ex-military brass figured prominently on the IRO staff. Another jingle went "A Brigadier is here to clear your cable. If you've any kind of work at hand, a Brigadier is always near at hand—ready to command!"

Daniel Clouzot wrote a clever French lyric to the tango *Perhaps.* Gene wrote the words for a poignant ballad to the tune of *I Can't-Advance.* I rhymed the names of many staff members in a ditty called *Bowens and Boes* based on the Doris Day hit *Buttons and Bows.* Bowen, one of the Latin American staffers of IRO, did a captivating solo on the Spanish guitar. And for the melodious *Mlle de Paris* we substituted *Mlle de Paquis*—named for the IRO's address on the rue de Paquis:

MADEMOISELLE DE PAQUIS
Lyrics by Edward B. Marks

I reside in the Ville de Geneve,
And I work on the rue de Paquis,
Though in winter I'm off to Megeve
Where I'm learning the French way to ski.

I've got a flat in the old part of town
And a cabana at ONU Plage;

I buy each hat and frivolous gown
And my per diem supports Grand Passage.

Chorus:
Sleek, chic, dressed in the fashion,
Alert, pert, charming and rational
And I think internationally.
Mademoiselle de Paquis
It's the truth, don't you know
It's the girls who make IRO go

We issued a casting call and recruited the best talent available, including a delectable international pony chorus coached by Irene Tissot, our Swiss Personnel Director. When the show was ready, we gave two well-attended performances for a local charity at the St. Pierre Cathedral in Geneva's old town. Survivors of that era still gather around the piano to sing the songs of *Outside the Mandate*, otherwise known as the *IRO Follies*. The cast included yours truly and Gene, who later garnered a Ph.D. at Columbia and went on to teach at Dartmouth. Mike de Sherbinin, a Dartmouth graduate from Chicago, and Sidney Shore from Pittsburgh were reliable performers. Mike and his genial wife, Polly, became our good friends. They eventually moved to Amherst where Mike bought and for some years edited *The Amherst Record*. Claire de Poret, a French countess of a certain age, played the role of a scrubwoman with a mop and great aplomb. Spencer Mapes sang and danced with rare charm. Warren Fuller brought down the house with his rendition of *We've Got Generals*. A tall man, he looked about nine feet high with an enormous shako topping his ridiculous uniform.

Warren, an American with unusual linguistic talent, became chief of mission in Rome after working for several years at headquarters. From there, he was transferred to Brazil. After a few days there, he decided one afternoon to visit a government ministry. When he got there he found the premises closed up. He finally spied a watchman and went up to him. "Don't you work in the afternoon?" he asked. The watchman replied, "We're not open in the afternoon. It's in the morning that we don't work." One night Warren ventured on his terrace to banish a yowling cat. In the dark, he tripped, fell to the ground below and suffered a fatal head injury.

In late 1950, the Greek government sought IRO's assistance in handling an avalanche of refugees fleeing communism. Geneva HQ decided to beef up its small office in Athens, and I was offered the job as Chief of the enlarged mission. I was happy in Geneva, but I liked the idea of running my own show and Margaret was enchanted with the notion of living a few years in Greece. So we took off for a sojourn of nearly three years.

We were genuinely regretful to leave Geneva. Our life there had become most pleasant, and we had made some close friends. We entertained frequently at the Route de Drize and were fond of our neighbors, especially the Meyer family who lived next door. Our children and their four sons were in and out of each other's houses and played together peaceably. Katie and Tom enjoyed their school and became really fluent in French. In winter, we skied with friends in the Swiss, French and Austrian Alps. Margaret and the children became graceful skiers, addicted to the sport. I never learned to ski with much style, but I became more sure-footed and courageous and could manage the intermediate trails at Megeve, Crans, Verbier, Val d'Isere, St. Gervais, Champery, Kitsbuhel, and other resorts. Winter weekends frequently found us at Villars, a relatively short drive from Geneva.

In summer, we swam at the United Nations *plage* on the lake, played many sets of tennis at the International Tennis Club, and enjoyed vacations touring in France, Switzerland and Italy.

Our friends on the ski slopes included Bill Shaughnessy, a Dartmouth graduate of about my vintage, whom I first met on the relocation staff of WRA. When a vacancy occurred in IRO's training shop I thought of Bill, a specialist in employment. He proved a welcome addition to our Geneva circle. For a time, he romanced Jeanne Simmons, an enticing American friend of ours, but he wound up marrying my secretary, Joy Mossop, a lovely looking British girl born and reared on a tea plantation in Ceylon.

When a second vacancy occurred in training and employment, I thought of Spencer Mapes who was not happy in his job, and responded eagerly to the prospect of living and working in Europe. Mary went along with the idea, and lost no time in getting a job in WHO's film division. Mapes was with IRO for about a year when the workload diminished and he was declared redundant. Mary kept on at WHO and Mapes, for a time, stayed at home caring for their twins. This led to family strains, and Mapes took off for the U.S. where he first did a night job at a bank and ultimately got a job with the American Cancer Society. An inveterate smoker, he had to sneak his butts! A year or two later, he and Mary divorced, and both remarried.

Another ski and tennis friend of Geneva days was Jan van Heerden, a one-time South African track star, who had a job at WHO. In the fifties he migrated to the U.S. where he met and married an American, Sandra Ingalls. Michael and Hilda Hacking, Sylvia Baverstock, Ineke Cronheim (Citroen's niece), Cairene and Jimmy Petrie, Vladimir Temnemeroff and Porter Jarrell were other IRO friends we sorely missed.

About this time, we had the sad news that my Dartmouth friend John Clark had been drowned. He had taken two of his children out in a canoe on Thanksgiving Day when the Connecticut River seemed placid, but they were caught up in a sudden storm. Linda, the daughter, managed to clutch a tree in the river and saved her younger brother. But John was swept away. His death at 40 was a great loss. John had almost limitless potential as a journalist or politician.

The prophets of doom at IRO had predicted correctly. After two extensions, IRO was to be phased out in December 1951. It had maintained hundreds of thousands of refugees in camps, repatriated about 75,000, and resettled more than a million for new lives in Australia, Canada, New Zealand, the U.S., Israel, Brazil and other receiving countries. The U.S. no longer felt it could make its annual contribution. The UN General Assembly had decided as early as December 1949 to plan for the establishment of a High Commissioner's Office (UNHCR) by January 1, 1951, with a modest budget of only $300,000 to cover administrative expenses. There was no provision for any kind of material assistance. Because IRO's life span was twice extended, UNHCR did not actually get off the ground until the end of 1951.

In effect, two organizations were created to take over IRO's unfinished work. UNHCR was a later model of the agency headed by Fridthof Nansen in League of Nations days. It could provide legal protection and provide aid to refugees still wishing to repatriate, but it could not resettle them. For this purpose, a new Western organization known as the Intergovernmental Committee for European Migration (ICEM) was formed.

When IRO left the scene, I joined ICEM, serving first as its chief of Mission in Greece, and later as Officer in charge of its New York Office, a receiving point for an additional influx of refugees from Europe, including several plane-loads of orphans.

Before taking leave of IRO, I want to cite its major significance in the administration of refugee problems. As stated in the monograph about IRO that Rene Ristelhueber wrote for the Carnegie Endowment, "IRO, in the community of nations, has represented a kind of superstate devoted to humanitarian and not political ends...Previously, the League of Nations agencies had been concerned mainly with questions of legal protection, and UNRRA, during its brief existence, with relief. For the first time through the work of IRO the problem was dealt with as a whole, from the arrival of refugees in the camps until their landing in the ports of the reception countries."

Louise W. Holborn, a Professor at Connecticut College and a friend of mine, wrote the full-scale, 805-page history of *The International Refugee Organization* in 1956.

In the next chapter, I deal with my golden days in Greece, first as Chief of the IRO Mission, and then in the fledgling period of ICEM.

VIEWED FROM THE ACROPOLIS

Greece is an integral part of the continent of Europe, though in the days I lived there Greeks traveling to Paris or London would frequently say they were visiting Europe. In addition to the isolation brought on by WWII and its bitter aftermath, Greeks often view their country as a special case. Though Greece today generally adheres to the institutions and principles affecting other European countries, it somehow remains aloof. It has its own special brand of hubris.

I knew virtually nothing about Greece when I arrived there. My knowledge of the Greek language was based entirely on my knowledge of Greek fraternity letters. At Dartmouth, I'd had a good course in Classical Civilization. Margaret and I were positively exhilarated at the prospect of living and working in an ambiance where we and the children could learn more about this historic country and its heritage.

It will help if I etch in some notion of the refugee dilemma facing Greece when it appealed to the International Refugee Organization for special assistance in the late fall of 1950. A rising tide of new refugees were fleeing the communist regimes of Eastern Europe, and, of these, a significant number were fleeing southward to Greece. Despite the poor state of its own economy, Greece was willing to give asylum to a fair number of these, but was not in a position to assure their long-term future. Indeed, Northern Greece was slowly recovering from occupation by the Italians and Germans and a civil war between the essentially right wing government and the Communist left wing political body, Andartis. During this period an estimated 25,000 children abducted by the Andartis were sent to Yugoslavia and other Communist countries for indoctrination. Through the intermediary of the International Committee of the Red Cross (ICRC), some were returned to Greece. Some remained in Yugoslavia or were sent to Tashkent for more intensive indoctrination.

The new refugees were of two kinds. Some, mainly single men from Bulgaria and Yugoslavia, were alien to the Greek culture, religion, language and way of life. But the larger number, from Rumania and Albania, were of Greek ethnic origin, whose language, religion and folkways were essentially Hellenic. Several generations of the Greek-Rumanians had flourished in Constanza and other cities. Some had functioned as bailiffs in the time of Turkish rule. Many had mercantile, even professional backgrounds. It was extraordinary that despite decades of Turkish rule and Rumanian influences, they retained their Hellenic heritage. They drank Turkish coffee and liked bezouki music but in their language, religion, taste in food and life style they remained solidly Greek.

The Greek-Rumanians boarded vessels at Constanza and came to Greece over the Black Sea. The Greek-Albanians were chiefly Northern Epirots coming from a province of Albania to which the Greeks laid claim. The Greek government apparently reasoned that if a substantial number of these Northern Epirots were retained in Greece they would bolster an irredentist claim which might one day command international recognition. Hence these refugees by and large were denied permission to leave Greece, though many sought to do so. The Northern Epirots arrived by land in Janina and other communities in Western Greece.

Despite its formidable post-war economic and security problems, Greece invoked its strong tradition of asylum to welcome these refugees. But as the flow intensified, they called on IRO to help in their ultimate resettlement. As a consequence, IRO's small office in Athens had to be significantly expanded to meet the rising need.

I flew to Athens in December 1950 to begin my new job. Márgaret and the children were to follow in a few weeks, driving from Geneva to Genoa and then proceeding by ship to Piraeus. I was met at the airport by Jane Moody, the IRO Welfare Officer who was acting director. Jane and her husband Jim had come to Greece from China. Jim was an official of the USAID Mission.

Jane was a breath of fresh air. Originally an Indiana farm girl, she was wonderfully natural and helpful, well informed, and extremely easy to work with. We became friends and colleagues, and after Margaret's arrival in January our families became and remained exceptionally close.

When I arrived, the IRO office on Omirou Street consisted mainly of Jane, Mirano Agopian, an Italian bookkeeper and controller who originated in Rhodes, Doreen Ardittis from Salonika, a general assistant, and George Tsamberis, a Greek administrator on leave from the government. To this mix we initially added a French medical officer, a Dutch eligibility specialist, a British resettlement worker, a New Zealander to handle individual resettlement, and two international secretaries. Hans Citroen, before leaving Geneva, had bequeathed me his most qualified aide, Joan Fillingham, a British lass from Lincolnshire, and Jane fell heir to Karen Ogendahl, a capable Danish secretary with a working knowledge of five languages. The international staff was supplemented by additional Greek, and later refugee workers, some of whom at a later date achieved international status.

Joan was much more than a secretary. She really functioned as a linchpin whose light restraint kept the office routine moving. One of her daily tasks was to dispatch the drivers. We had four or five of these at one time. I wouldn't say they feared her, but she kept them on a pretty tight schedule and they conformed to it. The exception was my driver, Poly, short for Polymachachis. He was a wonderfully effective operator whose knowledge of English was a distinct asset. When I was not using him, he was subject to Joan's dictum.

Among the more interesting local acquisitions were the Pierracou twins, Adelina and Maria. I never met their father who lived in Germany, but their mother of Polish/Italian parentage was a femme fatale who, during the Italian occupation worked underground with British Intelligence and helped many refugees to escape. She was an attractive, fascinating woman. Adelina in time married Andrew Ardittis, Doreen's brother, who headed our regional office in Salonika. Maria fell for, married and moved to America with an ensign she met after she left Greece in 1953 to work for NATO in Naples.

Mimi Bensi joined our team and became a supervisor for the Greek interviewing staff. Cliff Wyatt, on temporary loan from headquarters, helped organize our transport service, training in a talented young Greek named Nick Kaloryopoulas. Cliff was still there when my family arrived and became known to my son Tom as "Clipped Wire."

For many of us the language barrier was formidable. Jane had learned very little Greek during her stay. Jacq Langoussis, our resettlement officer, was a Brit of Greek origin but disdained the language. One way or other we all coped, but our first casualty came from an unexpected source. Mrs. Van Bielandt, the eligibility officer, was actually a Dutch countess. A highly cultivated woman, she spoke fluently the principal Western European languages, but had never encountered Greek. It positively threw her, and she was seriously troubled by her failure to comprehend it. After a month or so of hard sledding she asked me one day for a transfer to another mission. I tried to dissuade her—she was a highly competent officer—but I was unsuccessful. We got an Egyptian in her place. It was a pleasant surprise to find a number of Greek stenographers who could work reasonably well in English, though we rarely found one sufficiently expert to write a satisfactory letter in Greek. Without going into the matter deeply, I learned that there were at least three variations of the Greek language: ancient Greek; Katharevoussa, classic Greek somewhat modified for formal correspondence and speech; and Dimotiki, the common parlance of the people. Most of the newspapers were still in Katharevoussa; a few were turning to Dimotiki. Letters to the government at that time were generally in Katharevoussa. Today Dimotiki is the used language both in parlance and in print.

I had expected to spend a year or so in Greece, but even if I had known I would be there for a longer time I don't think I would have studied Greek. After a while I picked up words and phrases and could often sense what people were saying, but my staff and most of the government people I dealt with could manage English. I also found my knowledge of French was useful, especially in talking with some of the older officials. I'm a poor linguist, but three years in Geneva on top of some French studied in college had penetrated, and I decided to build on that by taking weekly French lessons from a creature who wore the most intoxicating perfume.

In my relations with the government I was fortunate to have my principal dealings with Michael Goutos, the Deputy Minister of Welfare. Michael was a huge, enlightened, capable man, blessed with compassion, understanding and humor. A native of Mytilini, he had gone to Ottawa right after the War as the first United Nations Fellow from Greece to Canada. There, under the tutelage of George Davidson, a former Canadian Deputy Minister of Welfare, Michael learned all about social welfare service. He and Davidson remained good friends through the years. Both in their time served as Presidents of the International Conference of Social Work. In a book about Michael published in 1989, a year after his death, Davidson described him as "smiling, urbane, genial and above all caring . . . truly he was a gentle giant."

Michael was a unique chap, and we became good friends. His wife, Arginy, who survives him, was from one of Athens' best families. She became a valued member of our IRO staff. For almost every question of policy or action—and there were many—I looked to Michael for guidance. Even on matters beyond his direct competence, Michael was sufficiently resourceful and well-connected to get me an answer. He helped us recruit worthy staff members, to find the larger office accommodation we soon required in Athens, to develop regional offices, and on many issues relating to security at a time when the Government was still highly sensitive to foreign influences. We once accompanied Michael and Arginy on a weekend trip to Mytilini (also known as Lesbos, the home of Sappho). He was warmly greeted as he pridefully took us around his native heath.

Michael's department was particularly concerned with the welfare of the refugees of Greek ethnic origin. The state and fate of the alien refugees fell within the province of the Minister of the Interior. I knew the Minister, and periodically had to deal with officials under him who supervised the camps for aliens maintained at Lavrion, on the tip of the Attic peninsula, and on the Aegean islands of Syros and Tinos. The aliens were mostly young men—this was a plus, but few of them were skilled in trades. Also most had only the ragged dirty clothes they wore in making their escape. The Greek police knew little about them, kept them closely confined in these grim internment camps where they lived in huge dark barracks with double-decker bunks, wholly inadequate sanitary facilities and no privacy. You can imagine the reluctance of country selection missions to accept candidates living under these conditions.

On one of my visits to Lavrion, I got talking to an executive of the mining company then operating on the scene. In ancient times, Lavrion produced abundant silver and was thought of as the treasure house of Greece. The contemporary mining company was producing nickel and zinc, but still extant were the tailings of the silver mined by the ancients and refined through their primitive refining methods. Out of curiosity, some of the tailings were put through modern refining machinery. Practically no additional silver was refined—the primitive methods of the ancients had done the job remarkably.

In giving asylum to aliens, Greece was accepting, if not exactly welcoming, some of its most ancient enemies, for example the Bulgarians. (A Greek once told me that in his country Bulgarians were barely considered mammals!) Sometimes aliens coming through to the final stage of selection were denied exit visas or simply disappeared from sight. You'd look for them on a certain day and they just weren't there. This kind of occurrence was not calculated to inspire confidence in the security officers of selection countries.

Michael did what he could to intercede for me with Interior to improve the condition and accessibility of the aliens but there were limits to what he was able to accomplish.

The refugees of Greek ethnic origin were considerably better off. Generally in family groups, most of them were quartered in abandoned hotels and warehouses in Phaleron and other locations near Athens. Families were partitioned off from each other by blankets hung from a wire. Each family had a cubicle for itself but, as in the alien camps, the sanitary facilities were extremely poor. However the ethnic refugees were not under police guard and had considerably more freedom of action. Some established small enterprises in the camps and worked as tailors, barbers, and shoemakers or set up stands to sell sundries. A few even found nearby employment and "commuted" from the camp.

The resettlement process was pretty much the same whether the candidate undergoing it was at the IRO Athens office, in a refugee camp, or in a community where a certain number of refugees had indicated their interest in migration to another country. There were two kinds of resettlement: individual and mass migration. To be eligible for individual migration one needed to have a potential sponsor in the country of choice or a skill highly desired in that country. For most refugees, the option was mass migration—meeting the criteria prescribed by a general offer of resettlement. The first step was determination by an IRO resettlement officer if the refugee and/or family were generally acceptable for immigration. If presumed acceptable, they would then be registered, physically examined by an IRO medical doctor, checked by a security officer and appraised as to their employment skills. Some would require vocational training to bring them up to a certain standard and virtually all would need language training. Refugees completing this process were classified as "pre-selected" and deemed suitable for presentation to the consular officer or selection mission of a receiving country. This was a sensitive procedure in which the IRO presenter would endeavor to portray the family in its best light, even if there were aspects which did not strictly meet the criteria. For example, Australia would normally reject a family if one of the children had a chronic health problem or even, in an actual case, a missing finger. Once an individual or family was accepted for migration there was need for documentation, including exit and entry visas. The refugee(s) would then be scheduled for transport and entered into a manifest. In those days, with rare exceptions, embarkation was by ship. IRO maintained its own fleet or sometimes made block bookings on other liners.

To our surprise, the first mass scheme was not for one of the larger receiving countries but for New Zealand. This was a country hardly known to the refugees, but as they learned about its advantages, they became enthusiastic and many applied. The selection team representing the Kiwis included Jim Stewart, in charge, and Dr. Derek Fair. They were both very personable and understanding and worked cooperatively with us to fill the initial quota.

Early in our Geneva stay Margaret and I had the good luck to meet Gina Fortunata, a young woman from Northern Italy then working in a pension. We took on Gina as a *bonne a toute faire* but she soon became an integral part of our household. The children adored her and we could leave them with her in confidence. When we drove to Italy for a holiday we dropped Gina and the children at her family home in Brescia where they were hopelessly spoiled by her parents when we returned from Naples and Capri a few days later. When we knew we were bound for Greece we asked Gina if she would like to join us. She spoke Italian and French but no Greek of course, but her sense of adventure and bond with us carried the day and she agreed to come. Margaret drove her and the children from Geneva and they arrived in the first weeks of 1951.

After some initial cultural shock (which we all shared), Gina absorbed a bit of the language and acquired a Greek sailor as a boyfriend. All went well for a while, but his frequent absences and obsessive jealousy blighted the romance, and an unhappy Gina returned to Italy. Within a short time she married a childhood friend, became the joint proprietor of the White Horse Inn, near Aosta, and raised a family of her own. We kept in touch over the years, and on a vacation in Italy at least a decade later Margaret and I kept a promise to spend a night at the inn as their guests. It was a heart-warming experience, not least relishing the ravioli we watched Gina make earlier in the day. Gina was right to leave Greece though we sorely missed her. Vera, Kate, Vera's daughter Vivian and I made a second visit in 1990 and it was a great pleasure to see her again. We were saddened when her family notified me of her death in 1993.

I put up at a hotel until Margaret and the kids arrived in Greece, and we then stayed with the Moodys for a few days before locating a temporary home in Kifissia, a suburb of Athens. That wasn't too satisfactory; it turned out not to have a proper heating system and we froze until we found a more congenial small house in the same area. We didn't have the heart to put the children in a Greek school. Instead, they entered the Anglo-American school, which was a good deal more British than American. There they had classes in Greek once or twice a week. They also played with Greek kids in the neighborhood, and before long were able to converse, at least to the point that long after they left Greece, they could still communicate in a secret language.

There certainly were aspects of "culture shock" during the first days of our life in Greece. Not long after the family joined me in Athens, "Ohi" Day, an annual holiday, commemorating the refusal of the Greek Army to surrender to the invading Italians, took place. Each year this is featured by a parade with many flags and the picturesque Greek Evzones strutting at their festive best. My secretary, Joan, arranged for us to see the parade from her apartment window. March 25th was Tom's seventh birthday and he gleefully assumed the celebration was taking place in his honor.

Several days after Margaret arrived in Athens we were invited to a state dinner for Trygve Lie, the first Secretary General of the United Nations. The UN was then fairly thin on the ground in Greece, represented mainly by the UN's first peace keeping body known as UNSCOB (established to maintain peace along the troubled Balkan/Greek border). The WHO had a representative in Greece and I qualified as another head of a UN mission. The dinner for Lie took place at the Grande Bretagne, Athens' leading hotel. Margaret, whose clothes had not yet arrived, would have been happy to skip the dinner, and could probably have done so, but her curiosity moved her to go. She was seated next to an imposing, highly decorated official who failed to make any small talk. After some minutes of silence she got up the courage to speak. "Are you connected with the government?" she asked. He regarded her sternly through his spectacles. "Madame," he said, "I am the leader of the opposition!" Tsaldaris was the recently deposed Prime Minister of Greece. (She dined out on that remark for some time.)

That evening we met a number of UNSCOB officials and their wives who became friends during our stay in Greece, including Jim and Joan Douglas, and the Arosteguis. Paz Arostegui, daughter of the Chilean Ambassador to the United States, was a talented, stimulating woman. Her Cuban husband, Martin, was spokesman for the UNSCOB delegation.

After a few nights in Athens we decided one evening to see a movie recommended by some friends. It was *Rashomon*, a Japanese feature, now a movie classic. The plot involves the recounting by several characters of an incident they have all witnessed. This was confusing enough, but when conveyed to us in Japanese with Greek subtitles it was unimaginably bewildering.

I'll never forget the experience of changing money those first days in Greece. At that point the *drachma* was quoted at 15,000 to the dollar: before long it went to 30,000 to the dollar. To change money you first went to a bank and changed your dollars into gold pounds. You then took the gold pounds to one of a dozen or more money changers who were sitting mostly cross legged on the pavement in front of scales. They proceeded to weigh your gold pounds meticulously and gave you *drachma* at the prevailing rate for dollar transfers. This was not a fixed rate—it fluctuated wildly under the prevailing inflation. I never understood the economics of all this but before long the government deflated the currency and the rate for the *drachma* was set at 30 to the dollar.

As soon as we were reasonably comfortable in the second Kifissia house, we began to explore on weekends some of the country's famous antiquities. We drove north on rough roads to Delphi and to visit Mount Olympus, timing one trip to include a rare and memorable performance of *Oedipus Rex* featuring the famed Greek actress Katina Paxinou. Heading south, we relished the glowering mosaic of the Christ Pancreator at Daphne which Osbert Lancaster in his book *Classical Landscape with Figures* calls "the most nearly satisfying portrayal of Our Saviour which Christianity has so far achieved...a much needed antidote to...those regiments of ginger-bearded, whey-faced scout masters which infest the children's corner in every church in the land." A favorite destination was Sounion, a gorgeous promontory near the tip of Attica. Further into the Peloponesus we explored Corinth, Tripolis, Mystra, Mycenae, Epidaurus and other famous sites. I recall a visit to Bourtsi castle on a small island near Tripolis, an unlucky spot said to have been the home for retired executioners.

Wherever we traveled we were charmed by the beauty of the land and the innate courtesy of the Greek people. With a few exceptions, we were also pleased to find the facilities well ordered and clean. You could get a passable and often delicious Greek meal in the smallest village. One custom was invariable: even at the most modest eatery you were immediately served a glass of cold, clear *nero* (water). The selection of food might not be large but one could usually count on fresh fish or tastefully prepared lamb.

Greek beer is very palatable and so were many of the local wines, especially the white varieties. I even learned to tolerate the resin-flavored retsina, much prized by the Greeks. There's a pretty story of its origin. The ancient Greeks kept their wine in goatskins. This left an aperture to seal, and they applied a closure of pine resin which imparted a unique flavor to the wine, continuing to this day. If it's cold enough I can tolerate retsina, especially the red variety, called *coccinelli*, but Margaret said it spoiled her taste for furniture polish.

For a time we patronized a Piraeus restaurant called Vassilena. It was important to arrive early. There was no printed menu. Instead the patron brought you, in surprising order, a succession of highly edible dishes. Main courses arrived at seemingly random junctions and instead of dessert the fifteenth course might be hors d'oervres or even a hearty soup.

A culinary treat that stands out in my memory was dinner with George and Naz Mardikian. When they phoned me one day on their arrival in Athens, I invited them for dinner. George declined, saying it would spoil his fun—we would accompany them instead. I knew that George, an Armenian, was the proprietor of the famed Omar Khayam Restaurant in San Francisco, and I wondered where he would take us. It turned out to be a tour of several places offering gastronomic delights. At each spot we would enter by the kitchen. George would then, in one language or another, talk a blue streak to the first person he encountered, meanwhile literally sampling the food and selecting a few items for our delectation. Then we would move on to the next place. He was in his element.

I first met George after the war in Germany where he headed the American National Committee for Homeless Armenians (ANCHA), one of the NGOs which helped IRO place refugees of varying nationalities. George himself as a young boy was a refugee during the expulsion of thousands of Armenians and others by the Turks in the early 1920s. He found temporary employment on a Greek Isle and managed to save enough money for passage to America. George washed dishes day and night in a New York restaurant, hardly ever seeing daylight. Finally, he realized his dream of California and bought a rail ticket to San Francisco. At a train stop near Kansas City, George saw a large group of men wearing red fezzes board the train. He was terrified and locked himself in a men's room. The conductor who found him there had difficulty convincing him that he was not being pursued by Turks. The men, of course, were Shriners.

George worked hard and with talent in San Francisco and in time became leader of the Armenian community, a very successful restaurateur and a wealthy man.

ANCHA was not among the NGOs active in Greece. I don't recall that we had any Armenian refugees. But from the start of our operation in Greece, a number of other NGOs supplemented our efforts to identify refugee candidates and help them on their way to resettlement.

I had exceptional cooperation from the World Council of Churches (WCC) and its related Church World Service (CWS), both closely allied to the Greek Orthodox Church. Mollie Rule, a tall, angular Irish social worker with many years experience was a solid rock of support. Assisting Mollie was Christopher King, who had come out from Geneva at my recommendation to become a close colleague and friend. Christopher was in a torture of indecision about whether to marry an American girlfriend who surfaced in Athens periodically. By the time he decided to do so she wisely abstained. A year later he achieved a union of NGOs by marrying Maria Tseleni, the first Greek Director of International Social Service (ISS). Norman Gilbertson, a British relief worker whose years in Greece had made him fluent in the language, was connected with the Quakers. He was a good friend, later went into business in Belgium. His first wife was Doreen Ardittis, sister of Andrew, who died.

Norman lives now in his retirement paradise with his artist wife, Diane Katsiaficas, on the coast of Greece, not far from Athens. Vera and I visited them there in 1999 and enjoyed good wine, good food and good company. They arranged a special luncheon in their garden and a number of my former staff came. It was a particular pleasure to relax in the garden that Norman lovingly tends. It was the time of Greek Easter and Norman and Diane took us to the island of Evia where we spent a delightful weekend at the home of their good friends, the Noel-Baker family. Edward Noel, a family friend of Byron, first came to the island in 1832. The story of his early life and problems as a foreign landlord in newly liberated Greece was written by Barbro Noel-Baker and published in 2001. She is the wife of Francis Noel-Baker, the current proprietor of the estate called Prokopi, formerly known as Achmetaga. Virginia Woolf visited there in 1906 and wrote in her book *The Grand Tour*, "Achmetaga stands on a flight of steps, with its garden and terraces, and a view far and wide to distant mountains, framed by tall trees." Francis was the son of Philip Noel-Baker, a

British cabinet minister who was one of the founders of the League of Nations. Philip received the Nobel Peace Prize for his work with Fridthof Nansen to provide relief to Armenian and other refugees displaced as a consequence of World War I. Francis himself was a former British MP. During World War II the estate was occupied by German and later Italian troops and was partially burned. The Noel-Bakers take paying guests who are encouraged to study Greek civilization, literature and practical arts. We celebrated that Easter in a hillside grove where wine poured freely as two whole lambs rotating on a spit gave promise of a feast in which the Noel-Baker family and neighboring Greek families participated.

Another stalwart NGO collaborator was CARE, whose representative in Greece was Fred Devine, so that it had the special aura of "Divine CARE." Several Greek agencies were also in the membership of the Greek Council of Voluntary Organizations Aiding Refugees, which I organized, and which met weekly. They included the Greek Red Cross, the Greek Refugee Council and the Queen's Fund. Refugee sponsorship by an NGO was a real asset in enhancing chances for selection.

NGO sponsorship was particularly helpful in the case of aliens. During my first two years in Athens there was no basic improvement in their miserable living conditions. However, many of them were single young men of considerable interest from a migration point of view, especially if they had some education or skill in a desired trade. I could expect, periodically, sometimes at night, calls from Jack Iams at the American Embassy. I never met Jack but I correctly inferred that he was the CIA officer. Jack would inquire about the status of a particular alien, say a Bulgarian, who was being processed by us. "Can you expedite the case?" Jack would ask. "He's hot." I never asked why he was "hot" but did what I could. What I understood was that there were people out to get him and his life would be in danger for political reasons if he stayed there. If the chap had been accepted by a mission and was awaiting transport, Jack asked if we could get him out on the next ship.

The U.S. Government had a special interest in these anti-Communist aliens and finally persuaded the Greek government that something should be done to improve their lot. The Greeks were willing as long as they bore no expense. The result was the U.S. Escapee Program (USEP) under which American funds were used to substantially upgrade the living and sanitary arrangements in the alien camps and provide clothing and other amenities to the aliens, making them more presentable to selection missions.

As IRO neared its end, the government and the NGOs shared our apprehension about the refugees in the pipeline. In the final weeks, we redoubled our efforts to obtain as many acceptances as possible, though we realized that some refugees would embark after IRO had ceased to exist. I knew that the government lacked the funds to do much more than carry on a clean-up operation. I was of course much concerned about the future of the Greek staff we had built up. I reasoned that the internationals would be able to transfer to other missions engaged in work with refugees. The locals were unlikely to find jobs that would pay as well. At that point, incidentally, two of our international staff had married Greek-Rumanian refugees. Karen Ogendahl had wed Mario Scrivanos and eventually they went to live in Connecticut. Jean Inglis, our individual resettlement officer, and the daughter of a New Zealand General, married "Podi" Podimatopoulos and they now live in Australia.

I was also concerned about the fate of "hard core" refugees for whom no permanent solution appeared to be in sight. The Scandinavian countries were generous in accepting a fair number of refugees with health conditions that made them inadmissible under the mass migration schemes of receiving countries. But there was also the problem of the aging parents of refugees accepted for resettlement. Australia, for example, had decreed that the parents of refugees accepted for labor schemes could not accompany their children. After two years, if satisfactorily adjusted, the settlers could call their parents forward. But there was clearly need for care during the two years.

IRO in its waning days was aware of this need and set up a fund to provide for it. I persuaded Kingsley to part with $100,000 to create a refugee home for the aged. I struck a deal with the Bishop of Rhodes to refurbish and equip an existing building for this purpose. Margaret and I visited the place, a former vocational training school. It was agreed that refugee aged would have priority in admission, but to the extent there were vacancies they could be filled by aged Greeks. About forty years later, Vera and I visited the home on a trip to Greece. The condition of the buildings had clearly deteriorated but it still served as a resource for, by now, mainly Greek aged. The Bishop I knew was long gone, but we were given a tour by the Archon of the incumbent Bishop. We made some specific suggestions for repairs and stressed to him the need for better maintenance.

During much of our stay in Greece, and especially during the last hectic weeks, we were fortunate to have Lia Galani as our *bonne a toute faire*. Lia is indeed a gentle soul. The Galani family met and entertained us when Vera and I made our last visit to Greece and we exchange greetings at Christmas and Easter.

Though IRO's demise was in sight our offices were as busy as ever. The influx of new refugees to Greece had slackened somewhat. However, word from migrants of their favorable resettlement in Australia, New Zealand, Canada and the United States had stimulated the interest of earlier arrivals who had not responded to previous calls.

With IRO closing down all over the world we wondered how this continuing demand for service would be met. Also, it would be a pity to break up our operational team of more than a hundred, at the peak of its expertise.

My last trip from Athens was a long delayed visit to Salonika where we had to close a busy office. My visit coincided with a dinner, given by the Jewish Community, to which I was invited. I was introduced to the group which was aware of our help to refugees. I knew that the well established and prosperous Jewish community had been decimated during the Holocaust. While they addressed me in English, the only other language spoken during the evening was "Ladino." This was described to me as a kind of Spanish Yiddish spoken by Sephardic Jews. It wasn't translated for me, so I have no idea of the context. It seemed one of their normal business/social meetings.

With IRO's end clearly in sight, I terminated the lease on our Kifissia house, regretfully sold our Studebaker and we packed up our household goods. It was a sad time for us and also for our children who would be taking leave of their school friends.

As we were heading into winter not knowing what our next destination would be, our family opted for a ski holiday in Switzerland. I had always been curious about the Orient Express, so we now booked passage on it for the northward journey.

We survived the usual round of farewell parties. Parting with the Moody family was particularly difficult. We had been in and out of our respective houses a great deal during our stay in Greece. When Margaret and I returned from a weekend trip, she made a point of thanking Jane for taking care of Tom. "Oh, really," said Jane, "To tell the truth I didn't realize he was here." So much was always going on in that house. We had greatly enjoyed the time in Greece and were reluctant to leave it, not knowing when, if ever, we would set eyes on it again.

I knew our train was scheduled to make a brief stop in Belgrade, so sent advance word of this to Myer Cohen, who was then the United Nations Resident Representative in Yugoslavia. He met us at the station for an all-to-brief reunion before we moved on through Austria and into Switzerland.

I had no job lined up, but I was confident Don Kingsley, Pierre Jacobsen (aka PJ) or others at the disintegrating IRO headquarters would come up with something attractive. IRO was finished, but it had been agreed that two international bodies would take its place. One, within the United Nations, would be non-operational and primarily concerned with protection for refugees, a kind of successor agency to the League of Nations High Commission for Refugees. The second, Intergovernmental Committee for European Migration (ICEM), would continue the resettlement of refugees.

Around this time, refugees resulting from the conflict between South and North Korea gave rise to a new UN agency: United Nations Korean Relief Administration (UNKRA). Kingsley was made its Director General and a number of IRO staff were joining him. That was a possibility.

After we'd been in Switzerland for several days I had a phone call from PJ. He wanted me to head a mission for ICEM that would be continuing to resettle refugees. Of course, I was intensely curious to know to what part of the world he wanted to assign me. Would it this time be one of the receiving countries, Australia or Brazil for example? PJ said, "I have a surprise for you. We want you to open the ICEM mission in Greece. We'll need a new agreement with the Government because this time they want our help in resettling Greeks as well as refugees. You're in a good position to achieve that and you should be able to bring back the staff that did such a good job resettling refugees."

I certainly hadn't thought of returning to Greece. We had just left and I was ready for something different, but PJ argued that the resettlement of Greeks would be an entirely new chapter. After some discussion with Margaret and the family I decided to accept the offer on the understanding that our return would be relatively short term.

I phoned Jane Moody as soon as I knew we were returning to Greece and asked her to line up as many of our IRO staff as possible before they found other jobs. I assured her that she would be staying on as my Deputy for Operations. I wanted to be sure we could hang on to the office space we had; indeed it seemed logical to me that we would need to expand it somewhat. I called Michael Goutos who was pleased at the news of my return, and told him I was counting on his help in developing the agreement with the Government.

I decided to spend a few days in Geneva before returning to Athens. I perceived the need for a second Deputy to deal with the Government on matters relating to our new responsibility, the resettlement of Greeks. For this critical role, I was fortunate in finding just the right candidate. Born in Alexandria, Alexandra Joannides, as a young woman, had been the administrative aide to Eleutherios Venizelos, several times Prime Minister of Greece and an important international diplomatic figure following World War I. After the war, she remained active in the Greek Red Cross and related activities until she retired. I found her at the Geneva home of her daughter, Athena, wife of a Swiss physician. When I met her, Alex was bored with inactivity and mustard keen to take up a new challenging assignment in Greece. Alex knew Michael Goutos and others in the Government. She was probably sixty at the time. She could be stern, doctrinaire, almost unbending at times, but she had class, and speedily won the respect of both the international and local members of our staff. She proved to be a purposeful, dedicated team worker.

As I contemplated my new job I wondered if the principal reception countries—Australia, Canada, the U.S. and Brazil—would be as receptive to Greeks as they were to refugees. In pre-war days Australia, for example, was primarily interested in Brits and other Northern Europeans. But it was said that fear of inundation by Asians had caused a change in their immigration policy. The U.S. had passed several measures admitting refugees but would they accept Greeks outside the minuscule Greek quota?

Reaching an agreement with the Government for the migration of up to 30,000 "allegedly surplus" Greeks, even with Michael's help, was more arduous than I had expected. Right from the start there was opposition from at least one political party and from *Athinaiki,* the popular newspaper. *Athinaiki* held that immigration of the youngest and fittest would represent a drain of some of the

best elements in the population. They maintained that the solution to the problem was internal social reform. I was for the program because I believed in immigration, and there were certainly a lot of unemployed. I believe that all countries need a periodic infusion of new blood. Moreover, resumption of Greek
settlement abroad would bring certain advantages to Greece in increased trade,
foreign exchange resulting from remittances of migrants to their families in
Greece and, eventually, increased tourism. I was told that in pre-war days the
foreign exchange produced by Greeks abroad was a big factor in balancing the
country's budget. These considerations weighed heavily with the Government
and much conservative public opinion.

Under the proposed agreement we would still not be able to move Northern
Epirots or, in principle, Greeks from sensitive regions in the north. A high official of the Ministry of the Interior opposed the migration of any single women
under the age of 35. We could not tolerate such a restriction because, for example, we planned to train young single women to become domestics in Australia
and Canada.

We finally settled on an agreement that took care of most of these problems.
I am happy to say that fifty years later the agreement, with very minor revision,
is still in effect.

Shortly after the agreement was signed, Harold Holt, Australia's Minister
for Immigration, demonstrated his lively interest in our selection process and increasing movements down under by making a visit to Greece with his wife. The
Holts were a delightful couple and we took pleasure in extending hospitality to
them. Holt was an enthusiastic swimmer and particularly enjoyed a day at the
beach. I was reminded of that day some years later when I read that Holt had
drowned on an ocean swim in his own country. The visit of the Holts to Greece
was helpful in loosening, somewhat, the rigid criteria of McGinnis and other
members of the Australian selection team.

It wasn't Holt, but Eugene Gorman, another official from Canberra, who
came up with an ingenious idea. On Kalymnos and Kos and a few neighboring
islands, Greek sponge divers were out of work because of a reduced demand for
natural sponges: people were buying the cheaper, synthetic ones. Gorman reasoned that some of the idle Greek divers might well be brought to Australia
where they could be retrained as pearl divers. Extensive research went on concerning the type of boat and other equipment used in both operations, the depth
of the dives, etc. In due course, a pioneer group was selected and embarked for
Darwin, including two boat builders. Some of the early placement was successful, but it was not a perfect fit. The Greeks were unhappy in their new location.
They complained that they had to dive deeper in colder, shark infested water.
The upshot was that most of them joined their countrymen who had immigrated
to Melbourne and other cities further to the south.

For our "second coming" to Greece we rented an attractive seaside villa
near Glyfada. Its only real disadvantage was the proximity of the Ellenikon Air-

port. Departing and incoming planes zoomed alarmingly close to our roof, providing a spectacle that never failed to delight the children. Fortunately there were not too many flights. (When I tried to find our house in later years it was nowhere to be seen, having been absorbed in the tarmac of the expanded airport.)

The house was fairly modern and the appliances worked! There was a sunny garden with fragrant lemon and pistachio nut trees tended with loving care by Prodromos, husband of the couple who came with the place ("Prodromos," we learned, meant "first on the road," which translated into "John the Baptist.") We had a constant supply of superb juicy lemons and, when they were ripe, delicious pistachios that Prodromos harvested and processed for our table.

I was lucky to pick up, at a reasonable price, the still relatively new Chevrolet of a departing expatriate. Incidentally, a Greek friend who had been to Salonika after our departure, reported sighting the '49 Studebaker I had sold. It was carrying the royal family on one of their visits to that city. This seemed amazing to me, but he knew the very distinctive vehicle. It was the only one in Greece so far as we knew.

Our medical officer had to enjoy the confidence of the selection teams, so when Dr. Leboyer left IRO, Athens, to take a job in Paris we were anxious to have a suitable replacement. Lutz Kessel, an Israeli M.D., filled in until December 1951 after which Geneva sent us Dr. Darrell Smythe, a short, wiry Australian of serious mien.

Darrell was a pleasant surprise. He was highly professional, incisive in action, and he quickly gained the confidence of the three Greek physicians he supervised. Apart from his medical prowess, he also demonstrated a team spirit that made him a valuable member of our senior planning group.

Several weeks after Darrell joined us, a younger friend of his, named James Robinson, arrived in Athens. Jim had worked with the YMCA in Australia and easily found a job with the same organization in Greece. Jim moved in with Darrell and it was soon apparent that they had a warm and binding relationship. We liked both of them. Darrell was taciturn, Jim of a sunnier nature, more open to the world. Darrell was with us close to a year performing superbly when I received a cable from Geneva informing me that the Australian government was asking for his recall. I protested—Darrell was working well with the Australian and other selection missions and as far as I knew he was enjoying the assignment. Geneva's first response was oblique, but when I pursued the matter I found the Aussies wanted to terminate Darrell because he was gay. That really enraged me. I pulled out all the stops in my reply insisting that Darrell's lifestyle in no way interfered with the excellent job he was doing. Fortunately my insistence prevailed, and our headquarters found the courage to persuade the Australians to back off.

I never told Darrell about the request for his removal, and if he knew about it, he never let on. I didn't see the necessity of upsetting him.

I hadn't heard from Jack Iams for some time when he gave me a call. "Not the usual," he said. "Will you be in Italy anytime soon?" he asked. "There's someone there who'd like to meet you. We'll fly you there and back." He didn't make any further explanation except to say it was not related to my present work.

I had been contemplating a weekend in Milan to meet my brother Herb and his wife who would be passing through there on a vacation trip. Why not, I thought, and I booked air passage. I arrived a day early in time for the lunch appointment Iams had made for me. A well-groomed man of about fifty picked me up at my hotel and bore me off to a small attractive restaurant. He introduced himself as "Browning." After an exchange of pleasantries, and some talk about sports, he came to the point.

"Jack told me quite a bit about you," he said. "He says you've been very helpful to him. I understand you'll be leaving Greece soon. Would you be interested in another assignment?"

"That depends on what it is and where it is," I replied. "I have a wife and two children."

"That can all be managed," said Browning. "We are looking for a few good people, and we'd like you to come with us."

I realized I was being recruited for the CIA and for the moment I didn't know how to react. "Are you talking about a job with the CIA?" I asked.

He nodded.

"Well, I thank you for your interest but I think I'll continue with what I'm doing."

I thought of that interview several months later when I received an interrogatory questioning my loyalty to the United States.

Our working hours in Greece were from 7:30 AM to 2 PM five days a week, returning on three days from 5 to 8 PM. As school let out at two, this made it possible for me to join Margaret and the children for a late, leisurely lunch at Vouliagmeni or another beach. Occasionally we met there Colonel Buck Williams, an affable, grizzled, 60ish chap whom I suspected of being another CIA contact. Buck was vague about his connection with the Embassy. He was lovely with our children and Margaret was intensely curious about his work. In those days, you didn't ask whether someone was with the CIA. Buck would disappear for some weeks, then return. When pressed, he told Margaret he was the coach for the Greek Army ski troops training on Mt. Olympus. Margaret was satisfied with this explanation. I remained skeptical.

Joanna, the wife of Prodromos, was an agreeable servant who cooked well, kept the house clean and filled it with fresh flowers. She accompanied Margaret to the market. Unfortunately neither Prodromos nor Joanna knew more than a few words of English.

One afternoon Margaret was on a deck chair in the garden warming herself in the Greek sun. Prodromos greeted her as he chanced to walk by. "Ahhh, madam," he said. *"Heliotherapia."* Most Greek was still a blur to Margaret, but when she heard *"Heliotherapia,"* she had a sudden flash. It was simply the Greek way of saying "sunbathing." The Greeks had a long word for it. Using the Greek-English dictionary she found that eyes were *"opthalmi,"* heart was *"cardia,"* and feet were *"podia"* (podiatry). In the market with Joanna, she further tested her theory. If she wanted to order kidneys, she'd ask for *"nephriti,"* except that we didn't eat kidneys. Or, if she wanted tongue she could ask for *"glossa."* Here the connection was more obscure until she thought of the English word "glossary."

With some excitement Margaret told me of her discoveries. Now we understood why "bishop" was *"episcopus"* (Episcopal) and church was *"eklissia"* (ecclesiastical). And we understood why it was *"ali baba k* (and the) *saranda* (forty) *kleptomania."* It also explained a puzzlement I encountered daily driving to and from the office. I would pass small delivery trucks almost invariably identified by the sign *"metaphores."* As an English major I knew the literary meaning of the term but had to come to Greece to learn that it also meant the common word "transfer."

Margaret developed her theory into an amusing article that was published in *Travel Magazine* as *Classic Style* in September 1958, though its original title was *The Greeks Have a Long Word For It*! It is reprinted in the next chapter.

My children were of ages when pets were important, so we "adopted" a friendly dog of no particular breed and called her Skylaki, the Greek word for dog. An attractive gray cat started hanging around with the encouragement of Katie, always a soft touch. We called it Grimatia. At first Grimatia was wary of Skylaki but before long they became friends. Skylaki succumbed to a neighboring dog with a roving eye, but unfortunately lost the resulting litter. Grimatia took advantage of the situation and dog and cat entered into a unique symbiotic relationship: every afternoon the cat would snuggle up to Skylaki and drink its milk. This went on for weeks. I inquired near and far but have never heard of a similar occurrence. This brings to mind the strange adventure of a cat belonging to the Llewellyn family (I have changed their name.) Major Llewellyn was a neighbor and their daughter Sharon was a friend and playmate of Katie's. The curious happening described in the chapter *The Major's Cat* occurred when the Llewellyns made their plans to leave Greece.

We found that Greeks, all over the country, were avid for migration. When recruitment for Australia was taking place, we had to call in the police to help us control the lines of applicants in our Athens office. We also had many candidates in Patras, Salonika and the islands.

One day Joan told me a woman on the next transport for Australia wanted to see me. "She wants to thank you."

It's always nice to be thanked. "Have her come in," I said. I presumed she was happy to be going to Australia but that wasn't what she had on her mind. She wanted to thank me for the chance to be married. The Australians had given us rather narrow criteria for this scheme. They wanted one third single men, one third young couples without children, and one third families with a bread winner under 45 and not more than two children. The initial scheme was for 3,000, and as McGinnis put it—they were all to be Greek Gods!

The young man in this particular case had applied to go as a single man, but the quota for that category was filled so he asked my visitor to go as his bride. He had thought of marrying her, but she came from a poor family and had no dowry. Now they could go as a couple.

One of my workers told me about a family she had presented to the Australian selection mission. They were the right ages, the man had a good skill, they were healthy and had passed the security requirement. Why then were they rejected as there was still room under the quota? I brought up the case to McGinnis when we were having a drink. He blocked and parried, but I bore in on him. Finally he confessed, "Touch of the tar brush," he said. I succeeded in shaming him out of it and the family left on the next transport.

When all three of Australia's selection categories were filled, they came back for a second helping with the same criteria. We insisted on greater flexibility permitting the acceptance of many worthy individuals and families. Because they were satisfied with the first group, the Aussies agreed.

So far as I know ICEM/Athens is still preselecting Greek migrants for Australia. Of course, by now, there are many Greeks in that country, and it's likely that new immigrants are admitted under family reunion schemes. I believe ICEM is still training young women to go as domestics.

ICEM some years ago had a change of name. It is now the International Migration Organization (IMO). Think of IMO as shock troops with the capability of moving almost anyone from one part of the world to another.

Near the end of my stay in Greece, the government relaxed its criteria against recruitment in several areas of the North. We found the impoverished agricultural workers in Serres were interested in migrating to Brazil. Up to that time we were sending 100 to 150 individual migrants monthly to the states of Parana, Santa Caterina and Rio Grande do Sul. Antonio Houaiss, the Brazilian Consul, had sought to develop a mass scheme, but it never worked out while he was in Greece. The selection of the Serres group seemed like a natural. But we were wrong. After they had been in rural Brazil for a short time, many of the Greeks requested repatriation. They couldn't tolerate the diet of rice and beans and actually felt the standard of rural living there was worse than they had had in Greece. The experience of the Serres group was the only instance I recall in which a resettlement scheme went sour.

About this time, our Deputy Director Pierre Jacobsen flew down from Geneva to pay us a visit. Unfortunately, his luggage got lost enroute and was not retrieved during his stay. He was not amused. I was reminded of the prevailing fable about breakfast in Paris, lunch in New York, dinner in San Francisco and baggage in Singapore! PJ was on the whole an excellent leader, though we battled with him over operational expenses and periodic delays in obtaining the transport we required. PJ ran the show, though the nominal head of ICEM was an ex-U.S. Ambassador named Hugh Gibson.

Gibson was well on in years, harking back to the generation of Herbert Hoover and other post-World War I care givers. Gibson took a special liking to me when I met him on one of my trips to Geneva. He insisted that I stay with him on my next visit instead of putting up at a hotel. A widower, he lived alone in a formidable, castle-like estate on the lake. When I told him my flight from Athens might get me there after his bedtime, he said not to worry. He would leave a "paper chase" at the door that would direct me to my bedroom, and even to his refrigerator, if I felt like a midnight snack.

Gibson was a gentle, thoughtful, wise and genuinely appealing man. I enjoyed our breakfasts and other personal contacts. It was fun to talk with him, especially about "the old days." He gave me a copy of his biography. Among other anecdotes it identifies him as the creator of the "Gibson Cocktail." As a young Foreign Service Officer in Washington he used to join his confreres after work at the old Ebbett Bar. He found the martinis they ordered were too strong for him, so he went to the bar early one evening and asked the bartender to make his martini weaker and identify it by inserting an onion instead of an olive. One evening a colleague noticed the change and told the barkeep he'd like to try one of those "Gibsons." The rest is history.

Gibson had been Ambassador to Belgium, Brazil and several other countries. His deceased wife was a Belgian. One year in Brussels when he hosted the usual Fourth of July party a young man in the reception line did the unpardonable when the Ambassador politely welcomed him. "If you know me, Mr. Ambassador," he said, "What's my name?"

"Young man," said Gibson, "If you don't know your own name how do you expect me to tell you?"

When I was going to NYC on home leave, Gibson asked me to deliver a letter to Hoover, then residing in the Waldorf Astoria apartments in NYC. It was mid-afternoon when I was ushered in, and it was apparent the ex-president had been napping. However, when he heard the name "Gibson" he snapped to: it was evident that he held the Ambassador in great esteem. He (then in his 80s) asked about "young Hugh's state of health" and what he had been up to and had me answer a few questions about ICEM.

Through the Moodys we met a number of Americans working in the Mission to Greece of the U.S. Agency for International Development (USAID). I liked Jim Moody a lot, but I'm not sure I ever really got to know him. Jim was tall, easy going, bright and always well informed on political events. It pained me, and it was devastating for Jim and Jane, when he got an interrogatory from the government alleging that he was suspected of un-American activities. We had read about the hearings of the Dies Un-American Affairs Committee of the House and the more recent witch hunting of Senator Joseph McCarthy. Jim answered the interrogatory to his own satisfaction but not that of the Committee, so he was summoned to a hearing in Washington. Among the serious allegations was that he was a homosexual. At that time the government was trying to weed out homosexuals from service. This accusation was hotly denied by Jim and Jane. Jim was never shown any corroborative evidence. I was among those who filed depositions attesting to Jim's integrity, good character and loyalty to the United States. Jim was not the only USAID official to receive an interrogatory. Another friend of mine, Alan Strachan, a likable mid-level official, got one. Strachan was a kind of Scottish socialist but I can't believe he was ever subversive so far as the United States was concerned. His daughter, Heather, was married to Tom Foley, a prominent Congressional figure for many years. Alan was called in for a hearing and he was ultimately cleared, but Jim was fired.

Jane put up such a battle to clear Jim's name that in 1954 while his case was still pending she got an interrogatory. It had no real substance and Jane was cleared without a hearing. Jim came back to Europe, selling securities for a time, but eventually returned to the United States without Jane, and died in Atlanta some years later. The interrogatory and alcohol destroyed him. Jim Moody Jr., the oldest of their four children, became a Ph.D. economist who taught at the University of Wisconsin and was elected to Congress for several terms. He served on Ways and Means and other House committees.

Another USAID friend was a fairly recent Dartmouth graduate—a tall articulate chap named Russell Hemenway. Always politically astute, Russ was among the chief organizers of an airport welcoming reception for Adlai Stevenson when he visited Greece. I was very pro-Stevenson and was pleased to attend. When he returned to the U.S., Russ became the Executive Director of the National Committee for an Effective Congress (NCEC), an NGO founded by Mrs. Roosevelt in the late 1940s to advise and support progressive candidates in close congressional election races. Charles Schumer, now a New York Senator, acknowledged the support he received from NCEC when he narrowly defeated Senator Alphonse d'Amato, a long time incumbent.

NCEC carefully watches and appraises the voting records of senators and congressmen, and publishes its findings at timely intervals. It is non-partisan in the support it gives. These days, most of its beneficiaries are Democrats, but it will also assist progressive Republican candidates in close electoral contests. In 2001 I was elected to the NCEC Board of Directors.

We were now back in Greece for a year—longer than I had expected to stay. I was happy with the job we were doing. We were still moving a fair number of refugees. With the help of the U.S. Escapee Program, the living situation and prospects for alien refugees were much improved. We had expected a lively show of interest in migration by Greeks, but were hardly prepared for the demand, not only in Athens but in our regional offices as well. As the migration succeeded, it intensified the opposition of *Athinaiki* and left wing parties, but the government was well satisfied with our accomplishments.

On the personal side it was time for a change. We had been nearly six years abroad and Margaret was anxious to rejoin her family and friends. I was very interested in the job, so I wasn't as avid as she was. The children had heard about the new sensation—TV—and keenly wanted the experience. The U.S. was on the threshold of passing legislation that would permit the immigration of refugees and nationals from a number of countries outside our quotas on an emergency basis. The situation was resolved when ICEM offered me a job in Washington or New York. We decided to leave Greece late in the summer so Katie and Tom could resume their U.S. schooling in September.

About a week before we were scheduled to leave Greece, a disastrous earthquake struck the Ionian Islands of Ithaca, Cephalonia and Zante (Zacinthos), resulting in a considerable loss of life. As the main shock occurred during the meal hour, when stoves were alight, the earthquake damage was intensified by a series of devastating fires. Many survivors took flight by sea.

ICEM had no office in the Ionian Islands, but we quickly anticipated that numbers of homeless refugees would be candidates for resettlement. Mrs. Joannides made immediate contact with the government, and on the third day after the earthquake she and I were invited to visit the islands in a gunboat furnished by the government. Others on board the tiny craft were two government officials, reporters from two newspapers and the French Ambassador. As we approached the islands we were met by several small boatloads of refugees. Some contained survivors who had lost their possessions and, discouraged at the future, were fleeing. Other boats contained refugees who had fled for immediate survival but were now resolved to return.

As I recall, Ithaca appeared to have suffered the least damage. In Cephalonia, a larger island, it was apparent that many buildings had been destroyed, but compared with these Zante was a basket case. Dating back to Venetian rule, Zante had been known for its distinctive architecture. In his book *The Greek Islands*, Lawrence Durrell calls the pre-earthquake Zante "one of the most splendid of the smaller towns in the Mediterranean...only in Italy itself could one find this sort of Baroque style, fruit of the seventeenth and eighteenth century mind." Now, as far as the eye could see, its buildings had been completely leveled with but two exceptions. The two stolid survivors were the Bank of Greece and a vocational training school, both completely undistinguished from any architectural standpoint. These two ugly structures now dominated the landscape. It was my first visit to Zante, but the French Ambassador, who had known the island in better days, was moved to say *"Que le bon Dieu a eu mauvais gout!"* (What bad taste the good Lord has had!)

From many parts of the world funds and relief supplies came to the stricken islands. We sent a team to register those wishing to emigrate. Australia took quite a few. So, eventually, did the U.S. and Canada. I haven't been back to these islands, but understand that they are substantially rebuilt. Fortunately there have been no more earthquakes of that magnitude. Zante, I'm told, bears little resemblance to the old Venetian style town.

This time we were really leaving. Cliff Wyatt arranged passage for us on an Italian ship, the *Roma*. The family looked forward to the return voyage by sea, a first experience for the children. Peter Gibson, the well-qualified officer who was to succeed me in Athens, was not yet on seat when we set sail from Genoa. The *Roma's* course included stops in Gibraltar, Palermo and Halifax before reaching New York. The voyage was pleasant and uneventful. As is customary, there was a lifeboat drill with all passengers required to report on deck. When the drill was about to start, twelve-year-old Katie was nowhere to be found. We weren't worried, but puzzled. We later found she had decided to make a visit to the engine room. I chastised her: "Didn't you know everyone was supposed to be on deck for a lifeboat drill?"

"Oh that," she said. "I did hear something about it, but I thought it was just for people who couldn't swim."

CLASSIC STYLE

(Written by Margaret Marks and published by
Travel Magazine September 1958.)

When I first went to live in Athens I didn't know a single word of Greek. This did not worry me though, as my husband, who had gone on ahead to settle into his UN job and find us a house, had written me, "Don't worry about the language. Everybody here speaks French or English."

And so they did—everybody *he* had anything to do with. But not on my low echelon. Nobody *I* had anything to do with—the maid, the gardener, the plumber, the man to fix the stove, the electrician, the carpenter, the plumber again, the ice man, the butcher, baker, vegetable man, fruit man, fish man— nobody spoke a word of anything but Greek. To be exact, nobody but Prodromos, the gardener. After the German occupation he had served under the British and knew *one* word of English—*"Kaput."* But this did not get us very far. I remember the cold damp day shortly after we arrived when Prodromos came in to light the living-room fire. He pointed to the lifeless ashes and said *"Kaput!"* To keep the conversation going, I pointed to the furniture which had been through the occupation, and said *"Kaput!"* So far it was good, if limited, talk. But then Prodromos pointed to Mount Parnes, visible from the window, and said something incomprehensible. Mount Parnes was not *kaput*, so what could be wrong with it? It seemed terribly important that I should know. Prodromos kept pointing and gesticulating. Finally, with sudden inspiration, he tore his newspaper into tiny bits and let them flutter to the floor. I got it—there was snow on Mount Parnes!

Feats of communication like this went on all day, every day. I could see I was going to waste an awful lot of time in Greece, unless I learned something about the language. In a country where they say *no* for yes, and *ochi* for no—I'd learned that much—the going was certainly going to be rough. Besides that alphabet! I couldn't even use a dictionary because the ones I'd seen took it for granted you'd had a classical education and could read Greek characters.

But one morning I was sun bathing on the marble terrace, forgetting my troubles for a moment in the fragrant beauty of the Greek spring when Prodromos strolled by. He looked me up and down in the friendly, flattering way of

Mediterraneans and said affably, "Ah! *Heliotherapia.*" Helio-therapy! I stared up at this simple peasant grinning at me so naturally—and suddenly light dawned. Didn't all our scientific and academic words come from ancient Greek? Maybe they were still the everyday words of the language? I resolved to try this theory out right away because, sun or no sun, I couldn't put off getting a plumber any longer. Leading Prodromos to the bathroom I pointed to the toilet, held my nose and wrung my hands. *"Hydrotherapia!"*

"Ne, ne, hydraulicos!" Prodromos beamed, shook my hand and trotted off purposefully. I had penetrated the sound barrier! And a week later the *hydraulicos,* pronounced *idravlikos,* actually came!

That same afternoon I experimented again, at the butcher's. All kinds of strange cuts of meat hung or lay about the shop, but I wanted liver—really because I planned on using "hepatitis" to get it, which seemed absolutely foolproof. *"Hep, Epa. Epa. Heepa,"* I said. Each time I enunciated, the butcher gave me an encouraging but bewildered stare.

"Nephritis!" I said recklessly. I knew it was the wrong disease but I was determined to prove my system.

"Ne, ne, nephri!" The butcher was as delighted as the gardener had been, went to his icebox and produced a dishful of sheep kidneys. How wonderful— except that we had to eat them. I was beginning to speak Greek.

From then on it was plain sailing, or should I say, fancy. I would think up a fancy word in English and more often than not I was understood. For the parts of the body I stuck pretty close to diseases and doctors. Encephalitis gave me— *cephalo.* Ophthalmologist gave me eyes—*ophthalmi*—a bit quaint but they understood me. Heart was *cardia,* chest *stetho,* blood *hemo,* Podi were the feet (podiatry), the joints *arthrosi,* the body *soma* (psychosomatic, of course) and so on. Liver, the imposter, turned out to be *sicoti.* I never knew why, but I remembered it because it sounded like cirrhosis.

Then there were the numbers. *Ena, dia, tria, tetra, pente, etc.* Child's play—or at most eighth-grade work. All I had to do was remember a bit of geometry—diagonal, pentagon, triangle, etc. And in modern Greek, *goni* still means corner.

For once I outstripped the children—natural linguists—but not nearly as well educated as I. In Geneva, where we lived before, their French had quickly put mine to shame, but now the tables were turned. How could they figure out their friends were their *philos,* and their brothers their *adelphios?* It didn't mean a anything to them when their teacher said she hated *caco phoni* (bad noises) or liked *caligraphia* (good writing). How should they know that *oligo* meant a few, never having heard of an oligarchy, *chromo* color, *chrono* year, *cosmos* world, *megalo* big, *micro* small, *anthropos* man, *gyneca* woman, *pedi* child and many many more. They couldn't share my joy, much less remember, that a delivery truck is called a *metaphor.* A transfer!

At times I would pick the wrong long word. Once a very wrong one. I had come home tired and grimy from an excursion with an American lad staying with us to find a Greek neighbor waiting at the house. To excuse my appearance I pointed at the young man and myself and said we'd been on a *taxidi* (trip) together and that *ego* was *poly porno*. I had rashly hit on pornography to get the word for dirt. My friend blanched, and is probably still wondering how I could so openly refer to myself as a fallen woman.

But on the whole everything went swimmingly. I had only to say *acouste* if I wanted to be heard, *schizo* if I split a seam, *trauma* if I'd broken a leg, *hypno* if I was sleepy, *dipso* if I was thirsty. If I didn't feel like going to market I would tell Antigone, the maid, that I had *agorapobia* and she understood. If I suggested she open a couple of cans for dinner she would express complete agreement by saying *"Symphony!"* And one memorable evening we took the children to the movies and saw *Ali Baba and the Forty Kleptomaniacs*!

So my advice to anyone planning a sojourn to Greece is forget about grammar—it's impossible anyway. Brush up on those polysyllables. *Calo taxidi!*

THE MAJOR'S CAT

Major Llewellyn had a pretty wife and three attractive children, but his proudest possession, with the possible exception of a glorious mustache, was his cat, Ajax.

We came to know and admire Ajax when the Llewellyns were our next-door neighbors in a suburb of Athens. His fur was a commonplace gray, but he had lovely green eyes and was exceptionally gentle. It was always a delight to watch him luxuriating in the warm Greek sun or stalking imaginary prey in the major's garden.

The solicitude with which the Llewellyns treated their pet was a source of amazement to the major's Greek driver and the maids of our respective households. The Greeks are wonderfully kind-hearted and generous to their fellow humans, but this warmth rarely extends to pets. In a land where life's necessities are often in short supply, they see little point in lavishing food and affection on a non-producing animal.

It was when driving along the Tatoi road one wintry day that the major had first glimpsed Ajax as a bewildered kitten, probably the victim of callous abandonment. With the humane instinct of a British officer and gentleman he had taken it to his hearth and made its transformation into a typical English house cat his special concern.

One day the major told me that he had been reassigned and would soon be returning to London. He was planning to make the journey in easy stages in the Hillman he always kept immaculate despite the dustiness of the Greek roads. His family was looking forward to the vacation trip. The only drawback was what to do about Ajax.

British law required that domestic animals on entering the country must be quarantined for six months in an approved kennel at the owner's expense. The major hit on the idea of shipping Ajax ahead, by air freight, so that the period of quarantine could be at least partly fulfilled during the family's tour. All this would be hideously expensive. We were surprised and touched at the major's deep loyalty. The Greeks just thought he was crazy.

In his well-ordered way, the major requisitioned some lumber and set about fashioning a special crate for Ajax's accommodation in the BEA Viscount that was to bear him aloft. The crate was generously proportioned so that Ajax could stretch out at full length. Mrs. Llewellyn lined its interior with quilting and cushioned it with an old bathmat.

The morning of the Llewellyns' departure there was a poignant ceremony witnessed by Tommy, my son. Ajax was gently installed in the crate along with provisions for the trip. The major fastened down the lid, peered through the air holes to make sure all was well, and bore off the uncomplaining Ajax to the airport amid the loud and plaintive caterwauling of the two smaller Llewellyn children.

A week or so after the Llewellyns' departure Tommy casually mentioned at dinner that he had seen Ajax in the garden next door. We brushed off his report as preposterous—he was given to wild and irresponsible utterances. But a few days later my wife, Margaret, glancing out of the kitchen window, spied a cat that looked like Ajax somewhat worse for wear. I scoffed at the idea, for even if, by some mischance, Ajax had failed to board the plane, the airport was a good fifteen miles from our home, with most of Athens lying in between. But at Margaret's insistence I called BEA and was given positive assurance that Major Llewellyn's cat had been shipped to England.

In the days that followed, Ajax's double kept turning up, usually hungry. My daughter Kate proved a soft touch—so soft, in fact, that some of the choicest bits in *our* diet were set aside for puss. Responsive to good nourishment, it began to look more and more like the old Ajax. Partly in self-defense (for I too liked chicken livers), partly out of concern for the major, and partly out of mounting curiosity, I resolved to get to the bottom of the matter. I called Captain Harvey, a British police officer, who had stayed with the Llewellyns much of one summer before his wife joined him in Greece. He would clearly recall Ajax, I reasoned. We chatted a bit, then I casually asked if the Harveys would take Saturday luncheon with us.

It was a heavenly day. In the distance, Mount Parnes was bathed in a shimmering haze, and the warm spring air gave a promise of early swimming. We ate on the terrace. During the meal I saw the cat eyeing us from next door, and as Antigone, our Greek maid, cleared away the dishes, he approached the table, hesitated a moment, then rubbed ever so gently against the Captain's leg.

"What a friendly cat!" said Mrs. Harvey to Margaret. "Is he yours?"

Before my wife could answer, the captain jumped up. "I say." He said, then with a growing excitement repeated the words, "I say, it's Ajax! It's positively Ajax. It's Llewellyn's...." His voice trailed off as he remembered the major's arrangements. "No, it can't be," he said, and sat down. He looked to Margaret and me in compete bafflement. We told him what we knew. He took out his pipe, sucked at it reflectively. " Poor George," he said. "He'll be terribly upset. We must do something about it."

"But can we be sure it's Ajax?"

"We'll damn well find out," said Harvey. He rose and plucked me by the arm. "Come along!"

We drove to the airport in record time and were lucky to find Bill Jewett, the BEA manager, at his desk. Harvey greeted him familiarly, then got professional and began his questioning.

Jewett nodded. "I remember the shipment. We don't fly many pets—it's deuced expensive. I wasn't here when Llewellyn brought the cat in, but I did see the outlandish crate he made for it. Quite outside our regulations. I had the beast transferred to one of our standard carrying cases. Lighter, and handles much easier."

"But are you sure Ajax was on the plane?"

"Dammit, of course I'm sure. Someone called us about it just recently and we confirmed it. See, here's the waybill, and the listing on the plane's manifest. What's more, we double-checked with London and got a letter certifying the cat's safe arrival. Matter of fact, London complained because the handler got a nasty scratch when the cat was handed over to quarantine."

Harvey reached for the documents and examined them carefully. He mused a long, silent moment, then suddenly said, "Scratched? That's odd." He jumped to his feet. "Look here, Jewett," he said, "Could I have a word with the chap that did the loading?"

"I suppose so," said Jewett, "though I don't see much point in it." He spoke to an aide on the intercom, and presently a small grizzled Greek walked into the room. "This is Spirides," said Jewett. "He handled the shipment."

Spirides glanced from one to the other of us, more puzzled than concerned. Under Harvey's polite questioning his story held up well. He carried out his instructions: transferred the cat from the crate to the carrying case, loaded the case with the cat inside it into the plane. Yes, he had fastened the lid securely. That was all there was to it.

Harvey moistened his lips, and I could see that he was about to step into character as a tough copper. He advanced toward Spirides menacingly. "When you moved the major's cat from the crate, he escaped, didn't he?" Pause. No reply. "Didn't he?"

Spirides faltered, just for an instant. "What do you mean, 'scaped?"

"Escaped. Ran away. Why didn't you go after him?"

"Did go after him," said Spirides, in the manner of one unjustly accused. "But he run too quick. Got away."

It was Jewett's turn to be incredulous. "But London received the cat. They said so." Spirides brightened. "That's right, boss. We know London plenty mad if no cat. But we find another cat—gray one, too," he said proudly. "And we ship him instead."

"*Another* cat?" said Jewett horrified. "A *stray* cat? How could you do such a thing?"

"Oh, we manage," said Spirides.

"I mean, how could you dare send the wrong cat?"

Spirides stood his ground stoically. Behind him was a great national tradition of artistic achievement. He raised his head with closed eyes in the classic Greek gesture. "What difference?" he said. "Cat is cat. Major happy when he find nice Greek cat waiting for him." He grinned, unrepentant.

Harvey was impassive; I concealed my amusement with great difficulty, But Jewett was speechless with frustration. He finally turned to the captain. "Of course," he said stiffly, "BEA will make good on this. We'll ship Ajax at no cost to the major as soon as you can have him ready."

"And pay the extra quarantine charges?" asked Harvey.

"Yes, and pay the quarantine," said Jewett, "Even if it comes out of my own pocket."

We took a BEA carrying case back with us in the car, and before the Harveys left us that afternoon we arranged that the captain would personally see to Ajax's shipment on Tuesday's plane.

He called me at the office on Monday.

"I don't think I'll be coming out for Ajax after all," he said.

"Anything wrong?" I inquired.

"No, not exactly, but I had a letter from the major this morning. The Llewellyns got back from their trip earlier than they had expected, and he writes of visiting Ajax at the boarding kennel."

"Good grief," I said. "He must have been furious."

Harvey cleared his throat. "He did get a bit of a surprise. Let me read you from his letter: 'I found Ajax in very good form indeed. Much livelier than he used to be—probably the climate. But we were wrong all this time in thinking he was a tom. The vet said he came up from Greece *expecting*, and he'll have a litter within the fortnight!'"

BACK IN THE U.S.A.

We stayed in New York for a few days after arrival. While I made a two-day visit to Washington, Margaret reintroduced Katie and Tom to their grandmother. Mimi was then 89, in reasonably good health, having recovered from an operation several years before when they had cut out several inches of her intestine. After a week or so in the Big Apple, we took off for Weston, Connecticut, where Margaret's older sister, Ellie; her husband, Sylvan Rich, and their daughter Carla, lived in a spacious house. I was always grateful to the Riches for giving us this month of respite before turning us loose on the realities of life in the 1950s in the USA. At that time, Sylvan headed a successful dress design firm. Ellie was a pleasant, placid hostess and a voracious reader. Sylvan, originally a Californian, went back to that state after his retirement. They lived in southern California until Ellie died. Sylvan lived on past a hundred before he died there in 2002.

Carla was a flower girl at my wedding to Margaret and has continued as a close friend, all these years, of my children as well as of Vera and myself. Trained as an actress by Uta Hagen, she worked all during the Depression and later as a social worker in Harlem. Now retired, Carla lives in Manhattan and in Southampton where her parents acquired a pleasant lakeside home before they moved to the West Coast.

While we were in New York the children were not only introduced to television but Katie actually performed on it. My brother's wife was Beatrice Landeck, a specialist in children's music, who taught at the Little Red School House in Greenwich Village. Beatrice also worked with children on TV and she arranged for Katie to participate in one of her programs. Beatrice was also the author of *Songs to Grow On* and other children's song books.

When Margaret and I arrived back in New York City, *My Fair Lady* had opened on Broadway to glowing reviews and was a smash hit. We were anxious to see it before going off to Connecticut, but there seemed little chance of getting a ticket. We went to the theater one afternoon on the faint chance of picking up a return, but they laughed us off—"booked solid." While we were standing near the theater a man appeared with two tickets for the evening performance. We wouldn't normally have considered such a purchase, but we were dying to see the show and the premium asked was not too high. I examined the tickets, which looked genuine and I was about to hand over the money when a brawny arm intervened. It was a NYC policeman. "I'll take those tickets," he said. "We'll use them as evidence." He collared the ticket seller. "You're coming with me," he said.

I had had a good look at the tickets and noted the seat numbers. As the cop and seller moved away, I got to wonder what would happen to the tickets. Perhaps the cop would take his wife or girlfriend to see the show. Maybe they really would be used as evidence. I decided to chance it. About fifteen minutes before performance time, we showed up at the box office. We pulled a long face. "We had these super tickets for tonight's show but lost them when my wife's bag was stolen." Box office was reasonably sympathetic. "Any idea of the seat numbers?" I told him what they were. "Well, stick around and if nobody shows up with the seats we'll pass you in." Nobody did, and we saw and hugely enjoyed *My Fair Lady* at the height of its run without spending a dime!

I could have elected to work in Washington, a city I knew well, where a small ICEM office was already in existence. But New York was where the action would be taking place. Congress had just passed the Refugee Relief Act, another piece of patchwork legislation designed to admit refugees outside the provisions of the malodorous McCarren-Walter Immigration Law. The newcomers would be arriving at the port by ship and at Idlewild (later Kennedy) Airport by plane. The sponsoring NGOs, both religious and non-sectarian, were based in NYC. And the families and many friends of Margaret and myself were mainly in the metropolitan area. So it seemed logical to establish the ICEM office in NYC. I took space at 11 West 42nd Street, a large convenient building, just a couple of blocks from Grand Central Station.

In the meantime I bought a commodious home in Mamaroneck, Westchester County, New York. The house was on Fairview Avenue, Orienta Point, several blocks from Long Island Sound. We had almost an acre of land, including two large copper beech trees that Tommy loved to climb. Less than a mile away was Harbor Island, where we could swim, and where I soon joined a weekend tennis group. Margaret tackled the Herculean task of consolidating our furniture and household goods. Some, from storage in New York, we hadn't seen for seven years; some came from the house we had rented to the Spingarns in Washington, and some we had shipped back from Europe. Margaret fell in with the Mamaroneck Artists Guild, and resumed painting. We had chosen Mamaroneck partly because of the good reports of its public schools. The children adapted pretty well to their new life, though Katie had some difficulty fitting into the well-established cliques at her new school. After we'd been back a few months the children pressed us to join a temple or church so they could go to Sunday school. We started first with the Larchmont Temple, veered to Ethical Culture when that seemed unsatisfactory, and made one more try with the Unitarians before we gave up entirely.

Mamaroneck was forty minutes from Grand Central by commuter train and it was easy enough for me to step back into the commuting pattern I recalled from Great Neck days. In the morning I read my *New York Times* or did a bit of work and almost resented interruptions. In the afternoon I would rush from the office for the 5:59, or next train, and enjoy the company of friends I was likely to meet. Sometimes Margaret would drive into town for dinner and a show or an evening with family or with friends. The life was less challenging than Greece but perfectly pleasant in its way and I was glad to be back.

As the refugee flow picked up, our small ICEM office expanded. My chief aide was Ruth Tropin whom I had known in NRS days. Ruth had been with UNRRA abroad, then with IRO for most of its life meeting transports of refugees arriving in NYC. Sometimes the ships would dock very early in the morning, but Ruth would be on hand checking the manifest and ensuring that the new arrivals were met by their relatives or representatives of the NGO sponsoring them. A graduate of the Washington University School of Journalism, Ruth was skilled in PR, and her wide contacts with the press led to many human interest stories about refugees that reflected credit on the agency.

Though she had no direct migration experience, Jean Gorman had a versatile look and we took her on. Shortly after, we heard from Geneva that they were sending us Vera Kalm, a seasoned resettlement officer. We sent Jean to the port to meet the ship bearing Vera and her mother. Jean called us some time after the ship was due. "They've arrived," she said, "But there's a bit of a problem." She couldn't explain on the phone.

We later learned that the two women were being held by Customs because one of the mother's suitcases had a double compartment in which Customs had found valuable contraband. Mrs. Kalm claimed it was not hers. Someone had asked her to bring in the suitcase with the understanding that it would be picked up in a few days at the address in the West 70s to which they were going. They were instructed by the authorities to go to the apartment as if nothing was amiss and wait a call from the owner of the suitcase. Meanwhile the FBI took possession of the apartment next door and drilled a hole through the wall for observation. In several days, the owner of the suitcase telephoned, then came to the apartment to pick it up. When he took it down to the street he was nailed. The FBI claimed a vital step in breaking up an active smuggling ring. Vera, who was unaware of her mother's action, was then permitted to come to the office and begin her work.

Vera, who spoke Russian, soon settled into her job. She got an assignment from Headquarters to escort a planeload of Old Believers from Hong Kong to the United States. The Old Believers were a Greek Orthodox sect that disputed the altered ritual of the church in the time of Queen Catherine of Russia. After the Soviets came in, they lived for a time in Mongolia, but now they were in Hong Kong anxious to migrate to new agricultural land. Brazil had accepted several hundred, most of them going direct from Hong Kong by ship. But a

planeload was scheduled to fly to Brazil via San Francisco, where supplies do-
nated for their welfare by various church agencies were to be picked up and
taken with them. As accompanied baggage this would alleviate the requirement
to pay Brazilian custom duty. None of the Old Believers had flown before, but
they awaited the flight with dignity and calm. Even the small children were well
behaved. An important factor in their discipline was the Elder of the group, a
gray-bearded patriarch well into his seventies, whose word was apparently law.

Vera flew to Hong Kong where she discussed details for the flight with the
captain, flight crew and the Elder. It was a Friday and she learned to her con-
sternation that the sect could only eat fish on Friday. This was not planned for
the menu, so Vera and several crew members made a frantic eleventh hour
search in the vicinity of the Hong Kong Airport which resulted in the triumphant
purchase of 86 tins of sardines. They just made it before the plane's departure,
and Vera spent the first part of the flight at the arduous task of opening the tins
in the plane's small galley.

About halfway through the flight the captain called Vera into the cockpit.
"In a few minutes," he said, "We will be crossing the International Date Line."
He paused but Vera made no comment.

"That means," he went on slowly, "that we lose a day and tomorrow is
again Friday—another fast day. The question is, shall we tell the Elder?" They
finally decided that while there was nothing they could do to alter the menu, the
Elder should be informed. When he heard the news, the Elder asked for some
moments of solitary reflection. Then he called Vera to him. Behind him was a
centuries-old ecclesiastical tradition. "We have considered the matter," he said
softly, "and we have decided that tomorrow shall be known as the day that has
no name."

Although ICEM was not an NGO, I found I was welcome to attend meetings of the Refugee Committee of the American Council of Voluntary Agencies
in Foreign Service. There I again met NGO colleagues I had known in NRS
days or during my years in Europe. Outstanding in my memory was Monsignor
(later) Bishop Edward Swanstrom. Swannie was chief of Catholic Relief Services (CRS) and a highly able and congenial man. Also with CRS were Monsi-
gnors Wycyslo and Landi and Jim Norris, a good friend with whom I once made
an Atlantic crossing. Roland Elliott of Church World Service (CWS) had his
thorny side, but when we had the same objectives he was a loyal ally. Paul Empie, who headed the Lutheran Refugee Service (LRS) was a wise and respected
leader. The Hebrew Immigrant Aid Society (HIAS) had regained its independence after World War II, and I had cordial relations with Isaac Astrofsky, U.S.
Director, Lewis Neikrug, European Director, and Jim Rice. Dominating the Jewish agency scene was Moe Levitt, boss of the American Jewish Joint Distribution Committee (AJDC).

Among the non-sectarian agencies I always had a high regard for Robert
DeVecchi and Carrel Sternberg of the International Rescue Committee (IRC). I

had a special bond with Read Lewis and Bill Bernard of the American Committee for Nationality Services (ACNS). I will tell more later about this agency, which resulted from a merger of the Common Council for American Unity and the National Federation of International Institutes. Read Lewis was considerably my senior: a gentle considerate man, a Quaker in temperament if not in origin. He enjoyed tennis and we played a number of times when he was in his seventies at an armory on 138th Street. Bill Bernard was an intellectual, a Ph.D. but he had the common touch. On more than one occasion, especially as a board member of the U.S. Committee for Refugees (USCR), he proved to be a friend in need.

Up to this point, virtually all migrants traveled by ship, but as larger planes became available and the cost of reliable air charter travel declined, more and more migrants were moved by plane. By the time the Hungarian refugees began to arrive in 1956, ICEM was shipping as many by air as by sea. New procedures were set up for the more expeditious clearance of migrants at Idlewild and other airports.

Air travel had several important advantages. It was no longer necessary to stockpile migrants in waiting centers until a full shipload was available. Moreover, air travel provided greater flexibility—e.g., ports of embarkation and destination may be inland.

As Hungarian refugees streamed across the Austrian frontier, the world responded with unprecedented welcome. Our U.S. quota laws at that time permitted the entry of less than a thousand Hungarians a year—by that means it would take over fifty years to admit the number of Hungarians we ultimately accepted. To bridge the gap, another makeshift formula was devised under which Hungarians were "paroled" into the United States. They were not admitted as immigrants, but after a certain time in the country, "parolees" with a clean record could qualify for permanent residence.

To facilitate sponsorship and placement, large numbers of Hungarians were flown directly to Camp Kilmer, an Air Force base at New Brunswick, New Jersey, where they were registered, examined, documented, trade tested and assisted to find sponsors. Public interest ran high and there were many visitors to Kilmer, official and unofficial. English classes were organized. Orientation films were shown. Prospective employers arrived with job offers, screening the new arrivals to find those qualified in a particular trade. The U.S. Department of Labor provided assistance. From the standpoint of job skills, this was an unusually attractive group of migrants. They spoke a language that was unintelligible to most people in the U.S. But, unlike the victims of Hitler who had spent months and even years in refugee camps, the Hungarians had been free living. They were energetic, resilient, eager to embark on their new lives and many of them possessed useful skills. In the end, the U.S. accepted about 75,000 Hungarian refugees. Within a relatively short time, most of the Hungarians moved into American communities and were at the threshold of a new life.

In my personal capacity, I served on a committee with some of the voluntary agency specialists who sought to change our immigration laws. The McCarren-Walter Act was clearly out of date, discriminatory, and much resented by
other nations of the world. We were not quarreling so much about the number of
immigrants, though we felt it could be higher. What shamed us was the highly
specious national origins quota system which so blatantly favored Western
Europe over Southern and Eastern Europe and the rest of the world. In the Congress, there was growing bipartisan support for a drastic change in the legislation. The old law died hard, but in time, thanks to our combined efforts, a new
law was finally passed which put an end to the quota system by national origin.
Immigration preference is now given to relatives, refugees and those whose
skills are in short supply in the United States.

I knew ICEM had me in mind for possible assignments abroad when my
family was once more ready to leave the United States. I was enjoying the active
posting in New York. What I didn't expect was a cable from Geneva Headquarters asking me to head up a temporary mission to Yugoslavia. Most of the Hungarians, escaping from Hungary in the wake of Hungary's abortive revolution of
1956, were making their exit through Austria. However, over 20,000 Hungarians
had managed to escape through Yugoslavia, and the Yugoslav government
wanted the assistance of IRO and ICEM in resettling them.

My good friend Dick Hazen and I had been busily engaged producing a 25-
year report of the activities of our Dartmouth classmates. It was nearly completed by April 1957, and we were looking forward to the class reunion in
Hanover in June. I wasn't anxious to take off on an assignment that might not
get me back in time. Moreover, I would not be permitted to take my family to
Yugoslavia. I hesitated but was tempted by the challenge of heading an ICEM
team in a Communist country. Duty called, and I flew to Geneva within 48
hours with a Yugoslav visa, leaving Ruth in charge of the New York office. If
the TDY (temporary duty) was prolonged I hoped Margaret and the children
might be able to join me in the summer.

My Yugoslav experience is related in the next chapter. Suffice it to say here
that the TDY extended to early November of 1957. At that point I returned to
the U.S. and resumed direction of ICEM's NY office. By then most of the Hungarian refugees admitted to the United States were arriving at Kilmer. A hastily
assembled team of interviewers was carrying out their registration and, to the
extent possible, referring them to sponsoring NGOs. Jane Moody, in the United
States on home leave, was recruited to serve as one of the interviewers at Camp
Kilmer. Ruth Tropin met some of the planes at Kilmer but also had to keep a
watchful eye on the refugees arriving at Idlewild Airport.

Among those who came to the United States under the new emergency legislation were a number of Greek orphans. Ruth arranged for extensive press
coverage when the first planeload was due. She and I went to Idlewild where we
were joined by Princess Sophia of Greece (later to become the Queen of Spain)

and Jane Russell, a bosomy film star and an active board member of International Social Service, the NGO sponsoring many of the incoming children. The plane was late, and while we were waiting in the VIP lounge another member of our welcoming party arrived. He was the American ex-Ambassador who had succeeded Hugh Gibson as Executive Director of ICEM. I had some apprehension about making the introductions but screwed up my courage. "Miss Russell," I said, "I would like to introduce my boss, Ambassador Tittmann."

When I returned to the U.S. in 1953 after six years abroad, my brother-in-law Edgar Simon and cousin Stephen Marks put a certain amount of pressure on me to enter the music publishing firm. I was by then a dedicated bureaucrat, and turned them down. Herb let it be known then and subsequently that he would be most happy to have me join him in the business, but I'm grateful that he never put any pressure on me to do so.

YUGOSLAVIA

Most of the refugees who fled from Hungary after the 1956 abortive revolution crossed the border into Austria, but about 20,000 made their exit through Yugoslavia. It seemed strange on the one hand that Hungarians would have sought refuge from Yugoslavs toward whom they had some historical animosity, and stranger still that one Communist country would have opened its border to refugees in flight from another Communist country. But there were valid reasons.

When the Russians entered Budapest to protect their domination, Hungarian Prime Minister Nagy was given asylum in the Yugoslav Embassy. He remained there until the Yugoslavs were assured that when released he would be given safe conduct to another country. With this understanding, Nagy was released from the Embassy, but the Russians went back on their word and executed him. Tito was enraged at this breach of faith and reacted by opening the Yugoslav border to fleeing Hungarians. It took courage for the Yugoslav government, endeavoring to maintain its precarious political balance between East and West, to risk the displeasure of its Eastern European neighbors by granting asylum to escapees from Communism.

At first, the Yugoslavs gave the refugees very acceptable accommodation in resort hotels and workers' rest homes, chiefly along the Dalmatian coast. Some were moved into improvised camps in the interior. But as the spring period approached, the resort hotels were needed for touristic purposes and the bulk of the refugees had to be moved into the crowded inland camps.

It was at this point that the government called on the United Nations for assistance in moving them to other countries. Pierre Brement of UNHCR was already in Belgrade, but UNHCR, essentially there for refugee protection, did not have the staff or capability to handle a resettlement operation. The Yugoslav government wanted the job done by the UN in preference to ICEM, a Western-oriented body. So the ICEM international team that I headed was fitted out with UN Laissez-Passers before we entered the country.

How this ICEM team of nearly twenty persons, drawn from twelve different nationalities, tackled the problem of refugee resettlement and completed the job before winter came, is our story.

I put up at the Excelsior Hotel in Belgrade and on my second day sought an appointment with the Minister of the Interior, whose office had the main responsibility for the refugees. We needed to have a working agreement with the Government to resolve such matters as our base of operations, transportation arrangements, employment of Yugoslav staff and the like. In Greece, we had found it relatively easy to reach an agreement with the government for our refugee operation, though it was sometimes difficult to count on them later for agreed logistical support. In Yugoslavia, by contrast, it took some tough bargaining until we had a piece of paper both could sign. But once the Government made a commitment, they lived up to it a hundred percent.

Myer Cohen had given me the names of two Yugoslavs whose cooperation he felt I could count on. One was a retired General. After I'd been in Belgrade a few days I sought out the General and he gave me some wise counsel. Happily I did not have to call on him for help. Myer's advice to join the Belgrade Tennis Club was also helpful and afforded me a chance for relaxation. I had the use of an Opel while I was in Belgrade and for the most part drove myself around.

We needed an estimated 50 Yugoslav staff for the national operation. Some applied to us directly; others were nominated by the government. We struck a bargain: anyone we recruited was subject to the Government's veto; anyone they proposed could be turned down by us. Myer Cohen had warned me that one or two of the staff would be "plants," but as we had nothing to hide this didn't particularly bother us. We knew to be especially careful when staff members or other Yugoslavs came to us seeking help in immigration to the U.S. or another country. However plaintive the case, we simply made it clear that we were there to help the Hungarians and that any Yugoslav applicants must follow the regular channels and procedures established by their own government. We were also scrupulous about changing money and in conforming to other proscribed procedures. Ultimately we spotted a woman employee who clumsily left around some notes reporting on our activities, but the contents were not incriminating. We never exposed her, but we knew who she was.

My chief international aide was Jean Schiltz, a capable, congenial Belgian officer of wide experience whose principal drawback was a harsh grating voice. Smythe had returned to Australia after IRO closed down, but in his stead we had another Australian medical officer, a pleasant more relaxed chap named Keith Watson. None of the internationals spoke Serbski, but we were fortunate to find Yugoslavs who knew enough English, or in several cases German, to work with.

It took me a while to get used to local customs and routines. The food was good, but very heavy and the portions of meat were enormous. When you asked for eggs at breakfast they brought you three with a heavy ration of bacon and potatoes, unless you changed the order. My hotel room was tended by a man whom I came to mistrust. He didn't take money but clearly kept helping himself to the limited supply of liquor which I kept in a closet and which got weaker and weaker as he diluted it. After I'd been in Belgrade for several weeks I made a trip to Athens to see the Moodys and other former colleagues. They gave me a bottle of fine Ouzo which I opened and sipped before putting it on the shelf with the other bottles. The next day there was telltale evidence that my houseman was indeed pilfering, for Ouzo turns cloudy with the addition of water. I never mentioned this to Josef, but in that regard, at least, he seemed chastened.

I found Belgrade, on the whole, a dull city. I walked around for miles on weekends and particularly enjoyed the district surrounding the Kalemegdan Fortress near the confluence of the Danube and Sava Rivers. Along with other members of my team, I traveled widely on the job, tracking the internal movements of the refugees. On a memorable trip to the coastal region I made a slight detour to see Plitvica, an enchanting locale in the Croatian National Park with a series of almost endless cascades. I had arrived in Yugoslavia in April. By late spring the refugees were scattered throughout the country. Some were still billeted in coastal hotels; others were located in a camp at Osijek, not far from the Hungarian border, while still others were in the depths of a wild forest region known as Gerovo in Western Yugoslavia.

One of our UN vehicles traveling in the dusk on the autoput between Zagreb and Belgrade hit the rear end of a farm cart with no tail light and pretty well demolished it. Fortunately, the cart's driver was not injured. However, he sought damages. We were advised to get a lawyer and were recommended to one in Zagreb. He went into the case very thoroughly and produced a long report. The result was that we had to pay a relatively small amount by way of settlement. I wouldn't mention this matter except for the surprise we got on receiving the lawyer's bill. He set forth every conceivable type of expenditure he had incurred in meticulous detail. The total amount was reasonable. What surprised us was that after summing it all up he added a minor charge for what he called "Cost of preparing this bill!"

One afternoon in Belgrade several of us were having a pleasant conversation when we had a phone call from ICEM's Geneva HQ. It brought the shocking news that Pierre Jacobsen, our leader, had been killed in an auto accident. PJ and Count Rossi Longhi were returning to the office after lunch. They stopped their car at a railway crossing while a train passed through. The gate keeper inexplicably then lifted the barrier, and they moved forward into the path of the Geneva/Lausanne Express coming full speed in the other direction.

PJ's death was a tragic loss to his family, ICEM, France and the world. Still a young man, he had already achieved a great deal, and who knows where he might have been headed. He could have been a President of France or a UN Secretary General. To have his potential extinguished in a senseless moment was inconceivable, his future held such promise. The news had a profound effect on us all.

While in Yugoslavia, I heard some good music, both folk and classical. A highlight was the concert given at the American Embassy by the visiting Minneapolis Symphony Orchestra.

The Minister of the Interior had designated Colonel Ljubo Stefanovic to be my principal liaison with the Yugoslav government, and throughout the operation Ljubo provided the same kind of helpful guidance that Goutos had in Greece. He had traveled widely; his English was almost idiomatic, and his charming wife was studying American Literature at the University of Belgrade. In a Communist country in those days, anything could happen, but it seemed to me he was wholeheartedly dedicated to our common objectives. A man with a passion for books, in later years he became an innovative, revered co-publisher in ventures all over Europe and in Japan and China as well.

The United States was very slow in accepting any of the Hungarian refugees who, mainly for geographic reasons, had found asylum in Yugoslavia. Congressman Tad Walter, who ruled the House Immigration Sub-Committee with an iron hand (and also headed the House Un-American Activities Sub-Committee) somehow suspected that Hungarians seeking asylum in Yugoslavia must be Communist sympathizers. As an American I was embarrassed when the well-meaning but tough Yugoslav officials asked me why my country was accepting so few of the refugees. I took the question to United States Ambassador James Riddleberger, who shared my conviction that the U.S. should take its fair share. He protested in Washington and we got an unexpected result: Tad Walter and General Swing, then Immigration Commissioner, decided to take a look for themselves.

Congressman Walter had a well-deserved reputation for being a lush. I gave advance information to Colonel Stefanovic, so he was prepared for the visit. The Yugoslavs greeted them with just the right blend of soft soap and slivovitz and before long the American selection began. It moved slowly at first, but in the final reckoning the United States accepted 2,412 refugees. They were paroled into the U.S. under criteria which were expanded from an initial "family reunion" scheme to include second and third degree relatives, unaccompanied youth who had relative-sponsors in the U.S., and persons having needed skills and trades. Although there had never been direct flights from Belgrade to any American city, ICEM-chartered aircraft made 27 direct flights from Belgrade to NYC, carrying more than 2,000 Hungarians.

The 30 camps which were in operation when large-scale resettlement began varied widely in their size, condition, and administration; some were well maintained and well directed; others were overcrowded. The camps were gradually consolidated as the refugees departed for new homelands; by October the number was reduced to three static camps, three processing centers, one camp for unaccompanied youth, a camp for convalescents, and two small transit centers. ICEM teams operated out of three processing centers—Gerovo, Osijek and Ecka—the third used exclusively for selection and embarkation for U.S. eligibles. Medical processing went hand in hand with selection. ICEM's medical program included the radiological survey of over 12,000 refugees.

At the outset, the traditional role of NGOs in assisting refugees to make their resettlement plans was not clearly understood. This was not unusual in a country with a strong, authoritarian central government. As a result, the agencies were impeded at times by the lack of status. The number of agency workers in relation to the number of camps to be visited was extremely limited. As a consequence they pooled their personnel so that a representative going into the field would, in effect, represent all the agencies in the centers he visited. As most of the refugees were Catholic, CRS became increasingly active in providing social services and sponsorships.

Before ICEM began its work, only 1,647 Hungarians had been moved to other countries; about 2,300 had chosen repatriation, and another 500 had asked for local integration in the Voyvadina, a Hungarian-speaking province of Yugoslavia. Before the operation ended another 400 repatriated. The vast majority, 16,537, were resettled in 29 countries, the largest numbers going to France, the U.S., Australia and Canada. Sweden sent a special mission to select hard core—TB cases. This gave rise to an ironic situation in the case of a few—their lung scars barred them from admission to other countries yet they were not sick enough to be accepted by the Swedes.

An outstanding contribution was made by France, which took the largest number except for the U.S., and accepted all comers regardless of their physical condition. Australia and Canada together accepted over 3,000 migrants. At one point about 700 bound for Australia under a mass scheme were collected in the Osijek camp. They were to go by train to Antwerp where they would embark on a ship for Australia. We needed an international Hungarian-speaking escort officer and I wired Geneva HQ to provide one. After a bit of a search they came up with George Klein, who had been with CRS in Austria. George met me in Osijek and we dined together. He was to leave with the transport early in the morning so there wasn't much opportunity to talk, but I liked him immediately and we became lifelong friends. George came to Lagos as my Deputy ten years later in the Nigerian refugee operation.

By late September, summer was over and it was getting chilly in Belgrade. Coming out on TDY I had not expected to be there that long and I needed warm clothing. In the news bulletin issued by the U.S. Embassy I noted that several bolts of English wool suiting were offered for sale. They had been ordered by a recently deceased Embassy official. I bought them and brought them to a recommended Belgrade tailor. After measuring me carefully he produced two suits. One of the features was cuffs that buttoned. The suits were wonderfully comfortable and I still have them.

With its diversity in politics, ethnicity, language and religion, Yugoslavia was nevertheless a united country while I was there. Presumably it was held together by Tito, for when he died all hell broke loose, giving rise to internecine conflict and serious refugee problems. This was a great tragedy in our time because it's a lovely land with strong, purposeful people. The mountain regions are quite beautiful and the Dalmatian Coast has extraordinary appeal. I made several vacation trips to Dubrovnik, which has a unique character—a fabulous vacation resort with a fascinating political history. At one time it was a city-state, known as Ragusa, precariously balanced between Venice and Russia. It was headed by a rector who was elected every year and during his term of office was kept almost as a prisoner by the members of his government so he would not become too powerful. Its mercantile fleet was laden with such rich cargo that it gave rise to the term "argosy" (derived from the name Ragusa).

I was happy at the result of our mission to Yugoslavia. It was unique in that a solution was found for each of the 20,000 refugees Tito had admitted to the country. They were resettled, repatriated or locally integrated.

INTERROGATORY

One morning, almost a year after my return from Greece, I had an unpleasant shock. There was a registered letter dated June 8, 1954 from the International Organizations Employees Loyalty Board accompanied by an "Interrogatory," a questionnaire concerning my loyalty to the United States. It contained "certain unevaluated information of a derogatory nature" to which I was asked to respond. A series of allegations, most of which had no foundation, purported to show that I had been influenced by relatives of known Communist sympathies.

I was pretty sure my wife's sister was a Communist—she and her husband had visited China when such travel was banned and had lost their passports as a consequence. The allegations concerning my brother's wife were less substantial. I didn't think Hortie, though she talked a good game, ever joined the Communist party. What I knew to a certainty was that neither of them had ever influenced me or altered my belief in the democratic process.

I was also queried about my subscription to the magazine *Social Work Today* and a small contribution I made to it. A list of cooperators was published in the February 1942 issue of the magazine, a special issue dedicated to the role of social welfare work in support of America's war effort. You became a "cooperator" by contributing $5.00 or more to the support of the magazine. This entitled you to subscribe to the magazine and receive any pamphlets published by it. I was one of hundreds of cooperators listed in that issue including the President of the National Conference of Social Work, the executive director of the National Urban League, an ex-Commissioner of Welfare of the State of New York, a Justice of the Domestic Relations Court of New York City, the General Chairman of the United Jewish Appeal, the former executive director of the President's War Relief Control Board in Washington, prominent faculty members at Columbia University, the University of Michigan and other institutions, and the former Borough President of Manhattan, a Republican currently serving on the New York City Council. Beginning in 1938, my primary vocational interest was in the field of social welfare. My interest in *Social Work Today* was purely for its reading matter.

In the Interrogatory, it was alleged that my brother Herbert attended Communist Party meetings, was affiliated with the American Peace Mobilization and sent communications and signed petitions sponsored by Communist organizations supporting the Communist Party line. My brother strongly believed in justice and tolerance, and he opposed discrimination in any form, but he was essentially non-political and not a "joiner," and it would be a great surprise to me if he ever became affiliated with any Communist organization. He certainly never attempted to influence me or alter my political views.

The final charge was that my mother "was acquainted with Irina Aleksander," alleged in the Interrogatory to be "an extremely dangerous professional Communist." My mother was 78 years old at the time, and not in the best of health, but in full possession of her wits. She unequivocally denied that she ever knew anyone bearing that name. My sweet mother was a housewife, almost completely devoid of outside interests. She certainly had never in any way taken part in subversive political activities.

I was outraged at the allegation that my loyalty to the United States was in question. Since I took the pledge of allegiance in school, I have unswervingly believed in democratic principles, and wherever I have been in the world had unquestioned loyalty to the United States. I had worked five years in sensitive programs of the U.S. Government, and in my work with international organizations always viewed myself first and foremost as a loyal U.S. citizen. To me, it was unthinkable that any relative or family member, however close to me personally, could have swayed or influenced my political beliefs.

Of course I read the newspapers of that time, and strongly disapproved of the, in my view, undemocratic actions of the Un-American Affairs Committee of Martin Dies, and the later reprehensible activities of the Senate Committee headed by Joseph McCarthy. I had known of several U.S. Government officials who were unjustly hounded and persecuted for alleged disloyalty or "guilt by association." I had a good friend working for the USAID in Athens who had lost his job as a consequence.

I vaguely knew that in the hysteria of the day an Executive Order had been issued requiring the investigation and clearance not only of U.S. Government officials, but also of Americans employed by public international organizations of which the United States was a member. But it never dawned on me that my complete loyalty to the United States would ever be impugned.

I was incensed and hurt by the accusation. It was a nasty, dirty thing. But I knew it had to be dealt with properly. If the Board was not satisfied with your response to the questionnaire, the next step was a hearing in Washington. I didn't fear the ultimate outcome, but deeply resented the idea that my loyalty was challenged.

I decided to seek legal advice, and went to Ben O'Sullivan, a lawyer friend of mine, who had handled other cases of this kind. Ben helped me to make a temperate response. He also urged me to obtain references from responsible people who knew me personally and were aware of my family relationships, as well as persons familiar with my work. Among the letters I gathered were one from my brother-in-law Edgar K. Simon, who wrote a convincing, supportive letter and another from a colleague in refugee work, Jim Norris of Catholic Relief Services. Statements on my behalf were also made by Myer Cohen, Augustine G. Elmendorf, William Schuman, and my brother-in-law, Sylvan Rich. I completed the questionnaire, sent it in, and some months later was given full security clearance. The letter I received from the Loyalty Board Chairman, dated November 26, 1954, said: "It has been determined that, on all the evidence, there is no reasonable doubt as to the loyalty of this person to the Government of the United States." It was the copy of a letter to the Director of the Intergovernmental Committee for European Migration. I had been ICEM's Chief of Mission in Greece, and was now Officer-in-Charge of the New York Office.

Because it was a significant symptom of the deplorable times through which we were then passing, I am reprinting a copy of the Interrogatory and the greater part of my response. I thought it was ironical that only a year earlier, while I was still in Greece, the CIA had shown interest in recruiting me.

UNITED STATES CIVIL SERVICE COMMISSION
WASHINGTON 25, D. C.

REGISTERED MAIL   June 8, 1954
RETURN RECEIPT REQUESTED
Mr. Edward Bennett Marks, Jr.
c/o Intergovernmental Committee for   PERSONAL AND CONFIDENTIAL
European Migration
United Nations
Sophocleous Street 1
Athens, Greece

Dear Mr. Marks:

As you know, each United States citizen who is employed or being considered for employment by a public international organization of which the United States is a member must be investigated in accordance with the standards set forth in Executive Order 10422, as amended.

The reports of investigation submitted to the International Organizations Employees Loyalty Board in your case contain certain unevaluated information of a derogatory nature which is summarized in the attached questionnaire. It must be emphasized that this information has not yet been evaluated and the submission of the questionnaire should not be interpreted as a statement of charges against you by the Board. The questionnaire is submitted so that you may have the opportunity to answer or comment upon the information received from others. The Board desires to have your answers or comments before it proceeds with its consideration of your case.

You are therefore requested to reply to the attached questionnaire under oath in such detail as you may deem appropriate. A reply within ten (10) days would be appreciated. There is attached for your information a copy of the Regulations of the International Organizations Employees Loyalty Board.

Very truly yours,
Pierce J. Gerety, Chairman, International Organizations
Employees Loyalty Board

REPLY OF EDWARD BENNETT MARKS, JR.
TO QUESTIONNAIRE OF THE INTERNATIONAL ORGANIZATION EMPLOYEES LOYALTY BOARD

QUESTION I
What is your full name and present address?
REPLY
Edward Bennett Marks, Jr 706 Fairway Avenue, Mamaroneck, NY (As my father died in 1945, I have used Edward B. Marks as a working name since 1950.)

QUESTION II
Where and when were you born?
REPLY
53 East 65th Street, NYC, NY April 22, 1911

QUESTION III
The magazine "Social Work Today" dated February, 1942, contains the following statement: "These men and women have made it possible for 'Social Work Today' to strengthen and prepare itself for the supreme test of today." Among the individuals listed in New York City was the name Edward Bennett Marks, Jr.
"Social Work Today" has been cited as a Communist magazine by the Special Committee on Un-American Activities in a report dated March 29, 1944.
What comment or explanation do you care to make regarding the above?
REPLY
This allegation apparently arises from the fact that I and some hundreds of other persons subscribed and made a small contribution to the magazine "Social Work Today," which contributions were acknowledged by the magazine in rather flowery language in its issue of February, 1942. "Social Work Today" was, as the name implies, a social welfare journal. The form of acknowledgment—that the contributors made it possible for the magazine to prepare itself for "the supreme test of today"—undoubtedly is a reference to the role of social welfare work in support of America's war effort. In fact, the February 1942 is-

sue of the magazine, which I have examined in the New York Public Library, was a special issue dedicated to this theme.

My subscription and contribution to "Social Work Today" are explained by the fact that beginning in 1938 my primary vocational interest was in the field of social welfare. I came into social work through the information field and despite an M.A. in sociology, sometimes felt the lack of a degree from a school of social work. I tried to compensate for this by endeavoring to learn as much as I could of the profession's jargon and techniques. I enrolled in 1938-39 for some courses at the New York School of Social Work, I read the magazines of the profession, and I attended several conferences of social work.

Two magazines of the profession to which I remember subscribing were "Social Work Today" and "Channels" a magazine issued by the Social Work Council. I can't remember whether or not I subscribed to "The Survey," a leading social welfare magazine, but I know that I read it consistently through this period and also wrote for it at a later date.

My interest in "Social Work Today" was purely for its reading matter. I never wrote for the magazine, or promoted it, or worked on its behalf. I recognized that it had a pinkish tinge, but I was interested in its contents as a practitioner, rather than from a political point of view. I don't remember for how long I subscribed, but I do recall that the magazine published irregularly for some period, due to lack of funds. When I received your letter, I checked with the New York Public Library to refresh my memory. I find that I was one of some hundreds of persons, including almost three hundred from New York alone, who were listed in the February 1942 issue as "Social Work Today" Cooperators. In an earlier issue bound in the same volume I read: "You may become a 'Social Work Today' Cooperator by contributing five dollars or more to the support of the magazine. This also entitles you to a subscription and any pamphlets published by the magazine." A subscription to the magazine alone was two dollars. In contributing the five dollars minimum, in response to urgent appeals, I'm sure I was motivated partly by the desire not to see the magazine fold up. I'm sure an equal or greater desire was to have the technical pamphlets, which included such items as "Re-thinking Social Casework," "Institutional Child Care," and "Group Work: Roots, Branches." I have no issues of the magazine, but several of these pamphlets are still part of my library.

Whatever the motivations in becoming a "Social Work Today" Cooperator, I note that a number of well-known and highly respected persons in the profession were similarly compelled, for the list also contains the following names:

Shelby Harrison, then General Director of the Russell Sage Foundation (1931-1947) and President of the National Conference of Social Work.

Lester B. Granger, executive director of the National Urban League, and recipient in 1954 of an honorary degree from Columbia University.

Robert B. Lansdale, ex-Commissioner of Welfare of the State of New York and formerly with the Community Service Society.

Justine Wise Polier, Justice of the Domestic Relations Court of New York City since 1935.

James Brunot, formerly executive director of the President's War Relief Control Board in Washington.

Arthur Dunham, Professor at the School of Social Work, University of Michigan, Ann Arbor since 1935 and at one time its Acting Director.

Edward M.M. Warburg, chairman of the American Jewish Joint Distribution Committee and general Chairman of the United Jewish Appeal; served as a U.S. Army Major with SHAEF.

Gordon M. Hamilton, associate dean of the New York School of Social Work of Columbia University.

Clara M. Kaiser, Professor at the New York School of Social Work of Columbia University.

Stanley M. Isaacs, former Borough president of Manhattan and at present Republican on the New York City Council.

Sidney Hollander, prominent Baltimore business man and civic leader; President of the National Council of Jewish Federations and Welfare Funds; vice president of the Family Service Association of America since 1938.

Also listed were such groups as the Family Service Association of Washington, the Greenwich Connecticut Public Welfare Department, and the staff of the Brooklyn Bureau of Charities.

By April 1942—two months after the issue appeared, I was in Washington working for the Government. I don't know how long the magazine continued to publish, but I'm positive that I never renewed my subscription, because I was involved in a new job with new problems, and the importance of being abreast of the latest social work terminology and practice had greatly receded.

QUESTION IV

The Board has received information to the effect that:

Hortense Eugenia Marks nee: Tyroler was an active member of and held various offices in the Communist Party;

Herbert E. Marks, your brother and former husband of Hortense Eugenia Marks, allegedly condoned Hortense's Communist Party membership and activities, attended Communist Party meetings, was affiliated with the American Peace Mobilization; advised the offices of the "Daily Worker," an East coast Communist newspaper, of a change of address to 33 West 12th Street; sent a communication in 1943 to Thomas E. Dewey urging the release of Morris U. Schappes, an admitted Communist Party member convicted on June 8, 1941 for giving false testimony; and has also sent other communications and signed petitions sponsored by Communist organizations and/or supporting the Communist Party Line;

Helen Levi Simon, your sister-in-law, admitted in 1946 that she was employed by the "Daily Worker" and that she had been converted to Communism in 1934. Further, it has been alleged that she has been actively engaged in Communist Party activities in recent years.

The American Peace Mobilization has been designated by the Attorney General of the United States as a Communist organization.

In view of the above, please state:

Your knowledge of the above mentioned or of any other affiliations with or activities or interests in the Communist Party, other Communist organizations or the Communist cause on the part of Hortense E. Marks, Herbert E. Marks and Helen Levi Simon.

The dates, nature and extent of any association you may have had with the persons named in item 1).

Whether or not you ever participated in any activities in behalf of the Communist Party or other Communist organizations with the persons mentioned in item 1). If you did, furnish details.

Whether you have ever subscribed to or been a reader of the "Daily Worker," the "Worker," or other Communist publications. If you did, please state details and indicate whether you advocate the policies of the Communist Party set forth in them.

Whether Hortense E. Marks, Herbert E. Marks, or Helen Levi Simon have ever influenced you to distribute or read subversive literature, attend Communist meetings, join Communist organizations or engage in any activities in the furtherance of the objectives of the Communist Party or the Communist cause.

Your attitude and views, both past and present toward the aims and ideologies of the Communist Party and the Communist cause.

REPLY

Since such knowledge as I have of the affiliations, activities and interests of Hortense E. Marks, Herbert E. Marks and Helen Levi Simon can best be understood in the light of my relationships with them. I will undertake to answer points (1) and (2) together for each of these three persons.

(1) and (2)—Hortense E. Marks

Until I received this questionnaire I had no knowledge that Hortense E. Marks was an active member of or held offices in the Communist Party. However, at one time I did have reason to believe that she was sympathetic to its point of view. Such knowledge as I have bearing on this point is stated below.

I have known my brother's former wife ever since he first met her in 1923 or '24. She has always been an attractive, gracious and intelligent person, with widely varied interests. During the early years of our association I never felt that she had any particular interest in political matters. She was always outspoken with something of a tendency to overstatement, but at that time I considered her a dilettante with several marked talents, rather than a person with a concentrated interest in social issues.

It must have been in 1938 or '39 that I noticed in my sister-in-law the development of new lines of interest and an increasing preoccupation with political affairs. She became greatly concerned with various domestic and international issues and began to express herself in terms seeming to correspond with the clichés used by Communist sympathizers. Apart from the rather didactic statement of her views, I also had the impression that she was carrying on some kind of new activity. As my sister-in-law was always a busy person who designed linen, did research in English literature, ran a thrift shop and carried on other enterprises, this in itself would not have been unusual. What distinguished it from her previous activity was that, although it obviously was taking up large chunks of her time, she never discussed its nature with me. I had the impression that during part of this time she was visiting or working at an office in Harlem, presumably on race relations problems, but I have no knowledge as to whether this had any relationship to the Communist cause, as the details were never disclosed. It is possible that one reason she never engaged me in any discussion on this point was because of her reluctance to involve me or my parents, or at a later date, my wife, in any way whatsoever.

Although I suspected that my sister-in-law was sympathetic to Communist views at this time, I would like to make it clear that my only knowledge in this connection was based on the rather dogmatic position she took on many social questions. Before long I tried to avoid discussion with her which would lead to argumentation, and politics tended to drop out of our conversations.

This relationship prevailed until my wife and I went to live in Washington from 1942 to 1947. While I lived in Washington I saw my sister-in-law only infrequently on brief visits to New York, where she continued to live, during which politics were not discussed. From 1947 to 1953 I lived in Europe with my wife and children. During this period I saw Hortense E. Marks only with other family members on my two visits home, and only once after 1950, when she visited us for a day or two in Europe in 1952.

During the eight months since my wife and I returned to the United States, we have seen my ex sister-in-law (she and Herbert were divorced in 1948) three or four times, at which times we have also seen my brother's children who live with her. These occasions always involved a social gathering of some sort. I have had no indication whatsoever that her opinions today reflect a Communist point of view, and would judge that her main interests now lie with her children, household and other non-political fields.

(1) and (2)—Herbert E. Marks

I have, of course, known my brother Herbert Marks all my life. Our family circle was always rather a close one. After my sister and brother were married they both came fairly regularly for Sunday dinner to the house in Great Neck,

New York, where I lived with my father and mother. I also dined at their houses. My affection for my brother has always been great. He has a warm and generous nature and has always had a host of friends, both in business and in his social life.

My brother has always had varied interests but preoccupation with social issues was not one of them, until about 1940 or possibly even later. Beginning at that time he began to hold forth occasionally on social questions, usually with more emotion than logic.

Since I did not know of Communist Party affiliation or activity by my sister-in-law, I cannot state that my brother knew of or condoned them. I can believe, however, from his general make-up and tolerant point of view on most questions that if such affiliations or activities existed and were known to him, it would be like him to feel that it was her right to hold such beliefs and carry on such activities if she so desired.

I have no knowledge of any affiliation or activity on the part of my brother, Herbert E. Marks with the Communist Party or any other Communist organizations, nor do I know anything concerning his alleged affiliation with the American Peace Mobilization. I do not know of any communication or signed petition forwarded by him. I find it difficult to believe that he attended Communist Party meetings as stated. Contrary to the situation in the case of my sister-in-law, Hortense E. Marks, it was my impression that my brother was not engaged in any outside activities. I had the feeling that my brother's political interest arose largely out of a well-meaning and generalized desire for civil liberties and social justice and was not that of an activist.

My inability to comment further on the specific information set forth in the questionnaire with respect to my brother arises in large part from the fact that I lived either in Washington or in Europe during the years 1942 -1953, and therefore saw him only very occasionally during that time, since he continued to live in New York. Also, as in the case of my ex sister-in-law, Hortense E. Marks, I tried to avoid discussion of social questions with my brother. Since he is a person of many interests this was never too difficult and I believe the same practice was followed by a number of his friends. It is of interest to note that, with no exceptions that are known to me, his old friends have always remained loyal and friendly to my brother, even though a number of them were and continue to be extremely conservative in the political views they apparently hold.

(1) and (2)—Helen Levi Simon:

I met my sister-in-law, Helen Levi Simon, in late 1937 or early 1938 during the period when I first knew Margaret Levi, who was to become my wife. My wife held anti-Communist views when I met her, which she has maintained continuously right up to the present day.

I have no knowledge that Helen Levi Simon was actually a member of the Communist Party. However, I did learn from Margaret of her sister's interest in various Communist-supported or "front" causes, of which the American Youth Congress and various programs in connection with Spain are all that I can presently recall. I had heard within the last year that she had written an article for the "Daily Worker," but know nothing of any other activities in which she may have engaged in recent years.

Both my wife and I have had slight and extremely sporadic contact with Helen Levi Simon since the time in 1937 or 1938 when I first met Margaret and Helen. I saw Helen on relatively few occasions both prior to my marriage and during the 18 month period when Margaret and I lived in New York. During the 5 ½ year period (1942-1947) when we lived in Washington, we saw Helen at most 5 times in all. While my wife and I lived abroad Helen Levi Simon moved to Detroit. My wife has not seen her since some time before we left for Europe in 1947 and they do not correspond. Since my return from Europe I have seen Helen only once while visiting Detroit to speak on migration at a social agency meeting there. On this occasion a family matter concerning my mother-in-law's estate was discussed.

(3) I have never participated in any activities in behalf of the Communist Party or other Communist organizations with the persons mentioned in Item I or under any other circumstances.

(4) I have never subscribed to or been a reader of the "Daily Worker," the "Worker" or other Communist publications. (I have already explained under Item III the reasons why I once read "Social Work Today," if this magazine is considered to have been "Communist" in nature.)

(5) With the possible exception noted in the succeeding paragraph, neither Hortense E. Marks, nor Herbert E. Marks, nor Helen Levi Simon ever influenced me or even tried to influence me to distribute or read subversive literature, attend Communist meetings, join Communist organizations, or engage in any activities in the furtherance of the objectives of the Communist Party or the Communist cause.

On a few occasions Helen Levi Simon sent pamphlets or newspaper clippings to my wife and myself, presumably out of a desire to inform us of her point of view. I do not recall any of these specifically, but she certainly failed in any intention she may have had to influence our thinking thereby. The last items came several years ago and evoked such a strong letter of protest from my wife that her sister has not written to us since.

(6) I have never approved of the aims and ideologies of the Communist Party or the Communist cause and for as long as I have had a specific opinion of them that is for most of my adult life, I have increasingly disapproved of and

been opposed to them. My attitude toward Communism and the Communist Party can best be summarized as follows:

I have always opposed Communism because it throttles the liberty of the individual, tries to control his thinking, and deprives him of the right of free speech and the free choice of his own leaders.

The Communist Party uses persons and organizations to further its own ends. I oppose such dishonest and deceitful methods even when, for a temporary period, they appear to serve desirable ends.

I always considered that in its doctrinaire inflexibility the Communist propaganda pretty accurately mirrors the totalitarian nature of Communism as a political system and lays bare its weakness. I cannot quote it exactly but I have always admired the characterization of a truly democratic government as one which is never *too* sure that it is right.

A somewhat more complete and affirmative account of the development of my thinking on this subject appears in the answer to QUESTION VII.

QUESTION V

Information has been received by the Board indicating that your mother, Miriam C. Marks, was acquainted with Irina Aleksander. It has been alleged that Irina Aleksander was an extremely dangerous professional Communist; that she had been arrested by the Royal Yugoslav Police as a Russian agent; that she was on friendly terms with a number of Russian Consulate officials in New York City; that the publication "Soviet Russia Today," which was cited as a Communist publication by the Special Committee on Un-American Activities, in its issues of January 1945, August 1946 and April 1948, contain articles written by Irina Aleksander.

You are requested to state your knowledge of any association which your mother may have had with Irina Aleksander. If you are acquainted with Irina Aleksander please state the period, nature and extent of any association you may have had with her.

REPLY

The information that my mother, Miriam C. Marks, was "acquainted with Irina Aleksander" is completely mystifying to me. My mother is 78 years of age and not in the best of health, but she has full possession of her mental faculties and she unequivocally denies that she has ever known anyone bearing that name. She said she could not recall at any time knowing any person whose first name was Irina.

My sister and brother-in-law, Mr. and Mrs. Edgar K. Simon, who since my father's death in 1945 have helped my mother with certain business and household affairs, have scanned back social security and other records to see if anyone of that name was ever employed by my mother as a maid or companion, but no trace can be found. I and they have searched our memories to recall whether in the period when my father was alive there was any person known to my mother who might have answered this description but we are positive that this is not the case.

From her marriage to my father in New York in 1897 until his death, my mother was a housewife, almost completely devoid of outside interests. She certainly has never in any way taken part in political activities or been affiliated with any organizations, aside from purely social ones. After my father's death my mother closed our house in Great Neck and since that time has resided at the Hotel Adams in New York.

It may be that the person providing the information has mistakenly confused my mother with another woman of the same or a similar name. While I cannot rule out completely the remote possibility that my mother met Irina Aleksander casually, it is impossible that they met in any context which would be significant of my mother's political views. Aside from voting at elections, my mother has never had and does not have today any political inclinations or interests.

Until I read it in your questionnaire, I had never previously heard the name of Irina Aleksander. I have never known anyone of that name and I am not acquainted with her writings.

QUESTION VI

Are you now or have you ever been a member of, or in any manner affiliated with the Communist Party, U.S.A.?

REPLY

No

Are you now or have you ever been a member of or in any manner affiliated with any of the organizations in the attached list?

(The list attached to the questionnaire was the list of organizations designated to date by the Attorney General of the United States in connection with the Federal Employee Security Program under the provisions of Executive Order No. 10450. The organizations listed also have been designated by the Attorney General as within the purview of Part II, Section 2 (f) of Executive Order No. 10422.)

REPLY

No

QUESTION VII

Please note hereon any comments you desire to make regarding your loyalty to the United States which you believe should be considered in determining your suitability for employment.

REPLY

I have never had occasion to draw up a statement of this kind before. As the question asked bears on my "suitability for employment," the simplest and most direct method I can think of is to supplement what I have said in earlier questions with biographical notes, giving special emphasis to the development of my political thought and to the work I have done.

My father was a self-made successful business man. My mother came from a conservative mercantile family. Both my parents were born in this country; in fact my father's father served with the Union Army in the Civil War. My father wanted me to follow my brother into his business but I developed other interests.

Since 1935, for a period of almost 20 years, I have studied and worked in the related fields of sociology and social welfare; from 1939 through the present, with the exception of one year in the National Housing Agency, I have been continuously engaged in the resettlement, placement and adjustment of displaced persons, Iron Curtain refugees and other migrants; since early 1942 I have been employed continuously in federal and international public service.

After graduation from high school, where I was awarded a medal for good citizenship, I worked as a printer's devil for 6 months before entering college. At Dartmouth, where I majored in English, my chief extra-curricular activities were the college daily, of which I was managing editor, and The Arts, of which I was vice-president. There were one or two public affairs discussion groups on the campus, but I was not a member. My era in college was before the day when left wing groups flourished on student campuses. If there were any such groups at Dartmouth while I was an undergraduate (1928-1932) I was unaware of it.

I do recall a flurry of interest on the subject of pacifism—some students were asked to sign the Oxford Pledge that they would oppose war and never bear arms. I was not greatly interested in the whole matter, and did not sign.

Upon graduation from college I used the savings accumulated from my work on the college paper for a 3 month summer trip to Europe. I visited 9 countries for brief periods, including Germany and Russia.

In Germany, Hitler was on the eve of triumph and there was deep apprehension among friends of my father and others I met there concerning the future of that country.

In Russia, although I was impressed by the manifest energy of the people and their artistic achievements, I was depressed by many things I saw and was in no way converted to the ideology. I was shocked at the poor housing and low standards of living and deplored the signs of disorganization and bureaucracy that were everywhere apparent.

Returning home I found America in the Depression, with jobs not easy to find. After some weeks' search I was employed by a new publication in the brewing industry and this eventually led to a job as associate editor of a wine and liquor journal. At first the work was interesting, but as the novelty of Repeal wore off, and the trade became pretty much like any other business, I felt the need to raise my sights. I decided to take an M.A. at Columbia and over the next 3 years, from 1935 through 1938, I took late afternoon and evening classes several times a week after work. I started with a course in Victorian literature and one in sociology. I found that my interest in the latter far exceeded my taste for Tennyson and the Pre-Raphaelites.

After I received my M.A., I became managing editor of "Better Times," the New York City Welfare Council's magazine on social welfare developments in New York. In one of the issues we did a story on the refugees who were coming to America in some numbers. I got interested in the problem, came to know some of the people working in the field of immigrant aid, and after a year with the Council I went with the newly organized National Refugee Service in September 1939.

My first job at NRS was as director of the Division of Social and Cultural Adjustment. I was in close touch with leaders in the field of English language training and Americanization. We showed films and arranged orientation lectures for new migrants on typical aspects of American life. I later worked as assistant to Dr. William Haber, NRS executive director on leave from his post as Professor of Economics at the University of Michigan, and after Pearl Harbor edited a special information bulletin designed to keep our cooperating agencies throughout the country informed on wartime regulations affecting aliens.

I remained with NRS until March 1942 when Dr. Haber, knowing of my interest to get into war work, recommended me to Milton Eisenhower, newly named director of the War Relocation Authority, who took me on as one of the first members of the WRA staff.

During the period 1935-1942 which I spent working in New York, it was inevitable that I should be aware of the constant effort of left wing groups to point up for their purposes such issues as the plight of the sharecroppers, the Scottsboro Boys, Spain, the Popular Front, etc. I didn't realize at first how fully the Communists were behind many of these causes. My principal concerns at that time were my job and my studies and I never got "involved" in these issues. I was an interested observer but had no personal program of social action. I tried to keep well informed from all points of view, though I am sure that I sometimes made judgments based on insufficient facts.

At the outbreak of the war in Spain I was pro-Loyalist and I remember attending a few money-raising "cause" parties for the Loyalists, although I was active in no organizations. As the Spanish conflict progressed I became increasingly aware of and irritated by the manner in which the Communists here were capitalizing the issue to their own advantage.

As time went on the Communist role in other front crusades became increasingly transparent to me and I felt more and more distaste for the methods used and the motives that prompted them. As far back as I can remember, the dogmatic approach of the Communists stuck in my craw. I felt it was inconsistent with our tradition of free discussion and the necessity of taking a new look at all the facts in the given case before reaching a decision. I did not like the manner in which, as I understood it; Communist decisions were superimposed by a higher party authority permitting of no dissent by persons down the line. This seemed un-American to me. Finally I became aware of some of the ridiculous flip-flops that resulted from this kind of party discipline.

I never knew whether the U.S. Communists were actually "receiving orders from Moscow" or if on their own they were desperately striving to follow the weaving Russian policy line. All I knew was that these turnabouts were making it crystal clear that U.S. Communists were not free to do their own thinking.

During this 7 year period, not withstanding all of this activity on the passing scene, I cannot recall that any particular influences were dominant in my own thinking. My academic work at Columbia during much of this period was undoubtedly a shaping factor. My courtship, engagement and marriage in June 1940 was certainly another. I read, I went to the theater, I talked with friends. During all of this period, until my marriage, I continued living with my father and mother in Great Neck, commuting daily to my work and studies in New York. Undoubtedly, home influence was still strong. I sometimes spent evenings and Sunday afternoons during this period with both my married brother and married sister and their families. I did not, however, feel that the influence of my relatives played any particularly significant part in determining my point of view.

No reasonably intelligent person living in that era could fail to recognize that it was a time of ferment, of many good strides forward; of advances checked and often blotted out by countermoves for other purposes. I was not among the earlier perceivers of the maneuvering of Communist elements, "front" organizations, etc., neither was I long unaware of their tactics. I simply never got involved; I was not a "joiner."

The job which I obtained in 1942 with the War Relocation Authority, which occasioned my move to Washington, was the most exciting one I had ever held. Fair treatment of Japanese-Americans in a country at war with Japan provided an acid test of democracy. One of the most poignant questions raised by their wholesale evacuation from the west coast and temporary confinement in relocation camps was whether the Government could retain the full loyalty of persons of liberty it has curtailed. During the first stage of the program I was in charge of the community activities section. It was my job to try to keep the Japanese American evacuees in step with America, even though they were living under military guard at 10 far flung and isolated relocation camps. We strove to bring about maximum evacuee participation in typically American recreational and group activities. We encouraged such national agencies as the Boy Scouts, Girl Scouts, YMCA and YWCA, USO and the American Red Cross to send field representatives to set up local chapters of these organizations at the camps which could carry on the same activities as Americans in normal communities.

The mass incarceration of a whole segment of our national population proved to be a severe test of loyalty. Some persons, especially among the younger generation of citizens, were discouraged about their future in the United States, and under the influence of pro-Japanese elements opted to be expatriated to Japan. Sent to a special segregation center, together with Japanese-born repatriants, a large number of these Nisei (American-born Japanese) reconsidered their action and requested the right of appeal. Hearings were held and the relevant data on each case was forwarded to Washington. During this period I was appointed by the director to serve on the WRA Central Office Board reviewing the loyalty cases of Japanese-Americans and recommending to him whether or not a given evacuee should have a chance to "return to America" from the segregation camp. I thought a lot in those days about the meaning of loyalty to the United States.

Another of my assignments with the War Relocation Authority was as refugee program officer for the Emergency Refugee Shelter at Fort Ontario, Oswego, New York. At the end of the war in Europe a question arose concerning the fate of a thousand persons given wartime asylum there under the legal fiction that they were not really in the United States. By that time the War Relocation Authority was a bureau administered by the Department of the Interior. On July 31, 1945, Secretary Ickes wrote identical letters to Secretary of State Byrnes and Attorney General Clark urging that a prompt determination be made as to the practicability of returning the refugees to their homelands. It was decided to set up a three-man board with representatives of the three Departments to evaluate each case. I was designated by the Department of the Interior, and the record shows that I consistently voted against the forced repatriation of these people. The following excerpt is from "Token Shipment," WRA's final report on the Shelter it administered from the arrival of the refugees in August 1944 until the Shelter closed in February 1946:

"*September 14-22, 1945* Representatives of the State, Justice and Interior Departments paneled the entire population of the Shelter to ascertain their desires for future residence and the practicability of returning them to their homelands. The classifications were reviewed in Washington by a review panel from October 4 to 10 and a joint report with findings went forward to the three Cabinet officers on October 24th.

"The panel found that 32 persons desired repatriation, 72 persons desired to seek admission to other countries, and the balance of 814 persons presented various reasons for not wishing to return to countries of origin. The panel agreed unanimously that 119 individuals in the last group should be classed as 'not practical to return' and the WRA representative dissented on 90 percent of the remaining 695 cases classed by the other two representatives as 'repatriable.' The difference of opinion was based on the desire of the persons involved—the State and Justice Departments feeling that this should not be taken into account in determining 'practicability.' The WRA representative held that, in view of conditions in Europe and the policy of UNRRA and the U.S. Army not to force involuntary repatriation, this group should be permitted to remain in the U.S."

I was the "WRA representative" referred to in the second paragraph who opposed involuntary repatriation. Substantially all of the refugees involved were, of course, from Communist countries. It was my position that they should not be repatriated against their will.

During my years with the Government, I was deep in the job I was doing and hardly aware of the activities of the U.S. Communists. Like all Americans at that time I admired the stand that the Russians were making against the Germans, just as I had admired the British stand after Dunkirk. I wasn't particularly apprehensive about the shape of things to come in the way of post war problems.

When peace came I wanted to use such skills and experiences as I had acquired in the constructive alleviation of the war's results. From its beginning I was also interested in the United Nations and hopeful of what it might be able to achieve. While I was still with the Government I made various efforts to get into UN work and finally, after a year with the National Housing Agency, went to Geneva in 1947 on the staff of the International Refugee Organization. Here I quickly found that what had started out as a program to help Hitler's victims was rapidly developing into an operation to help refugees who did not wish to be repatriated to Eastern Europe. Furthermore there were new refugees all the time. I felt from the outset that anti-repatriation desires had to be respected and for the next 6 years my work was largely devoted to helping refugees resettle elsewhere. My particular job at Geneva Headquarters was as deputy chief of the Division of Voluntary Societies. This included liaison with such large international and U.S. agencies as the World Council of Churches, National Catholic Welfare Conference, American Joint Distribution Committee and the Lutheran World Federation. It also took in a host of smaller agencies having an interest in special nationality groups—Polish, Russian, Ukrainian, Czech, Yugoslav, etc. IRO entered into agreements with these organizations and supported them financially and otherwise in their efforts to assist in the resettlement of their co-nationals in the free world.

When I went to Greece in December 1950, as chief of the IRO Mission to that country, I continued to work on behalf of Iron Curtain refugees. The task of our Mission there was to register such persons very soon after their arrival in Greece, examine them and prepare their cases and assist them wherever possible to qualify for resettlement opportunities. As IRO drew near its close, I was among the chief founders of the Refugee Service Committee for Greece, through which IRO residual funds were used to improve the living conditions of aged, sick and other refugees from Eastern European countries whose resettlement was not immediately possible. This included establishment of a home for aged refugees at Rhodes. I was honored by being made the first Life Member of the Committee.

During all of this period I could not help but be impressed by the sincerity of most of the escapees. The fabric of their experiences represented to me another first hand indictment of the totalitarian methods of the Communist rulers of the countries from which they had chosen to escape, often under conditions of extreme danger. Unfortunately, their welcome to the free world was far from auspicious. Greece could offer asylum, but its funds for support of the new arrivals were very limited. The squalor of their daily life in government camps, the low standard of nutrition, the ragged clothing, etc., made the refugees less acceptable to the selection missions of resettlement countries. IRO funds expended through the Refugee Service Committee were a helpful supplement but insufficient for the purpose.

Long before the establishment of the U.S. Escapee Program, I reported to my headquarters and also discussed with various U.S. Embassy officials in Athens, the gross inadequacy of the Greek government's refugee camp facilities and the low standard of assistance given to Iron Curtain refugees. An informal arrangement was worked out whereby certain other funds were made available to improve camp conditions. I was entrusted with the responsibility of implementing this program in Greece and arranging for expenditure of the funds in the most constructive manner. George Warren of the State Department, Lawrence Dawson of FOA, and particularly, John Imes of the U.S. Foreign Service, now on duty somewhere in the middle east, are fully acquainted with this interim project and the role I played in it. When the USEP program was established and opened offices in Greece I cooperated fully with its officials. This continued after I joined ICEM in 1952.

I have dealt above with my family background, my education and my work; and have tried to trace the development of my approach to social questions. Before closing I should perhaps add a word concerning the character of my personal associations.

Until my marriage virtually all of my close friends were persons I had met in school, camp and college. During the period between my graduation from college in 1932 and my marriage in 1940, I added to my friends a few people I met on the job, but in general these new contacts were more transient. I also met people in Great Neck, where I lived with my parents. I never went with any particular crowd—certainly not with any group whose major interest was politics or political questions. During our engagement and after our marriage my wife and I saw her friends as well as mine, but they were, and are, a miscellaneous assortment with no particular common denominator. In Washington, where we renewed old contacts and made some new ones, the same general principle prevailed.

In making this brief review of my life and work in the field of social welfare, I have pondered why it was that I did not get involved in the espousal of causes which brought so many of my generation under Communist influences. In part I feel this was due to my increasing distaste and distrust for Communist ideology and methods. But beyond this, I have always seemed to have the temperament to derive sufficient satisfaction from accomplishment of the specific job at hand, without the necessity of emotional identification or involvement with a more generalized "cause."

***

This is one of the very few occasions since I regularly pledged allegiance as a schoolboy that I have been asked to affirm my loyalty to the United States. I welcome the opportunity to do so, even if I regret the circumstances. Let me state, then, that I am and always have been completely loyal to the United States. Despite my long absence from the United States and my status abroad as an international official, I was always extremely conscious and proud of my American citizenship, heritage and beliefs.

My reverence for this country and its democratic form of government is profound and unwavering, and it is unthinkable to me that I could ever, for one moment, consider any other national or political allegiance.

(Signed) Edward B. Marks Jr.

CLEARANCE BY THE U.S. GOVERNMENT

I received the copy of a letter dated November 26, 1954 that was addressed to the Secretary of State for transmission to the Director of the Intergovernmental Committee for European Migration:

"SUBJECT: Information furnished under Executive Order 10422, as amended by Executive Order 10459, with respect to: Edward Bennett Marks, Jr, born April 22, 1911.

Employee, Intergovernmental Committee for European Migration, Geneva, Switzerland.

Sir:
The person named above, who has been reported to be a United States citizen employed or under consideration for employment by the foregoing public international organization, has been the subject of a full field investigation under the provisions of Executive Order 10422 of January 9, 1953, as amended by Executive Order 10459 of June 2, 1953, and the reports of investigation have been duly considered by the International Organizations Employees Loyalty Board.

It has been determined that, on all the evidence, there is no reasonable doubt as to the loyalty of this person to the Government of the United States.

Sincerely yours,
Pierce J. Gerety,
Chairman International Organizations Employees Loyalty Board

SPEAKING OF POLITICS

My first vote was cast for FDR when I was 21. Ferd, Bill and I went to Washington to witness his inauguration. We stood a long way off, but we were there. I voted four times for FDR and as I think back, never for a Republican candidate for President. But I always fell short of enrolling in the Democratic Party and cast ballots for LaGuardia, Keating, Javits, and other worthy Republicans. I should include among them, Stanley Isaacs, Borough President of Manhattan, and later a member of the New York City Council, whom I knew personally and greatly admired. I relished his scrappy political spirit as well as his love for Gilbert and Sullivan, an enthusiasm he imparted to his son Myron, a Dartmouth classmate and friend of mine. I also knew his daughter, Helen, through most of her life. Known as Casey, she for a time edited an English language newspaper in Geneva. She once took Margaret and me to the Geneva airport when we were bound for Helsinki. Her comment: "I'll watch you disappear into FinnAir."

I never met FDR, Truman, Johnson, Ford, Reagan or the Bushes. I was in a small group received by Jimmy Carter in the Rose Garden during the UN Year of the Child. It was a reception for the U.S. Commission established to promote the Year. The Commission was headed by Jean Young, wife of Andrew Young, who was then U.S. Ambassador to the United Nations. I met Dwight Eisenhower briefly when he received in the Rose Garden a group of NGOs involved in refugee work. Nixon I met when he was Vice President. I never liked or voted for the man, but have to credit him for his sage advice when three of us called on him in the White House to sort out a problem relating to refugee resettlement. Roland Elliott of Church World Service, Jim Norris of CRS and I had given him advance notice and were cordially received, and were pleased that the Vice President had indeed done his homework.

I don't recall the specific matter we discussed with him, but it probably concerned the resistance of officials in the State Department or the Immigration and Naturalization Service to the admission or status in this country of a particular group of refugees. The Refugee Committee of the American Council of Voluntary Agencies for Foreign Service (ACVAFS), consisting of the principal religious and non-sectarian organizations assisting refugees, was constantly seeking a change in our prejudicial quota laws. The basic struggle was with

Congress—our efforts to gain repeal of the obnoxious, grossly unfair, McCarren-Walter Act, which essentially restricted quota immigration to Western Europeans. Indeed, under that law, nationals of most Asian countries, including Japan and China, were deemed inhabitants of a huge area, not found on any map, that was dubbed the Asia-Pacific Triangle. With very rare exceptions, these people were excluded under our immigration laws, and those who managed to come could not become U.S. citizens unless they were U.S. Army veterans.

I had two memorable contacts with Mrs. Roosevelt who has always been one of my heroes. During the years just prior to World War II, our immigration laws were quite restrictive, but a certain number of refugees from Hitler were admitted to the United States mainly under the prevailing German and Austrian quotas. The majority was well educated, and a number were of high professional attainment. The National Refugee Service developed special committees to focus on the orientation and placement of doctors, lawyers, and musicians and other persons in the arts. Dr. John Lovejoy Elliott, then head of the Ethical Culture Society, organized a Good Neighbor Committee to help these newcomers meet their American counterparts and accelerate their adjustment in this country. Mrs. Roosevelt, a Committee member, invited the group to Hyde Park, and as another Committee member, I got to go. It was one of her famous picnic lunches. The President was not there, but she was a buoyant and hospitable host, and we had a productive meeting, as well as the chance to wander about the presidential mansion and estate.

When I was its Executive Director, the U.S. Committee for Refugees decided to join with other national committees to celebrate the 1961 centenary of Fridthof Nansen, who had won the Nobel Peace Prize in 1922 for his work with refugees as the Norwegian delegate to the League of Nations. In 1931 the League had honored him by establishing the Nansen International Office for Refugees. During his service as High Commissioner, Nansen created the passport issued to stateless refugees that bears his name, and the Office won the Nobel Peace Prize in 1938. I interviewed Mrs. Roosevelt in a United Nations office—she was then our chief delegate at the UN. She recalled our association nearly 20 years before on the Good Neighbor Committee, and graciously agreed to join our Nansen group as part of the U.S. observance of the UN's 1959 World Refugee Year.

I look back on Prohibition as a serious mistake and deplore the pernicious influence and actions of the Dies Committee and Senator McCarthy. But I have come to believe that when things become too outrageous, the American people seek and find a remedy. Sometimes it takes too long and there is a dreadful toll. I've never been active in politics but serve on the Board of Directors of the National Committee for an Effective Congress (NCEC) which provides funds and strategic support for progressive candidates in close electoral races. NCEC is headed by Russell Hemenway, an old friend whom I first met back in the 1950s when he was on the staff of the U.S. Agency for International Development in Greece. NCEC was established in the forties by Eleanor Roosevelt.

I was bitterly disappointed when Nixon beat Humphrey, Eisenhower bested Stevenson, and Gore lost to Bush. While I voted for Gore I thought he performed poorly in the campaign. Since Bush came in, I have been increasingly disenchanted at the efforts of the Democrats to retake the leadership. It is discouraging to think of a Bush Republican administration extending to 2008.

As a citizen I have favored social legislation, the march towards civil rights, a substantial increase in our aid to developing countries, and strong American support for the United Nations. Through the years, I've had a special interest in a generous immigration policy which includes the welcome of a fair share of the world's refugees, as well as assistance to people in limbo, wherever they are.

GUN CONTROL—ANTI-MAIM

With every shooting tragedy I have become more and more impatient with the National Rifle Association. I contribute money every year to the Brady Campaign to Prevent Gun Violence and was moved to write the following verse. The title parodies the name of a 1958 theatrical escapade starring Rosalind Russell—*Auntie Mame*.

ANTI-MAIM

Fifty persons every day
Meet their death by handguns;
Some while hunting, some at play,
Some as thieves' and muggers' prey,
Some who just happen to stand in the way —
Isn't it time we banned guns?

Every time you pull a trigger
There's a risk of mortis rigor.

They shot John Lennon, the Pope and Ronnie;
Look what happened to poor Jim Brady!
The diet doctor and his lady
Re-enacted Frankie and Johnnie.

Pursuants of this lethal hobby
Finance a highly effective lobby.
They fail to see the firearm
Brings dire harm to friend and foe alike.
Brandishing fast and slow guns,
Those jingoistic shoguns
Are quite insanely pro guns;
For them, the iron's always hot; they strike!

The National Rifle Association
Doesn't favor assassination,
But holds this truth self-evident:
Man has the right to shoot.
This well-upholstered institution
Quotes freely from the Constitution,
But when it comes to safety first
It doesn't give a hoot!

Guns, they say, are not to blame;
It's *people* who kill people,
Whether they fire for fun or fame,
From hip or a Texas steeple.

In this embattled fairyland
Who needs a neutron bomb?
A three year old in Maryland
Managed to shoot his mom.

NRA's busy on the hill;
Last year the Congress passed a bill,
Without much heed of public will,
An NRA bill—fit to kill.

While NRA may shrilly claim
It's people who should get the blame
When handguns massacre and maim
Their slogan is "WE PLEASE TO AIM."

The end result is quite the same.

THOUGHTS ABOUT COLOR

As a kid growing up in Manhattan, I never thought about race relations. I never had playmates of color. My father encouraged black songwriters and performers but I don't remember any that he brought home. I did know and respect Rosamond Johnson when he was a professional employee of my father. He was the brother of James Weldon Johnson, and co-writer with him of many songs— *Under the Bamboo Tree, My Castle on the River Nile*, and the Negro National Anthem, *Lift Every Voice and Sing*. I certainly did not grow up in a home of prejudice. I never heard my parents speak disparagingly of African-Americans. But it was my brother, probably during my high school years, who first alerted to me to the evil of discrimination.

I went to DeWitt Clinton High School where the most prominent personality of my time was George Gregory, a star basketball player and student leader. I never got to know him, but my first black friend was Reginald Weir, number two on our Clinton tennis team, who later became a good tournament player and respected physician. My bosom friend Ferd and I went to Gray's drugstore in Times Store almost every Friday night and bought cut-rate tickets for 50 cents that admitted us to the second balcony for great plays. It was common parlance then—and we were as guilty as anyone—to call that seating area the "Nigger Heaven." We also shamelessly and thoughtlessly referred to a black as a "coon," "smoke" or "dinge." My brother and his wife took me one night to the Cotton Club on my first visit to Harlem. It was an eye opener seeing the mix of skin colors.

When Bill Schuman and I were at Camp Cobbossee in Maine in the 1920s, we wrote, directed and acted in a minstrel show that was produced not only in the camp but as a benefit performance in the nearby town of Winthrop. We thought nothing of blacking up and going through the end man routine. I never attended a proper minstrel show, but I did see Eddie Leonard, one of the last great minstrels, in vaudeville, and heard him sing *Roll dem Roly Boly Eyes* and *Ida, Sweet as Apple Cider* two songs published by my father.

In college I had one black classmate in a class of over 600 students. Bob McGuire was the son of a prominent Washington DC mortician and a likeable guy, though we never became close friends. In my first jobs I had no meaningful contact with blacks. I did have a Korean co-worker who told me at length of the bitter experience that led to his exile from that country, but the cause was political.

I was a junior in college in 1931 when the Scottsboro Case became a cause celebre, and with many of my generation recognized the injustice in the charges against the accused. But I can't say the trial, or other events of the times, woke me to the indignities that later brought on the civil rights movement in the south.

It was my first government job, beginning in April 1942, that forcibly brought home to me the true outrage of racial prejudice. In this case, it was not blacks who were the victims of prejudice but the Americans of Japanese ancestry—more than 110,000—who were summarily evacuated by military order from their homes on the West Coast and confined to ten inland relocation centers. Right after Pearl Harbor, the Japanese *aliens* suspected of disloyalty and thought to be security risks were interned by the Department of Justice. But the evacuees—men, women and children—against whom there was no charge, were forced to leave their farms, homes and businesses merely because they were labeled "Japs." Two-thirds of them were Nisei, of Japanese ancestry and first generation American citizens. I tell their story in another part of this narrative.

In later employment with the Federal Government and the United Nations I came to know and work closely with many Americans of color as well as those of other nationalities. A colleague and friend of many years was John Thomas, of mixed African-American, American Indian and white heritage. We first worked together in the UN refugee program after WWII, then in resettlement of Cuban refugees, and finally when he became the Director of the International Organization for Migration (IOM). John was a counselor and mentor for my first few weeks in Saigon when I was sent there in 1965 to direct the AID program for refugee relief.

My brother was a friend of Harry Belafonte and published *Banana Boat Song* and other songs he sang. In 1989 when Vera and I were in Berlin we enjoyed a Belafonte show witnessed by a huge audience. We went backstage afterwards and had a very pleasant talk with him. I never thought of Amos and Andy and the vaudeville team of Moran and Mack as denigrators of a racial type. I heard the poignant plaint of the great comedian, Bert Williams, the first Negro star of the *Ziegfield Follies*. As a light skinned African-American he had to black up each night to make a convincing portrayal. The obverse of that sad story was the 1929 Fats Waller song popularized by Ethel Waters called: *What Did I Do to be so Black and Blue?* It was the mournful tale of a dark African-American woman agonizing because she was not light-skinned.

It's difficult today to understand the popular acceptance early in the 20th century of "coon" songs such as *All Coons Look Alike to Me, Every Race has a Flag but the Coon* and *Coon, Coon, Coon, How I Wish My Color would Change.* Even more anomalous is that the first of these songs was written by an African-American, Chris Smith.

In the early 1960s, my second incarnation in Washington DC, I invested in "integrated" housing and served with Joe Rauh and others on the board of a civic group that promoted it. Under the leadership of Morris Milgram, we bought properties in the Washington area that, up to that point, had been restricted. They included a large apartment house on Connecticut Avenue, and residential clusters in such areas as Culpepper, VA and Silver Spring, MD. We then encouraged the occupancy of a certain number of African-Americans in those buildings, taking care that there was a racial balance in each case. It was our experience that if the percentage of blacks passed a certain ratio of the tenancy, white tenants would leave, defeating our objective of integration. In one case this actually happened and we were threatened with a suit from an African-American to whom we had been compelled to deny access. Milgram, the author of *Good Neighborhoods—the Challenge of Open Housing*, devised a number of schemes to promote integration. In 1975 he and James Farmer, the founder/director of CORE—the Congress of Racial Equality, created OPEN, a program I helped to support. In this case, no property was acquired, but mortgages we subsidized were made available to minority homebuyers.

Working in Washington in the Kennedy administration in those years one couldn't help but be inspired by the advance in civil rights. I was working in my office in USAID on the day, on August 28, 1963, when the great march took place. I literally grabbed a colleague at the lunch hour and we jostled our way to a place where we could hear some of the speeches. We weren't present when Martin Luther King inspired the assembled thousands by proclaiming from the steps of the Lincoln Memorial: "I have a dream that one day this nation will rise up and live out the true meaning of its creed: 'We hold these truths to be self-evident: that all men are created equal.'" However, we were much moved by the occasion, and I'm glad I was able to be at the scene. I'm happy that my children and grandchildren exist in a country that has come a long way in its endorsement of civil rights. Too much racial prejudice still prevails, but it is fighting a losing battle.

U.S. COMMITTEE FOR REFUGEES AND WORLD REFUGEE YEAR

In 1958 there were more than 2 million refugees living in limbo in Europe, the Middle East, North Africa and Asia. Dr. Elfan Rees, of the World Council of Churches (WCC) aptly said, "Refugees are not a stagnant pool of statistics but a slowly moving river of human beings." He also called the twentieth century "the century of the homeless man."

The member states of the United Nations—only 59 at that time—voted for a General Assembly resolution designating a Year—July 1, 1959 - June 30, 1960—in which, through the increased efforts of governments, private agencies and individuals, many of the homeless of the world might finally find a permanent haven. World Refugee Year (WRY) was envisioned as a "human year" in contrast to the scientific emphasis of the recently concluded International Geophysical Year.

Instead of slackening, the refugee situation in the world was intensified by the Cold War. The UN asked its member states to form national commissions to widely disseminate information about refugees and stimulate efforts to provide timely relief. The State Department called a meeting of government and NGO bodies to accomplish this purpose and the United States Committee for Refugees (USCR) was established.

The U.S. Committee, by proclamation of President Eisenhower, was given the task of coordinating private efforts during WRY. The organizing group which met at the State Department included government officials, the chairmen or directors of the religious and non-sectarian NGOs, and a number of nationally recognized individuals. The Committee set itself the following tasks:

To inform the public about world refugee issues,
To consult regularly with government leaders and UN officials,
To stimulate research on refugee problems,
To work closely with American voluntary agencies in the refugee field,
And, to further American participation in World Refugee Year.

The "waiting people" in 1958 were the refugees of mid-century Europe, Algeria, Palestine, Tibet and China. In particular focus during the 1959 United Nations Refugee Year were the 30,000 refugees remaining in Austria, Germany, Greece and Italy, some of whom had been in camps for more than a decade. Another hundred thousand unsettled "out of camp" refugees languished precariously in these countries and in other parts of Europe.

The diversity of membership is reflected in the makeup of the Committee's original slate of officers and its Board of Directors. The Very Reverend Francis B. Sayre Jr., Dean of the Washington Cathedral, was named Chairman. Sayre, the grandson of Woodrow Wilson, had long been an outspoken refugee advocate. Maxwell M. Rabb, Secretary of the Cabinet and President Eisenhower's point man on refugee affairs was made President. The Vice Presidents included ex-Governor of New York Herbert H. Lehman, who had been Executive Director of UNRRA; Henry Labouisse, who headed the UN agency for Palestine Refugees and was to become U.S. Ambassador to Greece and later Executive Director of UNICEF; George Meany, chief of AFL-CIO representing labor; Samuel W. Meek, an advertising executive from J. Walter Thompson, and Roderick O'Connor, a former Undersecretary of the State Department.

The 36-member board included such well-known public figures at the time as General Alfred M. Gruenther, Clare Boothe Luce, Ambassador Eugenie Anderson, Jacob Blaustein (a U.S. Delegate to the UN), and Senator Arthur V. Watkins. From the business community came J.Peter Grace Jr., William L. Batt, Mary G. Roebling, David Sarnoff, John B. Ford III and Spiros Skouras. Jurists included Judge Juvenal Marchisio, Judge Francis A. Swietlik and Doctor Philip C. Jessup who later became American Representative on the World Court. J. Donald Kingsley, who had directed IRO, was a member. Among the voluntary agency representatives were Monsignor (later Bishop) Edward E. Swanstrom (CRS), Richard W. Reuter (CARE), Clarence E. Pickett (American Friends Service Committee), Alexandra Tolstoy (Tolstoy Foundation), Lowell Thomas, travel writer and explorer who headed the American Emergency Committee for Tibetan Refugees, William T. Kirk, International Social Service, James P. Rice (HIAS), Angier Biddle Duke (IRC), later White House Chief of Protocol, Dr. Paul C. Empie, Lutheran Refugee Council (LRC), Moses A. Leavitt (AJDC) and Dr. R. Norris Wilson (CWS). Distinguished additions to the Board in subsequent years included Robert D. Murphy, former Undersecretary of State for Political Affairs, Mrs. John Foster Dulles, Robert R. Nathan, economist, George Elsey, who became President of the American Red Cross, George Mardikian, restaurateur and President of the American National Committee for Homeless Armenians and Frances Humphrey Howard, sister of Hubert. Hyman Buchbinder, Jacob S. Potofsky and Joseph Beirne sustained Labor's interest on the Board.

USCR was always fortunate in the support received from movie and theatrical personalities such as Madeleine Carroll Heiskell, Myrna Loy, Faye Emerson, Marsha Hunt, Lorne Greene, Eddie Albert, Marian Anderson and others. Educators included Dr. Luther T. Evans, who had headed both UNESCO and the Library of Congress, and Dr. Buell Gallagher, President of CCNY. Mrs. Howard was Chairman of the active Maryland State Committee. Walter H. Bieringer, long associated with refugee work, was Chairman in Massachusetts. The New York Committee, early in WRY, sponsored a dinner at the UN at which Secretary-General Dag Hammarskjold was the principal speaker.

USCR was a truly nationwide body with a National Council supplementing the Board, and 72 state, area and local committees in 45 states.

I was named Executive Director of the Committee, and a resolution was passed to request ICEM to grant me a leave of absence. I decided that both ICEM and USCR could be accommodated in the 42nd Street office and that became our headquarters during WRY beginning early in 1959. Ruth Tropin would continue in charge of ICEM's office in New York.

One day in the spring of 1960 I had a phone call from Donald Swan. I knew the name, having hugely enjoyed on Broadway the appearance of Swan and Michael Flanders in *At the Drop of a Hat*. We had also bought and were enjoying their recording. I couldn't imagine why Swan wanted to see me, but he explained. They had given a benefit performance for an organization serving the handicapped in which Flanders, a paraplegic, was interested. Swan wondered if we would like them to do one for refugees, his special concern. They were just completing a successful eight-month run at the John Golden Theater after which they would be returning to England. We loved the idea, but it was getting close to Memorial Day and I didn't see how in such a short time we could corral both a theater and an audience in Manhattan.

A friend had an inspiration to book the auditorium of the Mamaroneck Junior High School for an evening performance on May 29th. The benefit would be sponsored by the Westchester Committee for the World Refugee Year (WRY) on behalf of the U.S. Committee for Refugees (USCR). The Westchester Committee, including most of our friends, worked hard on the sale of tickets, resulting in a sell-out producing nearly $20,000 for WRY. Flanders with his attractive wife and Donald Swan came to our home for dinner before the performance. They were very pleased with the arrangements and, of course, the capacity audience, and they gave a great show.

I didn't know Frank Sayre, but found him congenial to work with, dedicated, innovative and amenable to suggestion. I made many visits to the cathedral to consult with him, in the course of which I learned a good deal about his continuing efforts to complete the cathedral with stone and stained glass of his selection. In later years we occasionally called on Frank and his wife at their Martha's Vineyard home and they were perchance present when I met Vera at the Vineyard home of some mutual friends, Felicia Lamport and Judge Ben Kaplan, in the summer of 1981.

Max Rabb was less involved in the direction of the Committee's affairs but always showed a lively interest in our activity and a desire to be kept informed. In later years when he was U.S. Ambassador to Italy, Vera and I called on him at the Embassy in Rome. He was fresh from a diplomatic triumph. The White

House had pressured him to obtain U.S. access to a military base in Italy. The Italian government refused permission several times until Rabb tried a new strategy: "If you grant me this request my government will be very pleased and you will make me an important man in Washington." This plea melted their hearts and the Italians acceded to the request.

I naturally did a fair amount of business with Abe Claude, our Treasurer, who was based in a New York firm. Abe kept our books straight and helped us at the outset to get financial support from a few corporations. Bill Breese, always the conscientious Secretary, was a scion of the Vanderbilt family who lived in Washington. When he came to New York he would sometimes ride out to Mamaroneck with me on a commuting train at the end of the day so we could discuss pending matters.

We got an early start on fund raising from Marsha Hunt, the film star, whom I had met through a friend. Marsha, a dedicated worker for humanitarian causes through most of her life, is still promoting worthwhile local and national projects from her home in the San Fernando Valley. When she heard about WRY she prevailed on fifteen Hollywood stars to contribute their services for a television film titled A Call from the Stars which she conceived and produced. The cast included Philip Ahn, Steve Allen, Harry Belafonte, Richard Boone, Spring Byington, Jeff Chandler, Bing Crosby, Burl Ives, Louis Jourdan, Phyllis Kirk, Paul Newman, David Nevin, Robert Ryan, Jean Simmons and Joanne Woodward. Copies of the film were widely distributed and used to inform the public about refugees and to raise funds for WRY.

Our Committee strategy was to work as much as possible through over a hundred national organizations, many of whom had never previously been concerned with refugee issues. This included the YMCA and YWCA, the Rotary, Lions, Kiwanis, and other service clubs, the American Association of University Women, Soroptimists, and other women's organizations, youth organizations including the Boy and Girl Scouts, religious bodies, schools and colleges and myriad other national civic groups. A goodly number of these requested speakers on the refugee theme and/or featured articles about refugees in their publications. USCR's joint campaign with the Advertising Council reached a wide audience through TV and radio spots, newspaper and magazine ads, and car cards using the slogan "The Homeless of the World Still Wait." Dean Sayre produced "a Litany for Refugees" based on the Book of Common Prayer which was extensively used in the churches. Five thousand teaching kits prepared by USCR for teachers of social science classes in junior and senior high schools were distributed by the National Education Association. We sent copies of the Eisenhower Proclamation to the state governors urging them to form state commissions and ensure that the WRY theme was aired and promoted in the schools.

Our original statement about WRY and the formation of the U.S. Committee was distributed and followed up with additional promotional material for the press, radio and TV. In one six-month period, USCR sent out more than 158,000 pieces of material in response to 3,084 requests from all the states and twelve foreign countries. Our Director of Information was Sutherland Denlinger, a veteran newsman who had been many years with Scripps-Howard. Throughout its life, USCR published authoritative pamphlets and releases on refugee situations globally. 1961 saw the birth of the Committee's annual survey on the state and fate of refugees in the world. Dean Sayre and others introduced salient points and statistics from the 16-page report at a hearing of the Senate Judiciary Sub-Committee on Refugees and Escapees held under the chairmanship of Senator Phillip A. Hart. Over time, the World Refugee Survey has attracted much favorable comment. It goes to every member of Congress and is annually read into the Congressional Record. It receives wide press coverage and is an invaluable resource for researchers, students and professionals in the field. The current issue (2003) of the Survey contains 258 pages and gives facts and figures about the refugee situation in every country.

Though established under government auspices, USCR has never requested federal funding. In its early years, the Committee received a good deal of support from CRS, CWS, AJDC and LRC. These religious agencies did not wish the committee to undertake a national fund-raising campaign in WRY which they believed might interrupt the normal pattern of annual giving by their constituents. Other contributors to the USCR budget were the AFL-CIO, the American National Red Cross and several interested foundations. With the assistance of Sam Meek of the J. Walter Thompson Advertising Agency, USCR developed an attractive holiday gift wrap featuring the USCR logo of the uprooted tree. The gift wrap sales in subsequent years increased to the point where the resulting revenue financed nearly half of the USCR budget. Some gift wrap purchasers also became contributors.

Special stamps (with a first day cover) were issued in WRY. There were many exhibits, lectures, public meetings, concerts and other events commemorating the Year. Highlights included a gala event at Blair House in Washington sponsored by Vice President Hubert E. Humphrey and a dinner at "21" Restaurant in New York for West Germany's Willie Brandt.

At an all-day conference in Washington on June 16, 1960, Dean Sayre and others reviewed the Committee's efforts during WRY. Speakers at the conference included Robert Grey, Secretary of the Cabinet, who conveyed President Eisenhower's greetings, John Hanes Jr., Administrator of the State Department Bureau handling refugee problems, Dr. Evans and General Gruenther. A representative of Doubleday & Co. awarded a $5,000 prize to the winner of its WRY-inspired contest for the best book by a refugee. There was lively discussion and much enthusiasm at the Board meeting on the following day and it was unanimously voted to continue the life and work of USCR indefinitely beyond the end of the World Refugee Year.

In that Presidential election year, Rabb and Meany wrote to the candidates of the two major parties asking for their views and recommendations for legislation on refugee problems. Thoughtful replies from then Vice President Richard M. Nixon, Republican Vice Presidential candidate Henry Cabot Lodge and President-to-be John F. Kennedy were given wide press coverage. In January 1961 Dean Sayre went on a month's trip to the Middle East countries to study first hand the issues that still baffle world leaders, and report back to the Government and to the USCR Board at its annual meeting in June.

The World Refugee Year was a success globally and in the United States. This was true not only from the standpoint of enlightenment about the problem but also in terms of increased resources. Both governmental and private contributions to refugee aid took a quantum jump in WRY and attained a new level. The UN followed WRY with a succession of other Years, many of which heightened public interest, action and needs. There were Years for Women, Population, the Environment, the Child, the Handicapped, the Family and other humanitarian themes.

I welcomed the extension of WRY and USCR, but in the early sixties I found it difficult to continue the promotional activity with the same enthusiasm. At this time, a certain amount of dissension about our future course and scope arose among the USCR board members of whom a number, including Frank Sayre, lost interest. I felt a certain pull toward a return to more operational activity. I resigned as Executive Director early in 1962 and took a job with USAID. The Committee continued to function, but a change in direction forced a move to Washington in the seventies. During most of its sojourn in the capital, USCR was closely associated with the American Freedom from Hunger Foundation. For much of the time the two organizations shared the same space, executive director and Board. In 1980 the Foundation was absorbed by Meals for Millions in California, and for a few weeks the future status of USCR was uncertain. Frannie Howard and I were determined that the Committee should regain its independence. I had a series of meetings with Wells Klein, who then headed the American Council for Nationalities Service (ACNS), coordinating the efforts of some thirty International Institutes in the principal U.S. cities sponsoring refugees, and assisting them after their arrival. Wells had long cherished the idea of an information and advocacy arm for ACNS. He also sought to acquire the USCR mailing list, which included purchasers of giftwrap. With the help of Victor Jacobs, USCR General Counsel and Board member, we worked out an amicable agreement and USCR moved back to New York as an active program of ACNS.

Wells put the icing on the cake by hiring Roger Winter as the Director of USCR. Roger came from a responsible job in the Department of Health, Education and Welfare, now Health and Human Resources (HHR), that provided assistance to refugees after their arrival. During the decade he ran USCR, Roger traveled tirelessly to Africa and other parts of the world, wrote and spoke eloquently about the world refugee situation, supervised a bevy of reporters/correspondents who also traveled widely, and produced a newsletter and a series of pamphlets describing the refugee scene. I resumed an active role in the governance of ACNS/USCR, serving as president (1980-82) and subsequently as Chairman of the Board (1983-1998); and I continue today as a board member. Wells headed the combined agency until his retirement. He retired to his home in Stowe, Vermont, and embarked on a second career of buying and selling quality rugs (of which Vera and I bought two.) After Wells' retirement, Roger directed the combined agency until he returned to government service in 2000. He is today Assistant Administrator, Bureau for Democracy, Conflict, and Humanitarian Assistance in the State Department. The current Director of Immigration and Refugee Services of America (IRSA—a changed name) and USCR is Lavinia Limon, who formerly directed the International Institute of Los Angeles and whose background included a key post in HHR.

Refugees are a cause of war and a result of war. The nature of the global refugee problem has changed since the USCR Board voted in 1960 to have the Committee continue past WRY. In 1960, and for a number of years after that, most of the refugees were border crossers, entitled to the protection and assistance of the United Nations High Commissioner for Refugees (UNHCR). The 2003 World Refugee Survey lists 13 million of these international refugees. The difference today is in the additional number of internally displaced persons (IDPs). They have not crossed a border, but turmoil in their own country has displaced them. Altogether the Survey lists 21.8 million of these IDPs making a grand total of 34.8 million uprooted human beings.

In his book *The Price of Indifference*, Arthur C. Helton puts it simply: "Refugees matter. They matter for a wide variety of reasons rooted in human experience and international relations. The grim plight of refugees increasingly commands attention by the international community. Refugees are a product of humanity's worst instincts—the willingness of some persons to oppress others—as well as some of its best instincts—the willingness of many to assist and protect the helpless...Today, they are the flesh-and-blood personification of the chaos and insecurities that we confront in the new century which now seems so suddenly fraught with danger." Arthur Helton, widely known for his expertise in humanitarian action, died when the UN compound in Baghdad was bombed in 2003.

The one bright spot reported in the 2003 Survey is the voluntary repatriation of an estimated 2,227,000 refugees. Of these, 1,800,000 returned from Iran and Pakistan to Afghanistan. In addition, a certain number of refugees were victims of *refoulement*—involuntary return and expulsion. There is no assurance that repatriates, whether voluntary or involuntary, become peaceably reestablished in the countries to which they have returned, although UNHCR makes some efforts to monitor the treatment given them after their return.

In 2002 Mrs. Sadako Ogata retired as UN High Commissioner for Refugees after ten eventful years on the job. I first met her when she was Chairman of UNICEF's Executive Board. Mrs. Ogata had an outstanding record as High

Commissioner, serving in a period when there were refugee crises of unusual political complexity. We at the U.S. Committee for Refugees recognized her fine achievements, and during her long incumbency gave two receptions in her honor. I regard Mrs. Ogata as one of the few heroes in our time.

In the course of my own long experience in aiding refugees, I was asked many times if I did not find it too discouraging, in view of their large numbers and unmet needs. I sometimes told the story of an old woman throwing back in the ocean some of the myriad small fish tossed up on the shore. A passerby said, "There are so many! How can what you're doing possibly make a difference?" The old woman scooped up a wriggling fish and threw it back. "It made a difference to that one," she said.

USAID

1962 represented a kind of benchmark in my career for that was the year I returned to Washington and began my service with the U.S. Agency for International Development (USAID). I had greatly enjoyed the European assignments with IRO and ICEM and hoped eventually to return to international work, but I liked the notion of a federal job that would be challenging, take me to other parts of the world, and, incidentally, build credits for my pension.

Before I left USAID in 1976 I would have spent 2 years in London, 2 years in Lagos, a year in Saigon and have ventured widely on short duty trips to more than 15 countries in Africa and Asia. Not to mention a helping of bureaucracy in Washington.

My first assignment was as Deputy Chief of USAID's office of Central African Affairs. Pliny in his *Natural History* wrote "There is always something new out of Africa." There have been many new things out of Africa in the scant fifty years since decolonization. Edmond C. Hutchison, Assistant Administrator of the USAID Bureau for Africa, in Congressional testimony in the early 1960s said, "Internal instability and weak governments; decreasing influence by ex-metropole states; strong domestic pressures for rapid economic strides and social change; insufficient trained Africans and democratizing institutions—all are a part of the current African situation." Another problem is the recurring phenomenon of people in flight. The refugee is a constant in Africa. Ceaseless tribal wars, man-made and natural disasters and political persecution have driven over 2.5 million international refugees from Angola, Sudan, Burundi, Congo-Kinchasa, Eritrea, Somalia, Sierra Leone and Liberia. An even larger number are displaced within their own countries.

My boss at USAID was a Harvard trained, affable, endlessly curious chap named Dick Cashin who had seen service in Libya and Ethiopia. We had the assistance of four personable young men, two of whom were exceptionally bright.

The new job gave me a respite from more than twenty years' concern with refugee problems. There were serious refugee problems in the former Belgium Congo, Rwanda and Burundi, but my attention was largely focused on development issues. The nations in our purview were just emerging from French, British and Belgian colonial rule. They were underdeveloped (we later used the euphemisms of less developed or developing). In some countries, USAID had its own specialists; in others, the programs were implemented mainly by university and commercial contractors such as Michigan State University, Arthur D. Little and Checchi and Company. The projects were many and varied. Some involved technical assistance in agriculture, education, vocational training, health and kindred matters. In the case of larger development projects in road building, dam construction and the like, we furnished capital loans, often in concert with other country donors or the World Bank.

I learned that most of America's foreign aid was in the form of dollar expenditures for salaries of U.S. personnel and for supplies and equipment of American manufacture. Expenditures in local currency for salaries of indigenous staff and locally purchased supplies made use of funds generated in large measure by in-country sales of U.S. surplus food shipped to the receiving country under U.S. Public Law 480.

I will mention just a few of the projects that particularly interested me. One was to provide an alternative to classical teaching methods in higher education. Fourah Bay College in Sierra Leone and Ibadan University in Nigeria were based largely on British university models. The USAID administration in Washington felt that new institutions of higher learning in Africa should serve a more practical purpose by teaching, for example, modern agricultural methods. So in both these countries, USAID contracted with U.S. land grant universities to transmit this philosophy and these techniques. In Sierra Leone, Nbele University was created in this mold, and in Nigeria, the new USAID-financed University of Nigeria with campuses at Nsuka and Enugu was similarly patterned. This change of emphasis was decried by some traditional British and African educators, but in my view it was a healthy innovation, and these new institutions have flourished. At the same time, USAID in Nigeria supported the agricultural and veterinary schools at Amadu Bello University in the north, the university agricultural school at the University of Ife and a dozen other institutions of higher learning. USAID also financed a project for the modernization of textbooks and other volumes used in Nigerian schools.

On a visit to Sierra Leone in 1963 I witnessed a scene that may represent the high water mark in the efforts of a former colonial power to retain its influence. In 100-degree weather, I watched students in a vocational training class patiently construct English fireplaces with bricks imported from the United Kingdom. This seemed completely bizarre until I learned that this was a required step in the qualifying British exam. By now, I hope they've found a more appropriate vocational test for aspiring bricklayers in that beleaguered country.

Another project that greatly interested me was the construction in Ghana of the huge Akosombo Dam on the Volta River. The U.S. provided an USAID loan, an Export-Import Bank (EXIM) loan and a political insurance guarantee. World Bank funding provided substantial underpinning. The resulting lake would displace several thousand area residents and have considerable impact on the environment. Around 1963, a multidiscipline research team was assembled to study the probable consequences. We met at the National Academy of Science in Washington, and I was the USAID representative. It was agreed that the advantages would outweigh the negative effects, and construction of the dam got underway with the Kaiser Corporation as the principal contractor. The Ghanaian government agreed to provide new homes for the families whose homes were inundated.

My three years in the Office of Central African Affairs involved several extended field trips to West and Central Africa and considerably broadened my experience. I visited USAID projects in Nigeria, Ghana, Sierra Leone, Cameroon, Chad, Congo Brazzaville, Zaire and the Central African Republic.

I also served on the U.S. Delegation for a meeting of the Organization of African Unity (OAU) held in the former Belgian Congo, later Zaire, in 1963. The chairman of the U.S. delegation was Walter Kotschnig, a highly reputable State Department officer. Born in Germany, Kotschnig was both wise and witty, and it was a pleasure to serve under him during our week in Kinshasa. The third member of the Delegation was Tony Ross, a mid-level officer who later became a U.S. Ambassador to several countries. We breakfasted together each morning, plotting our strategy for the day.

In memory's haze I also recall my one visit to the Central African Republic (CAR) which in French Colonial times had the picturesque name of Ubangi-Shari. Situated on the Ubangi River, a tributary of the Congo, Bangui was surely one of the most attractive capitals in Africa. I had seen the Congo in Brazzaville, muddy and choked up with a great deal of water hyacinth. In Bangui, the river seemed cleaner and more inviting as it flowed lazily by in those pre-Bokassa days.

I was traveling to the CAR with an USAID agriculturalist named Harry some years my senior, although I was then in my 50s. The USAID country director, whose surname I forget, was a nice young American of French origin named Jean. He had arranged for us to take off the following morning on a chartered flight to view several up-country USAID projects. When he greeted us at breakfast, I could see that something was amiss. He told us the charter plane was in for repairs and no other charter was available. "But," he said brightly, "I have a friend who flies his own plane, and belongs to the Aero-Club. He's offered to take us." With some misgivings we boarded the tiny, one-engine plane and took off. Jean sat with the pilot and Harry and I squeezed in behind. It was a beautiful day. On the way up, the plane precipitously dipped. "Look," said the pilot and directly below we saw a magnificent waterfall, inaccessible by any other means. We arrived a bit late at our destination. They gave us lunch and a tour of inspection, and as often happens, we were late in starting back to Bangui. The weather had changed; ominous clouds hovered overhead. Half an hour out, with another hour still to go, the heavens opened and we were bobbing about in a torrential thunderstorm and heavy wind. The agriculturalist turned to me. "You know," he said, "Our insurance is no good in this private plane!" It was getting dark, and the skies ahead seemed impenetrable, even when lightning flashed all around us. Suddenly the pilot began a dizzying descent, veering swiftly to the right. It just about tore up our guts, and it seemed interminable, but eventually we found ourselves in a more placid area. We were way off course, but we had skirted the storm. We arrived back in Bangui an hour late. At the airport, they were seriously worried. They had made frantic efforts to track us but we had flown out of the range of their primitive efforts to communicate.

In Yaounde, the capital of Cameroon, I stayed with the American Ambassador, Leland Barrows, with whom I had worked closely in the War Relocation Authority. The country at that time had one of the sounder prevailing governments. A German colony up to World War I, it was shared out between England and France under the Versailles Treaty. West Cameroon went to France, and East Cameroon, across the Douala River, became a British colony until 1960 when the State of Cameroon was constituted from the two former colonial possessions. East Cameroon especially interested me. I had read Gerald Durrell's very amusing books about it—*The Fon of Bafut, The Bafut Beagles* and *A Zoo in my Pocket*. Gerald, the brother of Lawrence Durrell, had spent some time in Cameroon collecting animals. I flew from Douala, Cameroon's largest city, across the river into East Cameroon. During the flight I glimpsed Mount Cameroon, which rises up very suddenly to 13,500 feet. It is the highest mountain in West Africa and was, a few years later, the site of a disastrous plane crash. As we neared Bamenda, our destination, I peered down, looking for an airport, but the plane made its way to a green pasture. One of the half dozen passengers on the plane must have been a chief or someone otherwise worthy of special attention. As we descended from the plane I heard *Ach du Lieber Augustine*, a nostalgically familiar German tune. The music came from what I can only describe as a little German band. Seven or eight musicians dressed in ancient Germanic garb with lederhosen and Tyrolean hats, looking absurdly out of context, were primed to greet the visiting dignitary.

By 1965 I had acquired a working knowledge of West Africa and was fairly literate in the language of development. I had also come to admire a number of the African Development officials I met along the way, especially the university-trained, younger men I dealt with. I regretted in later years that corruption and autocratic rule obliterated this high promise in so many African countries. But a change in assignment was in the wind for me. Ted Kennedy and a few others in Congress were concerned about the rising number of refugees resulting from the war in Vietnam, at least partly due to the burgeoning U.S. military presence. They urged the creation within USAID of a special division headed by an Assistant Director in Saigon, and refugee representatives in about half of the South Vietnamese provinces where the refugee total was on the increase and there was a mounting need for relief supplies and other assistance.

Fred Hahne, in USAID's administrative office, knew of my background in refugee work, and offered me the job. The normal tour of duty was two years, but I was reluctant to leave my family for that long. USAID staff were, by then, not permitted to bring their wives and families. When I said I would go for a year Fred signed me up. I can't say I was delighted at the prospect of going to Vietnam. The sentiment against America's participation in the war was by no means as strong as it became later, but doubts were already creeping in about the validity of the struggle and the justification there was for U.S. intervention. It was only a few months after the Gulf of Tonkin resolution. The building up of American forces was just starting.

In preparation for the Vietnam assignment, I interviewed a number of USAID and other candidates in Washington, Boston and New York who were interested in joining the new team. I also met Eric Hughes, a Foreign Service officer, who was to be my deputy. I asked if an old friend with longtime refugee experience going back to UNRRA and IRO could join me as a consultant for the first few weeks. Permission was granted, and it was gratifying to have the input of John Thomas. Before going to Saigon, I attended a Senate Judiciary Hearing at which Wells Klein testified on a recent visit to Vietnam he had made for the International Rescue Committee (IRC), an NGO. Kennedy and the people at USAID were impressed with Klein and wanted him to follow me to Saigon as a member of my staff. I didn't know him, somewhat resented this gratuitous gift, but when Wells arrived we hit it off, and his previous experience in Vietnam proved enormously helpful. Wells and I were friends for 35 years, and for at least ten of them we worked together as Chairman and Executive Director of a leading NGO in the refugee field. But I am getting ahead of my story.

FLIGHTS OF FANCY

Travelers tell such doleful tales of the shortcomings of airlines that I would like to redress the balance. To be sure, in logging untold thousands of air miles I too have been plagued by monstrous delays, wretched meals, ghetto-like cabin crowding and occasional incivility. But there have also been serendipitous delights.

Public officials, except those in the very highest reaches, fly Economy. I suppose I could afford to pay the difference some time and go First or Business, but the urge is never quite that strong. That makes it particularly sweet when, as sometimes happens, you are thrust into First Class, through no fault of your own, on an international flight.

Although several airlines have dubbed me a Frequent Traveler, with the limited perks that distinction provides, I've never been awarded a First Class passage. But several times, when least expected, it's befallen me.

Some years ago Margaret and I were on a dismally long line at JFK, waiting to check in for an Air France flight to Paris. For no reason I could fathom, an attendant plucked at my sleeve and redirected us to the much shorter First Class queue. We thought it was just to equalize the service load, but instead we were graciously processed, whisked into the V.I.P. lounge and ultimately cradled into First Class seats on the plane, where we enjoyed all the goodies without any pangs of contrition.

***

My second, more intriguing experience took place several years later on a TWA flight from London to Dulles. I checked in reasonably early, but when I boarded the plane I found the economy seat assigned to me occupied by a delectable young woman of Asian mien. I verified the seat number, then mildly suggested to the occupant that she was in error.

Instead of replying, she raised her lovely eyes and handed me a boarding pass which not only bore the correct seat number but also, to my astonishment, my own surname. I showed her my pass—same name, same seat number—and it was her turn to be surprised. I called over an air hostess and asked for another seat. While she was seeing about it, I found out that my charming fellow passenger was the daughter-in-law of a recently deceased namesake and acqaintance of mine. His son had met and married this treasure, Premila by name, while a Peace Corps volunteer in India.

The hostess returned after some time. She looked unhappy. "The seat was double-booked," she said, "because of the similarity in names. I'm terribly sorry—but as the plane is full, one of you will have to get off and take the next one. Of course we'll make all the arrangements." She looked at each of us in turn.

"I can't possibly," said Premila. "I've only just been married, and my husband's meeting me."

"I'm due at an important meeting," I said. "What's more, I booked that ticket over three weeks ago. How about First Class?"

"No way," said the hostess. "We're booked solid there too. I thought we might have a cancellation, but not this time."

"Can't you bump somebody else—some late arrival?" She shook her head no. The time of departure was near. The hostess stood there impatiently.

"Wait a minute," I said. "This is a 747. What about that upstairs lounge? You've surely got seats up there."

"That's against regulations," she replied. "It would require special permission from the Captain. "

"Well, this is a special situation," I countered.

"Please try," said my beauteous namesake. "I would grieve to see this gentleman forced off the plane."

The hostess melted. A few minutes later she returned.

"The Captain agrees," she said, "exceptionally. You can sit in the lounge. But we serve a very special luncheon up there to First Class passengers who have made advance reservations. You'll have to leave the lounge while lunch is being served. After that, you can return."

"And meanwhile?"

"Meanwhile you can sit on a hostess' jump seat where we'll serve you some lunch."

I warmly thanked the hostess, Premila flashed her a smile of gratitude, and I was straightaway borne aloft to the vacant First Class lounge. I sat there a few minutes in solitary splendor. My first visitor was another hostess. After a brief introductory nod she went through, for my personal benefit, the complete oxygen mask/life jacket flotation device routine as if she were addressing a full cabin load. I gave her my undivided attention. Under the circumstances I could do no less.

The next arrival was the Purser. "TWA is terribly sorry about all this," he said. "And I'm afraid up here you won't be able to watch the movie."

The news didn't shatter me.

"But we want you to be as comfortable as possible," he went on. "How about a welcoming cocktail?"

I soon had an excellent Bloody Mary, compliments of the airline, which I drank in unconvivial silence until the plane took wing.

Perhaps an hour after take-off a steward appeared. He took no notice of me as he busied himself meticulously setting three tables of four and one of two for the select diners. Everything looked posh and sparkling, with fresh flowers on each table. On his way back to the bar, he noticed my empty glass and offered a fresh drink which I accepted. We began to chat, mostly about his work, while I drifted into a warm and pleasant haze.

The re-appearance of the original hostess brought me back to reality.

"It's time," she stage-whispered. "The luncheon guests are coming up any minute. I'll take you to your seat."

"Just a moment." I had an inspiration. "While the First Class diners are up here, what happens to *their* seats below? Couldn't I slip into one of those?"

"Oh," she said, followed by a long "Hmmm." Finally, "Well, I suppose so, but you'll have to leave before they return."

Result, I was ushered into the First Class compartment, arriving at the precise moment that champagne, caviar and other delicacies were being served to the passengers who had lacked sufficient foresight to book a table in the lounge. Never mind. Downstairs on this occasion fared as well as upstairs.

As I was relishing my post-prandial cognac, a familiar voice hissed in my ear, "It's time!" Before returning to the lounge I made a short visit to Economy to assure Premila that I was being well cared for.

Back in my eyrie, I once again enjoyed the steward's company as he cleared the tables. He preferred another friendly glass, but I decided not to push my luck. Then he, too, left, and I was alone with my thoughts until we had crossed the Atlantic.

As we overflew Boston, one of the plane's officers appeared. "So sorry we've inconvenienced you," he said. "Can't recall anything like this ever happening before."

"Me neither," I replied.

"I hope you'll fly with us again."

I assured him I had passed the voyage without undue hardship.

At the baggage claim I looked for Premila, but as First Class passengers were the first to disembark, she hadn't appeared by the time I cleared Customs. I scanned the waiting greeters for a glimpse of her husband whom I did not know but had cause to congratulate on his exquisite choice.

***

Several years ago, I was leaving Geneva with a colleague of mine who was an inordinate smoker. We had business to discuss on the plane, but as our taxi approached Cointrin Airport I turned to him.

"I hope you won't mind, John. We can get together during the flight. But I'm going to sit in non-smoking."

He preceded me in the check-in line. At the Swiss Air counter the girl asked for his seat preference, to which of course he replied, "smoking." She looked at her chart. "Oh, dear," she said, "We've such a lot of smokers today. I'm going to have to put you in First Class." It was now my turn. John, at the side of the counter, boarding pass in hand, fixed me with a quizzical gaze.

She asked the inevitable question.

"Smoking, please," I answered without batting an eye.

I enjoyed every moment of that flight, every crumb and sip. Perhaps my casual observation that there were empty seats in non-smoking Economy added to the pleasure.

And while I haven't taken up smoking, I learned that the aroma of tobacco, taken in moderation and under the right circumstances, is not injurious to the palette.

***

One evening Vera and I went to LaGuardia Airport with the shuttle flight to Boston as our destination. After we checked in, I hung behind to see what free magazines were available to passengers. As there were no reserved seats on the Delta Shuttle, Vera said she would board the plane and save one for me.

Armed with *The Financial Times* and *The New Republic* I proceeded to the gate in time to see a white haired woman resembling Vera pass through. I followed, boarded the plane, trying to reach the white haired woman, but I was stopped by the stewardess ushering me to the nearest seat, as the plane was about to leave the gate. The plane rolled on to the tarmac. Meanwhile, Vera on the Boston plane about to leave the gate, asked the stewardess to try to find me. The public address announcement came through to the Washington plane where I was peacefully settling in with my reading material. When I heard it I identified myself.

Delta rose to the occasion. I was whisked out of my seat and escorted to the rear of the plane where an open door permitted me to descend to a small car that transported me across the runway to the waiting Boston plane. I entered that plane through the rear staircase and the plane took off as soon as I was seated next to my much relieved Vera.

***

In 1994, Vera, Michael and I booked passage to Amsterdam on KLM. Vera was watching her weight at the time and decided she preferred the delicious calories available in Europe to run-of-the-mine Economy airline food. In consequence she ordered a vegetarian dinner when we purchased the tickets. We were late in checking in for the plane. At the desk we were informed there were no more Economy seats available and we would have to sit in Business Class! There we enjoyed the free drinks and were looking forward to a gala dinner. But just as we were making our selection from the menu, a steward appeared calling out Vera's name. "We haven't forgotten about you," he said. "Here's your vegetarian meal." Vera's face fell. She thanked him, then sweetly protested that she was willing to put up with the Business Class food. "Very sorry," said the steward, "but we reserved this meal especially for you." We were hardly in a position to complain. Vera ate half my chocolate dessert.

A CHAPTER IN VIETNAM

It was a strange feeling in the summer of 1965 to be working in Vietnam. At the time I arrived there was no more than a flurry of protests about the war on U.S. campuses but somehow my gut told me that all was not well. About one thing there was no doubt. The heightened U.S. military presence had brought about an increase in the number and needs of the refugees. The "search and destroy" operations were partly responsible. Some refugees fled the fighting zones or were forced out; others escaped through the lines to avoid the pressures of the Vietcong, the heavy taxation, the forced labor, and the conscription of young teenagers.

Upheaval has been chronic in this beleaguered land, and each crisis has brought its own wave of refugees. In 1954, when the Geneva Accords finally settled the war with the French, 900,000 refugees abandoned their former lives and trekked south, rather than live under a Communist regime. Many entered South Vietnam as complete families, often as parishes and hamlets with strong religious (usually Catholic) or secular leadership. On the whole they settled in well, with many fertile acres available for colonization. Now many of these former refugees, and a great many others—the estimated total in all parts of the country was 700,000—had been again displaced. Unfortunately, the responsibility for refugees was split between two government ministries, neither of which considered the refugee to be its chief concern. Many essential services, including schooling and medical care, were either not provided or made available only on a hit or miss basis. If the Diem and Ky regimes were more reliable, and more cognizant of humanitarian needs, they would have taken earlier action to alleviate the burgeoning refugee problem.

As I said in an article published in *The Reporter* of January 12, 1967, "It used to be said in Vietnam that the Emperor's law ended at the bamboo hedge around the village. But nearly 700,000 peasants are now refugees living in camps or temporary shelters, and some will never return to their hamlets. Almost all are dependent for a time at least on the support of the national government."

With the encouragement of Washington (notably Ted Kennedy and the Senate Judiciary Special Sub-Committee on Refugees and Escapees) a Refugee Commissariat was finally set up under Dr. Nguyen Phuc Que, an able adminis-

trator (though he lacked Vietnamese Cabinet rank). Que set up new criteria of
eligibility and standards of assistance. He also succeeded in putting together a
budget of roughly 12 million dollars, the first consolidated budget for refugee
purposes.

On the U.S. side, I arrived in the summer of 1965 with a team prepared to
complement and reinforce Dr. Que's efforts in Saigon and in the provinces having the most serious refugee problems. My Deputy was Eric Hughes, a seasoned
Foreign Service officer who had been U.S. Consul General in Belfast. As consultant during the first few weeks, I had John Thomas, an old friend from
IRO/ICEM, who in later years headed the U.S. program for Cuban refugees and
then became ICEM Director. Wells Klein, who had visited Vietnam for IRC,
was a skilled advisor and became a new friend. In the field, the provincial refugee aides we recruited were beginning to make their presence felt. This wasn't
so easy when other aspects of the program were given priority. Often they battled with the USAID province chief to retain for refugees supplies he would
have preferred to release for other purposes. Bill Egan, Carl Harris, Phil Aschner
and Steve Cummings were outstanding in this role. Some years later Egan, Harris and Aschner would work again with me in the Nigerian refugee operation.

It wasn't as if the refugee situation was static. The relentless tides of war
complicated the situation. New military actions resulted in new refugees. Only
very occasionally were we given advance warning so we could be prepared with
supplies. More frequently, we were informed only when an action had been
completed and the refugees clogged the roads. Some areas containing refugees
were retaken, and they once again found themselves in villages controlled by the
Vietcong (VC).

In the February 8, 1966 issue of *Look Magazine* Ted Kennedy writes of a
village elder he spoke with in a small village. By that time, Kennedy had made
several exploratory visits to Vietnam. As Kennedy put it, "This man had seen
thirty years of continuous conflict, two sons had been lost in long-passed military engagements, and his crude farm implements lay useless behind his home.
He was an exhausted man in an exhausted country. Without my asking, he related the needs of his village—but he was really speaking for Vietnam. 'We just
want to be free from the terror and weapons of soldiers,' he said. 'We want our
children to read, we don't want them to be sick all their lives, and we want to
grow our own food on our own land.'"

Our USAID team worked closely and congenially with Dr. Que to provide
emergency relief food, medical, and some amenity supplies and to assist in the
resettlement in other provinces of refugees displaced from their homes. We tried
to move in supplies by truck, water transport or air as soon as possible after the
fighting stopped. Sometimes the target area was inaccessible for security reasons
and we had to make emergency drops by air. On more than one occasion, while
munching K-rations in the plane, I derived satisfaction from seeing the bundles
we dropped retrieved by refugees. When the situation stabilized in a given area

we could stockpile and move in regular supplies to encamped refugees, but in numerous cases the VC penetrated camp borders by night. Our second function was to resettle refugees who could not return to their villages or remain in the areas to which they had fled. We consulted with the Vietnamese authorities, with the military, and with our USAID agricultural and economic specialists to locate areas suitable for resettlement. It was important to know something about the refugees affected. What kind of farmers were they? Did the group include some artisans or people with construction skills? Were they willing to quit the general area of their former homes? We then had to match these findings with the location of an appropriate resettlement site.

Several key factors were involved. Was the proposed site arable and reasonably similar to the land they left? Was it secure and likely to remain so? Was it available from the standpoint of ownership? We found some parcels of land were tightly held, in some cases by absentee French landlords. Finally came the question of moving the refugees and any of their remaining possessions. Was it safe enough to go by truck, by coastwise or river craft, or would an airlift be necessary? Some refugees could stay for a time where they had trekked. In other cases, a move to an adjoining province was indicated, but there were some instances where the best solution was a move to a totally different area. In such case it was advisable to have an advance party of community leaders view the proposed site.

The odyssey of a group of several hundred refugees dislodged from their home in Phu Yen Province serves as an example. They had to move some distance from their homes for security reasons. I went with Dr. Que and an USAID agriculturalist to a recommended seaside area in Ninh Thuan Province. When Que saw the vast expanse of sandy ground he felt it was unsuitable. But the American agriculturist spoke glowingly of its potential. Yes, it would need irrigation and some fertilizer but it was capable of growing market produce of a value far exceeding that of crops grown in Phu Yen. Still skeptical, Que finally agreed.

We were able to truck the refugees to Cam Ranh Bay, a huge naval resource developed by the U.S. Military. There they boarded a U.S. navy vessel that took them to Ninh Thuan. I didn't make the overnight voyage, but on board the vessel before its departure I viewed the arrangements for the shipment of farm animals, baggage and several hundred refugees. While still in Vietnam, some months later, I learned that it was hard scratch at first for this pioneer group, but in time the irrigated soil yielded a harvest of onions and sugar baby melons that brought high prices in Saigon and other urban markets. The colony succeeded, and I understand that few of the resettlers returned to Phu Yen at the war's conclusion. Not all relocations were as successful as this one. As the VC gradually prevailed, there were rapid shifts in the occupation of land and in the ability and willingness of the displaced to resettle very far from their native heath.

The experience of a group of about 600 Catholic fishermen and their families who moved in 1955 from North Vietnam to the maritime province of Binh Thuan is worth recalling. The VC began harassing the settlers as early as 1960, but it was not until May of 1965 that the villagers, with their boats, nets, and other possessions, took off down the coast and reestablished their village on a bleak, uninhabited point near Vung Tau. Here they made a rapid comeback. The men resumed their fishing, but some of them, as well as some of the women, were employed in construction work or service trades in Vung Tau, with its major U.S. and Australian support facilities.

Meanwhile in Washington, President Johnson was in a torture of indecision about whether to accede to General Westmoreland's request for 19 additional American combat battalions—100,000 more men by the end of 1965—plus more in 1966. The President encouraged full debate on the question at a number of meetings in the Cabinet Room and at Camp David. Defense Secretary Robert S. McNamara strongly backed Westmoreland, as did Dean Rusk, Secretary of State; General Earle Wheeler, Chairman of the Joint Chiefs of Staff; U.S. Ambassador Henry Cabot Lodge; the Bundy brothers and Walt Rostow. The "Domino Theory" that other Asian countries would give way if we showed weakness was then in vogue. Dean Rusk expressed uncertainty that "the Communist world will stay their hand if they find that we will not pursue our commitments to the end." On the other hand, Undersecretary of State George Ball, almost uniquely but persuasively, voiced his doubts about the war and the Westmoreland/McNamara proposals. His view at that time was supported by General Maxwell Taylor and by Clark Clifford, friend and confidante of Johnson, who with Richard Holbrooke wrote a long article in *The New Yorker* describing the President's efforts, in a series of pivotal meetings, to resolve the question.

In the end, the McNamara view prevailed. According to Clifford's report, our troop strength in Vietnam grew from 75,000 in the summer of 1965 to 485,000 at the end of 1967. Casualties grew even faster, from about 500 killed in action before July of 1965 to more than 16,000 by the end of 1967. Clifford notes that "domestic controversy over the war effort also grew dramatically, with a handful of campus teach-ins giving way to large demonstrations in front of the Pentagon." The escalation certainly had its effect on the number of refugees and their vulnerability.

In Saigon, I was periodically invited to the Embassy by Ambassador Henry Cabot Lodge and later by his successor, Ellsworth Bunker. General Westmoreland, my USAID boss Charlie Mann, Phil Habib and the CIA Chief were present at a luncheon when I was asked to report on the refugee situation and give my opinion of the Vietnamese Commissioner, Dr. Que. While I was present there was no discussion about the pros and cons of escalating the U.S. participation in the war.

On the personal side, I enjoyed somewhat the companionship of men without women. While John Thomas and Wells were there, we had long bull sessions about the work and speculated about the future. We dined together, went bowling several times and watched a few movies. When they left, I joined Le Cercle Sportif and enjoyed some tennis on Sundays. It was mostly an expatriate club carried over from the time of French rule, but there were some wealthy Vietnamese members. Most evenings I went to my comfortable apartment on Doan Cong Buu for dinner and a quiet evening. I was fortunate in my household arrangements. I'll tell about Nam, my *boyesse*, in another chapter. The sounds of bombardment sometimes distracted my thoughts. I would go up on the roof to watch the flight of the tracer bullets and the flares. I had not been in military service in World War II and, in a funny way, Vietnam was my war.

Occasionally I dined with Eric or refugee representatives from the provinces who were in Saigon for a night or two. I periodically lunched with Charlie Mann. Born in Germany, Charlie spoke with the accent of that country but his speech reflected the tough vernacular expressions of a veteran USAID executive. He somehow reminded me of Charlie Chaplin in the Great Dictator. Once in a while visitors from the outside would lend spice to the routine. One was Florence Boester, an IRO friend, who came out to establish a branch of International Social Service (ISS) in Vietnam as she had in Greece. I spent a pleasant evening with Ulf Wickbom, a prominent Swedish journalist who interviewed me for a Swedish paper. Years later, when I was with UNICEF, we met again in Stockholm. By an amazing coincidence his charming wife, Ulla, directed the Swedish Committee for UNICEF. Vera and I dined in their home in Stockholm. It was a convivial evening and we were served the most delicious salmon we've ever tasted. Among the members of Congress who came out to report on Vietnam to their constituents was John S. Monagan of Connecticut, a Dartmouth friend who had been the mayor of Waterbury. I took John for a Chinese meal in Cholon and we had a most agreeable reunion.

During my Saigon days, I avoided the hotel dining rooms and the more expensive restaurants. I occasionally lunched in a seafood restaurant on a boat moored in the harbor. One day it was heavily damaged by a Claymore bomb. Away from the main part of town I found a Corsican restaurant that seemed unaffected by the progress of the war. The strapping owner served a limited menu, but everything on it was good. His gazpacho was the best I've ever tasted. Cholon eateries served very acceptable Chinese meals. And of course there was Cheap Charlie's for a quick bite.

While on duty in Saigon I took one R & R (Rest and Relaxation) in Bangkok. I knew no one there at the time, but it was my first visit and I enjoyed wandering about the city with its bizarre, eclectic architecture. That I resisted the temptations of that wicked city was not due to any lack of effort by the taxi driver who drove me from the airport. We had gone but a few hundred yards when he turned around and said: "Like a girl?" I declined, but after a few minutes he persisted. "Nice young girl," he said. "Only sixteen—we bring her right to your room." I was more vehement in my denial. He didn't ask again until we were near my hotel. Then he swung around once more, "Maybe like boy?" he asked hopefully.

When I was there in 1965-66, two years before the Viet Cong's crucial Tet offensive, there were many South Vietnamese who abhorred communism and nourished the hope that despite known corruption in Ky's government the South Vietnamese would prevail. This was especially true of the mainly Catholic Vietnamese who streamed from the North into South Vietnam when there was an exchange of population following the liberation of Vietnam from the French. Nearly a million had headed South, voting with their feet. Less than one tenth of that number trekked North from their homes in the South.

POSTSCRIPT

I reluctantly left Saigon in the summer of 1966, but I had fulfilled my agreement with USAID Washington. By then we had put in place the infrastructure of a satisfactory refugee operation, and were working harmoniously with Dr. Que and his team, but it was perfectly clear that the refugee crisis would end only when the war ended. As a matter of fact, subsequent military action in the next few years brought the refugee total to nearly 2 million.

I was out of it, and didn't revisit Saigon for nearly ten years. Before leaving I made a small gesture, contracting with Foster Parents Plan (Plan) to contribute a couple of hundred dollars a year towards the support of a Vietnamese child I had never met. I then left Vietnam for a reunion with Margaret and a delightful vacation trip in Scandinavia. We ended up in London where, for the next two years, I enjoyed one of the few USAID assignments in an industrialized country. I didn't return to Vietnam until early in 1974 and then only for a few days. My USAID job had changed. We were encouraging the NGOs in Africa and Asia to come up with worthwhile projects in line with the objectives of our USAID program. If the project was acceptable to USAID and the NGO was prepared to provide at least 25% of the needed funds, USAID would make up the difference. By partnering an NGO, USAID would get an extra dividend and the refugee client would enjoy the more personal association with an NGO. We had the pot boiling with a number of projects at one time. My visit to Vietnam was shortly before Saigon fell. I made a plane trip with Martin Sandberg and another UNICEF officer to view several NGO projects that our agencies were helping to support. It was a routine visit but one that we found very memorable. Our pilot miscalculated the landing; one wing of the plane came within two feet of the ground before he was able to set the plane right and come in for a proper landing. My UNICEF friends said they had never had such a close shave. It was terrifying.

Less fortunate was the initial flight of Operation Baby Lift (OB) on April 4, 1975. The tragic crash of Air Force C-54 on that day took the lives of 78 of 228 Vietnamese and Cambodian orphans on board; six staff escorts also perished in the crash. Subsequent flights on Pan American chartered planes safely carried a total of 2,547 children. Of this number 602 were enroute to other countries, leaving the total of 1945 for adoption in the U.S. under the sponsorship of seven private international and U.S. adoption agencies. During the Baby Lift there were nine deaths, including seven orphans under 20 weeks of age. Fifteen percent of all orphans processed required hospitalization during the operation at Pacific locations enroute to the U.S.

Over half the orphans involved in the lift were under the age of two; over 91% were under eight. Fifty seven percent were male orphans. Twenty percent of the orphans were racially mixed, of whom 173 were of black paternity. However, the OB report states only 34 of these were placed in black homes.

Altogether the Military Air Command (MAC) chartered a total of 46 planes between April and June 1975. There was a great deal of public interest in the baby lift, and many offers to adopt children were sent to OB's Washington office and to the individual adoption agencies. There was a "last chance" aspect to the lift because it took place at a time when the military outlook for South Vietnam and its American ally was rapidly deteriorating.

When I returned briefly to Saigon in 1974 I told the representative of Plan that I wanted to meet my foster child. They arranged for a car to take me to Bien Hoa on Sunday with a driver who could interpret for me. Xoi was five when we "adopted" her. In the eight years since, we had exchanged photos and learned of her progress through bulletins from Plan. Through Plan we sent Christmas presents to her.

Xoi's family, consisting of her parents and several siblings, lived in a crude structure mainly consisting of one room and a courtyard. Although none spoke any English, I was greeted and pressed to accept some cake and a glass of warm Coca Cola. Xoi's father proudly showed me the tin roof that my contributions had helped to provide. I continued the support for another year, but when Saigon fell in 1975, the Plan office was abandoned and I had no further communication with the family. Plan in fact substituted a child from Haiti that I helped support for several years.

When Vietnam opened up somewhat I thought of Xoi and of the country in general. I wondered if the family was still in Bien Hoa and how they'd been affected by the war. In 1998 Vera and I decided the time was opportune for a trip to Vietnam. There were no direct flights, so we booked passage via Bangkok, arriving in Hanoi December 4th with a schedule taking us south to Hue, Hoi An and Ho Chi Minh City (HCMC, formerly Saigon). It was of course my first visit to Hanoi, and that was an eye opener I'll discuss a bit later.

I had brought with me two photographs of Xoi and her family taken at the time of my 1974 visit. I had no address and little expectation of locating them, but when I mentioned this to Rima Salah, the UNICEF Country Director, she said: "Give me the pictures. We'll find them. I'll send your photos to our HCMC office and they'll put a message on the TV." After a most interesting trip, we arrived in HCMC a week later, and I went to the UNICEF office. "We haven't yet located your family," said Frances Kostick, "but if you visit Bien Hoa you may have better luck." We drove out there but the local Child Protection Office was unable to locate the family. They did, however, send the photos to a TV station for broadcast.

We returned to HCMC and heard nothing for several days. We were leaving on Tuesday for Hong Kong. On Monday morning, I was in the room nursing a miserable gut and Vera was preparing to leave for a long-anticipated day of shopping, when the hotel informed us that four non-English-speaking Vietnamese were in the lobby. It was a thrill to find Xoi, now an attractive woman of 32 with her husband, brother and cousin. A neighbor had told them of the television broadcast and they had come into the city on two borrowed motorbikes to meet us.

It was a moving occasion. We recognized her immediately from the photo. She produced photos I had sent her after my 1974 visit, letters written to her by Margaret and some long outdated papers from Plan. Through an interpreter provided by the hotel and over orange juice, she told of her father's death, her marriage two years before and her sometimes work as a seamstress. She expressed her fond hope of returning to America with us. Xoi's brother, a truck driver, spoke a smidgen of English. Her farmer husband did not. They were very keen for us to come back with them to Bien Hoa for a visit, and though it was the day prior to our departure, and I was feeling poorly, we arranged through the hotel to hire a car and an interpreter to do so. Xoi rode in the car with us and en route expressed the hope we could continue to help her. Above all, she and her husband wanted a home of their own. Vera and I thought she might ask for $500, since the structures we were passing were small and mostly made of simple cement blocks; we would have been prepared to help. The interpreter said he handled this kind of transaction for other people; it would cost $20,000 and he would get a percentage. He went into great detail about the situations in which he helped and apparently he had a thriving business.

I explained that I could not possibly meet that expectation but that when we returned home we would do what we could to help her. In Bien Hoa we first went to Xoi's family's house that I had visited in 1974. We met her mother, now virtually blind, and other family occupants including a number of children. There were perhaps a dozen in the room plus numerous curious neighbors outside crowded around the windows. The house and meager furnishings looked very much the same. When I asked the brother about the roof, he laughed and said it was now called "the roof of a thousand stars!" Prominently displayed was a photo of Xoi's father who had died two years before. On the floor was an older child patiently tying up vegetables for sale in the market.

We then took off for a visit to the modest home of her in-laws, where Xoi and her husband resided. While Vera traveled in the hired car I was encouraged to make the short journey on the back of the motorbike driven by her brother, skillfully maneuvered through an incessant flood of oncoming traffic. There we met Xoi's gracious mother-in-law and a host of other relatives and onlookers. It was easy to understand Xoi's desire to have her own home.

These are poor people. They were dressed simply but neatly. The family did not appear to have been greatly affected by war. Work is hard scratch. Xoi said she finds only occasional customers for the clothing she sews. She supplements her income by selling in the market some of the vegetables grown by her share-cropper husband. Xoi's brother, a markedly bright young man, works only sporadically and yearns to have his own truck.

We left Bien Hoa with warm goodbyes and entreaties to return. We knew this probably would never happen. We had not anticipated their expectations of what we might be able to do for them; their hopes were that we might make a significant difference in their lives. For all the 23 years since I had visited her, Xoi had treasured, like a hope chest, the photos and letters we had sent her. We knew, especially after our visit, that we could never meet her dreams. We lived in two different worlds. In the end we said we would send her some money when we returned home, and through the UNICEF office we sent $300 to her She bought a pregnant sow to produce piglets she could sell and made a party for her neighbors.

HAVING A LOOK AROUND VIETNAM

When they heard we were going to Vietnam, our American friends were surprised. "What makes you want to go there?" they asked. "Well, we have several reasons," I replied. "I was there in the 60s for almost a year heading an USAID program for relief and resettlement of war-created refugees. I also hope to locate a 'foster' child we helped to support after my return to the U.S. Vera has a healthy curiosity to experience that part of the world, especially to see where I had been. And our exposure to many Vietnamese refugees in America has set us wondering about the emerging unified country from which they had fled. Have the wounds been healed?"

Vietnam today has many attractions for the tourist. On our fortnight's visit, Vera and I met Australians, New Zealanders, Canadians, French, German and Dutch, but also a fair number of Americans. Meeting Vietnamese, excepting those assisting foreigners, was not easy, but we did make a number of contacts. As Americans, we were treated very well, both in Hanoi and in the towns we visited below the DMZ line: Hue, Hoi An and Ho Chi Minh City (Saigon). These towns I knew in my year's tour in 1965-66. Hanoi I saw for the first time.

Quite a few Vietnamese now have relatives in the U.S., and even those who don't, like to show off any English they've acquired. English is clearly the second language of choice and the key to many jobs in the burgeoning economy. I was told that all government employees under the age of 50 are required to study English, and the government is receptive to modern techniques of teaching English to school children. Working closely with the Business Alliance for Vietnamese Education (BAVE), the Vietnamese Ministry of Education is experimenting with a new modern textbook for children beginning English language study. We learned this from Adrie van Gelderen, then the BAVE representative in Hanoi. Adrie was a Dutchman we had met ten years before when he was directing the school program for Vietnamese refugees in Hong Kong.

HANOI

We started our trip in Hanoi, flying in from Bangkok on Vietnam Air. One doesn't find many passenger cars in this city of a million people, but the constant, close order stream of motorbikes, bicycles, trucks and busses, with relatively few stop signs and traffic lights, was intimidating until, from our hotel window, we watched other pedestrians warily cross the busy streets. We did some walking, but got around mainly by taxis; once we hired a car and driver for a day's tour. We never did get used to the perpetual horn blowing.

We spent much of our first day in the compound around Ho Chi Minh's mausoleum. Uncle Ho's nearby house-on-stilts, where he spent the last twelve years of his life, is delightfully situated on a small lake. He lived there simply in peaceful surroundings. The dwelling has a loggia with a conference table below, and upstairs two sparsely furnished rooms, his bedroom and study. The teak building has graceful lines, in great contrast to the ponderous, glitzy HCM Museum designed by the Soviet Union to celebrate the leader's life and revolutionary career. We had a new concept of HCM when we found on sale a slender volume containing poetry he wrote when he was in prison.

The visitor to Van Mieu, the Temple of Literature, finds himself in a placid, scholarly retreat that goes back a thousand years. Dedicated to Confucius, it was founded in 1070 to honor scholars and writers. Eighty-two stelae, each mounted on a stone tortoise, record the scholastic achievements of sons of mandarins educated at Vietnam's first university established six years later in 1076.

Shaded avenues, lovely parks, and several lakes adorn the Hanoi landscape. A delightful feature of Hoan Kien Lake, the largest, is the Ngoc Son Temple (1225-1400), also known as the Tortoise Pagoda. Located on a small island it is reached by a wooden bridge named The Huc (Flood of Morning Sunlight). A huge stone tortoise, symbolic of a 15th Century legend greets the sightseer. Heaven, it is said, presented the Emperor Ly Thai To with a sword he used to expel the Chinese from Vietnam. The day after peace had been declared, the Emperor went boating. To his astonishment, a golden tortoise swimming in the lake seized the sword and vanished with it. Since then the lake has been called the Lake of the Restored Sword.

The Army Museum is an unsparing reminder of American participation in the late war. The museum's courtyard is filled with captured American planes, tanks, jeeps, guns and other military equipment. The interior contains hundreds of exhibits, photographs, maps and scale models giving a graphic picture of Vietnam's bloody history including occupations by the Chinese, Japanese and

French. Several rooms are devoted to mothers who lost two or more sons in the war, and these are particularly moving.

Near our hotel in Hanoi was a street with at least a dozen outdoor pool tables actively in use day and night. *Billards* (sic) is popular everywhere and we had a game in the bar of a classy restaurant. Many bars advertised karaoke.

Before leaving Hanoi, we took in the hour-long performance of the Thang Long Water Puppet Theater. Puppets swim, leap, fish, ride in boats and generally cavort most amazingly on a huge water stage, motivated ingeniously by out of sight puppeteers who appear only at the end of the 17 scene program. One witnesses such features as Dragon Dance, On a Buffalo with a Flute, Catching Frogs, Rearing Ducks, and an enactment of the "Restored Sword" legend mentioned above.

As in most third world countries, the tourist is bombarded in the street by all kinds of hawkers, many of them children, offering a variety of T-shirts, souvenirs, cheap jewelry, head gear, etc. For those spending a few days in the city, there are shops to purchase tailor-made clothing with a variety of fabrics and styles. Vera bought a jacket and blouse and I found men's shirts of a good quality. We found, however, that much of the material identified as silk was actually inferior in quality or rayon.

HUE

Hanoi is Vietnam's once and current capital, but Hue on the Perfume River held the stage as the country's political capital from 1802 to 1945 under the thirteen emperors of the Nguyen Dynasty. We flew to this attractive but war-ravaged city of 250,000 from Hanoi and put up at a riverside hotel. The top floor restaurant served a variety of Vietnamese and Western dishes. My wife's vegetarian tastes were gratified at a small, unpretentious restaurant, one of the culinary highlights of our trip. We ate hearty mushroom soup, deliciously wrapped spring rolls and outstanding tofu noodles. Our cyclo driver first took us to another "Vegetarian" restaurant. Vera took one look at the menu, that featured "Vegetables with pork uterus...vegetables with snake heads...vegetables with..." and we fled! Hue's principal tourist attraction is the Citadel—a huge moated structure dating from 1804 with high walls on a ten-kilometer site and many interior royal buildings. Within the Citadel is the "Imperial Enclosure" where the Emperors performed official duties, staged court ceremonies and received visiting dignitaries. Also within the Enclosure is the Forbidden Purple City, largely destroyed during the Tet offensive, which housed the royal concubines. UNESCO has included the Citadel in its World Heritage Program.

We made the trip to the Citadel in the rain in two cyclos. Unlike Vietnamese couples, we didn't fit into one! These are bicycle-driven pedicabs—a slow, inexpensive but reliable means of transportation. One generally bargains an agreed rate with the driver. We arranged for our driver when we exited the City Hall and the civil servant with whom we were talking hailed him. The rate from downtown Hue to the Citadel and return was 10,000 dong an hour, or slightly less than a dollar. While we were in Vietnam the dong's value fell to 14,000 per dollar. One cyclo driver, who spoke pretty good English, told us he had been a high school chemistry teacher; however, because he had worked with the Americans during the war he was sent to a re-education camp and was then unable to get his job back. On the other hand, we met several wartime sympathizers with South Vietnam who said their careers had not been visibly affected by the war's outcome. In Hue we visited a new school and library financed with outside assistance. The classrooms are somewhat smaller than those in other schools with the object of promoting a better teacher-pupil ratio. The children were alert and well clothed and knew enough English to delight in a question-answer session the teacher invited us to hold with them.

I hit some balls with the manager of the tennis court connected with our hotel. A congenial chap, he was a retired math teacher. At the court I also met a Vietnamese ear, nose and throat specialist. It was one of the few opportunities to chat with Vietnamese professionals.

Before leaving Hue we visited the Heavenly Lady Pagoda, a seven-tiered structure, built by the Emperor Thieu Tri on a rise overlooking the Perfume River. This Buddhist pagoda has witnessed many anti-government demonstrations. On exhibit is a car which carried the monk Thich Quang Duc to Saigon where he immolated himself by fire in 1963. We hired a car with an English speaking driver to take us some 80 miles to Hoi An, with a brief stop in Danang. The scenic route took us through lovely farm country and three mountain passes with spectacular views. We saw water buffalo plowing rice paddies, dogs, cows, ducks and pigs, but no horses.

HOI AN

Once a busy port, Hoi An today is a quiet town of about 60,000. It was undamaged in the war and is said to look much as it did a century ago. Over 800 structures have been designated as of historical significance. We toured half a dozen of these. One, a sixteenth century Japanese covered bridge on the Bach Dang River, was built to connect the Japanese and Chinese communities of that day; two, the Phuac Kien Assembly Hall serving different elements of the Chinese population has a mural depicting the leaders of six Fujian families who fled from China after the overthrow of the Ming Dynasty; three, the elegantly furnished ancient home of Tan Ky, constructed by Chinese, Japanese and early Vietnamese builders, has housed seven generations of the same family; four, the Chuc Thanh Pagoda founded in 1454 is the oldest in Hoi An.

We hired the same guide and a good-sized boat to visit several nearby islands. On the first island, a pottery was producing large flowerpots for a Canadian contractor. The price was $3.00 for 6 pots. Hordes of children engulfed us there offering small clay animal figures. At a second location, we witnessed the making of incredibly carved and elegant oriental-style furniture. A beautifully carved bedroom set ordered by an American was priced at $3,000.00. By this time it was pouring, but our guide bought us a gift of plastic ponchos so we could press on to a third location where two children aged ten were patiently weaving large straw mats. There were no adults in sight. In response to our question, the children told us they went to school in the morning and did their weaving in the afternoon. We bought a mat.

Back in Hoi An we spent some time in the large and labyrinthine local market. We were able most days to buy a copy of the English language Vietnam News, but it was not until we got to Ho Chi Minh City that we were able to catch up with the International Herald Tribune. We did get CNN on the tube and that kept us reasonably up to date. We read quite a bit at night and soon ran out of books. We had no luck finding a store with English language books in Hue or Hoi An. Several times, however, street kids offered us paperback copies of Graham Greene's *The Quiet American* and a newer book called *The Sorrow of War* in which a North Vietnamese veteran writes bitterly about his wartime experiences. We both read it.

Because it rained almost continuously we went on to Ho Chi Minh City a day early. Tan Son Nhat Airport is modern, attractive and completely unrecognizable to Americans who flew in and out of it during the war years. The ride to our downtown hotel in an air conditioned taxi cost us $5.00. We had booked at a small hotel which reminded us of the choice small hotels of Switzerland, clean, simple and modern with good food and exemplary service.

HO CHI MINH CITY

It was good to see the sun again in Saigon but the weather became very hot, in the 90s. We visited the War Remnants Museum. As in Hanoi's War Museum, the surrounding yard was awash with captured American planes, guns, bombs and other lethal souvenirs. Inside the museum are small arms, exhibits of various kinds, enlargements of news stories, photographs and documentation of Vietnam's other wars of liberation. However the accent is on the last war, and deals less with the civil strife between the south and the north, than with the effects of American intervention. The illustrated pamphlet given to visitors is frank in its mention of My Lai and other "wrongdoings." There are pictures of Robert S. McNamara and quotes from his book, e.g., "We were wrong, terribly wrong. We owe it to future generations to explain why." One of the rooms featured posters, newspaper headlines and other forms of protest from all over the world of America's entry into combat, including scenes of peace demonstrations at Kent State and elsewhere in the U.S.A.

As a more peaceable antidote, we visited the Cercle Sportif where I occasionally played tennis during my Saigon year. It is now Cong Vien Van Hoa Park, open to the public. I hoped to visit the apartment house at Doan Kong Buu where I had lived. I recalled that it was some distance from downtown Saigon, going out Avenue Pasteur. We actually found the small street on the map, but discovered the whole area was now a military reservation with soldiers on guard. While I could see the building's rooftop through the barred gate, an armed guard would not permit us to enter.

Before leaving HCMC we visited the impressive Jade Emperor Pagoda built early last century by a Cantonese congregation and filled with grotesque papier mache statues of Buddhist and Taoist characters. We were there on a Sunday morning, and the many worshipers shaking their joss sticks in the direction of one or another image suffused the air with the aroma of smoky incense.

The reunion with Xoi pre-empted our plans for a last day's shopping and sightseeing, but we were satisfied. Our visit to Vietnam was a superficial one, but we had seen many things. This country of 70 million lively, literate and industrious people, with its fascinating history and current forward thrust, has a lot to offer, despite its authoritarian form of government. In the main cities and recreational areas the infrastructure is already in place. There are modern hotels with satisfactory cuisine and all, or nearly all the expected amenities. Many Vietnamese, certainly the hotel people and tour guides, speak passable English. Taxis are abundant and inexpensive. Decorative fabrics, lacquer ware, woodcarvings, pottery and other crafted creations are available, and the dollar goes far. Retail trade goes on at a feverish pace. As Vera put it, "Vietnam may have a socialist government, but it has a capitalist heart." You can pay in dollars instead of dong if you wish. Above all, you will find the Vietnamese to be bright, friendly and engaging people. It's a poor country, still third world in many respects, but it's clearly on an upswing.

BONJOUR BOYESSE

(Written in 1970 by Edward B. Marks)

I found Nam waiting in the apartment assigned to me the day I arrived in Saigon in the autumn of 1965. Barefoot, and wearing a loose fitting brown pajama suit, she was washing the dishes and utensils issued to Embassy personnel. As I walked in she looked up, giggled pleasantly and said, "I your boyesse." The term "boyesse" puzzled me until I realized it was the feminine for boy, or house boy.

Nam's references showed she had worked for several American families in the days when Americans on official duty in Vietnam could have their dependents with them. I had no particular use for the baby-tending talents described by her former American employers, but I sparked to the mention that she could both cook an American style meal and turn out a first-rate Chinese dinner. Anyway, I had little choice about the matter. She came with the apartment.

According to regulations, I had to check Nam's papers with Security to make sure she wasn't V.C., dishonest, or both. She passed the test, and thus began a classic master-boyesse relationship that can have had few rivals in domestic tranquility. Nam was everything her references said and more. She was honest, perceptive, reasonably industrious, sunny, reserved when the occasion called for it, adaptable, and possessed of a certain whimsicality. Language of course was a problem. Vietnamese I soon discovered was impenetrable. Nam's French vocabulary included *bonjour* in the morning, *bonsoir* at night, but not much in between. She had picked up a small amount of English, but mainly we communicated through gestures.

I am not a demanding person, and the job was an easy one. I was frequently out for lunch or dinner and also spent considerable time out of town.

Shortly after I moved in, Nam introduced me to her younger sister, Sau, who worked for a family several floors below. The two sisters and the other maids in the house had small cell-like rooms facing on a back yard court that also included a battery of laundry tubs. Sau actually lived there with her baby, paying only Sunday visits to her husband in Cholon, Saigon's huge Chinese district. Nam kept her room mainly for afternoon siestas; she motor biked daily to and from the small house she occupied with her soldier husband and young daughter. I would watch her sometimes from the window as she rode off through the blue miasma of engine fumes, skillfully threading her way around potholes in the almost unbelievable tangle of taxis, private cars, scooters, bicycles, Army vehicles, trucks and donkey carts that was Saigon's traffic. Sometimes she rode with her child seated precariously behind, tightly clutching Nam's rather ample waist. On school holidays, the child often stayed overnight with Sau. The children of the boyesses were supposed to remain in the servants' quarters but despite the objections of the grumpy Indian concierge they ran about pretty freely in the apartment courtyard.

Nam always had my breakfast ready on time, even on the mornings I rose at 5:30 or 6 to take an early plane up-country. Cleaning the one-bedroom flat didn't take long, and if I wasn't home for lunch there was no real call on her time until evening. She polished my shoes, pressed my suits, washed and mended my clothes, occasionally shopped in the neighborhood and talked incessantly with the other boyesses. She worked a six day week, but I often let her off after Saturday lunch. I paid her what she asked, 3000 piasters a month (about $40 at the old rate), and at Tet, the Buddhist holiday which is celebrated as if it were a combination of our Christmas, New Year's and Fourth of July, I gave her the usual bonus of half a month's salary.

As a department head in the office of the USAID Mission to Vietnam I was obliged from time to time to entertain members of our staff, Washington visitors (of whom there were a great number) and Vietnamese officials with whom we worked. I had no home phone, and was often unable to give advance notice, but she rose uncomplainingly to the occasion when I brought home unannounced guests. Sometimes I was amazed at how well she coped. With a few hours' warning, she was capable of producing a banquet—often with droll combinations, but always delicious and well balanced.

The simple china and stainless steel utensils issued to me were all right for personal use but hardly suitable for more gala occasions. I thought Nam would point this out the first time I told her I was giving a dinner for ten including two Vietnamese Ministers and their wives, but she never batted an eye. "You eat Chinese or PX?" she asked. "PX," I said, signaling that the meal would be American-style mainly based on items bought in the commissary. "You make list what you need," I said, falling in with her pidgin dialect. Next morning Nam appeared with a list I can only conclude was the result of collaboration with some of her more literate associates. Some words were in French; some in English, and some in a delightful *drolerie* part way in-between. The staples—milk, salt, coffee, butter, were writ large and clear. I was surprised at the orthographic accuracy of such items as Bab-O, Masola Pure Corn Oil, Hunt's Tomato Juice and Alcoa Wrap, but presumed these trade names were copied off the can or package. Family Napking was quaint but sufficiently understandable. Lime beans and asperge were clear enough. But what about Jujube apple and doliquelabla? When I was a child we ate tiny chewy gelatinous candies called "jujubes," but that didn't seem to help. I looked up "jujube" in the French half of my

French-English dictionary, but it was translated simply as "jujube." I then consulted the English half, but it just played back "jujube." The Concise Oxford, my one English dictionary, told me jujube was the "edible berry-like drupe of certain plants." I looked up "drupe" which turned out to be "fleshy or pulpy fruit enclosing stone or nut with kernal, as olive, plum, cherry." I don't suppose an apple, despite its core and seeds, qualifies as a drupe, but it suddenly dawned on me that Nam meant applesauce. I never did dig *dolique-labla*, nor is it in the French dictionary, so I still don't know what I missed. Nam apparently managed without it. The food was superb. But what really surprised me was the service, the more so since, when I first spoke to her about dinner, Nam had spurned my suggestion to engage someone to help her.

On the evening of the dinner party I came home a bit early and, and it must be confessed, apprehensive. I needn't have been. The table was beautifully laid; indeed, for a moment I wondered if I was in the right house. Some of the objects had a familiar look, but there was a handsome centerpiece and candlesticks I'd never seen before. My stainless steel basked in unaccustomed luster on a gleaming white linen table cloth I seemed suddenly to have acquired. And the half dozen napkins I'd picked up in the Manila Airport had been nicely supplanted by four almost matching ones.

I relaxed and let events take their course. First came a delicious crab and asparagus soup from an unfamiliar tureen. I did a double take, then I realized that the server was not Nam, but sister Sau. Both sisters served the succulent chicken which arrived reassuringly, but less glamorously, on my own dinner plates, though the gravy boat was an added starter. Salad was served on my "other" plates, and I wondered how Nam would prepare the dessert of fruit salad and sherbet. It made its appearance in attractive cut glass dishes. About this time I spied a third girl stealthily making her way from the front door to the kitchen. I recognized her as the maid who worked for a colleague of mine who lived down the hall. She had come to assist with the cleaning up.

The next day I tried to give Nam some money to pay the two helpers, but she refused. In time I learned that there was nothing unusual about this type of floating contingent. The girls always helped each other, and when I dined soon after at the apartment of a friend in the building, Nam was one of those who served me.

When a maid's employer gave a cocktail party or dinner, there was a general rallying around of the other boyesses. On such occasions it seemed perfectly *au fait* to "borrow" any article required to bring the service up to a certain standard. I once watched the startled reaction of a dinner guest in another's home when he suddenly recognized the implement in his hand as one of his own soup spoons. In our Embassy group, those who had maintained a household in Saigon prior to the evacuation of dependents were better fitted out than those who had come without their families. A friend of mine in this more fortunate situation constantly dined out on his own china.

This charming communal spirit among the boyesses extended to food as well. There was never any problem about "borrowing" a couple of eggs, a loaf of bread, or a few cans of beer, and I recall at least one occasion when Nam met the crisis of unforeseen company at a late hour by producing—from sources shrouded in mystery—a glorious Chinese feast.

In household matters, Nam stuck to the old ways. She never could get used to an American-style broom, much preferring the short-handled native type. She frequently sat on the marble floor when she scrubbed it or shined my shoes. She also ironed many things on the floor although we had a small ironing board. She played the radio incessantly—every time I turned it on I was greeted by the cacophonous chant of the latest Vietnamese pop singer.

Nam was always good-humored, often buoyant, and at times downright fey. Let me illustrate what I mean. As I had brought no household goods to Saigon, I used the furniture on general issue, much of which was in its declining days. To brighten up the place I got some colored drapes, a few pictures and knick-knacks. On top of an otherwise barren table I assembled a small zoo I had accumulated—two little stuffed birds someone brought me from Hong Kong, several small furry seals acquired at the Anchorage Airport, a tiny plastic beaver, two silly African chipmunks made of bone, and a floppy Danish rope lion. Nam and I never spoke of these animals. But every week or so I noticed they had been rearranged. Sometimes I found them in fighting poses, sometimes they were paired off in couples, sometimes they were just charmingly, if improbably, juxtaposed—a bird perched on a seal's head; the beaver astride the lion or nibbling its paw. Nam occasionally added touches of her own—green leaves or bits of colored paper to perch on, a shallow saucer to serve as a water hole, a ribbon for the lion's hair.

One day Nam's mother came in from Mytho in the Delta to visit her and Sau. I took some pictures of the family and offered them to Nam when they were printed up. It was the only time I ever saw her lose her composure. She positively squealed with delight, grabbed the pictures from my hand, and ran off at a gallop to show them to Sau and the other boyesses. I really think she had never been photographed before.

There was much friendship and conviviality among the boyesses—indeed they functioned in their off-hours as a kind of extended family unit. They took care of each other's children, covered for each other in case of sickness, kept track of each other's whereabouts. If I came home unexpectedly, the boyesse bush telegraph would summon Nam from her room, the nearby market, or wherever in the neighborhood she happened to be. When there was a party on the roof the boyesses would bring up their children to share the excitement. The roof had seen better days but it was cool, and from its seven storey vantage one had an excellent view of Saigon and, incidentally, the war. On a "good" night, when flares obligingly lit up the sky, you could see planes and helicopters in flight, occasional shellfire, and the projectory of tracer bullets. This held a curious fascination for those whose work never took them out of Saigon or for visitors just passing through.

In the Saigon of 1966 you heard and read about occasional "incidents" involving Claymores, grenades, or "plastique." As you walked the streets you were all too aware of military vehicles and G.I.s: both American and Vietnamese. You saw Army billets and public buildings sandbagged and guarded twenty four hours a day by sentries on the alert. But in those days you could spend a whole year in the city without being involved in an "incident" or even hearing an explosion near at hand. And if you sometimes awoke at night to find your bed reverberating to the distant thud of aerial bombardment, you could take some comfort in the realization that the aircraft were "ours."

I wondered how Nam felt about the war, but lack of a common language made it difficult to find out. She seemed to take it in her stride, but once or twice, haltingly, she made known her hope that it would stop. She was certainly upset the day someone threw a grenade into a B.O.Q. (Officer Quarters) several miles away. Sometimes I would find her motionless on the balcony, staring into space.

One evening when she served me dinner I noticed Nam was unusually quiet. This mood prevailed for several days and I wondered if I had offended her, or if she wanted a raise. When she finally got up the courage, she let me know she was leaving the very next day for Kontum where she and their child would join her husband who was being transferred to that area. She announced that Sau would replace her. I supposed that Sau would have to give the usual notice to her employer, but next morning there she was, bright and early, ready to serve me breakfast. Sau was younger than Nam, actually next in line in the family. Nam, which means five, was the fourth child, and Sau, meaning six was the fifth. In many families the first born child is named Hai (2), the second is Ba, (3), the third Tu (4), the fourth Nam (5) etc., without regard to sex. Mot, the word for one, is never employed as a name, being reserved for Number One or the Deity.

So Sau took over and served me during my remaining months in Saigon. She was prettier than her sister but very timid, and spoke no English. Although she did the housework creditably enough, she lacked Nam's versatility as a cook. The third sister, Bay (7), who couldn't have been much more than fifteen, came to live with Sau and spent most of her time tending Sau's baby. He was a handful. He trotted up and down the apartment, clad only in a small striped shirt, with nothing conveniently below the waist. One day Sau looked worried and I learned that the boy was sick with a rash and high fever. I offered to arrange for someone to see him at the hospital, but to my surprise she declined. The boy's fever grew higher and higher during the next few days but she still refused, saying that on Sunday she would take him to the Chinese doctor. I had little faith in the procedure, but she carried out her plan and, amazingly, whatever the treatment given, the child speedily recovered.

Sau picked up some English and grew more confident on the job. But when the time came for me to leave Vietnam, I found she was quite apprehensive about her future. I thought she might want to find work in Cholon where she could live with her husband. But her only wish was to continue at the apartment, so I recommended her to a new office associate who was moving in after my departure. He gave her the job, and so far as I know, the family dynasty is still installed in the flat.

Shortly before I left Saigon, Sau told me Nam's husband had been moved from Kontum to Tay Ninh, a province somewhat nearer to Saigon. I really didn't expect to see Nam again, but on my last Saturday in Saigon, after a long day at the office and a dinner with friends, I found all three sisters in the apartment when I returned. I learned that Nam had been waiting since early afternoon to give me a parting gift, a handkerchief that she had embroidered. Now she had missed the last bus home. She looked thinner and tired, but her eyes still had the remembered warm and candid gaze. I felt sad about things in Vietnam, but never more poignantly moved than when Nam pressed her farewell gift into my hand and said goodbye in words I didn't know but understood.

ENGLAND

My two years at the American Embassy in Grosvenor Square, London were among the most enjoyable I have ever spent. My job as AID Coordination Officer was less demanding than a field assignment but it had its fascination. Ambassador David Bruce, who had already served as Ambassador to Germany and to France, was my boss. Strictly speaking my boss was Willis Armstrong, the Economic Counselor, but I attended the weekly staff meetings chaired by Bruce and relished his sophisticated, relevant views and comments on the world scene. The Vietnam War was at its height. The VC's devastating Tet offensive took place while I was in London. FDR's statue in Grosvenor Square looked down on a number of serious demonstrations protesting our role in the war.

Bruce had surrounded himself with a bevy of accomplished aides, several of whom became ambassadors in the years ahead. The DCM (Deputy Chief of Mission) was Phil Kaiser who later became Ambassador in several African countries. Mike Pistor, a light-hearted fellow who was a good friend, became Ambassador to Malawi. When I heard about it I sent him the verse of unknown origin reading as follows:

Said Livingston to Stanley,
Looking rather wanly,
We've just got to Malawi–
Where the hell are we?

Arthur Hartman was later our Ambassador to the Soviet Union. Ron Spiers, Dartmouth 1950, became Ambassador to Turkey and Pakistan and an Assistant Secretary of State in Washington. Perhaps our closest friend at the Embassy, and theater-going companion, was Monteagle (Monty) Stearns. Monty was married to the daughter of Jimmy Riddleberger who was Ambassador to Yugoslavia when I was there. Monty ultimately became U.S. Ambassador to Greece. The Embassy Cultural Attache was Bob Goodell whom I had known at Dartmouth. He opened the door for us to a succession of interesting cultural events. Unfortunately Bob was not well and died a few years after his tour at the Embassy. I was lucky to have as a secretary Darinka Trbovic. Reared in Pennsylvania, Darinka had served two of my predecessors, and was a fountain of information about the job, the Embassy and London. She was also an extremely nice and co-operative person and Margaret and I grew very fond of her.

Briefly stated, my main work at the Embassy was consultation with Sir Andrew Cohen and the desk officers at the Ministry of Overseas Development. As they reached independence, the UK was divesting itself of its colonies in Africa, the Caribbean and elsewhere and, after giving them a golden handshake, the U.K. was turning to Uncle Sam to continue development aid. This extended to a few countries such as Jordan that Britain never colonized but where it maintained a sphere of influence. Cohen was a huge presence, both physically and intellectually. He was not exactly a hail-fellow-well-met, and could be gruff at times, but I found him reasonably civil (after all, the Brits were asking us to take on some of their burdens).

I had extensive contact with Dudley Sears, Director of the Institute for Overseas Development at the University of Sussex, and his associate Richard Jolly who later came to UNICEF as Deputy Director. With Dudley, I crafted a well attended two-day conference at Sussex on "International Development and American Aid."

While in the U.K. I filled a large number of speaking engagements, mostly at universities. That included a ten-day conference on development aid at Cambridge during which I resided at Peterhouse College. I visited Ditchley, Oxford, Leicester, York, Liverpool and Southampton; also, Edinburgh and Londonderry. The American Consul General in Belfast drove me to Derry along the coast, pointing out the Devil's Highway en route. Derry itself was a pleasant provincial town. The Consul General told me about the famous siege and gave me a chapter of Macauley's *History of England* describing it. Macauley used the term "aborigines" to characterize the Irish. On an Easter weekend Margaret and I flew to Dublin for a look at the Republic. It was wonderfully green, as we had heard. Dublin was an attractive town architecturally; we walked around a good deal of it and relaxed afterwards in a friendly pub. Unfortunately, the Abbey Theater was dark that weekend; I had nostalgic memories of the troupe's visit to Hanover when I was a Dartmouth student. We hired a car on Easter Sunday and drove to Limerick. My college friend Charlie O'Neill had been named for his uncle who ran a pub there, and Charlie had urged me to look him up if we ever got to Ireland. In mid-afternoon we found the pub, but it was closed. I hailed a man in the street and asked if by chance he knew where Charlie O'Neill resided. "I haven't a clue," was the reply, "but you'll find him in the pub." When I told him the pub was closed, he said, "Pay no mind. Just go around the back way." We did so, and had a couple of congenial hours with Charlie, his blind son, and a few of the patrons. Later, in a mellow glow we drove to Cork.

We made a number of rewarding excursions while in England, some with our British friends Stanley and Trudy Brown. Standouts were Brighton and Bath. We corralled Cairene Petrie, widow of an IRO doctor friend, Jimmy Petrie, and she met us for several nights of the Edinburgh Festival. I've never been fond of the bagpipe, but it was a thrill to hear the lone piper perform in the stadium at the launch of the festival. We also enjoyed some of the "Fringe" attractions.

With a small subsidy from the Embassy, which encouraged a number of officers to live in town, we rented an attractive house in Markham Square, Chelsea. It belonged to an executive of British Airways who was posted to India. We were a few steps from the swinging King's Road, with the Chelsea Cinema, Mary Quant, the Soldier's Retirement Home, a host of appealing restaurants and pubs, and Sloane Square nearby. I could park in our square at night and at the Embassy during the day, which made life easy. We saw a wonderful lot of theater at the Royal Court, the Savoy and theaters in the West End as well as some of the smaller playhouses. Many of the attractions later came to Broadway. We also saw some fine exhibits and got to visit a few museums previously unknown to us—the Courtauld, the National Portrait Gallery and the John Soane Museum. I love London. I didn't get there on my first trip abroad, but subsequently made up for lost time. In recent years Vera and I made two memorable trips there. I have found the Brits almost invariably courteous and friendly.

Willis Armstrong was an agreeable boss whose introductions to several of the key officials I'd be dealing with were most helpful. His gracious wife invited us to dinner and helped orient Margaret to London. In my work I pretty much stuck to the development theme but there was one notable departure. An international conference to reschedule Ghana's debts was called in London. The economist on Armstrong's staff who would normally have gone was on leave, so Armstrong asked me to cover it with a junior member of his staff. I had visited Ghana twice on USAID trips but really didn't know the country.

Each of the delegates of the creditor nations had received instructions from his government as to just how far he could go in reducing Ghana's debt. The conference opened with statements by two Ghanaians offering persuasive reasons why their debts should be substantially reduced. They were extremely eloquent and put forward their arguments most convincingly. The debt reduction they sought was far beyond the figure we were instructed to settle for. We creditors—U.S., British, Dutch, Swedish and one or two others—discussed the matter among ourselves. All of us then cabled our governments for greater latitude. In the end, Washington and the other governments agreed to significant debt reduction, though they were unwilling to meet the figure urged by the Ghanaians.

In its desire to acclimate personnel to the local scene, the Embassy subsidized our membership in a London club. I could have joined the Reform or another in-town club, but on the advice of Charles Rubens, a relative of Margaret's, we became members of Hurlingham. In its second century, the Hurlingham Club was located in a lovely suburban area half an hour from London. It had everything one could wish for in a country club: a pool, access to a fine golf course, lawn bowls, croquet, a pleasant dining room and, best of all, ten carefully tended grass tennis courts. I had played on grass only once before, in

Bermuda, and it was a great treat for me and my feet to have this luxury. Hurlingham claimed to have been the birthplace of croquet, and while we were there, Margaret took in its hundredth anniversary celebration attended by the Queen.

In November of 1968 I received a cable from Washington asking me to leave post haste for a TDY (temporary duty) in Nigeria. The civil war with Biafra was at its height. The Federal government had retaken a fair amount of territory, and USAID Washington wanted an assessment of the refugee situation and the relief needs. The assessment involved an adventurous journey to Eastern Nigeria, following which I made certain recommendations. As sometimes happens in such cases, when I returned to London I found a message asking me to go to Lagos to do what I had recommended. My two-year tour in London was at an end. Margaret was willing to make her first trip to Africa. My children were out of college and into the world, so I agreed.

NIGERIA'S CIVIL WAR

Nigeria has the largest population in Africa (more than 130 million today), substantial economic resources (including oil), and has long been considered among the brightest stars of the continent. President Kennedy pledged more than 200 million dollars in American aid toward realization of the country's six-year development plan. But tribal rivalries exacerbated by competing external influences brought on a succession of blood baths in the late sixties, culminating in the secession of the Ibo-dominated Eastern region. Many millions of words have been written about the Nigerian Civil War. I will limit my account mainly to what I did and witnessed.

I was vacationing in Yugoslavia in the summer of 1968 when I received a call from London, where I was then employed at the American Embassy. Washington wanted me to do a TDY in Nigeria. The Nigerian Federal Government had retaken Port Harcourt and much of the southeastern state. It was reported that the retreating Biafran army had left in its wake thousands of malnourished people, with small children the most seriously affected. I was asked to survey the situation and make recommendations for U.S. assistance. Winging my way to Lagos in a Nigerian Airways VC-10, I was reminded of my previous visits to Nigeria for USAID, especially a trip that took me by car through the busy and prosperous area that was now a battleground.

Returning to eastern Nigeria would not be easy. Air schedules had not been resumed, and road routes from Lagos to the war zones were bisected by the Biafran enclave. Through a lucky circumstance, I met Dr. Wolf Bulle, a Lutheran medical missionary who was about to drive with his team by a circuitous route to the very area I wanted to visit. He asked if I could drive a Land Rover, one of the vehicles in the supply convoy. I said I'd be glad to. Ulla, a young Swedish nurse, was assigned to accompany me. Part of the convoy set out early one morning for the Lokoja Ferry, one of two points north of the enemy lines where one could still cross the Niger. After eight hours of mad driving, much of it on battered roads, we reached and managed to cross on the ferry. The ferry's motor had long since expired. It was powered by a wheezy tug. We pressed on to Nsuka in recently recaptured territory. We were challenged at various checkpoints, but finally reached our destination, the temporary billet of a Swiss Red Cross worker. The next day Bulle and the others drove on to Enugu, the recaptured capital of the East Central State, while the Swiss and I sadly viewed the destruction wrought by the war at the University of Nigeria. AID had made an extensive investment in this "land grant" type of university and was anxious to know how it had survived. I had a small "spy" camera with me, and though the campus was alive with vigilant Federal soldiers, I managed to get a few photographs of the destruction. The ground floor of the Continuing Education Building which AID had built for a million dollars was gutted by fire and bomb damage. The floors of that and other buildings were strewn with exam books, academic materials and all manner of waste paper and bits of school equipment.

I rejoined Bulle in Enugu and we drove south to Awgu, very near the front lines, where we discussed the war and relief situation with the Nigerian commander in charge. It had been proposed that Awgu be one terminus of an internationally controlled land route that would permit the safe conduct of badly needed food and other supplies to Biafra. The Federal authorities were willing, but the Biafrans balked, expressing fear that once the road had been sanitized and land mines removed, the Federal army would use some pretext to invade the corridor. Besides, they argued that food brought in through Federal territory would have been contaminated or even poisoned. This was the first of a number of attempts on the part of the International Red Cross and others to establish a land, sea or air corridor for the safe conduct of relief supplies. Each time one or the other of the adversaries raised an objection.

In Enugu our caravan was assembled, consisting of four Land Rovers and a huge truck to transport two Red Cross medico-relief teams and a load of urgently needed medical supplies from Enugu to Uyo in the South Eastern State. Uyo was part of an area unreachable from Lagos (or from Enugu for that matter) except for a wide swing on rough roads including a stretch of 22 miles in the Republic of Cameroon. We had permission from the Cameroonian authorities to negotiate this leg, but no one to our knowledge had, since the war began, traveled the dubious road from the Cameroonian border to Calabar, capital of the South Eastern State.

In retrospect, the trip was like a grade B movie called "The Road to Calabar." We were still in the rainy season. We were twice delayed because bridges were out; in one instance a six-hour detour resulted. We had great difficulty negotiating the slippery terrain; the truck got stuck twice and had to be pulled out of the muck by a combination of Land Rovers. The Cameroonians gave us no trouble, but we had to talk our way through an over-zealous Nigerian in charge of the border crossing point near Ikom. Beer, freely used as a lubricant, finally convinced the soldier that we were authorized to pass.

Our hopes of reaching Calabar on the third day were thwarted by a torrential storm which flooded the road. We stayed the night in the cold and damp of an abandoned school house and finally made Calabar the next morning. While the rest of the party dried out and rested, Bulle, his Deputy Bill Foege, another member of the group and I boarded the Calabar Ferry for a long meandering trip that took us to the mainland. Here we saw some of the grimmest sights that I have ever seen. A handful of missionaries were desperately trying to cope with malnutrition of epidemic proportions. The refugees were packed into schools, warehouses and other abandoned structures. Hospitals and sick bays were hopelessly overcrowded. The food ration was minuscule. The people had the look of hunted animals. Many of the children were listless. Everywhere one saw kwashiorkor, the protein deficiency disease which is marked by swollen limbs and, in many cases, orange hair. Wholesale importation of high protein food was essential if these children were to survive.

Two days later, the two Red Cross teams were at work, establishing the priorities for medical care. For some of the children it was too late, but most could still be saved. Food was diverted from other destinations, shipped coastwise from Lagos to Calabar, and then carried by helicopter and barge to the stricken area.

We returned to Lagos by a somewhat less arduous route. I then made my report to Washington with a number of recommendations. I flew back to London, but agreed to make a second TDY in October when a former U.S. Ambassador to Nigeria, in his role as Assistant Secretary of State for African Affairs, would be visiting Nigeria to take a first hand look. In the end, I agreed to come back for a two-year tour as Assistant Director of the AID Mission in charge of relief and rehabilitation.

My boss in Nigeria was Mike Adler, a seasoned USAID official I had first met in Greece, some fifteen years before, when he was there as an official for the Marshall plan. Mike had been USAID Director in Pakistan and Korea before coming to Nigeria. He was bright, articulate, well organized, fair-minded and fun to work with. He has passed on, but the last I heard, his widow, Ada Adler, was still working for USAID in Washington. Mike's writ covered a variety of programs, but he had a special interest in refugees, and that was helpful. He gave me considerable latitude in running my own show. Mike had a good sense of humor. My back gave me trouble from time to time, and riding in a Land Rover on Nigeria's miserable roads exacerbated the condition. Fortunately, I had brought with me a special corset prescribed by Dr. Alan McKelvie in Washington, who said I had "an angry joint." The corset helped a lot. When Mike's back went out he used the corset with a favorable result. Then a third staff member borrowed it to alleviate his back pain. Mike issued an order that no two staffers were permitted to have back trouble at the same time.

Mike of course reported to the Ambassador, Elbert Matthews, with whom I had relatively little contact, but both Mike and I consulted frequently with Clint Olsen, the Deputy Chief of Mission (DCM). I liked Clint, even though from time to time, with Washington's ceaseless badgering, his patience gave out. He was married to Hoov, the daughter of Herbert Hoover.

The first person I met in Lagos was Peter Bloom, who fetched me from the airport. Peter is a graduate of Yale Law School, but in Nigeria was working in refugee relief. He became my trusted assistant. We had many a good laugh together. I recall my first visit to Oma Bare, the Minister for Refugee Affairs. Peter and I waited in his outer office long past the time he had set for the meeting. A young woman on his staff said she would find out what was delaying him. To our surprise, she stepped forward, leaned down, and peered through the keyhole. "He's just winding up his appointment—he'll be with you in a minute." Peter was dark and swarthy in appearance and a marvelous mimic. He later served in Sri Lanka, and can give a priceless imitation of a civil servant in that country. Peter was an excellent tennis player and persuaded me to join the mostly Nigerian Lagos Tennis Club. He left Lagos for a job dealing with capital loans and legal matters in USAID's regional office in Abidjan. We have remained good friends.

USAID sent George Klein as Peter's replacement. George had had much relevant experience in refugee work in Austria and later in Vietnam. I had first met George in Osijek, Yugoslavia, when he came down to escort a trainload of Hungarian refugees to their Antwerp port of embarkation for resettlement overseas. After service with USAID, he did a year of graduate work at Harvard, then spent several productive years with the International Fund for Agricultural Development (IFAD) in Rome. He and his wife, Helga, are close friends of ours. Helga was an important official at the UN Office for Human Rights in Geneva and headed the Secretariat for the 2001 World Conference Against Racism in Durban.

The U.S. Government took no part in the shooting war but aided both sides with relief supplies, including most of the high protein and other food imports. The principal remedy for treatment of kwashiorkor was a compound of corn, soya and milk (CSM) which could be served as a soup or cereal or mixed with other foods. The Center for Disease Control (CDC) in Atlanta regarded the prevalence of kwashiorkor as a kind of epidemic and sent out several highly qualified medical officers to deal with it. Among these were Dr. Stan Forster and Dr. David Miller, both of whom became friends. Miller's wife, who was there much of the time, was Reina Schweitzer, daughter of the famous doctor. The CSM and other food supplies were distributed by the International Red Cross (and cooperating NGOs) on the Federal side, and some was flown from the islands of Fernando Poo and San Tome directly into the Biafran enclave on night flights arriving at Uli airport. The Federal government was not happy about our aid to the Biafrans; they knew the airlift was prolonging the war, but they gave their grudging acquiescence, as long as a definite flight plan was followed. If relief planes deviated from this plan while flying over Nigerian territory, they were warned by the air force and, if necessary, fired upon. The downing of a relief plane in early 1970 resulted in the decision by the International Committee of the Red Cross (ICRC) to suspend future relief flights, and from then on the lift was carried solely by Joint Church Aid, a combination of church agencies, courageously flying in from San Tome, always at night.

One of the ICRC representatives who served in Lagos but frequently made visits to the other side was Gus Lindt, the former UN High Commissioner for Refugees. (His daughter, Gillian Lindt, was Dean of Graduate Studies at Columbia University.) I knew Gus pretty well from his previous service, and admired his accomplishments, but he was a stormy petrel in the Nigerian picture who ruffled the feathers of the government with his independent stance. One day he flew in from San Tome with his little Red Cross plane without giving advance warning to the authorities. They forced the plane down, clapped him in jail, and gave him 24 hours to quit the country. Nothing the Swiss Ambassador or ICRC Geneva could do would stay the order. He was ejected.

Another demonstration of Nigerian obduracy occurred when Washington was concerned about hunger in the retaken portions of Biafra, and Nixon sent off a shipload of wheat without clearing with the Federal Nigerian government. The ship was denied permission to land. It went on to Cotonou, in the Benin Republic, while negotiations took place, but the Nigerians stuck to their guns and some 15,000 tons of wheat had to be diverted to another African country.

I was based in Lagos but, as in Vietnam, made frequent trips to the war zones to view the general situation, observe the use of USAID-contributed food and relief materials, and assess the further requirements. As in Vietnam, we assigned refugee officers to the principal areas; in fact our small staff was recruited largely from those who had had comparable experience in Vietnam. These included Bill Egan, Carl Harris and Phil Aschner. Phil, who was in Enugu with his wife, had rigged up out of war-damaged materials a kind of Rube Goldberg living arrangement, complete with bathtub. These representatives worked closely with the Red Cross teams in a particular area, moved precariously from check-point to check-point, lived and traveled under relatively primitive conditions. The medico-relief teams representing a wide spectrum of nationalities functioned under the aegis of the ICRC. The number of Federal teams reached a high of about 25. They were moved from location to location as the Biafran enclave became smaller. At the war's end a number of the teams were assigned to Owerri, Orlu and other towns in the final enclave. Many of these seasoned relief workers saw grim sights, especially in hospitals and sick bays abandoned by the Biafrans in their panicky eleventh hour flight. Transport was disorganized; roads were still mined or in distressing condition, and it was difficult to move in the desired supplies. The Federal officials did not help in this situation by barring use of the former Biafran airfields.

Our USAID unit was called "Relief and Rehabilitation," and almost from the outset of our work we were as much concerned with the latter as with the former. We reasoned that satisfactory rehabilitation of war-devastated areas would do much to sustain morale and might to some degree hasten the end of the war. As early as October 1968, we pledged a million Nigerian pounds (some $2.8 million) for a series of projects to be agreed with the National Rehabilitation Commission in Lagos. As the war neared its close, this budget was increased: we ultimately committed 25 million dollars for a wide assortment of projects aimed to restore essential infrastructure: to re-equip schools and hospitals, provide tools, fishing boats, road and shop machinery, temporary bridging, seeds, orthopedic equipment, vehicles and a variety of other items.

We did many of these projects with NGOs. Sometimes they originated the projects and we co-financed them. They were expected to provide 25% of the cost. When the war ended we pressed forward with the rehabilitation program. Of course, relief needs came first. It took some time before the malnourished children who survived could be brought back to health. In this endeavor we were greatly aided by an Ibo doctor named Aaron Ifekwunigwe who had performed miracles in the Biafra period, saving the lives of countless children by a method of treatment he developed with limited nutritional supplies. Later, Dr.Ifekwunigwe went to the U.S. and had a distinguished career at UCLA.

Major General Yakubu Gowon was the leader of Nigeria during my two year stay in 1968-70. I met Gowon twice and had a strongly favorable impression of him. The first time was shortly after I had arrived in the country. There was already a fair amount of pro-Biafra sentiment in the U.S. when I left, and I guess some of that showed when I met the general. "Look at it this way, Mr. Marks," he said. "You had to fight a Civil War to keep your country together. We're going through much the same thing here."

When the war was over, Gowon refused to impose sanctions on the vanquished Ibos. He wished truly to reunite the country, and he decreed that there would be no medals, no military cemeteries, no reparations, no visible reminders of the bitter struggle. In general, Ibos would be allowed to regain their previous positions without prejudice. That seems very statesmanlike to me, and I was pained to hear, a few years after I left Nigeria, that Gowon had been deposed in a military coup. He then spent a few years in England teaching at a provincial university before being allowed to return to Nigeria. Now, as an elder statesman, he is back in grace and called on by the government for various diplomatic assignments.

The Biafran propaganda effort was so successful that some people, years after the war, still referred to Nigeria as Biafra. Enormous sentiment was whipped up to support the rebel cause. In the face of this propaganda barrage, we in Lagos tried to keep our perspective.

After the war, those who had backed the losers feared a cataclysm. The Cassandras said there would be bloody reprisal, continuing guerrilla warfare, mass starvation. Fortunately, none of these disasters occurred. There was some looting and misbehavior by individual soldiers. There were pockets of neglect which, with the best will in the world, it would take some time to revive. But the Nigerians, who took over the relief responsibility from the ICRC, took the cue from their leader, and showed an astonishing lack of revenge symptoms. However, many on the outside refused to believe that Ibos were not being persecuted and starved. We had a steady drum beat of cables from Washington offering us heaven and earth, including offers of food far beyond what was needed or could be equitably distributed.

Margaret was apprehensive as to what Nigeria would be like after her long, torturous ride from the Lagos airport, but she was reassured when she saw the pleasant USAID house assigned to us in Ikoyi. It was of good size, and the appliances worked. Downstairs was an exceptionally large living room, with a decent kitchen and half bath. There was a graceful staircase that led to two bedrooms and bathrooms on the second floor. A short distance behind the house was a second building occupied by Adie, the houseman assigned to us. Adie was about 50 and had a wife and eight children. He spoke a pretty good broken English. He had served several USAID families and before that, British colonials, and he had an answer for everything. He made great efforts to please, and you couldn't help liking him, though we knew he kept something for himself on purchases he made for us. With children spilling out all over the place, Margaret earnestly spoke with him and his wife about birth control, and once even got her to a clinic, but less than a year after we came on the scene they had their ninth child. Margaret had more success teaching English to several school children.

There was a friendly expatriate crowd at USAID, the UN agencies, the embassies and the NGO community. We had an active social life, though it included boring evenings when your hosts after dinner insisted on showing you too many slides of their vacation trips. This practice was thwarted somewhat by an inspired friend who stipulated that his guests were welcome to bring not more than fifteen slides of their own.

There was a local Thespian group in Lagos that helped pass the time. I recall one production, I think it was a Noel Coward play, when an actor bit into an apple. The audience gasped! You don't find apples in Lagos! It must have been specially imported.

A USAID officer named Bob Huesman who played the viola had managed to find three other string players, including a Nigerian, and we heard them one night performing very creditably. That gave us the idea for a concert at our home for the benefit of a Nigerian children's institution. The setup was ideal for the purpose. A large crowd was seated in the living room and in the balcony that led to the bedrooms on the second floor. Most Lagos expats, and a number of Nigerians turned out for the event, and we made quite a lot of money for the charity.

Nigeria doesn't have many tourist attractions, but we visited Kano and Kaduna in the north, and made trips to Ibaden and Oshogbo in Yoruba country. At the Lagos home of Dick Wolford, we had attended an exhibition of objets d'art fashioned by Oshogbo artists instructed by a German professor named Ulli Beier and his wife Genevieve. Oshogbo, when the Beiers arrived, was a nondescript market town of about 80,000 population. They cultivated a group of young men in creative artistic pursuits with astonishing results. Twins-Seven-Seven, allegedly the seventh twin of a seventh twin, who had been the barker for a medicine show, became a talented painter. Another young man learned to make sculptures in cement; a third worked in beads, a fourth in tapestry, and so on. In Oshogbo we met Twins-Seven-Seven, bought a couple of his paintings, and also acquired a colorful tapestry depicting an airport, and a work in hammered aluminum illustrating Noah's Ark. In Washington a few years ago I witnessed a fine exhibit of the works of Oshogbo artists at the Smithsonian. I found that the Hood Museum of Art at Dartmouth was interested to build up its modern African collection and gave them, in memory of my son Tom, Class of 1965, a Twins-Seven-Seven painting and a tapestry.

On Sundays, we sometimes went with friends to a beach on the Atlantic Ocean where, for the first time, I enjoyed riding the gentle surf on a boogie board. It was a hand-carved board, rented for a shilling from one of the young native boys. When we returned to the U.S. we used store-bought boogie boards at Martha's Vineyard, and once in the Caribbean, but never quite recaptured the long, undulating thrill of the African experience.

We got to know one of the beach boys named Julius who taught people how best to use the boards. He gave us a few tips one day, then somehow ascertained that we were Jewish and identified himself as a Jew. He arranged for us to meet the Israeli Ambassador, and we were invited to the residence for Seder. There were a dozen guests of various ages including Julius and two other Nigerians. It seemed incongruous, in an African setting, but was an enjoyable experience.

If you could put up with their frequently bumpy surfaces, the roads in Nigeria had a special appeal. We savored the sight of the colorful mammy wagons encountered along the route. Each bore a distinctive message in a sign blazoned in big letters. My favorite was "No Condition is Permanent." An indisputable truth! And there were others: "No Telephone to Heaven" and "Man Proposes, God Disposes." Some of these luridly painted wagons carried whole families. Others brought produce down to the Lagos market. The introduction of the transistor radio has been a godsend to the up-country farmers. They listen to the market broadcasts before they set out and can no longer be duped in the matter of fair prices. Most of the trading is done by women. I was told that they keep floating but strict accounts with their urban customers, to be settled up at intervals in an exchange of mutual trust.

In recent years the talents of Nigerian and other African writers, artists and musicians have met with well-deserved attention in the West. The books of Achebe, Soyinka and others have eloquently portrayed the conflicts faced by Africans seeking to relate to Western life and thought without abandoning their native cultural roots.

Near the end of the war I made a second trip to the east with Haven North, USAID Director in Ghana and Steve Tripp, USAID Disaster Relief Coordinator. We traveled around the edges of the front lines to assess the relief situation and the attitude of the Federal military towards the Biafrans in flight. We talked with one army commander and were impressed with his concern about the refugees and our efforts to provide relief supplies. As we moved through the villages by car we saw instances of starvation as well as kwashiorkor. We interviewed a number of local chiefs, and then were picked up by helicopter, causing quite a stir. When we returned to Lagos we wrote a report that expressed our concern about the hunger we witnessed and the relief needs and the importance of Federal troops not taking revenge on the local population. We gave the report to Ambassador Joseph Palmer to show to General Gowon to impress him with the needs of the region and the importance of restraint. I believe Gowon was already of this mind but it probably influenced him and supported his post-war efforts to obliterate distinctions arising from the war.

In those days we used to say the war was over in Nigeria but not yet in Washington. The ultimate was reached one day when the Embassy received a message saying: "What are you doing about the rainy season?" They meant, of course, are you doing forward planning to ensure the safe delivery of adequate supplies when the rains begin? But in our weakened state, we took it more irreverently, more in the mood of Mark Twain when he was asked what he was doing about the weather.

It's unlikely that I'll ever return to Nigeria, and I'm sorry about that. All is not well there, but I keep hoping true democracy will assert itself, and that Nigeria will realize its potential as a leader among African nations.

FINAL ASSIGNMENT AT USAID

In my last two years with USAID I had a change of assignment from the Africa to the Asia Bureau. The new job called for field trips to a number of countries I had not previously seen, including South Korea, Laos, Cambodia and Indonesia. I reviewed ongoing USAID projects and initiated others including a number that called for Operational Program Grants to cooperating NGOs.

I had always wanted to visit Bali, and when I found I was going to Indonesia I booked passage to fly there the weekend I arrived. But the USAID Director meeting me at Jakarta Airport on Friday night had different ideas. "If you don't mind," he said, "We're taking a 6 A.M. plane tomorrow for Medan. We're going to visit USAID projects in Sumatra." It turned out to be a fascinating day, but I never got to Bali.

My last days at USAID, including retirement from my final government job, were passed pleasantly. USAID Administrator Daniel Parker called me into his office to receive USAID's first Distinguished Career Award.

UNICEF

During my tour in Nigeria, Harry Labouisse and his wife, Eve Curie Labouisse, came out to assess the situation of children in the Federal Republic. I had first met Harry at the State Department meeting a decade earlier when the U.S. Committee for Refugees had been established. He had been elected one of the USCR vice presidents. He was now Executive Director of UNICEF. I didn't know Eve, except by reputation. She was a daughter of Marie Curie and had written several books, including one about her mother. I took the Labouisses to several camps where they could see children recently liberated from Biafra. I knew quite well the UNICEF representative in Nigeria, a congenial Dane named Paul Larsen whom I had also known in Greece, but for some reason he was not in Nigeria when they visited. I told Labouisse that when my Nigerian tour was up I was keen to return to work with the United Nations. He said to keep him informed.

At that time, State Department officials (including USAID) could apply for a lateral transfer to an international agency for a two-year tour if there was a suitable job they could fill. If you did this, you retained your government grade and salary but were required to return to State at least two years before retirement to protect your pension rights. I applied for a transfer and landed a job with UNICEF beginning in mid-1970. I had two good friends on the UNICEF staff: Sherry Moe, an old refugee hand who had been with Labouisse in the UN Palestine agency, and Jack Charnow, one of UNICEF's longest serving employees. Jack's specialty was liaison with NGOs. Knowing of my close link with voluntary agencies over the years he wanted to have me in UNICEF's European office to deal with the international NGOs. I was amenable to the idea, and Margaret looked forward to another stretch in Europe. However Dick Heyward, UNICEF's Deputy Director, had a different idea. He wanted me—at least at first—to serve as UNICEF's Emergency Desk Officer, based in New York.

While still with USAID, I had for two sessions been a member of the U.S. delegation to the UNICEF Board meeting in New York, so I had a pretty fair understanding of UNICEF's structure and programs when I came to work there.

It was refreshing to be back at work with an international organization. On my first or second day on the Emergency Desk I drafted a cable to be sent to one of UNICEF's field missions. At USAID, most cables went out over the signature of the Secretary of State, or at least the USAID Administrator, so I drafted my cable for the signature of Labouisse. It came back to me from his office with the word that the cable should be signed by its originator—in this case, me. After I'd been a few days on the job someone sent me a memorandum I thought should receive special handling. "Put this in the confidential file," I said to my secretary. "We don't have such a file," she replied, "But I'll mark it 'Confidential.'" At USAID, of course, it would have been filed in a restricted filing system going up to Top Secret.

After I had been on the job for a couple of weeks, Heyward sent me to Bangladesh. I flew to Dacca where I saw many of the Bengalis who had been in the Great Salt Lake Camp I had visited in the North of India. I arrived when the people were still in a festive mood, celebrating the country's independence from West Pakistan. Before this happened they were in East Pakistan, separated by India, and they didn't get on with each other, being of different nationalities, Bengali and Punjabi. It wasn't absolutely clearcut because there were Hindus in there as well. Flying over Bangladesh, one had the impression that the country was inundated, and indeed, one of the periodic floodings took place at the time of my visit. I was taken around to see some UNICEF projects by Glenn Davis, who had been UNICEF Chief in India and several other countries. One was a class in sewing machine operation to make women more self sufficient; a second offered nutritional training to nourish young children. We also saw some infants being immunized against measles and other child killers.

When I returned to New York Headquarters, Heyward took me out to lunch and released me for the assignment in Europe, apologizing for the delay. After briefing by Charnow I took off. UNICEF's European Headquarters at that time was in Neuilly, a somewhat independent community at the end of a Paris Metro line. I found a furnished apartment owned by a fussy French landlady within walking distance of the UNICEF office and moved in. I also bought a small Peugeot III to get me around. Margaret was delayed but would be coming in another month. I had been in the U.S. just briefly after the Lagos experience and now enjoyed the reprieve of Paris. Most of the NGOs were based in Geneva, but there was enough activity in France for me to start my liaison work. The UNICEF office was in France because it was the home country of Dr. Faure, an early UNICEF supporter and at one time Chairman of its International Board. UNICEF had outgrown the building it occupied and space was limited. I shared a tiny office with Doris Phillips. Doris cracked that if the office had been a few centimeters smaller it would have been adulterous. She was a great sport, had lived in Paris for years with her writer husband "Phil." They were friends of Man Ray and other artists there. Other UNICEF friends were Flo Dunoyer and Nano D'Abo. Nano was in charge of the European greeting card operation. Her beautiful daughter played the ingenue in one of the James Bond movies. We all shared a dislike for the European Director, a rigid Dutchman named Twigt.

Dr. Faure died while I was working at Neuilly, and Harry Labouisse decided to move the European Office to Geneva where a number of the other UN organizations were located. I rented a pleasant flat at Avenue Bude, near the InterContinental Hotel and the Palais des Nations, where the UNICEF office was established in a new wing. I had found the enormous Palais confusing enough when I worked there in the Library Building for IRO in 1947. This time it was even more so—it was a real hike to get to the cafeteria and the main entrance hall. But we had more office space.

I lost no time in getting in touch with the many NGOs based in Geneva and joined the well established International Committee which met regularly and to a certain extent coordinated their activities. I was quite active on a subcommittee which dealt with children in emergency situations that was chaired by P.C. Stanissis of the League of Red Cross Societies.

I represented UNICEF at an International Red Cross Conference held in Teheran. I was amazed to see the amount of traffic in that city. I also traveled to Germany and Denmark with Victor Beermann, UNICEF's chief fund raiser and a good friend of mine. We were successful in getting several of the huge evangelical NGOs to make substantial contributions to UNICEF's budget.

While in Europe, and after my return to the U.S., I initiated a series of Recognition Agreements between UNICEF and the national committees representing UNICEF in the affluent countries of the world. These committees, through sale of greeting cards, galas, exhibits and special events, raised a significant amount of money for UNICEF. They had their own boards of directors and were very independent—so much so that a certain amount of friction resulted between UNICEF and them. Some of them called themselves "UNICEF" and gave the impression *they* were the international agency. This sometimes led to misunderstanding when they gave voice to statements at variance with UNICEF policy. On the other hand, they bitterly resented it when UNICEF officials or PR people visited the country and dealt with the government or the press without consulting the national committee. Sometimes UNICEF and the Committee would disagree in the matter of retention—how much the Committee could retain for administrative expense of the revenue resulting from the sale of UNICEF greeting cards. There were exceptions, of course. Nils Thedin, long-time chair of the Swedish committee and twice chairman of UNICEF's board was a lovely fellow. I recall with pleasure a dinner he gave me at the Opera Restaurant when I came to Stockholm. But the general situation needed repair and UNICEF set me to work on it. No two Recognition Agreements were exactly the same. The agreements for the Soviet Union, Poland, Czechoslovakia, Hungary, Rumania and Bulgaria had to take into account the authoritarian governments in those countries. Perhaps the thorniest negotiation was with the U.S. Committee (now called the U.S. Fund for UNICEF). They wanted a higher retention because they claimed they had higher administrative costs.

I left UNICEF after two years of lateral transfer to return to USAID. At that time the required retirement age for Foreign Service personnel was 65. As I neared that age, the notion of retirement did not appeal to me. I once more applied to UNICEF and they took me back under a Special Service Agreement. I had the same salary as previously but no pension rights, as the UN's retirement age is 60.

BACK AT UNICEF

Back at UNICEF Headquarters I finished up the Recognition Agreements with the U.S. and Canadian Committees for UNICEF before tackling my new assignment as Associate Director of the Secretariat for the UN's 1979 Year of the Child (IYC). The UN Secretary General had designated UNICEF as the lead agency for the Year. This was not altogether pleasing to Labouisse who had to be assured that IYC would not interfere with UNICEF's regular program or its sources of income. We were part way into 1977 but reckoned it would take a year and a half to gear up for a successful Year. Mrs. Fanny Aldaba Lim, Minister of Social Welfare in the Philippine Government, was selected to head the office as the SG's Special Representative. Fanny Lim was qualified for the post because of her work as a Philippine Cabinet Minister. She was capable and easy to get along with and she was a hard worker who visited 65 national capitals during her incumbency to spur the creation and activation of national IYC Commissions. My boss was John Grun, a seasoned official who had served UNICEF for more than 30 years in Europe, Central America, Mexico and Nigeria and as Deputy Director in New Delhi. John was Dutch but had lived in England for many years and had an English wife. We hit it off well from the beginning. I deferred to his knowledge of UNICEF and the international scene. He recognized that I was in familiar territory with the central objective of firing up others to make meaningful contributions to the Year.

My considerable duties as John's Deputy for IYC were agreeably lightened by the assignment of Pauline Bessell as my Secretary. Well versed in UNICEF lore, Pauline performed expertly and became a close family friend.

John and I backed up and extended Fanny Lim's efforts to stimulate establishment of national IYC Commissions, working with their Ambassadors at the UN. We also made visits to some countries to stimulate formation of commissions. Some were spontaneously formed. In the U.S., President Carter designated Jean C. Young to head the U.S. Commission. Jean had been a classroom teacher, a supervisor for the Teacher Corps, and coordinator of elementary and pre-school programs for the Atlanta School System. She was the wife of Andrew Young, onetime Mayor of Atlanta and U.S. Ambassador to the UN. An active branch of the IYC Secretariat flourished in Geneva under the direction of Jim McDougall, another experienced UNICEF hand. In 1978 Jim and I visited Moscow for a consultation with the Soviet Red Cross that officially represented UNICEF in that country. We were told that in the Soviet Union every year was a year for the child; there was no need for a special year. However our visit led to a notable effort on their part to celebrate IYC, despite frenetic Soviet activity at that time preparing to be hosts for the 1980 Olympics.

Margaret had never been to the Soviet Union so I arranged for her to join me there after the first official week. During our consultation with the Red Cross they had put up Jim and myself in the former Hall of the Nobles, a kind of Blair House. It was red carpet treatment, old fashioned, elegant and immaculate. When I told them Margaret was joining me they expressed regret that I couldn't stay where I was, but they would arrange for suitable alternative accommodation. This they did, in a humongous hotel with 3,000 rooms. Somehow, my glasses got lost in the car they provided to make the transfer. They arranged for me to see an ophthalmologist who could check my eyes and make me a new pair. She clearly knew her business. When she had finished the examination, she asked me if I was planning to be in Finland. She explained that the lens I required was just between two of the standard lenses made in the USSR. My eyes were pretty good and I decided not to fill the prescription she gave me until I got home. On the Saturday morning after my return I took it to an optician in Leesburg, Virginia, a town of about 20,000 people. He said the prescription was exact and if I wanted it filled to come back in an hour.

When Margaret arrived in Moscow, I took a two-week break from my UNICEF work for some sightseeing in the Soviet Union. We were not allowed to travel on our own, but were assigned to an Intourist-sponsored party of about a dozen, including Americans and Europeans. We would also be visiting Moscow, Leningrad, Kiev and Yalta. Our principal guide, who traveled with us most of the way, was an intelligent, sophisticated woman of about 50 who spoke excellent English. Local guides assisted her in the cities we visited. In Moscow, we saw the usual attractions, including parts of the Kremlin, St. Basil's Cathedral, Lenin's Tomb and the Tretiakov Gallery. In Leningrad, Margaret was thrilled to see the Hermitage, and I was glad to make a second visit to Peterhof. We followed the Intourist itinerary until we got to Kiev. A number of us wanted to visit Babi Yar, but it was not on the schedule. At first our guide said it wouldn't be possible, but when we insisted, she reluctantly agreed to have one bus go there; in the end, both went. We were curious to see this area near Kiev with its huge mass grave where Jews and others were put to death by Nazi troops and, some say, by Ukrainians as well. Yevtushenko wrote a famous poem about it from which excerpts are given here:

Babi Yar

By Yevgeny Yevtushenko 1961

No monument stands over Babi Yar.
A drop sheer as a crude gravestone.
I am afraid.

Today I am as old in years as all the Jewish people.
Now I seem to be a Jew...
I seem to be Dreyfus.
The Philistine is both informer and judge.
I am behind bars.
Beset on every side.
Hounded, spat on, slandered.
Squealing, dainty ladies in flounced Brussels lace stick their parasols into my
face...

O my Russian people!
I know you are international to the core.
But those with unclean hands have often made a jingle of your purest name.
I know the goodness of my land.
How vile these anti-Semites—without a qualm
They pompously called themselves
The Union of the Russian People!...

The wild grasses rustle over Babi Yar.
The trees look ominous, like judges.
Here all things screen silently,
And, baring my head, slowly I feel myself turning gray.
And I myself am one massive, soundless scream
Above the thousand thousand buried here.
I am each old man here shot dead.
I am every child here shot dead.
Nothing in me shall ever forget!...

The government refused to raise a monument to the thousands of Jews executed there. All one sees there now is a kind of park, with a dramatic downward
slope.

Yalta was a delight. We liked our hotel, the weather was beautiful, and for
me as a lover of Chekov, it was exciting to visit the streets, parks and haunts
with which he had been familiar.

Our Intourist tour finished in Moscow. We were being taken to hear a concluding, sum-up lecture. "By whom?" we asked the junior guide who was escorting us in the bus. "By a Senior Official of the Ministry of Information." We
smelled a rat: that sounded like indoctrination. "Can we ask questions?"

"Yes, this is a highly qualified official. You can ask any question you wish
and you'll receive a highly qualified answer." Of course, she didn't know what
she was saying—her English wasn't that good! We were greatly amused and our
conjecture was correct. We got a hard sell on the Soviet way of life.

Before we left Moscow, the President of the Red Cross made good on the promise he made to me at the IYC meeting. He and his wife invited us to attend a performance of the famed Moscow circus. It turned out that he was a real circus buff, well known to the circus people. We sat in choice seats, clearly visible to the performers, and during the first act, our host was greeted by the principal clown. Several stars and the circus manager were among those we met in the green room after the performance. It was a rare treat—and a great show!

ORIGINS OF THE CHILD WELFARE MOVEMENT

Back in New York, I did some research on the history of the child welfare movement. For centuries the child was thought of as the chattel of its parents and not as an individual with rights. Child cruelty and exploitation were as common as the 16-hour workday, and children all over the world were subjected to child labor. The first anti-cruelty laws were enacted on behalf of animals. The American Society for the Prevention of Cruelty to Animals (ASPCA) was established in 1866. Within a few years, some saw the applicability to human needs. *The Northern Budget*, a publication in Troy, New York, in 1867 said, "It is not alone the lower animals that are subject to ill-treatment and cruelty."

In the winter of 1873 a rooming house janitor in Hell's Kitchen, a seedy section of New York, told Etta Walker, a church worker, about a case of child cruelty. She went to the police and others but no one was willing to intercede. She finally approached Henry Bergh, who had founded ASPCA. He involved Elbridge T. Gerry, a lawyer, who made ingenious use of an obscure section of habeas corpus. Within 48 hours there was an investigation; Mary Ellen, the child, was removed from the home, a temporary placement was arranged, and criminal prosecution was underway. The journalist, photographer and social reformer Jacob Riis (author of *How the Other Half Lives*) who was in the courtroom when Mary Ellen testified, said, "As I looked, I knew where the first chapter of children's rights was written." The New York Society for Prevention of Cruelty to Children (NYSPCC) was founded in 1874 and incorporated the following year. It claims to be the first such organization established anywhere in the world. England's National Society for the Prevention of Cruelty to Children was formed in London in 1884.

In its first year, the police referred to NYSPCC several hundred cases of child maltreatment, and the agency rescued 72 children from abuse and neglect. The need for protective legislation was apparent, but it was some years before adequate child welfare laws were enacted. The Child Labor Committee first met in New York in 1904. The first White House Conference on Children was convened by President Theodore Roosevelt in 1909. The U.S. Children's Bureau dates from 1912, and the first Child Labor Law was passed in 1916. It was a long slow process!

Children were an early concern of the United Nations. Dr. Ludwik Rajchman, a Pole who had headed the League of Nations' Health Organization for 18 years, proposed the establishment of UNICEF in 1946 to provide relief for children in Europe who had been adversely affected by World War II. Audrey Hepburn in Belgium was one of those children. She later became an active Ambassador for UNICEF.

By 1950, Europe's children, with UNICEF's aid, were well on the road to recovery, but Pakistan's delegate at the UN's Social, Cultural and Humanitarian Committee pointed out that post-war needy children in Europe were in no worse state than millions of children living so-called "normal" lives in underdeveloped countries. UNICEF, with a broadened mandate, turned its attention to these, and today provides assistance to children in more than 160 nations and territories.

In 1923 an Englishman named Eglantyne Jebb proposed a charter for the newly formed International Save the Children Union. Adopted the following year by the League of Nations, this charter contained some of the provisions that later found their way into the 1959 UN Declaration of the Rights of the Child.

Universal recognition that the child has rights as an individual was embodied in the Declaration that was issued by the United Nations in 1959. The Declaration was the internationally agreed synthesis of the essential rights and needs of children; but in many parts of the world its fine sentiments were still mostly honored in the breach. As the years passed, it became evident that there was no long-term improvement in the lives of some 400 million children living in appalling conditions of neglect and deprivation. A Belgian priest named Canon Joseph Moerman, Secretary-General of the International Catholic Child Bureau in Geneva, came up with the concept of a UN Year of the Child. Moerman felt that a year focused on children might generate a "second wind."

UN Years for Refugees, World Population and Women had, each in its way, resulted in favorable action and increased support. Moerman's idea appealed strongly to the International Union of Child Welfare, which had led the crusade for the Declaration. Other NGO organizations of stature, such as the YWCA and the World Council of Churches, joined Moerman's growing bandwagon. Norway and Holland became champions of a Year for the Child, and a number of countries in the developing world fell in line. By 1976, there was overwhelming sentiment for the Year. At the UNICEF Board meeting that year, it was agreed that while IYC in the developing world would be a vehicle for the promotion of basic services, the Year should be a Year for all children. The IYC Resolution passed the UN General Assembly on December 21, 1976, and the date for the Year was fixed for 1979. There had been growing awareness that children were short-changed in the bank of life.

INTERNATIONAL YEAR OF THE CHILD (IYC) 1979

IYC was conceived as a Year for advocacy—to heighten awareness of children's special needs among decision- makers, parents and the public, and to encourage practical measures to prepare children to participate fully in the development of their societies. The active role in IYC of voluntary bodies not normally associated with UN programs, or even directly with children's concerns, was particularly encouraging. They included many professional societies such as those composed of pediatricians, dentists, judges and lawyers, psychologists, journalists and architects. Almost all of the men's and women's service clubs adopted "special emphasis programs" related to the child.

An outstanding example was the Junior Chamber of Commerce (Jaycees), which set a goal of $12 million for the organization's first-ever international fund raising campaign. The Jaycees' program was scheduled to extend over a three-year period and affect the lives of some five million children. A number of universities scheduled special symposia, conferences, seminars and research studies for the Year. The Yale University two-day conference was notable in this regard. The national IYC Commissions chose different ways of celebrating the Year. Many at least issued stamps and displayed posters in the principal cities. A 100 foot- banner proclaiming the Year stretched across the road in the highlands of Papua New Guinea. Commissions raised funds for the enhancement of their own children's programs. Some undertook a national diagnosis of their children's situation (Guinea-Bissau, Saudi Arabia); studied their nutritional condition (China, Haiti, Oman); took steps to eliminate polio (Malawi); or, immunize newborn children (Bhutan). Others made a census of the children of migrant workers (Luxembourg); set up centers for "latch-key" children (UK) or street children (Colombia). Still others tried to do more for the orphaned (Chad and the Philippines), the nomadic (Botswana), the victims of war (Nigeria, Lebanon), and refugee children (Finland). Benin campaigned to start pre-school programs; Ghana and Kenya got children off the streets and into school; Gambia lowered the age of school entry; India abolished elementary school fees; Vietnam and Korea focused on the care of the handicapped; Bahrain, Chile and the Congo emphasized aid to the mentally disabled.

Togo and Barbados put a Family Code on the statute books; Bolivia revised its code for minors; Indonesia passed new legislation on legitimization and adoption; the Dominican Republic adopted laws for the protection of minors, and Liberia took action to protect victims of child neglect; Bulgaria moved to provide free medicine for children up to 3 and for pregnant women having medical treatment at home; Brazil increased its budget for dietary supplementation, day care centers and services for the handicapped. Sri Lanka's President decreed that IYC activities must extend beyond the Year for at least five years. These included establishment of children's parks in rural areas, extension of immunization programs, special aid to school dropouts and rehabilitation measures for the handicapped. Sweden's Commission had two committees, one for children at home, the second for needy children overseas. Algeria was one of the countries turning its Commission into a permanent body. Barbados enacted legislation providing equal status for every child, whether born to married or unmarried parents.

There was no international conference in the Year of the Child. The strategy of celebrating the Year through a myriad of NGOs, service clubs, women's and youth organizations, civic and religious bodies, and other groups worked very well. Sometimes our contacts with the organizations' international headquarters would trigger the activities of its national branches and chapters. In other cases the national branches and chapters would respond to the appeal of the national IYC commissions.

Before IYC ended, every country in the world with four exceptions had a National Commission, or comparable body, promoting its participation in IYC. North Korea and Equatorial Guinea were two of the four exceptions; I forget the names of the others.

Our IYC offices at HQ and in Geneva produced a vast amount of informational material for newspapers and magazines, for use on radio and TV, and for speakers. Almost from the beginning, an IYC journal heralded special activities and forthcoming events. Grun and I and others on the staff did a fair amount of barnstorming. Notable among our publications, printed in English, French and Spanish was a series of issues papers on various topics. Dani Adjemovitch, a talented editor in the IYC Secretariat, searched far and wide to select authors who were authorities in their various fields.

Some idea of the quality of these papers can be gained from our experience with one that we commissioned on child abuse. We prevailed on Dr. Eli Newberger of Boston to write us a paper on this subject with the understanding that he would receive printed copies in the three languages. Before he delivered his paper we had a call from Dr. Newberger asking if he could be released from his agreement to prepare it for IYC. The prestigious *New England Journal of Medicine* had seen the text of the article and wanted to publish it. The *Journal* had an inflexible rule that *it* had to be the first to publish an article. Newberger said that publication in the *Journal* would mean a great deal to him. I phoned the *Journal* editor saying that I saw no problem in having the article appear simultaneously in both publications. They were completely non-competitive. He graciously agreed to this suggestion and Newberger was extremely satisfied.

Most of the issues papers were concerned with the problems of children in the developing world. The child abuse paper was applicable to the industrialized world as well. So were two excellent papers on children and TV which had two authors, Peggy Charren of Action for Children's Television and Cecily Truitt, a specialist from South Carolina Public Television. We had many requests for these publications.

In the United States, as Jean Young put it, "IYC was a year of many faces. Hundreds of projects and special events were undertaken by all sorts of people." The Report to President Carter from the U.S. National Commission refers to the activities of IYC Commissions in every state and in Guam, Puerto Rico, the Virgin Islands and American Samoa. It also lists 425 NGOs, service clubs, women's and youth organizations, professional societies and other national organizations which participated in the Year.

"The flavor and scope of the Year," to use Jean Young's phrase, can best be captured by a few examples of the events its inspired: Colorado launched a statewide campaign to identify migrant children, enroll each one in an education program, reduce the high dropout rate, and provide necessary health service. In Seneca, Missouri, programs were initiated to counsel potentially abusive mothers, to provide shelter to battered wives and to recruit foster grandparents. In New Mexico, the chair of the state IYC Commission mobilized opposition to a proposed revision of the state juvenile code that would have allowed punitive incarceration of juveniles with adult criminals. Prompted by the IYC Commission, the Governor sent the state legislature a package of proposed legislation for children and was successful in getting three million dollars earmarked for children's programs.

In Pennsylvania, a day-long celebration of IYC, sponsored by the Commonwealth, involved all 67 counties and 5,000 young people. A weekly newsletter on the status of children's legislation was published by Kansas Action for Children.

Early in its deliberations, the U.S. National Commission decided to form a Children's Advisory Panel to give "a direct, clear sense of how young people in the U.S. see themselves, their opportunities and their constraints." The panel had a balance of boys and girls, of city dwellers and rural youths. The Panel met in Washington in August and December 1979. Among the topics covered in the Panel's report were: child abuse, education, parental involvement, the media, drug abuse, teenage pregnancy and adult/youth communication. The title of the Panel's report was *No Time for Mud Pies!*

Jean Young did an outstanding job coordinating the work of the many organizations that were involved in the U.S. program. A few years after IYC's conclusion I was saddened to hear that she had died at an early age.

INTERNATIONAL YEAR FOR DISABLED PERSONS (IYDP) 1981

The situation of handicapped children was a priority concern of many national commissions of IYC, so it was possible to build on this foundation when the UNs Year of the Disabled came along in 1981. We had also published an excellent Issues Paper in IYC on the disabled child. *One Out of Ten* was the slogan adopted for the Year, meaning that one out of every ten persons had some kind of disability. The ongoing studies of the World Rehabilitation Council pinpointed aspects of the problem and recommended measures that could be taken to alleviate them.

During IYC I got to know Dr. Michael Irwin, an articulate Englishman and an activist who spoke out, somewhat rashly on occasion. At one time he was the Chief Medical Officer at United Nations Headquarters and he was later employed in the same capacity at the World Bank. Michael was involved with health matters at UNICEF in 1981 and was named the point man for the Year. I don't recall why he left UNICEF part way through the Year but before he did he recommended that I take his place. Although I was not a physician he thought my experience in two previous UN Years would more than compensate for this deficiency.

I followed the same strategy in IYDP that I had used in the two previous UN years I helped to promote. I worked through governments where possible but mainly through NGOs, service clubs, professional societies and other groups that might or might not normally deal with the problems of disabled children. An example would be architects, who were encouraged to make allowance in their structural designs for the access of disabled children. In this connection, the symbol of the wheelchair now universally adopted as the logo for the handicapped has been a great asset in spreading the message.

As in IYC, it was decided not to have a UN-sponsored international conference for IYDP. The emphasis was placed on national and local initiatives. Probably the closest thing to an international conference was scheduled to take place at Rennes in Brittany. The French invited participants from other European countries, Canada and the United States including a goodly number of handicapped persons. I went, representing UNICEF. The opening plenary session was held in the ground floor auditorium of the vocational training school where the meeting took place. Those attending were then divided into subgroups to meet in smaller rooms. About half of those attending were assigned to convene in rooms on the second floor. A sizable cluster of the handicapped collected at the bottom of a staircase. They were speaking angrily in loud voices and some were gesticulating wildly. Inconceivable as it seems, the French had arranged for the use of a building which had no elevator. Of course there were apologies galore, and the conference staff found a building not too far away with small ground floor rooms that could be used for meeting. But the egregious oversight left an indelible stain on the proceedings.

THE CONVENTION ON THE RIGHTS OF THE CHILD

While the Declaration on the Rights of the Child contained lofty principles, it had no standing in international law. In 1979, Poland's proposal for a Convention on the Rights of the Child was taken up by a Working Group of the UN Commission on Human Rights. Over the next years, many governments, UN agencies, and a network of some 50 NGOs serviced by Defense for Children International contributed suggestions for the Convention's provisions. One of the controversial points was the minimum age allowable for induction into a nation's armed forces. Agreement on the Convention draft was reached in 1988 and it was approved by the General Assembly in November 1989, thirty years after the issuance of the Declaration. The Convention has been ratified by the requisite number of nations (20) and is now part of international law. The U.S.

signed the Convention but up to now has not ratified it. All nations of the world, except for the U.S. and Somalia, have ratified the Convention.

At the end of IYC, Harry Labouisse retired as Executive Director of UNICEF. He was succeeded by James P. Grant, a high principled man of enormous energy. Grant, the son of missionaries in China, displayed much zeal in establishing goals for UNICEF to attain in a number of fields. He also sought to capitalize on the impact of IYC by staging a Child Summit at the UN to which heads of state would be invited. The Summit was held in 1990; many heads of state attended, ambitious new goals were set and the situation of children received a high degree of world attention.

In the post-IYC period attention was focused on a number of controversial problems. Taking a stand against female excision is a case in point. Another was the adoption of a policy to curb the injurious advertising and merchandising practices of certain infant food producers. A third was to come into the open on child abuse and face that issue squarely. UNICEF and the cooperating groups, as a result of the Year, are working more closely to detect and combat gross exploitation of children.

THE U.S. FUND FOR UNICEF

I was enjoying retirement in 1985 when I had a phone call at ten o'clock one evening from Hugh Downs. Hugh called me in his capacity as Chairman of the U.S. Committee for UNICEF. The Committee had fired its president after a stormy passage and needed someone to calm the waters and serve as the CEO until a new president was recruited. The search agency took some time coming up with suitable candidates, so I was interim President for most of the year. Morale was low, but picked up considerably as I got the chance to meet with the staff and consult with the heads of various departments, some of whom I had known in my UNICEF days. Preparing (and living within) a budget was a useful discipline; I also got to know the nuts and bolts of such fund-raising activities as the sale of greeting cards and Trick or Treat. Fortunately, there was a well established staff association, and I had a congenial relationship with its chairman, Chip Lyons, who became a good friend.

I was on the small selection committee that interviewed candidates for president. We had several good ones but settled unanimously on Lawrence Bruce, an exceptional young man of considerable relevant experience and an engaging personality. Larry traveled widely and introduced many outstanding reforms in his brief term of office but tragically became ill and died.

Some time after I left, Chip joined UNICEF and served in Mozambique and elsewhere before returning to its New York HQ as administrative aide to Carol Bellamy, who became UNICEF's Executive Director after the death of Jim Grant. In a curious turn of fate, the U.S. Committee for UNICEF again had CEO problems and Chip was given a temporary assignment to help sort them out. He performed so capably that he was elected president and is doing a most commendable job. During all this period—a ten-year stretch—Hugh Downs held a steady course for the Committee. His experience as a top radio, then television host, enabled him to preside easily over the fortunes of the Committee. His warm, attractive personality carried real conviction for the cause of children.

An added pleasant feature of my year with the U.S. Committee was the chance to meet for an exchange of views with the CEOs of other UNICEF Committees. There were two such occasions, one in Warsaw and one in London.

As interim President I got better acquainted with Helenka Pantaleoni, who had preceded Hugh as Chair of the U.S. Committee and was, in a sense, its patron saint. Helenka was a delightful woman, bright and innovative even in her later years. Born in Poland, and a friend of Paderewski and his family, Helenka was briefly on the New York stage in her salad days, but early on became attracted to UNICEF and began working in its behalf. Everyone adored Helenka, and many tributes were paid to her at her retirement party which I attended. When I finished my work with the U.S. Committee I was gratified to receive the Helenka Pantaleoni Award for service to the world's children.

It was interesting, and somewhat challenging, to find myself on the other side of the fence, that is, representing a UNICEF Committee instead of UNICEF itself.

LATIN AMERICA

I don't speak Spanish and I never worked in a Latin American country. It's a source of regret to me that I never really came to know that part of the world. Margaret and I honeymooned in Mexico and I returned there several times, once to Mexico City when the UNICEF Board met there, once with Vera on holiday, and again with Vera and our families to Cozumel for our group honeymoon. It is a wonderful country and I wish I knew it better. Thinking of Mexico puts me in mind particularly of the visits I made with both Margaret and Vera to picturesque Oaxaca.

In 1956 when I was heading up the ICEM office in New York, I was asked to represent the agency at a UNESCO Conference in Havana on the adjustment of migrants. It was the year before Castro took power. The Batista government was a genial host and we were well treated; at the weekend they took us by bus to Varadero beach, some 80 miles to the east and one of the finest beaches I've ever visited.

I had to give a talk about the work of ICEM on the first day of the conference. I was nervous about that, but it went quite well and I was able to relax the rest of the week. Many speakers followed me and the discussion was brisk. Our chairman was an Australian, a knowledgeable academic who kept us in line. Unfortunately, there was no arrangement for simultaneous translation, with the result that we had to sit through two language versions in addition to the original speech in English, Spanish and French. A whispered translation would probably have sufficed for the single delegate from France but characteristically he insisted on a full French interpretation.

We were hosted at parties given by the Cuban government, the U.S. Embassy and Walter Bieringer, an old friend of mine who was then chairman of the Massachussetts Commission for incoming refugees. It was a fun week, I learned quite a lot, and I was glad for the chance to see Havana, a beautiful city, not suspecting that the prevailing autocratic government would soon be overturned. I never returned to Havana, though I've been tempted to; my grandson, David Marks, who shares my enthusiasm for Cuban music, had a great visit there recently. Margaret and I enjoyed a vacation trip to Costa Rica, despite being badly sunburned by the deceptive tropical sun.

In the winter of 1978, Margaret and I decided to spend a week in the Caribbean city of Baranquilla. She hadn't been feeling quite right and we thought a week in the sun might knock out the winter's chill. We enjoyed the tropical weather, then decided to take a train to Colombia's capital city. Bogota is picturesquely located high on a mountain-rimmed plateau of the Andes. I have three memories of our short visit there. Its famous Gold Museum, housing a noted collection of pre-Columbian goldwork, is on view in the Department of the Treasury building. We saw the window from which Bolivar escaped while his valiant mistress held off a searching party of his adversaries. The man who rented us a car gave us elaborate instructions on how to avoid being mugged. That was our last out-of-town junket. On our return to New York, doctors discovered Margaret had ovarian cancer.

In April, 1989 I had an opportunity to visit UNICEF projects in Guatemala and Honduras on a trip arranged for seven board members of the U.S. Fund for UNICEF. In Guatemala we witnessed major efforts to implement the Child Survival Plan by improvements in health management in the maternal/child field. UNICEF sought a decrease in the 1985 child mortality rate of 66 per 1000 live births. This was to be achieved by increased immunization of children under five against the ten preventable diseases that are the chief causes of child mortality. We visited income-generating projects at Canabaj with community leaders, including production of ceramics, fuel-efficient stoves, a bakery and a tree nursery. Some of these were designed to benefit displaced families. We also visited the urban marginal area of El Mezquital to see health, sanitation and income generating projects. In the municipality of Todos Santos we inspected projects for mini-irrigation and soil preservation in the El Rancho community and others involving women in Batzalom.

When we visited there, Honduras was the poorest country with the lowest standard of living in Central America. Its 1985 rate for infant mortality was 79 per one thousand. The rates for Nicaragua (71) and El Salvador (68) are the next highest. This contrasts with Panama (22) and Costa Rica (18) as examples of what can be done. On the Honduras portion of our trip we were especially impressed by the knowledge and enthusiasm of the UNICEF staff, their patience with our innumerable questions, and their warm relationship with community leaders. Clean water is probably the greatest need. People pay one third of their income for water and the same for firewood which doesn't leave much pocket change on a yearly income of $750. In the country at large, 45 percent have no clean water source and as many as 85 percent lack adequate waste disposal. We visited urban water, basic services and community organization projects in the poor urban communities of Colonia Villa Nueva and Altos de San Francisco. Then, after a three hour trip south to Choluteca, we saw additional projects for integrated child care/early child stimulation and women's activities including education, informal day care and income generation.

The Honduras barrios don't house as many internally displaced people as those in Guatemala, but many occupants have moved to the barrios from rural areas because they hope to raise themselves above the poverty level. This urban drift has given rise to many street children in Tegucigalpa. As in other cities, UNICEF is developing a number of projects to alleviate this trend.

UNICEF was continuing to support a basic services program to improve the plight of displaced children and families in Guatemala, Nicaragua and El Salvador. Some of those displaced from their homes by war and political strife are living within their national borders but others fled to neighboring countries where, for the most part, they are confined to camps. Because of my background in refugee work and status as a board member of the U.S. Committee for Refugees, I was anxious to visit one of the camps and stayed an extra day to do so.

We took in a Honduran camp for 6,000 Nicaraguan refugees near Jacalapa on the road to Danli. As the situation in Nicaragua improves, the refugees displaced by the struggle are returning home and it was expected that those at Jacalapa would soon be repatriated. The camp was no better but no worse than the average refugee camp I've seen in Asia and Africa and so far as I could ascertain the refugees were well treated. They were reasonably clothed, their health and sanitary facilities seemed adequate and the communal lunch I had was spartan but acceptable.

I was later briefed by Ulrich von Blumenthal, deputy UNHCR representative, who had arranged for my visit to the camp. He said the situation of Salvadoran refugees at two main camps was such that UNHCR was, for the first time, seeking third country solutions. This was partly due to the capricious brutality of Honduran Army guards who had killed several refugees by indiscriminate firing. While these charges were officially denied, the fact remains that a third alternative was needed for some refugees who refused repatriation but were endangered by their continued camp stay. It wasn't possible for me to visit these camps during my brief visit.

I regret that I never got to Brazil, though I've been responsible for sending hundreds of refugees and Greeks to that country, mainly to the southern states of Parana, Saint Marguerita and Rio Grande do Sul.

VERA AND FAMILY

In the summer of 1981, a year after Margaret's death, I drove solo from Virginia to New England, visiting a number of friends en route. I had had some correspondence with Ben and Felicia Kaplan, and they invited me to spend a few days at their Martha's Vineyard home. Ben was then a judge on the Massachusetts Supreme Court, after a brilliant career as a professor at Harvard Law School. Felicia (nee Lamport) was known for her delicious, satirical light verse, but also for her lively wit, capacity for friendship, and consummate skill as a welcoming hostess. The Kaplans had a recently divorced friend who was visiting her children on the Vineyard. They invited her for a drink on August 8th, noting that she might be interested to meet a somewhat older house guest from New York. Several others were invited, including Francis Sayre, a former boss of mine when as Dean of the Washington Cathedral he was also chairman of the U.S. Committee for Refugees.

People at the gathering were talking about the movie, *Raiders of the Lost Ark* which was playing at a Vineyard theater. I hate *Star Wars* and other science fiction movies, but I had fixed my gaze on a woman across the room, admiring her looks and poise. I started a conversation with her and almost immediately asked if she'd like to accompany me to the film. She agreed, and we spent a romantic dinner and evening, winding up in the moonlight on Squibnocket beach. The next day I visited her at her campsite, and that evening followed her back to the Cambridge apartment where she was living with her children. In subsequent weekends, I visited Cambridge and she drove with her children to visit me in Virginia. I hadn't thought of remarrying but I was strongly attracted to Vera and her children, and after I retired from UNICEF (and the U.S. Fund for UNICEF) I found I was spending more and more time at 4 Channing Street, Cambridge, and was in love with its owner. I proposed, gave her Mim's emerald ring, and we were married November 28, 1987, EB's 122nd birthday and Thanksgiving weekend. Vera's children, my children and grandchildren accompanied us on our honeymoon in Cozumel, Mexico a month later, during the Christmas vacation. With all aboard the plane returning to Cancun airport, we had a scare when the pilot was unable to get the landing gear down. We hovered for quite a while watching the shadow of the airplane against the buildings below, and he finally made it.

Vera June Barad was born in Brooklyn on March 27, 1936, and brought up on Long Island. Her father was an attorney. Her mother, a Spanish major in college, worked on Ellis Island before her children were born. After graduation from Hempstead High School, Vera went to Mount Holyoke College, where she roomed with Katie Butler Jones, whom she had known since they were both counselors at Camp Felicia. After college, Vera enrolled at Boston University's School of Social Work and emerged with an MSW degree. One summer she worked as a volunteer for the American Friends Service Committee office in Chicago serving Native Americans. After a few years working as a psychiatric social worker, Vera established her own clinical practice as a psychotherapist, which she maintained for nearly forty years, working mostly from an office in her Cambridge home. She helped scores of patients, and on her retirement received warm tributes from many of them. Vera is a fantastically well organized person, and has an innate talent for innovative cooking, knitting and other home crafts. She's an ardent and attentive mother and grandmother, shares my interest in travel and the theater, and has many friends, including a number she has met since we moved to California.

In *Hero and Leander* Marlowe asked "Whoever loved, that loved not at first sight?" Shakespeare used the same phrase in *As You Like It*. I fell in love with Vera the day I met her on the Vineyard. I have a wonderful family of my own but meeting Vera and her great kids gave me a new lease on life.

I've written many verses in celebration of my Vera. Here's one from the 80th birthday bash she made for me in Cambridge:

THE LADY IS A CHAMP (Tune: *The Lady is a Tramp*)

I get too hungry for dinner at eight:
When Vera's cooking, the food's always great,
Only one problem, I'm gaining some weight,
That's why the lady is a champ.

She's hard at work each morning at nine
Looking divine
Tip top, non-stop;
She's just the mate for this born-again gramp
That's why the lady is a champ.

She's done a swell job raising her young
To the top rung;
They'll star—go far!
Her radiant smile lights up days that are damp,
That's why the lady is a champ.
She solves the problems of many a miss;
They find new boyfriends, once more savor bliss!

And brawling couples depart with a kiss;
That's why the lady is a champ.

I count my blessings:
Kids I adore, friends by the score;
Sweet wife, good life;
When you reach 80 and limbs start to cramp,
You're lucky living with a champ.

Then there are my step-children: Amelia has many fine qualities that have been evident in her past work and currently in her homemaking and gardening skills, but at this moment her maternal instincts and super performance as a mother reign supreme. She is a graduate of the University of Massachusetts and finished the course at the Culinary Institute of America (C.I.A.) in Hyde Park, New York. Her husband, Todd Humphries, is chef-partner of Martini House in St. Helena, California and is recognized nationally as a leading chef. He also is a graduate of the C.I.A.

Vivian's sparkling personality is a constant source of purposeful, creative energy reflected in her work and in her life stream. I'm confident of her leadership in her chosen field of industrial design. She graduated from the University of Michigan and is finishing her studies in design at the California College of Art. She and her husband, Jason Thompson, live in the Mission District of San Francisco. Jason moved from London to San Francisco and is now a California convert. He is doing free-lance writing and working on his first novel. He is an Oxford graduate.

I've known Michael more than two-thirds of his life and like to think I've been a favorable influence. He's a straight shooter, a thoroughly nice guy, well put together and embarking on a promising career in hydrology and environmental engineering. He has completed course requirements for his Ph.D at the University of California. He has an engineering degree from the University of Colorado (where he minored in skiing) and a Master's Degree from Berkeley. They all live in the Bay Area, have demonstrated their affection in many ways and were the reason we moved across the country.

GRANDSONS

I've been blessed with eight grandsons. Six by direct descent and two from Amelia and Todd. Tom and Lucky's quintet bear witness to their parents' creative guidance in the field of music and also in the quality of their lives. After he was graduated from Indiana University, Jethro studied at the Manhattan School of Music where he received an advanced degree and was mentored by Pinchas Zukerman. Jethro is already a recognized success as associate principal violist of Canada's National Arts Centre Orchestra. Paolo and Theo are formidable cellists; Paolo is also a skilled string instrument maker. David is an accomplished violist, a member of the esteemed Hilversum Radio Orchestra of Holland. First of my grandchildren to wed, David married long time friend Fanny Bray at her parents' home in France in December 2003. Fanny is a talented cellist who has performed at Verbier and other festivals. David and Theo have displayed marked talent in the visual arts. Theo is spending his junior year at the University of Utrecht specializing in print making. Vincent, at 17, is a promising violinist in the State Youth Orchestra and Loudoun County Orchestra. He plans to matriculate at the University of Indiana following in his brothers' footsteps. All five inherit their father's love of the outdoors and tennis. Thomas Branczyk, 32 year-old son of Tom and Yvette Branczyk, was raised in France, educated in California and now lives in London with Keiko Takatani. He is an able real estate entrepreneur.

Desmond Finn Humphries at 4 is an irrepressible delight and Wyatt James Humphries at one is a joyful early walker and talker.

HAMLET

The following parody of Shakespeare's *Hamlet* is one of the humorous gems written by Newman Levy in his *Opera Guyed*, published by Knopf in 1923. Having committed this verse to memory I willingly inflict it from time to time on command at family dinner parties or to entertain the young:

Last night the boss slips me a ticket
Fer one o' them opera shows
An' the name o' the show is called Hamlet,
So I breaks out my glad rags and goes,
Well, it's gloom from the moment it opens
Till the time the theater shuts,
An' the company's half o' them looney,
An' the rest o' the cast is all nuts.
The tenor's a goof known as Hamlet,
But his real name's George W. Gloom.
He's a regular Life o' the Party;
He's as jolly an' gay as a tomb.
His old man was King o' the Denmarks,
An' the poor simp's gone weak in the bean,
Fer his dad had been croaked by his uncle
Who, right afterwards, marries the Queen.
So, young Hamlet just hangs around sad like,
An' he talks to hisself like a nut.
But as yet he ain't hep that his father
Was bumped off by his uncle,--the mutt.
One night he slips out o' the castle,
An' goes up on the roof fer some air,

When along comes the ghost of his father,
An' he shoots him an earful fer fair.
"That lowlife, your uncle, has croaked me,
An' he went off an' married your ma.
Will you let that rat hand you the haha?"
Says Hamlet. "Just notice me, pa!"

Young Ham has a frail called Ophelia,
An' her pop is a dreary old goof,
An' they can't dope why Hamlet's gone batty.
They don't know what he seen on the roof.
Well, Ham goes an' calls on his mother,
An' he bawls the old girl out fer fair,
Then he sees somethin' move in the curtains,
An' he thinks that the uncle is there.
So he jabs with his sword through the curtain,
An' he cries "Now we're even, my lad."
But it isn't the King but Polonius,
An' he's killed poor Ophelia's old dad.

Then, Ophelia, poor kid, just goes daffy
When she hears how her old man is crowned,
An' she goes around singing like crazy,
Till she walks in the lake and gets drowned.
There's a jolly old scene in the graveyard
Where Prince Hamlet gets into a scrap
With Ophelia's big brother, Laertes,
Who wants to muss up Hamlet's map.

Then the King says, "Now boys don't act nasty,
I know how to fight this thing out.
I've got some tin swords at the castle,
An' we'll frame up a nice friendly bout."
Then he winks at Laertes an' whispers,
"We'll knock this here nut fer a gool,
I'll smear up your sword with some poison,
An' we'll make Hamlet look like a fool."

So they pull off the bout like they plan it,
But the King thinks his scheme may slip up,
So he orders a cold drink for Hamlet,
An' some poison he sneaks in the cup.
Then Ham and Laertes start fighting,

An' the King slips Laertes the wink.
But the Queen she ain't wise to what's doin',
An' she swallers the King's poisoned drink.
Then Hamlet gets stuck in the shoulder,
An' he sees how he's framed from the start,
So he switches the swords on Laertes,
An' he stabs the poor bum in the heart.
Then he runs his sword right through his uncle,
An' he says "Well, let's call it a day."
Then the Queen dies, the King dies, an' Ham dies,
I call it a helluva play.

HEALTH

I was pretty healthy most of my life, and my health was of no particular concern. In 1951 while I was in Greece, I had a severe abdominal pain during a hectic week, but it went away. Several days later, on a duty trip to Geneva, the pain recurred with greater intensity, and I was rushed to the hospital at midnight to have my appendix removed. One morning in 1955 I picked up the phone and found I couldn't hear in my left ear. The doctor said I'd had a vascular accident. Fortunately I have good hearing in my right ear despite the fact that I was operated for mastoid in that ear when I was 4 years old.

In 1970 after a visit to the Great Salt Camp in India to which millions of Bengalis had fled from East Pakistan, I came down with cholera despite having taken a cholera shot before my departure. After a week in a New Delhi hospital, being fussed over by tiny nuns, I was invited to spend a second week recuperating at the home of Alvin Roseman, then heading the Ford Foundation in India.

In 1981 I had a double hernia operation. The recovery was very painful.

Ten years later, we were skiing at Steamboat Springs and I got terribly fatigued. They found my blood pressure was over 200. That led to the installation of a pacemaker. I dreaded the idea of that, but found that I was almost entirely unaware of it. I could continue with an active professional life and still play a relatively strong game of tennis.

Some years later, my dermatologist, Dr. Michael Whitlow, found a melanoma behind my left ear, and that had to be operated. In the winters of 1999 and 2000, I came down with bad pneumonia. The second attack took me to the Mount Auburn Hospital, and while there I had a silent heart attack. Since then, I've been in cardiac rehabilitation, first in Cambridge and more recently in Marin County. The most serious consequence is that my wind is severely cut. I went to a tennis "clinic" once a week at Mill Valley's Boyle Park, and found I could hit the ball reasonably well, but it didn't take much to get me out of breath. Vera has been a loving and conscientious caretaker, ensuring that I drink the proper amount of water, stick to a low sodium diet, and keep taking the numerous pills that have been prescribed. I was able to go to my 70th Reunion at Dartmouth in 2002, and felt in better shape than most of my classmates who were able to attend. One said: "If you can move it, it hurts!"

Several years ago while traveling in St. Croix, Virgin Islands, with Vera and a group of retired UNICEF friends, I fell ill and had to be hospitalized for a night. The hospital was pleasant enough, but there were no single rooms and I was put in with an older local gentleman who kept mumbling aloud passages from the bible. This was terribly annoying, and I asked him if he could please read to himself. He seemed to agree, but went on as before until the time came to turn out the lights. After that, peace and quiet prevailed and I looked forward to getting some rest. I was dozing off when I felt some presence hovering over me. In the dim light from the corridor I recognized my neighbor from the adjoining bed. He was fixing me with a steady gaze. After a long moment, he spoke: "Are you ready?" he said. When I failed to answer, he repeated the question: "Are you ready. You *must* be ready!" After I sleepily said I was as ready as I could be, he seemed satisfied and shuffled off to his bed.

In February 2003 we flew from California to New York City. The major purpose was to have some theater time and enjoy a visit from Tom and his family. While there I looked forward to the installation of a recommended biventricular pacemaker at NYU Hospital. In pre-operative tests before its installation, it was discovered that my kidneys had failed badly. The doctors kept me in the hospital while they experimented to see if I could get by without dialysis. Unfortunately the answer was "no," so the nephrologist began it and it was five weeks before I was able to leave the hospital. Vera was with me the whole time and even moved into the room to sleep on a cot next to me. It was about four inches lower than my bed but we were able to hold hands. In the middle of a delirious dream she reports that I complained, "Well, they gave us the honeymoon suite BUT why the hell are you on the floor below mine?!"

I was much weakened by the hospital stay and our flight back to California was a real trial. There after several months, I regained a good deal of my strength and weight. The new pacemaker has been working well. I am now dialyzed three times a week, three hours each session.

I feel fortunate in having optimum medical care in these recent years when my health has been a major concern. I could have wished for no better attention than that given in Cambridge at the Mount Auburn Hospital by Dr. Matthew Carmody in general practice, Dr. Robert Campbell, a cardiologist, and urologist Dr. Paul LaFontaine. At New York University Hospital, in the emergency room one night, I was lucky to find cardiologist Dr. Norman Risinger and in subsequent visits profited by his creative medical knowledge. In California Vera and I share an internist, Dr. William McAllister, a competent and compassionate practitioner. My cardiologist in California is Dr. Jerald Young. It took a bit of shopping to find someone I liked as well as the cardiologists in the East.

I don't really expect to be able to get back on the tennis court. I take no consolation in Andre Gide's remark that he never had to give up anything because of age that he wasn't already tired of.

FRESH PURSUITS

When I left UNICEF in 1981 at the end of IYDP it was a strange feeling to be without a job and an office. I was 70 years old but still in pretty good health. I had just met a wonderful younger woman who was still working full time and I was dividing my time between her gracious home with three lively teens in Cambridge and my NYC apartment. I was still very much imbued with the spirit of UNICEF, which always seemed to me a can-do organization. By 1981 I had completed my part of the final report on IYC. I knew that Jack Charnow had in charge the preparation of the history of UNICEF, and I told him I was ready to do some of the interviewing involved. This fitted in with his plans, and for the next couple of years I did half a dozen extended interviews with retired and still active UNICEF officials.

In 1985 I served a year as interim President of the U.S. Committee for UNICEF. After that I served on the Board of Directors for six years.

I gave more time to the U.S. Committee for Refugees (USCR), not only serving on the Board but also having frequent consultation with Wells Klein who now directed the American Council for Nationalities Service which had incorporated USCR. In 1988 I was elected President of ACNS and two years later became Chairman of its Board.

I knew that a number of European countries and Canada had formed national refugee committees to consult with the government and with other NGOs dealing with refugee and asylum problems. I suggested to Wells that it might be useful to take soundings with these committees. He was encouraging but didn't feel ACNS was in the position to finance the project. I nevertheless went ahead, combining the interviews with private travel in England, Germany, Switzerland, Ireland, Holland and the Scandinavian countries.

While undertaking this project, I booked a sleeper berth on a night train proceeding from Utrecht to Copenhagen. The date was June 25, 1986. I mistakenly assumed that I would be the sole occupant of the sleeping compartment, but when I boarded the train I found I would be sharing it with a fearsome stranger who was already there. I don't use the term "fearsome" lightly. Seated, smoking his pipe, was a huge, mustachioed chap with locks of unruly hair. I don't scare easily but it took much of my courage to mutter a weak "Good evening" as I entered. In return I got a rude stare and single grunt. We rode silently for a few minutes while I claimed my berth and opened my small suitcase. Then I gave him a steady gaze and mouthed the single word "English?" He shrugged his massive shoulders and answered with "Venig," which I understood as the German for "Just a little." We started a polyglot dialogue—his limited German, obviously not his first language, my rudimentary German, and a bit of English he was able to summon up. He looked to me to be in his early forties. When I asked what he did he replied that he was a revolutionary. That set me back—you don't meet so many of those! He guessed I was an American, but it took some time to determine that he was from East Timor, traveling in western Europe to drum up foreign support and funds for independence from Indonesia. From an initial, sullen quiet, his eyes flashed as he warmed to his subject with words in a number of languages that I failed to understand though I mostly grasped their meaning. He was an ardent champion of the cause—the more so when he comprehended that—in a much milder way—I was working in the same vineyard. By now I no longer viewed him as fearsome but as picturesque and redoubtable.

Our halting dialogue continued until we finally retired and it continued the next morning until we quit the train and went our separate ways. In recent years when East Timor erupted and ultimately threw off the Indonesian yoke, I wondered about my friend whose name I had forgotten but whose formidable presence lingered in my memory. I believe today he must be one of the leaders of the liberated country.

In 1987 I was named to serve in a voluntary capacity as a member of the United Nations Panel of Counsel. This body was set up as an important element in the UN administration of justice to represent a staff member in disciplinary and appeal cases before the Joint Appeals Board at Headquarters or the Administrative Tribunal. Because I had already left the Secretariat I was called on only once to act in this capacity, but it was an interesting experience.

This is not to say that I wasn't enjoying life to the full. Vera and I spent a considerable amount of time in NYC going to museums and to the theater nightly. We also traveled to Europe and the Caribbean. We tolerated Cambridge winters with the relief of a week or two on Anguilla, introducing our friends Justin Kaplan and Anne Bernays to the pleasant, laid back Rendezvous Bay Hotel. Some ski trips and summer holidays in Martha's Vineyard included my children and grandchildren. We also visited my son and his family at my former residence in Leesburg, Virginia, and my daughter in Switzerland where she was then residing. We established a comfortable life in Cambridge where Vera enjoyed entertaining at congenial dinner parties.

In addition to Ben and Felicia Kaplan, classmate Frank Westheimer and wife Jeanne, and Victor and Juliette Brudney, whom I had known previously, I was soon welcomed by other of Vera's friends. Derek Polonsky and Cathie Ragovin were helpful arbiters in a troubled moment of our courtship, and continued as firm friends along with David and Ellen Blumenthal, David and Alex Harrison, Gerry and Terry Hass, Howard Wishnie and Cathy Mitkus.

Vera's children were teenagers when I met her, heavily involved in soccer, basketball and other sports, so we spent a great many hours at athletic events. Despite my advanced age I found it easy and greatly pleasurable to participate again in the upbringing of children. Amelia and Vivian were twelve and fourteen and Michael ten when I came into their lives. All three were and have remained loving and devoted to our relationship.

A WORLD OF ART

In 1989 I had an idea for a book about the United Nations. Although I never had an office in the thirty-eight storey UN Headquarters, I was in and out of it a great deal and had ample opportunity to see the works of art given to the World Organization by its member nations. They included some rare antiquities as well as more modern objects by such artists as Picasso, Rouault, Matisse and Dali. The antiquities included a statuette of Osiris from Egypt with original paint showing (700 BC), a vase of the Geometric Period given by Cyprus (600 BC), a Roman mosaic representing the four seasons from Tunisia (2nd C AD), and an almost priceless embroidered burial mantle from the Paracas region of Peru (2-3000 years old).

Outstanding among modern works is the stained glass window created by Chagall, representing a gift of the UN Staff Association and the artist in memory of Dag Hammarsjkold, Secretary-General of the United Nations, whose plane was shot down in the Congo in 1961. Sculptures by Henry Moore and Barbara Hepworth were also given to the UN as memorials to Hammarsjkold.

I wrote up the project and presented the idea to the UN Publications Board which, after several months, gave its approval. I combed through the files of the photo unit but found they had shot relatively few of the objects d'art. Most of the photos they had were of the dedication ceremonies featuring not so much the object itself as the ambassador presenting it. Through a Secretariat friend I was given entrée to a Sotheby's Vice President who assigned Ben Cohen, their top photographer to shoot the objects of greatest value. By happenstance his wife worked in the UN Information Division, which was a plus, and he gave us two full days. Vladimir Kartsev, then the UN Chief of Publications, was enthusiastic about the project and made an appointment for us to see Paul Gottlieb, CEO of Harry Abrams, the most successful art book publishers. Gottlieb agreed to publish the book, but wanted an estimate of how many copies the UN would sell. We consulted the manager of the bookshop at Headquarters and he gave us a figure, as did the manager of the shop at Geneva's Palais des Nations.

On her return from leave, Susannah Johnson, the Secretary of the Publications Board, not only questioned the estimate of the HQ shop manager but bawled him out for giving it to us without clearing it with her. She was heartily disliked throughout the Secretariat but she wielded a considerable amount of power and was feared by her subordinates and other associates. Kartsev outranked her and certainly did not fear her but she had a vendetta against him and made life difficult.

Gottlieb assigned one of his editors to work with me, and as I concluded portions of the text and selected the photos I wanted I passed them on to her. Abrams listed the title of the book—*A World of Art*—in *Editor and Publisher* as a forthcoming publication. It was a moment of great exhilaration for me. Meanwhile the UN contract office negotiated with Gottlieb. As the negotiation dragged on, Gottlieb became exasperated at what he considered were needless roadblocks in the process. He was not used to dealing with a bureaucracy. One day he sent me a letter saying he was pulling out of the project. I was greatly disappointed and urged him to reconsider, but it was no use.

We approached several other publishers but found they were reluctant to undertake, without subsidy, a project involving a large number of color reproductions. The revised estimate of UN sales also discouraged them. I had succeeded in raising $25,000 from the Luce Foundation. After Gottlieb abandoned the project I was able to obtain another $40,000 from the Japanese and Austrian Governments. Finally we made a deal with Il Cigno Galileo Galilei, a small Italian publisher of quality art books. They produced a handsomely printed volume but unfortunately lacked the experience and resources required for global distribution. The book did become a best seller at the UN.

To promote the book in America (and supplement my dwindling income) I worked up a slide show illustrating the book's most interesting features. In the next couple of years I gave a series of lectures at state and local chapters of the UN Association of the United States including Boston, New York City, six chapters of the North Carolina Association in Raleigh and chapters of the World Affairs Council in San Francisco, Washington, DC and New York City. Most of these places Vera and I were going to visit anyway. She not only accompanied me but kept track of the books and arranged for the book signings. In most venues I received an honorarium or an agreement to purchase a certain number of books. I varied my spiel with anecdotes. It included Harry Truman's reaction to the two abstract Leger designs in the General Assembly chamber. He called one "Bugs Bunny" and the other "Scrambled Eggs." I told of the two gifts presented by the Peoples Republic of China when that government displaced Taiwan at the UN. One is an ivory sculpture made of the tusks of four elephants that depicts the area from which Mao started his "Long March." The second is an outsized tapestry showing the Great Wall. When a representative of the Secretary-General received the tapestry at a ceremony in China he cabled UN Headquarters to say it was an amazing, wondrous work on which scores of artisans had labored, that it required so many hundred miles of thread, etc, etc. He ended the cable by saying "Unfortunately, it's life size!" The tapestry now hangs in the Delegates' Lounge.

I also tell the story of the sculptor who tranquilized a massive male elephant in Africa, enveloped it in a plaster cast and shipped the cast in more than 30 pieces to the U.S. It resided in a Long Island warehouse for some time while the sculptor canvassed ambassadors seeking sponsorship from countries wishing to make a contribution to the UN in recognition of its 50th birthday. He lined up Kenya, Namibia and Nepal and got to work assembling and casting the huge pachyderm in metal. Unfortunately, a warehouse fire damaged some of the pieces in the plaster cast, and that set him back. He missed the anniversary deadline, but early in the following year he notified Alvaro de Soto, Chairman of the UN's Arts Committee, that the elephant was on the way. In anticipation of its arrival, the UN had constructed a concrete platform in the northwest corner of the UN park. The sculptor advised de Soto that only half of the sculpture was being delivered. It turned out to be the rear end, and de Soto indignantly sent it back until the entire work was assembled. The completed elephant was shipped some months later and installed at the prepared site. The ambassadors of the three sponsoring nations and the Secretary-General were on hand for the dedication. The elephant was clearly visible to passers-by on First Avenue, and that gave rise to another dilemma. It was huge and lifelike in every detail. Mothers complained to the UN that its prominent genitalia created too much curiosity on the part of their children, and they were troubled by that. The UN gardeners had to screen off the sight by planting a clump of masking bushes.

The selection of objets d'art from those offered by UN member nations is a minor part of de Soto's job, but it can become irksome at times if the work is unsuitable. National sensibilities are easily ruffled if an item is rejected. Sometimes an inferior work is offered to the Secretary-General when he visits a member state.

In choosing the illustrations for *A World of Art* I decided the book would be a whole lot richer in content if I included photos of some of the fine objects in the various UN agencies as well as at HQ. I visited Paris, Geneva, The Hague and Washington to make a selection on the spot from UNESCO, ILO, WHO, the World Bank, the World Court and other UN agencies in those locations. I wrote to the UN offices in other places and had them send me photos or slides. The final volume contains at least one photo from each of the different agencies around the world.

FOR A BETTER WORLD

In 1991 I had the idea for a second book that even more than *A World of Art* would illustrate what the UN is and does. I began collecting United Nations posters, not just from the HQ but also from the specialized agencies and regional offices. I found there was no poster archive at the New York HQ. Individuals had posters in their offices relating to their own programs, and in the basement there was a display of about 20 outstanding examples, but for the most part I had to beg and borrow the posters I wanted, sometimes literally taking them off the walls.

Susannah was still running the Publications Board, but I decided to go over her head. I broached the concept for the book to her boss, the Under-Secretary-General for Public Information, Kensaku Hogen, and got his endorsement. I also got warm letters of endorsement from two other high UN officials. Judy Brister helped me get one from Nitin Desai, Under-Secretary-General for Economic and Social Affairs. The second came from Gillian Sorensen, Assistant Secretary-General for External Relations. I first met Gillian during IYC when she was the Mayor's liaison person with the UN. Gillian is the wife of Ted Sorensen, friend and advisor of Jack Kennedy.

I was encouraged to find an outside publisher, with the understanding that the UN would have a chance to review the final text. Tom and Katie Burke of Pomegranate Communications of California were attracted by the idea of publishing the book and also producing a calendar based on it. I liked their style and their ideas, so we made a deal. They produced an attractive volume in the millennial year, reproducing over 150 posters. Several of the posters in the book were derived from works of art in the UN collection. A UNICEF poster shows a detail of the Chagall stained glass window. Another poster illustrates the mosaic based on Norman Rockwell's painting *The Golden Rule*, which depicts people of different nationalities and races. Rockwell portrayed himself twice in the picture, once as a young man, and a second time, as he was in later life. The mosaic was a gift of the United States in 1985, dedicated by Nancy Reagan and Secretary-General Perez de Cuellar.

In my search I was able to locate black-and-white reproductions of the very first posters issued by the UN in 1945-46. They mostly illustrate the UN flag and commemorate the first UN Days. I also obtained on loan a poster portraying Ralph Bunche, an early UN hero, whose centenary is being celebrated in 2004. As was the case with *A World of Art*, I was able to obtain posters from the various UN specialized agencies and associated bodies. The book continues to be a best seller at the UN Bookstore. Incidentally Susannah Johnson, our bete noir, was removed from her position on the Publications Board, demoted and left the UN.

I had, from the first, the notion that the book could give rise to a splendid exhibit portraying the manifold activities of the UN in peacekeeping, human rights, famine relief, conserving the environment, fair labor practices, health and sanitation, aid to children and refugees, civil aviation, etc. Joseph Verner Reed, another UN Under-Secretary-General, shared my vision, organized a poster exhibit team, and set about raising money for the project. The UN could provide technical assistance, but no cash. The posters needed to be framed, exhibited in New York, then sent on their way to a series of venues.

Reed currently supervises the Staff-Management Coordination Committee and carries out a variety of trouble-shooting assignments for the Secretary-General. He was formerly U.S. Ambassador to Morocco and Chief of Protocol. He involved me in his fund-raising efforts for the poster exhibit. One day he made a date to see David Rockefeller, with whom he had once been associated, and he brought me along. I was feeling poorly that day, but got dressed and met Reed at the appointed time. Going up in the elevator at Rockefeller Center to the 56th Floor, Reed notice that my coat suit pocket was not in order. Very deftly he put it in place, saying, "Chief of Protocol, you know!" David Rockefeller was on the phone when we reached his office, and while we waited, his aide escorted us through a fabulous collection of mostly French impressionist masterpieces.

When we entered Rockefeller's office he was looking over a copy of my book, *For a Better World—Posters from the United Nations.* Reed introduced me as the author and mentioned that I had known David's brother Nelson at Dartmouth. I told Rockefeller I had known Nelson but was better acquainted with his roommate, John French, who was editor of *The Dartmouth* when I was a freshman board member. I also told him that my father had been one of the first tenants in Rockefeller Center. Rockefeller put me at my ease, then turned to Reed. "I like this project," he said, "and we are prepared to give you $15,000." He looked at Reed. "Are you prepared to match that?" I don't know what Reed expected, but he agreed, and we emerged with a nest egg of $30,000. Rockefeller, Reed and Katie Burke of Pomegranate were present when the Secretary-General and I cut the tape to open the HQ exhibit in December 2000. From there it traveled to Europe, where it was seen in Paris, Geneva, Berlin, Warsaw, Oslo and Vienna. Vera and I were present in Geneva when Nane Annan opened the exhibit at the Palais des Nations in July 2001. A number of my old friends turned out for this occasion including George and Helga Klein, Daniel and Cristina Lopez, Rusty Hauben and Ineke Cronheim. The Secretary-General and Mrs. Annan were present in Oslo where the exhibit coincided with the award to the UN of the Nobel Prize. In Poland, the Foreign Minister said he had never seen a better illustration of what the UN is all about. In Asia, the exhibit was seen in South Korea, four venues in Japan, Myanmar and Thailand before coming back to the U.S. for a showing in San Francisco's City Hall.

I arranged with the San Francisco Association for the UN and the UNICEF office in California for a children's UN poster competition to be held at the same time, with the prizewinners on display along with the UN posters. From San Francisco, the UN posters were briefly shown at the Bruce Museum in Greenwich, Connecticut before being shipped back to Europe for successful exhibits in Prague and The Hague. In 2004 it will travel Switzerland and probably other countries. So the exhibit has had a great run, bringing the message of the UN to thousands of people.

I was pleased to receive a personal letter from Secretary-General Kofi Annan, on July 24, 2000, reading as follows:

"My wife and I would like to thank you very much for sending us copies of your beautiful new book and calendar, *For a Better World: Posters from the United Nations.* It is indeed inspiring to see, in one volume, visual representations of so many of the issues that our Organization has been devoted to over the years. I have no doubt that your book will spread the message of the United Nations to some who would not otherwise have received it...We would both like to commend you on a job well done."

On our last trip to Europe in May 2002 we spent a few days in London, then flew to Rome for a long delayed reunion with Peter and Gretchen Bloom. Gretchen was working for the World Food Program and awaiting a transfer to Kabul, her last posting before retirement. From Rome we took a sleeper train to Paris where, arriving early in the morning, we had an inordinate wait with a whole trainload of taxi seekers. The highlight of our Paris stay was the first meeting and dinner of the Oyster Foundation, brainchild of our friend Stephen Banker. Outstanding talks were given by Oyster Foundation members David Levering Lewis, biographer of W.E.B. DuBois, and long-time friend George Klein.

A MEMOIR

With the encouragement of family and friends I began work on this memoir in 2002. It summarizes a long life, lived mainly in the 20th century in a variety of locales, in Europe, Asia, Africa and at home in the U.S. I was fortunate to have survived a tempestuous period of two world wars (and several smaller ones), a cold war, a major economic depression, as well as periods of relative economic, social and political tranquility. I outlived my parents, my two siblings, my first wife, a son tragically lost in an accident, and the death of most of my best friends. In my lifetime I have seen enormous changes in personal relations, many for the better but some for the worse. We have passed through revolutions in the style of dress, tastes in music, art, literature and food, prevailing standards of morality, and in general, designs for living.

If I just think of the advances in means of locomotion—from the early cars and trolleys to high speed autos, bullet trains and airplanes to the advances, (I guess they can be called that), in media proliferation and telecommunications. To have survived all this lends no particular distinction, but I hope it has given me a modicum of perspective, of tolerance, and—I would hope—a small ration of wisdom.

It's difficult to measure one's own accomplishments. Aside from family, I believe I've made a positive difference in the life of a number of individuals I've worked or studied with or have encountered, sometimes by mere hazard, along the way. I'm confident that my work has benefited, directly or indirectly, a large number of refugees and children.

When my son-in-law, a writer, read several chapters of this memoir, he said it needed to have a central theme. That set me thinking. Was there a thread that tied together at least most of the work experiences of my life? After some reflection, I decided the binding thread was helping people in limbo to get back on track.

In the case of refugees, "back on track" usually meant reestablishment of their lives somewhere other than the place they originated. In IRO we helped nearly one and a half million Europeans displaced by the Nazis to find new homes, mostly in overseas destinations. In Greece and Yugoslavia, working for IRO and ICEM/IOM, I helped thousands more refugees and unemployed Greeks to resettle overseas. These refugees were mainly in flight from Eastern European Communist countries. Part of the satisfaction on other jobs came from the orientation and placement of refugees and other migrants coming to the United States both before, during and after World War II. Our immigration laws creaked with prejudice, but fortunately enough legislation of a patchwork nature finally let a reasonable number of refugees through the cracks.

My experience with refugees in Vietnam and Nigeria was of a different order, but equally poignant. These people were war victims, caught in the maelstrom of civil strife in those two countries. They were not forced to cross a national border but were seriously buffeted by military action in their own countries. In the case of the Vietnamese, I was keenly aware that U.S. military strikes were, to a considerable degree, responsible for their displacement. In Nigeria a protein deficiency made critically urgent the delivery of nutritious food supplies to malnourished children. It was immensely gratifying to see infants snatched from death by an infusion of corn, soya and milk precariously brought in from the United States.

Of all my refugee experience, the one which perhaps had the most significance for me was the relocation of Japanese-Americans. The 110,000 evacuated from the west coast were never in any danger of starvation. They were not, as in Vietnam or Nigeria, refugees from a shooting war. They were not compelled to leave their country of residence. But they were hapless victims of discrimination compounded by war hysteria. The government acknowledged—but only after 40 years—that they had been unjustly treated. It was an unfair test of their loyalty to the United States, yet all but a very few passed it, despite loss of pride, dignity and in many cases personal property. I am satisfied that the War Relocation Authority, and I as an American, did everything we could to ameliorate their relocation experience and return them to normal life. But no monetary compensation can ever extinguish the shame of what this country did to them.

My work with refugees and immigrants was channeled through three kinds of agencies: non-governmental, U.S. government and international. Having had the experience of all three I preferred working in an international setting though I found it can and does have its share of bureaucracy. I greatly relished the association with people of a wide spectrum of nationalities and races. In the government agencies in which I worked I was lucky to experience a minimum of bureaucracy, though of course it existed. An extreme example I've heard took place at the Pentagon. During a periodic efficiency drive it was finally decided to toss the documents pertaining to the French and Indian Wars. However the order stated that before shredding, a copy of each document should be placed in the file! In Washington and in the field I worked with colleagues I respected. I found that changes in national administration didn't seriously affect policy or performance at my job level. Of course, budgetary restrictions can always be a hazard; in USAID we sometimes had to wait for our pay.

I found that working in an NGO framework offered certain advantages, the chief of which is that it offers the client a greater degree of direct, more informal contact. I also found that a blend of NGO and government (or UN) sponsorship makes possible the realization of worthwhile projects that neither could achieve on their own.

Whether refugee assistance is international, governmental and/or includes the sponsorship of a voluntary agency, I like to think democracy's door has been opened just that much wider. Our treatment of refugees is a fair measure of how far we've come in realizing our goals for human rights.

FUNNY BONES

I guess I've hung up my track shoes, but like to think I can still carry on useful pursuits. One project I want to return to is *Funny Bones*. Having a fondness for comic songs, and knowing quite a few myself, I thought up the idea of a series of half hour radio programs designed to celebrate the American comic song. A rich and varied tapestry of humorous songs extends through our history and is an important part of our national heritage. Throughout the last century, comic and novelty songs gave lighthearted and relevant witness to our follies and foibles. There are funny songs joshing the family, love (requited and unrequited), food and drink, jobs, animals, vehicles, places, dance crazes, styles of dress, new inventions and just plain nonsense. Unfortunately, many of the most appealing humorous songs are no longer performed or even recollected. I made contact with a radio producer, and with a small grant from the National Endowment for the Arts we made a live pilot with Julie Wilson, Kaye Ballard and Arthur Siegel. I wrote a lyric for the *Funny Bones* theme and Arthur composed a jaunty tune. One of the pleasures of working on the project was association with a Cambridge neighbor and friend, Tom Lehrer, whose encyclopedic knowledge of songs, especially show tunes, was of enormous value. Over time I worked with two hosts and produced a total of eight tapes on various themes. Several were played on a radio station in the Boston area. We kept hoping for a grant to complete a series of thirteen. I still think the project has merit and plan to return to it, so stay tuned to your local PBS station!

ACRONYMS

AAUW	American Association of University Women
ACLU	American Civil Liberties Union
ACNS	American Council for Nationalities Service
ACT	Action for Children's Television
ACVAFS	American Committee of Voluntary Agencies in Foreign Service
AFL-CIO	American Federation of Labor - Congress of Industrial Organizations
AFSC	American Friends Service Committee
AID	Agency for International Development
AJDC	American Jewish Joint Distribution Committee
ANCHA	American National Committee for Homeless Armenians
ASCAP	American Society of Composers, Authors and Publishers
ASPCA	American Society for the Prevention of Cruelty to Animals
ASPCC	American Society for the Prevention of Cruelty to Children
BMI	Broadcast Music, Inc
C & G	Casque and Gauntlet
CAR	Central African Republic
CCNY	City College of New York
CDC	Center for Disease Control
CRS	Catholic Relief Service
CWS	Church World Service
DCM	Deputy Chief of Mission
ECOSOC	Economic and Social Council
ESL	English as a Second Language
EXIM	Export-Import Bank
FAO	Food and Agriculture Organization
FPHA	Federal Public Housing Authority
FSA	Farm Security Administration
FTP	Federal Theatre Project
HCMC	Saigon/Ho Chi Minh City
HHR	U.S. Department of Health and Human Resources
HIAS	Hebrew Immigrant Aid Society
HUAC	House UnAmerican Activities Committee
ICCB	International Catholic Child Bureau
ICEM	Intergovernmental Committee for European Migration
ICRC	International Committee for the Red Cross
IFAD	International Fund for Agricultural Development
ILO	International Labor Organization
IOM	International Organization for Migration
IRO	International Refugee Organization
IRC	International Rescue Committee
IRSA	Immigration and Refugee Services of America
ISS	International Social Service

IUCW	International Union for Child Welfare
IYC	International Year of the Child
IYDP	International Year for Disabled Persons
JACL	Japanese-American Citizens League
JayCees	Junior Chamber of Commerce
LRC	Lutheran Refugee Committee
LWF	Lutheran World Federation
MAC	Military Air Command
MOD	Ministry of Overseas Development
NCEC	National Committee for an Effective Congress
NGO	Non-Governmental Organization
NLRB	National Labor Relations Board
NRA	National Rifle Association
NRS	National Refugee Service
NSRC	National Student Relocation Council
OAU	Organization for African Unity
OB	Operation Baby Lift
OSS	Office of Strategic Services
SSEU	Social Service Employees Union
USAID	U.S. Agency for International Development
USCR	U.S. Committee for Refugees
USCRI	U.S. Committee for Refugees and Immigrants
USFU	U.S. Fund for UNICEF
UN	United Nations
UNDP	United Nations Development Program
UNESCO	United Nations Education, Scientific and Cultural Organization
UNHCHR	United Nations High Commissioner for Human Rights
UNHCR	United Nations High Commissioner for Refugees
UNICEF	United Nations Children's Fund
UNKRA	United Nations Korean Relief Agency
UNRRA	United Nations Relief and Rehabilitation Agency
UNRWA	United Nations Relief and Works Agency for Palestine Refugees
UNSCOB	United Nations Special Committee on the Balkans
WCC	World Council of Churches
WCCA	Wartime Civil Control Administration
WCTU	Women's Christian Temperance Union
WFP	World Food Program
WHO	World Health Organization
WRA	War Relocation Authority
WRC	World Rehabilitation Council
WRY	World Refugee Year
YMCA	Young Men's Christian Association
YWCA	Young Women's Christian Association

BIBLIOGRAPHY

BOOKS:

American Voluntary Aid for Germany 1945-1950, by Edward Mc Sweeney, O.P., Caritas-Verlag, Freiburg im Breisgau, Germany, 1950, 141 pp.

Arena—The Story of Federal Theatre, by Hallie Flanagan, foreword by John Houseman, Limelight Edition, NY, 1985 475 pp. (Original by New York Times Company, 1940)

Beauty Behind Barbed Wire—The Arts of the Japanese in Our War Relocation Camps, by Allen H. Eaton, Harper & Brothers, Foreword by Eleanor Roosevelt, 1952, 208 pp.

A Bed for the Night—Humanitarianism in Crisis, by David Rieff, Simon and Schuster, 2002, 351 pp.

The Brutality of Nations, by Dan Jacobs (Problems in providing food and medicine to children of rebel Biafra.), Alfred A. Knopf, 1987, 383 pp.

Childhood is not Child's Play—Illustrations from International Poster Competition, German Poster Museum, Essen, Germany 1998

Circle of Song: Sings, Chants, and Dances for Ritual and Celebration, compiled by Kate Marks, Full Circle Press, Amherst, Massachusetts, 1993, 280 pp.

Citizen 13660—Drawings and Text by Mine Okube (Depicting her life at Topaz Relocation Center), Columbia University Press, 1946, 209 pp.

Classical Landscape with Figures, by Osbert Lancaster, Illustrated by the author, John Murray, London 1947, 224 pp.

Contemporary Art in Africa, by Ulli Beier, Frederick A. Praeger, 1968, 173 pp.

The Dartmouth Story—A Narrative History of the College Buildings, People, and Legends, by Robert B, Graham, Dartmouth Book Store, 1990, 250 pp.

The Disciplined Bow—A New Practical Approach to Learning Violin Technique, written and published by Tom Marks, 2001, 89 pp.

Don't Fence Me In—Fort Ontario Refugees: How They Won Their Freedom, by Joseph H. Smart, (Former Director, Oswego Refugee Shelter), Heritage Arts, Salt Lake City, Utah 1991, 280 pp.

Food and Wine, Issues of 1995, 1997, 1999 and 2000, edited by Hugo Dunn Meynell, International Wine and Food Society, London

For a Better World—Posters from the United Nations, by Edward B. Marks, foreward by Kofi Annan, Secretary-General of the United Nations, Pomegranate Communications, San Francisco, 2000, 159 pp.

Good Neighborhoods—the Challenge of Open Housing, by Morris Milgram, W.W. Norton and Company, 1977, 248 pp.

The Governing of Men, based on experience at Poston Japanese-American Relcation Center, by Alexander H. Leighton, Lt. Commander, Medical Corps, USNR, Princeton University Press 1945, 404 pp.

The Greek Islands, by Lawrence Durrell, Faber and Faber, London 1978, 287 pp.

Haven: The Unknown Story of a Thousand World War II Refugees, by Ruth Gruber, Crown Publishing Group, revised 2000, 352 pp.

Homo Migrans, written and illustrated by G. Tortora, Published on Occasion of Twentieth Anniversary of the Intergovernmental Committee for European Migration (ICEM), Geneva, Switzerland, circa 1971, 100 pp.

Hugh Gibson—1883-1954, edited by Perrin C. Galpin with an introduction by Herbert Hoover, Belgian American Educational Foundation Inc., 1956, 163 pp.

The International Refugee Organization—Its History and Work (1946-1952), by Louise W. Holborn, Oxford University Press, London and New York, 1956, 805 pp.

Ljubivoje V. Stefanovic, A Graveside Appreciation by Twenty Friends and Associates, Belser Verlag, Stuttgart und Zurich, 1983, 94 pp.

Journey of a Johnny-Come-Lately: Biography of John McLane Clark, by David Bradley, foreword by Earnest Martin Hopkins, Dartmouth Publications, 1957, 215 pp.

Michael Goutos, edited by Arginy Goutos, Athens 1989, published in Greek with some English, 270 pp.

Paper Walls—America and the Refugee Crisis 1938-1941, by David S. Wyman, Pantheon Books, 1968, 1985, 307 pp.

Posters—A Concise History, by John Barnicoat, Thames and Hudson, 1972 (Reprinted 1998), 273 illustrations and 288 pp.

Prejudice—Japanese-Americans, Symbols of Racial Intolerance, by Carey McWilliams, Little, Brown & Company, 1944, 337 pp.

The Price of Indifference—Refugees and Humanitarian Action in the New Century, by Arthur C. Helton, Oxford University Press, 2002, 314 pp.

The Redbook of the Wine and Liquor Trades, edited by Edward B. Marks, Atlas Publishing Company, 1936, 630 pp.

Refugees Today, edited by Barry N. Stein and Sylvano M. Tomasi, In Spring-Summer 1981 issue of Center for Migration Studies, includes article on Refugees: a New Approach by John F. Thomas, 1981, 441 pp.

La Representation de l' Humanite—Collections des Oeuvres d' Art de l' Office des Nations Unies a Geneve, by Annaleen de Jong, 2001, 512 pp.

The Saving Remnant—an Account of Jewish Survival, by Herbert Agar, Viking Press, 1960, 269 pp.

Snow Falling on Cedars, by David Guterson, Vintage Books, 1995, 460 pp.

Token Refuge—The Story of the Jewish Refugee Shelter at Oswego 1944—1946, by Sharon R. Lowenstein, Indiana University Press, June 1986.

Token Shipment—The Story of America's War Refugee Shelter, by Edward B. Marks, U.S. Department of the Interior 1946, 106 pp.

The State of the World's Refugees—In Search of Solutions, by UNHCR Editorial Team, Oxford University Press, 1995, 264 pp.

Visions—Fifty Years of the United Nations, editor Jan Ralph, introduction by Boutros Boutros-Ghali, Smallwood and Stewart, NY and Hearst Books, 1995, 257 pp.

Warming up for Fifty years—Reflections of Some Members of the Class of 1932 Dartmouth College, Edited by W.H. Ferry, published by James R. Cook, Santa Barbara, California, 1982, 215 pp.

We Wish to Inform You that Tomorrow We Will be Killed with Our Families—Stories from Rwanda, by Philip Gourevitch, Farrar, Straus and Giroux, 1998, 356 pp.

The Wild Place, by Kathryn Hulme, Published by Little, Brown, Boston, 1954, 233 pp. (Won Atlantic non-fiction award for 1953)

WRA—A Story of Human Conservation, War Relocation Authority, U.S. Department of the Interior, 1946, 212 pp.

A World of Art—The United Nations Collection, by Edward B. Marks, foreword by Boutros Boutros-Ghali, Secretary-General of the United Nations (1992-1996), preface by Brian Urquhart former Under-Secretary-General, Il Cigno Galileo Galilei, Rome, 1995, 214 pp.

World Refugee Survey 2003, published by U.S. Committee for Refugees, 258 pp.

PAMPHLETS AND ARTICLES:

"American Assistance to Victims of the Nigeria/Biafra War: Defects in the Prescriptions on Foreign Disaster Relief," by Beverley May Carl, *from Harvard International Law Journal*, Volume 12 1971, pp. 191-221.

"Americans All Immigrants All—A Handbook for Listeners," by J. Morris Jones. Published by Federal Radio Education Committee in Cooperation with U.S. Office of Education. Circa 1938, 120 pp.

"Art at Home in the United Nations," by Edward B. Marks from *UN Chronicle #4*, 1998, pp 76-78.

"As We Do Unto Others," by Charles H. Seaver, National Council of Churches, circa 1954, 31 pp.

"Century of the Homeless Man," by Elfan Rees, for International Conciliation Series, Carnegie Endowment for International Peace, November 1957, pp. 193-254.

"The Drys Crusade Again but with New Tactics," by Edward B. Marks, *The New York Times Magazine*, October 25, 1936, pp. 6 and 21.

"The Physician in America," 1941, Report of the National Committee for Resettlement of Foreign Physicians, from *Journal of the American Medical Association*, November 29, 1941, pp. 1881-1888.

"Europe's Homeless Millions," by Fred K. Hoehler, in Headline Series, Foreign Policy Association, November-December 1945, 96 pp.

"The Hardcore DP's," by Edward B. Marks, *The Survey*, September 1949, pp. 481-486.

"How the Yugoslav Camps for Hungarian Refugees were Closed," by Edward B. Marks, November/December 1958 issue of *Migration News*, published by International Catholic Migration Commission, pp. 19-21.

"Immigrants and Refugees: Their Similarities, Differences, and Needs," by Dr. William S. Bernard, Published in *International Migration* issued by ICEM and the Research Group for European Migration, Volume XIV, #4, 1976, pp. 267 to 281.

"The International Committee for World Refugee Year, 1959-1961," by ICWRY, Geneva, 74 pp.

"Internationally Assisted Migration: ICEM Rounds out Five Years of Resettlement," by Edward B. Marks, From *International Organization*, Volume 11, #3, 1957, pp. 481-494.

"The International Refugee Organization," by Rene Ristelhueber, International Conciliation Series. *Carnegie Endowment for International Peace*, April 1951, pp. 165-228.

"Paths to the New World: American Immigration Yesterday, Today and Tomorrow," by Edward Corsi, *Freedom Pamphlet of Anti-Defamation League of B'nai B'rith*, 48 pp.

"The Refugee: A Staggering World Problem," special section of *UNESCO Courier* of March 1955.

"The Refugees in America," by Dr. William Haber from *The Menorah Journal*, Summer 1940, pp. 1-9.

"Refugees in Philadelphia—A Study of their Adjustment in a New Land," by Philadelphia Study Committee on Refugee Integration, 1962, 20 pp.

"Reminiscences of a Born-Again Wine Lover," by Edward B. Marks, International Wine and Food Society, London, *Food and Wine*, Volume 24, 1999, pp. 59-65.

"Saigon: The Impact of the Refugees," by Edward B. Marks, *The Reporter*, January 12, 1967, 4 pp.

"Through a Wineglass Hazily—A Staggering Account of One of the Wettest Junkets in History," by Edward B. Marks, *Playboy*, February 1965, pp. 149, 150 and 168.

"Two Against the Pre-Packs," by Edward B. Marks, *The New Yorker*, November 15, 1958, pp. 192-196.

"USAID Nigeria and the Book Gap," from *USAID/Nigeria Newsletter #32*, June 1965, pp. 1-14.

"Vietnam's Contradictions," by Andrew J. Pierre, from *Foreign Affairs*, November/ December 2000, pp. 69-86.

"The Volunteer in Auxiliary Services with Refugees," by Edward B. Marks, from September 1941 issue of, *The Jewish Social Service Quarterly*, 3 pp.

INDEX

325; Ninh Thuan Province, South
Vietnam, 315; Pleiku, 1, 2; Que, Dr.
Nguyen Phuc, 313; Saigon, 313;
STAL Planes, 1; Tunney,
Congressman John V., 1; Tydings,
Senator Millard, 1; Vietnam Refugee
Commissariat, 313; Vung Tau, 316;
Westmoreland, General William C.,
2, 316; Wickbom, Ulf (Swedish
journalist), 317
Vietnam - 1974 EBM: *Reporter, The,*
313, 386; Rostow, Eugene V., 165;
Rusk, Secretary of State Dean, 316;
Xoi and family, 319, 320, 321, 326
Vietnam - 1998 Visit with Vera:
Danang, 1, 2, 324; Hanoi, 319, 321,
322, 323, 325; Hanoi traffic
intimidating, 322; Hanoi, Army
Museum, 322; Hanoi, Tortoise
Pagoda, 322; Hanoi, Van Mieu,
Temple of Literature, 322; Hanoi,
Water Puppet Theater, 323; HCMC,
Jade Emperor Pagoda, 326; HCMC,
War Remnants Museum, 325; Ho
Chi Minh City (HCMC) Formerly
Saigon, 189, 319, 321, 325, 382; Hoi
An, 319, 321, 324, 325; Hue, 319,
321, 323, 324, 325; Hue, Perfume
River, 323, 324; Saigon, 325;
Saigon's revised Cercle Sportif, 325;
van Gelderen, Adrie, 322
Vietnam Refugee Commissariat, 313
Volunteers at NRS, 150
Votes for Republicans, 285
Vung Tau, 316

W

Waiting people in 1958, 293
Waller, Fats, 290
Walsh, Natalie, 56
Walter, Congressman Tad, 262
War Refugee Board, 173
War Refugee Division (WRA), 169
War Relocation Authority, 153, 155,
165, 205, 278, 279, 280, 304, 379,
382, 385

Wartime Civil Control Administration
(WCCA), 156
Washington Post, 169, 184
Washington, D.C., 145, 301
Waterman, Josephine, 38
Watson, Keith, 260
Webster, Daniel, 48
Weir, Reginald, 289
Welfare Council of New York City, 133;
Beckleman, Moe (AJDC), 134;
Better Times Magazine, 133, 134,
135, 148, 278; Boretz, Mary, 134;
Foster Home Bureau, 134; Granger,
Lester B., 135, 269; Hine, Lewis W.,
133; Kellogg, Paul, 134, 214; Lane,
Marie, 134, 211; Lane, Robert P.,
133; Mayo, Leonard, 133;
*Metropolitan Diary, Better Times
Magazine,* 133; Motherwell, Hiram,
133; Riis, Jacob, 353; Robison,
Sophia, 134
Welles, Orson, 113, 128, 130
We're Dressed Up for the Visitors, 33
West Africa, 3, 304
West, Herb, 52
Westchester Committee for WRY, 295
Westchester County, 9, 19, 252
Westhampton, Long Island, 17
Westheimer, Frank, 54, 372
Westmoreland, General William C., 2,
316
Wet-dry issue, 109
White River Junction, 45, 55
Whoever loved, that loved not at first
sight?, 364
Wickbom, Ulf (Swedish journalist),
317
Wild Place, The, 215, 385
Williams, Bert, 21, 102, 290
Williams, Colonel Buck, 236
Willowcroft Wine, 101
Wilson, Christopher and Dagmar, 146
Wilson, Helen, 145, 214
Wine and Liquor, 93, 102, 384;
American Wine and Liquor Journal,
39, 92, 94, 100; American Wine
Institute, 100; Gibson Cocktail, 239;
Gorman, Jean, 253; Jameson, Right